A MULTIDIMENSIONAL APPROACH TO POST-TRAUMATIC STRESS DISORDER - FROM THEORY TO PRACTICE

Edited by **Ghassan El-Baalbaki**
and **Christophe Fortin**

A Multidimensional Approach to Post-Traumatic Stress Disorder - from Theory to Practice
http://dx.doi.org/10.5772/61874
Edited by Ghassan El-Baalbaki and Christophe Fortin

Contributors

Larry D Sanford, Laurie L Wellman, Richard Ross, Heike Gerger, Jens Gaab, J P Ginsberg, Ana Starcevic, Alessandra Simonelli, Chiara Sacchi, Laura Piccardi, Anna Maria Giannini, Pierluigi Cordellieri, Emanuela Tizzani, Umberto Guidoni, Francesca Baralla, Roberto Sgalla, Sandro Vedovi, André Marchand, Katia Levrier, Carolyn Leathead, Sophie Lacerte, Geneviève Belleville, Delphine-Emilie Bourdon, Layla Tarazi Sahab, Mayssa' El Husseini, Claude Belanger, Caroline Dugal, Natacha Godbout, Noémie Bigras, Melanie Vachon, Prudence C. Bessette, Christine Goyette, Stephane Guay

Published by InTech

Janeza Trdine 9, 51000 Rijeka, Croatia

Publishing Process Manager Romina Rovan

Technical Editor SPi Global

Cover InTech Design team

First published October, 2016

Printed in Croatia

Additional hard copies can be obtained from orders@intechopen.com

A Multidimensional Approach to Post-Traumatic Stress Disorder - from Theory to Practice, Edited by Ghassan El-Baalbaki and Christophe Fortin

p. cm.

Print ISBN 978-953-51-2728-4

Online ISBN 978-953-51-2729-1

For EU product safety concerns:
IN TECH d.o.o., Prolaz Marije Krucifikse Kozulić 3, 51000 Rijeka, Croatia,
info@intechopen.com or visit our website at intechopen.com.

Meet the editors

Dr. Ghassan El-Baalbaki is a professor of psychology at the University of Quebec at Montreal and an adjunct professor at McGill University. Prior to this, he held a position as an international consultant in psychology for a humanitarian project, where he undertook clinical projects with victims of violence, harmed by landmines and war. He also trained healthcare providers in CBT for patients with PTSD and with serious injuries, including amputation, and in working with families to improve support for patients. With his team, he runs several research projects, financed by governmental and institutional grants with the Trauma Studies Center, the Scleroderma Patient-centered Intervention Network, and the Louise Granofsky Psychosocial Oncology Program. He is the author of several scientific publications.

Dr. Christophe Fortin is a professor of psychology at the University of Ottawa and an adjunct professor of psychology at UQAM. He currently holds several governmental and institutional research grants supporting his work on PTSD and has been, for the last 15 years, studying several aspects of the disorder. His current research interests focus on the efficacy of psychotherapy and the healthcare costs associated with this disorder. He is actually codirecting, at the Trauma Studies Centre in Montreal, a randomized control trial on the efficacy of two length-flexible cognitive-behavioral therapies for PTSD. His expertise led him to give several trainings to first responders, and he is currently developing a psychological first aid program for firefighters with PTSD or with subclinical symptoms.

Contents

Preface

Since thousands of years, humans have been experiencing traumatic events, leaving many victims and those who come to their rescue with emotional and behavioral disturbances. Just in the last decade, we unfortunately witnessed many of those events, to which people could be exposed to during a lifetime, occurring all over the world, serving as a cruel reminder of their unpredictability and their frequency. Whether it be natural disasters such as tsunamis that devastated the coasts of Japan in 2011 and of Southeast Asia in 2004, the various terrorist attacks, acts of war, and violent crimes, or the many human or technological errors occurring on a daily basis, traumatic events make countless victims each year. The events, beyond the regrettable deaths and victims that they entail, are the basis of the etiology of post-traumatic stress disorder (PTSD).

In the early 1980s, the *Diagnostic and Statistical Manual of Mental Disorders* (DSM) and the *International Classification of Diseases* (ICD) included PTSD in their taxonomy and nosology of mental health disorders. PTSD has since seen several revisions of its definition. The detrimental effects and high prevalence of PTSD made it a well-known and widely researched theme.

The collective work you are about to read presents a biopsychosocial perspective of PTSD and offers research results from quantitative and qualitative approaches as well as from different schools of psychotherapy (i.e., psychodynamic, humanistic-existential, and cognitive behavioral). We believe it will be of great interest for researchers, clinicians, and graduate students working with PTSD or wanting a starting point to do so.

The first section covers some of the latest research on brain structural and hormonal changes (Starcevic, A.—Chapter 1), showing that biomarkers may indicate the presence of PTSD, a predisposition for, or an increased risk of, developing this disorder. The first section also sheds light on the neurobiology of sleep disturbances in animal and human experiments (Wellman, L.; Ross, R.; and Sanford, L.—Chapter 2) that have been linked to PTSD. Based on several of their studies on the significant causes and predictors of hyperarousal in combat veterans with PTSD, Ginsberg, JP. and Nagpal, M. close this first section by proposing a model to account for the symptoms of disinhibition, hyperarousal, and attention bias. They also discuss heart rate variability biofeedback as a promising intervention in reducing symptoms and argue for the need to study it (Chapter 3). Following this fundamental and neuro-bio-physiological tour, you will find in the second section of this book a focus on clinical and methodological approaches.

In a comprehensive and extensive literature review, Dugal, C.; Bigras, N.; Godbout, N.; and Bélanger, C. describe the various forms of childhood trauma and explain the underlying mechanisms linked to the development of comorbid psychopathology and challenged interpersonal functioning (Chapter 4). One aspect of childhood trauma is investigated by Simonelli, A. and Sacchi, C. who were able to show that early experiences of emotional abuse and neglect have deleterious impacts on the development of PTSD as well as on the development of romantic attachment and well-being of adult women (Chapter 5).

The prevalence of PTSD is known to be higher in women and acute stress disorder seems to be a predictor of PTSD. Guay, S. et al. (Chapter 6) run a study to verify the predictive power of full and partial acute stress disorder (ASD) diagnosis for PTSD and to verify whether or not its predictive power varies according to the gender of victims of violent crimes. They found no gender differences in the predictive power of ASD and present data supporting the importance of ASD diagnosis early on in order to prevent the development of a full-blown PTSD.

The victims of a traumatic event or of childhood trauma or of abuse are not the only ones at risk for developing PTSD. First responders and rescuers often witness the horrific event and its devastating consequences and hence are also at risk of developing PTSD. Giannini, A.M. et al. share the results (Chapter 7) of their study on the protective factors (i.e., personality traits, social factors, and cognitive strategies) in emergency rescuers in three communities in Italy. Moreover, psychotherapists have to emotionally and mentally deal with the trauma narratives of their patients, manage their countertransference reactions (El-Husseini, M. et al., Chapter 8), and—from a humanistic and existential perspective—go beyond symptoms and diagnosis and work with the meaning of the traumatic experience by focusing on the subjective experience of the patient in the present moment (Vachon, M.; Bessette, P.C.; and Goyette, C.—Chapter 9). In the two case studies reported by Vachon et al., though the emphasis is on the process and not the symptoms, we can easily see that nightmares are part of the two patients' suffering experience and that their reduction in frequency is reported as a marker of betterment.

In fact, post-traumatic nightmares are recurrent symptoms and can be difficult to treat, hence the use of medication with or without psychotherapy. Until recently, there were no meta-analyses looking at the efficacy of such treatments. Levrier, K. et al. (Chapter 10) share their meta-analysis on the impact of prazosin compared to cognitive behavioral therapy on the reduction of post-traumatic nightmares and general symptoms of PTSD. They found that both medication and therapy were effective, with prazosin demonstrating a larger effect. However, Gerger, H. and Gaab, J. (Chapter 11) argue that in meta-analyses, extra-therapeutic factors act as moderators and may impact the conclusions favoring one treatment over another. Hence, they say that no particular PTSD treatment is proven to be the best and that even non–trauma-focused treatments may be beneficial to diagnosed victims.

Finally, we would like to thank all the contributors who generously shared their work and who were responsive and patient with the several back-and-forth versions of the manuscripts. We know how hard it is to conduct sound research and want to laud your passion and efforts invested in studying PTSD. We would also like to thank the InTechOpen team who got involved in this book, particularly Mrs. Romina Rovan who made this project an agreeable experience by taking charge of all the administration and publishing communication.

Last but not least, we want to thank our wives and children: Pascale, Noemi, and Sophie, and Julie, Isaac, and Charles-Antoine. Without your patience, tolerance of our absence, encouragement, and love, we would have never made it.

We love you.

Ghassan El-Baalbaki, PhD
Université du Québec À Montréal, Canada

Christophe Fortin, PhD
University of Ottawa, Canada

Section 1

Biological and Fundamental Perspectives

Chapter 1

Structural Brain Changes in PTSD

Ana Starcevic

Additional information is available at the end of the chapter

http://dx.doi.org/10.5772/64080

Abstract

Chronic stress induces structural and hormonal changes in the various brain structures: caudate nucleus, putamen, hippocampus, amygdala, prefrontal cortex in participants with post-traumatic stress disorder. Based on the results of recent neuroimaging studies on post-traumatic stress disorder, hippocampus, amygdala, and prefrontal cortex play a key role in triggering the typical symptoms of PTSD. Cortisol, as the primary stress hormone, together with dehydroepiandrosterone, tries to return the body to its original state of homeostasis, but its disturbed concentration levels can modify brain structures volumes. The scanning was performed using a 3.0 T whole-body scanner (Philips Medical Systems, Best, The Netherlands). Saliva was taken from all examined participants, for the determination of cortisol concentration and its effect on volume changes of the examined brain structures. The strongest headache that might occur during the day was marked on the pain rating scale (0–10). Hamilton depression rating scale was used for rating the depression level. Studies are moving toward the recognition of different biomarkers that would indicate the presence of clinically significant symptoms and a predisposition or increased risk of developing post-traumatic stress disorder, which can be made by increasing the number of studies, number of participants, and number of different methodologies.

Keywords: Brain, chronic stress, posttraumatic stress disorder, rats, psychosocial stress

1. Introduction

One in two people will be exposed to a life-threatening trauma event in their life [1]. Prolonged stress results in neuroendocrine deficiency axis and defensive mechanisms are weakened, and stress hormones are activated. Definition of neuroanatomical or morphological substrate is crucial in defining any condition, illness or disorder in medicine and psychiatry. There is almost no area of the brain that is not directly or indirectly affected by the stress or trauma impact [2–5]. The field of neuroimaging has made tremendous advances in the past decade and has contributed greatly to our understanding of post-traumatic stress disorder (PTSD). Recent neuroimaging investigations have shown significant neurobiological changes in PTSD. The areas of the brain that are different in patients with PTSD compared to those in control subjects appear to be: hippocampus, amygdala, and prefrontal cortex. The amygdala appears to be hyperreactive to trauma-related stimuli. The hallmark symptoms of PTSD may be related to a failure of higher brain regions to dampen the exaggerated symptoms of arousal and distress that are mediated through the amygdala in response to reminders of the traumatic event [6–8]. The findings of structural and functional neuroimaging studies of post-traumatic stress disorder are reviewed as they relate to our current understanding of this disorder. Some volumetric investigations show that some other subcortical brain structures are also involved in trauma impact such as caudate nucleus, putamen [9–11].

2. Methods of investigation

2.1. Magnetic resonance imaging

Magnetic resonance imaging generally presents the most important volumetric and structural assessment tool in general evaluation and determination of morphological substrate in post-traumatic stress disorder. The MRI scanner detects the radiofrequency energy emitted and energy level changes represent different brain structures. T1- and T2-weighted images are used for differentiating the white and grey matter and for delineating hyperintensities, respectively. The advantage of this procedure is its safety in the first place, since it does not involve ionizing radiation. Neuroimaging investigations mostly involve a magnetic field varying from 1 to 3 Tesla (T). Various MRI techniques are available for clinical use such as fast spin echo, high-performance gradients, echo planar, and diffusion weighted imaging. In a study of male therapy-naïve participants with PTSD, Starcevic et al. [12] performed the scanning using a 3.0 T whole-body scanner (Philips Medical Systems, Best, The Netherlands). After the scanning, all the participants were coded in order to blind the volumetric evaluation team, and sent for the subsequent volumetric analysis. MIPAV software with three integrated software tools (brain extraction, Talairach alignment, tissue segmentation) was used for brain volume estimation. Volume measurements of the cerebral structures examined in the study were performed on 3D T1-weighted MR images (acquisition parameters were as follows: TR = 9.8 ms; TE = 4.6 ms; flip angle = 8; section thickness = 1.2 mm; number of sections = 120; no section gap; whole-brain coverage; FOV = 224 mm; matrix = 192; reconstruction matrix = 256). Routine T2-weighted MRI and FLAIR were performed to rule out a mass lesion as a contributory factor to memory loss or cognitive decline. After the data had been collected, the input data (3D T1 images) were transformed to 152 common spaces, using transformations based on 12 deg of freedom (i.e., three translations, three rotations, three scalings, and three skews). After subcortical and cortical registration, we applied the subcortical mask to locate the cortical and subcortical structures of interest, followed by segmentation. The total, absolute volumes of structures of interest were calculated, taking into account the transformations made in the first stage. As for the certainty of precision of segmentation, boundary correction was used to determine whether or not the boundary voxels belonged to the structure examined. That was one of the most important steps through which the accuracy of the delineated measured cerebral structures were determined using the Z-value of 3, corresponding to a 99.998% certainty that the observed voxels belonged to the particular structure. After all MR scans were registered and segmented, all segmented regions of interest were visually checked for errors during registration and segmentation.

2.2. Determination of cortisol levels

Secretion of cortisol shows the circadian rhythm characterized by a sudden increase in concentration early in the morning and a gradual decrease until the end of the day. Since stress induces higher levels of cortisol, the concentrations remain elevated until the cause of the stress is eliminated. The main role of cortisol is to help the body under stress to adapt to the changing conditions. Steroids can be determined in a sample of blood, urine, and saliva. Salivary cortisol is a measurement of active free-cortisol concentration which follows a diurnal rhythm of serum or plasma cortisol. Saliva sampling protocols are simple and noninvasive. Proper sample preparation is important for the accurate determination of cortisol in saliva. There are various commercially available saliva sets: simple sterile containers, containers with cotton pellet (Salivette), or specialized systems for collecting saliva. Salivettes are mostly used for saliva sampling. This system includes cotton rolls to be placed in the mouth and the patient chews on them for about 30 s to 30 min followed by transferring the sample to the test tube. With regard to the stability of cortisol, patients can store the samples in their home refrigerators at a temperature between 4? and 8? for up to seven days before taking them to the laboratory for testing. Before psychological testing and magnetic resonance imaging, all patients underwent a structural psychiatric interview and ventilation psychotherapy without taking any medications. The disorder was diagnosed according to the guidelines of the 10th revision of the International Classification of Diseases (ICD 10). Saliva was taken from all participants for the determination of cortisol concentration. The concentration was determined by the available commercial kit (Salivette) twice a day in the morning (7 h) and the evening (21 h).

3. Neuroanatomical substrates and structural, volumetric changes

3.1. Hippocampus

The animal stress model investigations showed that stress produced damage to the hippocampus, a brain area involved in learning and memory, situated in the medial temporal lobe just under the cortical surface, with associated memory deficits. The hippocampus contains high levels of glucocorticoid receptors which make it more vulnerable to chronic stress than most other brain areas [13]. The mechanism involves glucocorticoids and possibly serotonin acting through excitatory amino acids to mediate hippocampal atrophy. Under normal conditions, hippocampus blends together all the elements of a memory from all the sensory areas. Short-term memories are stored in the hippocampus, but when they are no longer required as conscious memories, the hippocampus processes these into other parts of the brain to create longer term memories. Patients with post-traumatic stress disorder from Vietnam combat and childhood abuse showed deficits on neuropsychological measures that have been validated as probes of hippocampal function [14, 15]. In addition, magnetic resonance imaging (MRI) showed a reduction in volume of the hippocampus in both combat veterans and victims of childhood abuse [5, 14, 15]. In combat veterans, the hippocampal volume reduction was correlated with deficits in verbal memory on neuropsychological testing. These studies introduce the possibility that experiences in the form of traumatic stressors can have long-term effects on the structure and function of the brain [4, 16, 17]. Stress related steroids like cortisol, as a primary stress hormone, affect the hippocampus by reducing the excitability of some hippocampal neurons, thus inhibiting the genesis of new neurons in the dentate gyrus and causing atrophy of dendrites in pyramidal cells of the specific CA3 region, which leads us the conclusion that humans who experienced chronic traumatic stress had atrophy of the hippocampus more often than of other parts of the brain. All above mentioned brain changes effects are present in post-traumatic stress disorder [18]. Hippocampal damage interferes with the proper processing of information coming from the amygdala making an individual very vulnerable to new disturbing stimuli. This has been confirmed by experiments on animals, where damage to hippocampal functions results directly in behavioral disinhibition [19–21]. The volume reduction of the hippocampal formation may be explained by a negative impact of cortisol at the level of the hippocampal cells. General reduction of any structure of the brain may be caused by the negative effect of cortisol to a cell of such structure [22, 23]. Intense stress is associated with the release of endogenous stress hormones and transmitters of cortisol, epinephrine, and norepinephrine, vasopressin, oxytocin, and endogenous opiates, and their role is reflected in the launch of altered metabolism and release of energy necessary to respond to stress. Then glucose is released and changes occur in the immune system. In a healthy organism, these changes are of short duration, and the baseline cortisol level of functioning is established as soon as the danger has passed, while in the case of prolonged stress, if it is very intense, there is a dysfunction of the system response to stress and to its desensitization [24]. Studies that have investigated the functions of neurohormones in post-traumatic stress disorder show reactions that are opposite of the normal response to stress. The sudden cortisol concentration increase is one of the standard elements of the response to stress and, as a result, can damage the hippocampal formation, which leads to cognitive deficits in the form of memory impairment. Glucocorticoids and catecholamines modulate the reciprocal effects in the manner that in acute stress the response regulates cortisol stress hormones via negative feedback through the hippocampus, hypothalamus, and pituitary gland. Based on the results of their study, researchers suggest that cortisol is a potent hormone that can even interfere with other processes in the body after the exposure to acute stress [22, 23, 25]. Alternately, released catecholamines and corticosteroids stimulate active behaviors necessary to overcome stress, whereas in the case of low levels of corticosteroids, the increased irritability is caused by inadequate and uncontrolled reactions of fight or flight. Chronic stress induces decreased basal cortisol levels. On the other hand, acute stress can be seen as a leading factor of decreased activation of pulsatile stress hormone release, and increased number of glucocorticoid receptors in the hippocampus structure [25]. Kuljić and colleagues showed in their study that chronic stress caused a reduction in corticosterone concentration indicating the exhaustion of the hypothalamic-pituitary-adrenal axis, as was shown in an experimental study in rats [26]. A study conducted by Resnick et al. [27] showed that reduced cortisol made people more susceptible to post-traumatic stress disorder, for example, those with a personal history of sexual abuse [27]. The occurrence of post-traumatic stress disorder was manifested after 3 months in individuals who suffered from reduced levels of cortisol immediately after the car accident [28, 29].

3.2. Amygdala

The amygdala is a structure described as a center of normal expression of emotions to external stimuli and realistic perception and response to stress and fear. Located deep and medially inside the temporal lobes, it is involved in processing memory, emotional reactions, and decision making [30]. There was a weak activation within the paradigm of experimental functional MRI imaging (fMRI) for war veterans. The occurrence of different blood flow consistent with the level of an emotional reaction is a common finding during the experimental paradigm performance in psychiatry; however, this was not the case for former warriors in whom it was shown in reduced amygdala complex and the lack of displaying the symptoms of PTSD [31, 32]. The exposure to a traumatic event results in autonomic activation, after which the amygdala evaluates information and, depending on that assessment, determines the emotional significance of the entrance and triggers a structure such as hypothalamus, hippocampus, and basal prosencephalon, which then determines the behavioral, autonomic and neurohormonal function and its manifestation. In a study conducted on forty-nine male patients, Starcevic et al. [12], found that both left and right amygdala volumes were statistically significantly different between individuals with PTSD and individuals without PTSD, with the emphasis on the volume of the left amygdala as more significant. LeDoux [21] discovered the crucial role of the amygdala in the emotional brain, which he called neural alarm, which can take control over behavior even when the prefrontal cortex is still at the stage of selecting an equal reaction to external stimulation. Rogers et al. [33] show that the left amygdala volume has a significant negative correlation with the severity of PTSD symptomatology as well as with the reduced gray matter density in the left anterior cingulate cortex. A smaller amygdala volume was associated with the presence of cancer-related intrusive recollections in a sample of 76 breast cancer survivors [34]. Normal amygdala volumes do not necessarily preclude functional abnormalities in the amygdala in participants with PTSD. As a case in point, the results of a functional neuroimaging meta-analysis in participants with PTSD found evidence of amygdala abnormalities, particularly in the left amygdala, where two distinct clusters of abnormal function were identified: a ventral anterior hyperactivation cluster and a dorsal posterior hypoactivation cluster [35, 36]. The amygdala has a great potential and therefore research should go in the direction of a more detailed examination of this structure.

3.3. Prefrontal cortex

With its executive function, the prefrontal cortex, a cerebral cortex that covers the front part of the frontal lobe, has been indicated by many authors and researchers as an integral link between an individual's personality and basic psychological functions of the frontal cortex [37]. Brain imaging studies have shown that the reduced volume and interconnections of the frontal lobes with other cerebral regions can be found in individuals with different mental disorders such as post-traumatic stress disorder [38, 39]. A structural neuroimaging research study indicates that marked improvements in prefrontal and hippocampal grey matter volume occur in individuals who have physical exercise [40]. Researchers, who have studied the prefrontal cortex as a part of the brain that suppresses memories, showed that it could not function at lower levels in people with stress related disorders like in healthy subjects. When individuals with stress-related disorders were asked to suppress their memory of certain words, their brains showed activation in the hippocampus, which was higher than normal [41].

The reduction of brain structure volume may occur as a result of molecular alterations in those specific brain areas. Researchers. [41, 42] showed increased blood flow in the upper prefrontal region of the brain in a study conducted on both men and women who suffered from post-traumatic stress disorder. This is to be expected because different structures of cerebrum are triggered in the same task paradigm in men and women. Cortisol, the main stress hormone, which is involved in the apoptotic actions in the brain and consequently reduction of solitary brain structure, has a great influence in bilateral and general reduction of brain volume at the expense of increasing the ventricles of the brain [43].

3.4. Caudate nucleus, putamen, and globus pallidus

Subcortical structures such as caudate nucleus and putamen have been described as structures involved not only in motor function, but in cognitive processes and that their volume decrease was associated with major depression and Alzheimer's disease. Chronic stress induces neuroendocrine deficiency and weakened defensive mechanisms which lead to post-traumatic stress disorder. Cortisol, as the primary stress hormone, together with dehydroepiandrosterone, tries to return the body to its original state of homeostasis, but its disturbed concentration levels can modify brain structures volumes. Negative effects of cortisol result in volume decrease of subcortical structures [44].

Globus pallidus, as a major subcortical grey structure, participates in the regulation of sleep via the nigrostriatal dopamine and through its connections with subthalamic nucleus [45]. Studies carried out on an experimental model of the rat have shown that damage to the globus pallidus leads to disruption of sleep. Sleep disorders, which are considered among the most severe symptoms of post-traumatic stress disorder, are leading to hypoxic changes and changes in metabolism in the brain, which alters, to a high degree, dopamine levels, and the degree of blood flow through the brain, which, in turn, leads to brain atrophy [46]. Sleep deprivation, one of the most annoying symptoms in PTSD suffering subjects, could not be neglected. Higher values of the Hamilton depression rate score in patients with more frequent headaches, who, in addition, have a greater decrease in volume, could be explained with the theory of sleep deprivation influence, and long-term cortisol effects after the stressing event, although insomnia and headaches are reported to be more frequent in women [47, 48] .

3.5. The link between stress, post-traumatic stress disorder, and cortisol

Cortisol is the primary stress hormone, a steroid hormone of the adrenal cortex, which participates in the regulation of metabolism of carbohydrates, fats, and proteins. It has a role in stress and a variety of inflammatory processes in the body [49]. Dysregulation of the secretion of this hormone triggers severe dysregulation mechanisms in the body during stress with far-reaching consequences. Hypothalamic-pituitary-adrenal axis activates during the stress. If the acute stress is not removed and is prolonged to chronic stress, such deregulated secretion of cortisol can lead to outbreaks of a disease caused by suppressive effects of cortisol on the immune system. Frequent infections and neoplasms can also occur [50]. The stimulative effect of cortisol on proinflammatory cytokines leads to autoimmune diseases and malignancies [51].

Endocrine imbalance is reflected in altered cortisol concentrations and increased sensitivity of the liver, which produces insulin in the case of increased cortisol secretion leading to the clinical manifestation of increased blood glucose levels [52, 53]. Hypercortisolism and cognitive deficits that can also occur are associated with obsessive compulsive disorder, panic disorder, or melancholic depression [54]. The ability to bind cortisol receptors in the hippocampus affects memory and consciousness. Excessive production of cortisol can lead to hippocampal atrophy that can be clinically seen in different dissociative disorders [55]. Yehuda et al. [56] showed the correlation of chronic stress and post-traumatic stress disorder with lower cortisol levels. They explained it as the huge influence of chronic stress on the hypothalamic-pituitary-adrenal axis, which is exhausted. Other research has shown that there is increased secretion of cortisol in those with PTSD. Such research has been conducted on veterans from Vietnam who had been diagnosed with PTSD. There is documented data from studies that have monitored the course and development of PTSD in abused children showing also increased secretion of cortisol due to the experienced and re-experienced trauma. This suggests that the levels of circulating basal cortisol may occur until a person develops a mechanism leading either to healing, in the sense that they will not develop PTSD, or to triggering the effects of increased cortisol concentrations in response to stress and consequently to the development of some psychiatric disorder like post-traumatic stress disorder or some other manifestation, for example, a somatic one. Despite previous studies, some researchers have documented normal levels of cortisol during stress [23, 25, 56]. Female population is still more affected by the post-traumatic stress disorder, but recent studies pinpoint the effects of the global situation that affects to a great extent the trauma level in male population. In a study of 49 male therapy naïve patients with PTSD, Starcevic et al. [12] documented decreased levels of cortisol, which induced decreased volumes of, especially, left amygdala, right putamen, total hippocampal volume, and prefrontal cortex.

Headaches, as primary manifestations of hyperarousal, are among the major occurrences in patients with post-traumatic stress disorder. They appear to be associated with decreased volumes of subcortical cerebral structures as well as with co-occurrence of anxiety and depression in male therapy naïve patients with PTSD [12, 44].

4. Future prospective

Researchers have made a significant progress in identifying neuroanatomical structures that could be defined as substrates or predictors of post-traumatic stress disorders. Given the complexity of the genesis of post-traumatic stress disorder, it is unlikely that it will be defined by only one biomarker. Neuroimaging investigation defined decreased volumes of most cerebral structures as neuroanatomical substrates in PTSD, and some of them, such as left amygdala, can be used as possible predictive structures for this psychiatric disorder [12].

Studies are moving toward the recognition of different biomarkers that would indicate the presence of clinically significant symptoms and a predisposition or increased risk for developing the post-traumatic stress disorder. Such recognition can be achieved by increasing the number of studies, participants and of different methodology like diffusion tensor imaging (DTI) or functional magnetic resonance imaging (fMRI) and then correlated with the results obtained from animal model studies.

Particular attention should be focused to further assessment of morphological predictive factors in establishing a definitive diagnosis of post-traumatic stress disorder.

Author details

Ana Starcevic

Address all correspondence to: ana.starcevic22@gmail.com

Institute for Anatomy, Medical faculty, University of Belgrade, Serbia

References

[1] Chopko BA, Palmieri PA, Adams RE. Posttraumatic Growth in Relation to the Frequency and Severity of Traumatic Experiences Among Police Officers in Small to Midsize Departments.J Interpers Violence. 2016 May 18. pii: 0886260516651089.

[2] Amunts K, Kedo O, Kindler M, Pieperhoff P, Mohlberg H, Shah NJ, et al. Cytoarchitectonic mapping of the human amygdala, hippocampal region and entorhinal cortex: intersubject variability and probability maps. Anat Embryol (Berl). 2005;210(5–6):343–352. doi:10.1007/s00429-005-0025-5

[3] Morey RA, Gold AL, LaBar KS, Beall SK, Brown VM, Haswell CC, et al. Amygdala volume changes in posttraumatic stress disorder in a large case-controlled veterans group. Arch Gen Psychiatry. 2012;69(11):1169–1178. doi:10.1001/archgenpsychiatry.2012.50.

[4] Bremner JD, Randal P, Scot TM, Seibyl JP, Southwick SM, Delaney RC, et al. MRI-based measure of hippocampal volume in patients with PTSD. Am J Psychiatry. 1995;152:973–981. doi:10.1176/ajp.152.7.973

[5] Bremner D. Does stress damage the brain? Biol Psychiatry. 1999;45(7):797–805. doi: 10.1016/S0006-3223(99)00009-8

[6] Newport DJ, Nemeroff CB. Neurobiology of posttraumatic stress disorder. Curr Opin Neurobiol. 2010;10(2):211–218. doi:10.1016/S0959-4388(00)00080-5

[7] Skelton K, Ressler KJ, Norrholm SD, Jovanovic T, Bradley-Davino B. PTSD and gene variants: new pathways and new thinking. Neuropharmacology. 2012;62(2):628–637. doi:10.1016/j.neuropharm.2011.02.013

[8] Milad MR, Pitman RK, Ellis CB, Gold AL, Shin LM, Lasko NB, et al. Neurobiological basis of failure to recall extinction memory in posttraumatic stress disorder. Biol Psychiatry. 2009;66(12):1075–1082. doi:10.1016/j.biopsych.2009.06.026

[9] Bremner JD. Traumatic stress: effects on the brain. Dialogues Clin Neurosci. 2006;8(4): 445–461. Review. [PubMed: 17290802]

[10] Filipovic BR, Djurovic B, Marinkovic S, Stijak L, Aksic M, Nikolic V, et al. Volume changes of corpus striatum, thalamus, hippocampus and lateral ventricles in posttraumatic stress disorder (PTSD) patients suffering from headaches and without therapy. Cent Eur Neurosurg. 2011;72(3):133–137. doi:10.1055/s-0030-1253349

[11] Qiu MH, Yao QL, Vetrivelan R, Chen MC, Lu J. Nigrostriatal Dopamine Acting on Globus Pallidus Regulates Sleep. Cereb Cortex. 2016;26(4):1430-9. doi: 10.1093/cercor/bhu241.

[12] Starcevic A, Postic S, Radojicic Z, Starcevic B, Milovanovic S, Ilankovic A, et al. Volumetric analysis of amygdala, hippocampus, and prefrontal cortex in therapy-naive PTSD participants. Biomed Res Int. 2014;2014:968495.

[13] Joëls M. Functional actions of corticosteroids in the hippocampus. Eur J Pharmacol. 2008;583(2–3):312–321. doi:10.1016/j.ejphar.2007.11.064.

[14] Orcutt HK, King LA, King DW. Male-perpetrated violence among Vietnam veteran couples: relationships with veteran's early life characteristics, trauma history, and PTSD symptomatology. J Trauma Stress. 2003;16(4):381–390. PMID: 12895021

[15] Regan J, Barrett D, Gordon S. Childhood trauma and combat-related PTSD. Tenn Med. 2007;100(10):47–48. PMID: 17966719

[16] Koenigs M, Huey ED, Raymont V, Cheon B, Solomon J, Wassermann EM, et al. Focal brain damage protects against post-traumatic stress disorder in combat veterans. Nat Neurosci. 2008;11(2):232–237. doi:10.1038/nn2032

[17] Stein MB, Hannah C, Koverola C, Yehuda R, Torchia M, McClarty B, et al. Neuroanatomical and neuroendocrine correlates in adulthood of severe sexual abuse in child-

hood. Presented at the 33rd Annual Meeting, American College of Neuropsychopharmacology; December 1994; San Juan, puerto Rico.

[18] Karl A, Schaefer M, Malta LS, Dörfel D, Rohleder N, Werner A. A meta-analysis of structural brain abnormalities in PTSD. Neurosci Biobehav Rev. 2006;30 (7):1004–1031. PMID: 16730374

[19] Han F, Xiao B, Wen L. Loss of glial cells of the hippocampus in a rat model of post-traumatic stress disorder. Neurochem Res. 2015;40(5):942–951. doi:10.1007/s11064-015-1549-6.

[20] Golub Y, Kaltwasser SF, Mauch CP, Herrmann L, Schmidt U, Holsboer F, et al. Reduced hippocampus volume in the mouse model of Posttraumatic Stress Disorder. J Psychiatr Res. 2011;45(5):650–659. doi:10.1016/j.jpsychires.2010.10.014

[21] LeDoux JE, Farb C, Ruggiero DA. Topographic organization of neurons in the acoustic thalamus that project to the amygdala. J Neurosci. 1990;10(4):1043–1054. doi:0270-6474/90/041043-1

[22] Yehuda R, Halligan SL, Grossman R, Golier JA, Wong C. The cortisol and glucocorticoid receptor response to low dose dexamethasone administration in aging combat veterans and holocaust survivors with and without posttraumatic stress disorder. Biol Psychiatry. 2002;52(5):393–403. doi:10.1016/S0006-3223(02)01357-4

[23] Yehuda R, Southwick SM, Nussbaum G, Wahby V, Giller EL Jr., Mason JW. Low urinary cortisol excretion in patients with posttraumatic stress disorder. J Nerv Ment Dis 1990;178(6):366–369. PMID: 2348190

[24] Kim E Barrett, William F Ganong Ganong's Review of Medical Physiology .New York, 2010;London by McGraw Hill Medical

[25] Yehuda R, Kahana B, Binder-Brynes K, Southwick SM, Mason JW, Giller L. Low urinary cortisol excretion in Holocaust survivors with posttraumatic stress disorder. Am J Psychiatry. 1995; 152(7):982–986. doi:10.1176/ajp.152.7.982

[26] Kuljić B, Savić V, Černak I, Leposavić Lj, Milovanović S. Chronic stress procedure-experimental model of depression or posttraumatic stress disorder (neuroendocrinological characteristics). Psychatry.dan. 1999;31(4):283–295. /2000/32/2-3/73-93/

[27] Resnick H, Yehuda R, Pitman RK, Foy DW. Effect of previous trauma on acute plasma cortisol level following rape. Am J Psychiatry. 1995;152:1675–1677. doi:10.1176/ajp.152.11.1675

[28] Lazarus RS. Psychological stress and the coping process. New York: McGraw-Hill, 1966

[29] Hawk LW, Dougall AL, Ursano RJ, Baum A. Urinary catecholamines and cortisol in recent-onset posttraumatic stress disorder after motor vehicle accidents. Psychosom Med. 2000;62(3):423–434. PMID: 10845356

[30] Eickhoff SB, Paus T, Caspers S, Grosbras MH, Evans AC, Zilles K, et al. Assignment of functional activations to probabilistic cytoarchitectonic areas revisited. Neuroimage. 2007;36(3):511–521. PMID: 17499520

[31] Koenigs M, Grafman J. Posttraumatic stress disorder: the role of medial prefrontal cortex and amygdala. Neuroscientist. 2009 Oct;15(5):540–548. doi: 10.1177/1073858409333072

[32] Koenigs M, Huey ED, Raymont V, Cheon B, Solomon J, et al. Focal brain damage protects against post-traumatic stress disorder in combat veterans. Nat Neurosci. 2008 Feb;11(2):232–237. doi:10.1038/nn2032

[33] Rogers MA, Yamasue H, Abe O, Yamada H, Ohtani T, Iwanami A, et al. Smaller amygdala volume and reduced anterior cingulate gray matter density associated with the history of post-traumatic stress disorder. Psychiatry Res.-Neuroimaging. 2009;174(3):210–216. doi:10.1016/j.pscychresns.2009.06.001

[34] Weiss SJ. Neurobiological alterations associated with traumatic stress. Perspect Psychiatr Care. 2007 Jul;43(3):114–122. doi:10.1111/j.1744-6163.2007.00120.x

[35] De Bellis MD, Keshavan MS, Shifflett H, Iyengar S, Beers SR, Hall J, et al. Brain structures in pediatric maltreatment-related posttraumatic stress disorder: a socio demographically matched study. Biol Psychiatry. 2002;52:1066–1078. doi:10.1016/S0006-3223(02)01459-2

[36] Doyère V, Debbie J, Monfils MH, Schaefer GE, LeDoux JE. Synapse-specific reconsolidation of distinct fear memories in the lateral amygdala. Nat Neurosci. 2007 Apr;10(4): 414–416. PMID: 17351634

[37] DeYoung CG, Hirsh JB, Shane MS, Papademetris X, Rajeevan N, Gray JR. Testing predictions from personality neuroscience. Brain structure and the big five. Psychol Sci. 2010;21(6):820–828. doi:10.1177/0956797610370159

[38] Liston C, Miller MM, Goldwater DS, Radley JJ, Rocher AB, Hof PR, et al. Stress-induced alterations in prefrontal cortical dendritic morphology predict selective impairments in perceptual attentional set-shifting. J Neurosci. 2006;26(30):7870–7874. doi:10.1523/JNEUROSCI.1184-06.2006

[39] Rajkowska G. Morphometric methods for studying the prefrontal cortex in suicide victims and psychiatric patients. Ann NY Acad Sci. 1997;836:253–268. doi:10.1111/j.1749-6632.1997.tb52364.x

[40] Erickson KI, Leckie RL, Weinstein AM. Physical activity, fitness, and gray matter volume. Neurobiol. Aging. 2014;35(2):S20–S28. doi:10.1016/j

[41] Wang J, Korczykowksy M, Rao H, Fan Y, Pluta J, Gur RC et al. Gender diff erence in neural response to psychological stress. Soc Cogn Aff ect Neurosci 2008;2:227–239. doi: 10.1093/scan/nsm018

[42] Reichel JM, Nissel S, Rogel-Salazar G, Mederer A, Käfer K, Bedenk BT, et al. Distinct behavioral consequences of short-term and prolonged GABAergic depletion in prefrontal cortex and dorsal hippocampus. Front Behav Neurosci. 2015 Jan 13;8:452. doi:10.3389/fnbeh.2014.00452

[43] Chen L, Qi R, Chen XY, Xue Y, Xu R, Wei HJ. Modulation of the activity of globus pallidus by dopamine D1-like receptors in parkinsonian rats.Neuroscience. 2011 Oct 27;194:181–8. doi: 10.1016/j.neuroscience.2011.08.011.

[44] Filipovic BR, Djurovic B, Marinkovic S, Stijak L, Aksic M, Nikolic V, Starcevic A, Radonjic V. Volume changes of corpus striatum, thalamus, hippocampus and lateral ventricles in posttraumatic stress disorder (PTSD) patients suffering from headaches and without therapy. Cent Eur Neurosurg. 2011;72(3):133–137. doi:10.1055/s-0030-1253349

[45] Goelman G, Ilinca R, Zohar, Weinstock M. Functional connectivity in prenatally stressed rats with and without maternal treatment with ladostigil, a brain-selective monoamine oxidase inhibitor. Eur J Neurosci. 2014;40(5):2734–2743. doi:10.1111/ejn. 12621.

[46] Nofzinger EA, Buysse DJ, Miewald JM, et al. Human regional cerebral glucose metabolism during non rapid eye movement sleep in relation to waking. Brain 2002;125:1105–1115. PMID: 11960899

[47] Basta M, Chrousos GP, Vela-Bueno A, Vgontzas AN. Chronic insomnia and stress syndrome. Sleep Med Clin. 2007;2(2):79–291. doi:10.1016/j.jsmc.2007.04.002

[48] Ohayon MM. Epidemiology of insomnia: what we know and what we still need to learn. Sleep Med Rev. 2002;6:97–111. PMID: 12531146

[49] Hoehn K, Marieb EN. Human Anatomy & Physiology. San Francisco: Benjamin Cummings. 2010. ISBN 0-321-60261-7.

[50] Meewisse ML, Reitsma JB, de Vries GJ, Gersons BP, Olff M. Cortisol and post-traumatic stress disorder in adults: systematic review and meta-analysis. Br J Psychiatry. 2007;191:387–392. PMID: 17978317

[51] Elenkov IJ. Glucocorticoids and the Th1/Th2 balance. Ann NY Acad Sci. 2004;1024(1): 138–146. doi:10.1196/annals.1321.010

[52] Gerald DG, Dominique C, Rheem AD. Post-traumatic stress disorder: revisiting adrenergics, glucocorticoids, immune system effects and homeostasis. Clin Transl Immunol. 2014(3);e27. doi:10.1038/cti.2014.26

[53] Baynes J, Dominiczak M. Medical Biochemistry. Mosby Elsevier. 2009. ISBN 0-323-05371-8

[54] Guilliams TG, Edwards L. Chronic stress and the HPA axis: clinical assessment and therapeutic considerations. The Standard. 2010;9:2.

[55] Lupien SJ, de Leon M, de Santi S, Convit A, Tarshish C, Nair NPV, et al. Cortisol levels during human aging predict hippocampal atrophy and memory deficits. Nat Neurosci. 1998;1:69–73. doi:10.1038/271

[56] Yehuda R, Bierer LM, Pratchett LC, Lehrner A, Koch EC, Van Manen JA, et al. Cortisol augmentation of a psychological treatment for warfighters with posttraumatic stress disorder: Randomized trial showing improved treatment retention and outcome. Psychoneuroendocrinology. 2015 Jan;51:589–597. doi:10.1016/j.psyneuen.2014.08.004

Chapter 2

Sleep Disturbances in PTSD

Laurie L. Wellman, Richard J. Ross and Larry D. Sanford

Additional information is available at the end of the chapter

http://dx.doi.org/10.5772/64189

Abstract

Stress-induced alterations in sleep have been linked to the development of post-traumatic stress disorder (PTSD) and sleep complaints and disturbances in arousal are continuing symptoms in patients. PTSD-related changes in sleep have not been fully characterized but involve persistent disturbances in both rapid eye movement sleep (REMS) and non-rapid eye movement sleep (NREMS). PTSD is considered a disorder of the fear circuitry, which includes the amygdala, dorsal anterior cingulate, hippocampus, and ventromedial prefrontal cortex. Currently, several animal models are used to examine the underlying neurobiology of PTSD; however, sleep has been characterized in only a limited number of models. Intense conditioned fear training, which may best model PTSD in rodents, can produce reductions in REMS as well as alterations in NREMS that may vary with mouse and rat strains. The amygdala, a central region in current concepts of PTSD, plays significant roles in regulating the stress response and changes in stress-induced alterations in arousal and sleep. This chapter reviews sleep-related findings in patients with PTSD and in animal experimental paradigms currently utilized to model the disorder, as well as the neurobiology that has been linked to disturbed sleep in PTSD. It will also discuss the impact of PTSD treatments on sleep disturbances.

Keywords: amygdala, animal models, conditioned fear, rapid eye movement sleep, stress

1. Introduction

Post-traumatic stress disorder (PTSD) is a neuropsychiatric disorder which develops in a significant subset of the population following psychological trauma. It is estimated that 70% of individuals will experience a traumatic event sometime in their lifetime; however, only an estimated 20% of those who experience significant trauma will go on to develop PTSD. Sleep complaints and disturbances in arousal are continuing and distressing symptoms in PTSD and stress-induced alterations in sleep have been linked to the development of PTSD. However, the exact role sleep plays in PTSD is unknown. This chapter will describe our current understanding of disturbed sleep in PTSD patients, how sleep is altered in animal models employed to study PTSD, linkages between the neurobiology of PTSD and sleep regulation, and current therapies for treating sleep disturbances in PTSD. Our review will discuss the complex effects of stress on sleep, stress parameters that appear to be important in determining post-stress sleep, and the neuroanatomical substrates important in regulating the relationship between stress and sleep. Lastly, we will discuss some of the limitations that need to be addressed in order to advance our understanding of the role that sleep may play in PTSD.

2. Sleep in PTSD patients

PTSD is unique among mental disorders in that a disturbance of sleep is included twice among the diagnostic criteria in the Diagnostic and Statistical Manual of Mental Disorders (DSM-5) [1]—as recurrent nightmares, a re-experiencing symptom, and also as insomnia, a symptom of hyperarousal. By self-report, 52–96% of individuals with PTSD have endorsed experiencing frequent nightmares [2, 3] while insomnia is reported by up to 70% of individuals with PTSD [4]. Unmentioned in the DSM-5, but well recognized by clinicians and PTSD patients alike, is excessive, disruptive movement during sleep [5].

In recent years, much has been learned about the clinical phenomenology and pathophysiology of PTSD, including the sleep disturbances. However, there have been remarkably few studies of the optimal approaches to treating the recurrent nightmares and insomnia that are so prevalent in the disorder and represent two of its major morbidities. We proceed to provide a description of the sleep disturbances experienced by individuals with PTSD, the brain mechanisms implicated by clinical studies, and the treatments, both psychotherapeutic and pharmacological, that have been proposed.

Largely because nightmares occur during rapid eye movement sleep (REMS) and are a distinguishing symptom of only PTSD, among all mental disorders, we (RJR; [5]) originally proposed that REMS mechanisms are essential to the pathophysiology of disturbed sleep in PTSD. At the same time dreams, albeit less vivid and more thought-like than nightmares, also emerge from non-REMS (NREMS) and as such a role of NREMS mechanisms must also be considered. The extant polysomnographic (PSG) literature provides no firm consensus regarding defining sleep abnormalities in PTSD. Enhanced, fragmented, and preserved REMS all have been reported [6–9]. Mellman et al. [10] have emphasized the likely importance of the duration of time following the trauma as an explanation of the diverse PSG findings in PTSD. In a non-clinical community sample of young adults assessed retrospectively by patient interview, both REMS percentage (amount of time spent in REMS/total sleep time) and average REMS segment duration were positively correlated with PTSD chronicity [10]. In addition, REMS latency (time from sleep onset to the start of the first REMS episode of the sleep period)

http://dx.doi.org/10.5772/64189

was negatively correlated [10]. These findings point to a view of PTSD pathogenesis in which REMS plays a prominent role, as a biomarker or perhaps as a central etiologic element.

Mellman et al. [10] suggested that increases in REMS percentage and continuity that occur over time post-trauma could indicate a role of REMS in promoting adaptation to, and recovery from, trauma. While acknowledging that this hypothesis fits well with independent evidence that REMS processes help in the processing of emotional memories, we (RJR; [11]) have suggested that the reconstituted REMS observed long after traumatization may be pathological and, in fact, a sign of poor adaptation to a severe stressor. In a psychoanalytic framework, the repeating traumatic dream would be an indication of the failure of the normal dream mechanism.

An increase in REMS continuity with the passage of time following trauma warrants consideration in the context of the extant PTSD treatment literature. The alpha-adrenoceptor antagonist prazosin is arguably the most effective pharmacotherapy for recurrent post-traumatic nightmares. Although PSG has not been carried out in most prazosin trials, Taylor et al. [12] reported that the drug increased total REMS time and average REMS episode duration in a civilian group with PTSD. This suggests that prazosin's therapeutic effect may depend on a normalization of REMS continuity. Pharmacotherapy for PTSD will be reviewed at greater length below.

Understanding the dynamics of REMS changes after exposure to a traumatic stressor must account for phasic as well as tonic REMS processes. REM density (number of rapid eye movements/REMS time) is the phasic REMS measure most often reported in clinical investigations. In a meta-analysis of 20 PSG studies of PTSD, an increased REM density was the strongest finding [13]. An emphasis on heightened REM density in PTSD is consistent with the early observation of a direct relation between rapid eye movement activity and the intensity of dream mentation in healthy subjects [14].

A greater frequency of phasic leg muscle twitches (calculated as the percentage of REMS epochs with at least one prolonged tibialis anterior twitch; REMS phasic leg activity (RPLA) index) also has been described in PTSD [15]. Although no clear association between RPLA and rapid eye movement activity was seen overall, a single recorded nightmare occurred out of a REMS episode with a particularly high REM density. This observation led to the hypothesis that, as a nightmare unfolds, diverse REMS phasic processes, which can otherwise be uncoupled, may be recruited en masse [15].

Largely because investigations in animals have implicated REMS phasic activity in the processing of fearful stimuli [16, 17], it is important to consider the possibility that severe psychological stress initiates processes in REMS phasic event generators that promote adaptation to trauma, or, alternatively, maladaptation in the form of PTSD. Studying fear conditioning in rats, DaSilva et al. [18] proposed that failure to mount a strong phasic REMS response in the early aftermath of a stressful experience could predispose individuals to the increase in REMS phasic activity that has been observed in humans with chronic PTSD.

PTSD is very often comorbid with other mental disorders, most commonly depression [19]. In addition, new to the criteria for diagnosing PTSD is a set of symptoms, including low self-worth and anhedonia, classed as "negative alterations in cognition and mood" [1]. This raises the question whether REMS abnormalities that have been described in PTSD are in fact a function of depression, for which heightened "REMS pressure" (analogous to increased REMS continuity in evolving PTSD), is the best characterized PSG finding [20].

In order to clarify the distinct roles of PTSD and depression in the REMS changes observed after psychological traumatization, Ross et al. [9] analyzed PSG data by thirds of the night and found increases in REMS percentage and REM density throughout the sleep period in a group of military veterans with chronic combat-related PTSD. These distributions were distinguished from shifts in REMS amount and REM number to earlier in the night, which characterize major depressive disorder [20]. Supporting the importance of brain mechanisms fundamental to PTSD in mediating REMS changes following traumatization, Mellman et al. [10] found that a positive correlation between REMS percentage and time elapsed following traumatization remained significant after excluding subjects with comorbid major depression. Nonetheless, the current emphasis by the National Institutes of Health on Research Domain Criteria (RDoC) in neurobehavioral research provides an alternative perspective, in which both PTSD and depression can be conceptualized as disorders of "dysphoric hyperarousal," sharing in elements of a common REMS pathophysiology.

3. Stress, sleep, and PTSD animal models

By definition, stress is a significant component of putative animal models of PTSD. However, experiments in animals have shown that virtually any stressful experience can significantly impact subsequent sleep [21]. Exposure to many experimental stressors induces a period of arousal [22] followed by subsequent rebound sleep (increases in REMS and/or NREMS) that occur at various latencies after the stressor is removed. REMS appears to be particularly susceptible to the effects of stress and can either be decreased or increased depending on stressor characteristics, for example, controllability [23, 24] or possibly individual resilience or vulnerability to stress [25].

Sleep disturbances, both before [26] and after [27, 28] a traumatic event, may be predictive of future development of emotional and physical disorders. This suggests that stress-induced sleep alterations in animal models may be critical for assessing their value for examining underlying neural mechanisms that produce long-term pathological alterations in behavior as well as for understanding the linkage between stress and continuing sleep disturbances in PTSD. Unfortunately, current efforts are hampered by a lack of full understanding of alterations in sleep associated with traumatic events that lead to PTSD. There also is relatively limited work examining sleep in animal stress models as well as an incomplete understanding of what those stress-induced alterations indicate with respect to successful or unsuccessful coping with stressful events. That is, although stress can have a significant, long-lasting negative impact on health, stressors are commonly encountered in daily life without producing permanent or pathological changes, and the majority of individuals cope with traumatic life events with only transitory effects. Many of the stress models that have been explored produce differences in subsequent sleep, as illustrated in the models discussed below; however, their actual relevance to PTSD, for the most part, is not known.

3.1. Fear conditioning stress

PTSD is viewed as a disorder of the brain's fear system [29]. As such, experimental fear conditioning is a leading experimental model of processes thought to be related to PTSD as it allows exploration of learned fear and anxiety in animals [30–35]. Fear conditioning occurs when a neutral stimulus or context becomes associated with the occurrence of a significant aversive emotional event; subsequently, those previously neutral stimuli and contexts alone can elicit behavioral and physiological fear responses similar to those induced by the aversive event itself. During training, animals are exposed to an aversive stimulus (unconditioned stimulus; US (usually footshock)) in experimental paradigms that utilize various numbers of trials, shock intensities, and durations. For cued fear conditioning a tone or light is utilized (conditioned stimulus; CS) to alert the animals to the shock. Contextual fear conditioning does not alert the animal to the shock and as such the animal simply associates the context (also a CS) with the shock. After training, the cued or contextual CS elicits physiological and behavioral response (conditioned response; CR) similar to those produced by the US. The animal can be tested for fear memory by presenting the CS and measuring the CR.

Fear conditioning models are particularly relevant for PTSD as they can engage fear memory processes without requiring a full re-experiencing of the stressful event. These paradigms are also valuable because they allow stressor parameters (e.g., duration, intensity, controllability) to be manipulated and allow fear memory processes to be assessed and manipulated. They have been highly used for explorations of the relationship between fear memory and sleep. However, it is important to note that conditioned fear also can underlie adaptive behavior that typically is extinguished when the fear-inducing situation is removed. Fear "extinction" learning creates a new memory that inhibits subsequent fear without erasing the original memory for fear conditioning [36]. It is the failure of extinction that has been linked to persisting symptoms of PTSD [37]. The effects on sleep of stress, conditioned responses, and extinction in paradigms related to fear conditioning are discussed below.

3.1.1. Footshock stress

Footshock has been utilized as a stressor in models relevant to anxiety and depression, as well as specifically to PTSD. Like some other stress models, the effects on sleep vary with stressor parameters as well as the putative resilience and vulnerability of the animal receiving the stressful experience.

A variety of studies have demonstrated enhanced REMS in rats [38–42] and mice [43] (and rats also denser ponto-geniculo-occipital (PGO) waves, a signature characteristic of REMS [38]) at various latencies after shock avoidance training in a shuttle box. In the avoidance paradigm, animals are signaled of imminent shock and can learn to jump to safety without shock ever being delivered. The increases in REMS have typically been viewed in the context of learning and interpreted as indicating a role for REMS in memory consolidation, but there is potential significant stress as the learning is motivated by footshock.

By comparison, Adrien et al. [44] in an early study using an extensive inescapable shock (IS) paradigm (60 footshocks of relatively high intensity (0.8 mA) and duration (15 s)) found greater

REMS latency, reduced REMS and increased light NREMS compared to the control group and their own baseline sleep. Afterwards, REMS returned to control amounts, but no REMS rebound was observed in recordings that night or the following day. We have also conducted studies utilizing extensive shock training in mice and failed to observe a REMS rebound over ten days of post-training recording [45]. This lack of recovery REMS is different than most other forms of stress (including water maze, exposure to novel objects, open field, ether exposure, cage change, and some types of social stress), which cause an initial REMS decrease followed by an increase (rebound) later during the recording period (reviewed in [21, 125]).

One of the significant differences between typical IS training used for fear conditioning and avoidance training is that animals can learn to totally avoid receiving shock. We have utilized a yoked footshock paradigm in which animals receive identical amounts of footshock, but one of a pair can learn an escape response (simply moving to the safe side of a shuttle box) whereas the yoked animal cannot. Escapable footshock (ES) can produce significant increases in REMS whereas IS can produce significant decreases in REMS (with variable changes on NREMS) [23, 24, 46]. Changing the paradigm (e.g., signaling the footshock) can modify subsequent sleep after ES [47].

Together, these studies indicate that the type of environmental information available to the animal, and the associated learning, are important factors in the effects of footshock stress on REMS. They also suggest that these factors can be manipulated to produce either increases or decreases in REMS, and potentially enable assessment of the role that REMS may have in mediating the effects of stress.

3.1.2. Fearful reminders

It is believed that PTSD patients have impaired contextualization, the inability to appropriately contextualize the traumatic events in autobiographic memory. That is, PTSD patients are unable to process traumatic experiences as time and context limited events. Therefore, it is beneficial to use a model which not only has a physical trauma (e.g., shock) but also enables probing memories of stressful events. Critically, evoking memories of shock training can produce alterations in sleep similar to those produced by the shock experience itself. That is, cues or contextual reminders of footshock training experiences that decrease REMS also decrease REMS (in mice [45, 48, 49] and rats [50–54]) whereas reminders of footshock training experiences that increase REMS also can increase REMS [23, 24, 46]. These directionally different alterations in sleep can occur even though behavioral freezing (the gold standard CR for measuring fear in this paradigm) is virtually identical for both reminders that decrease REMS and those that increase REMS. Pawlyk et al. [54] also showed that cue exposure at day 14 following IS training produced greater freezing than cue exposure on day 1 suggesting that the fear memory can strengthen over time.

3.1.3. Extinction

PTSD patients are generally deficient at learning that stimuli previously associated with adverse outcomes no longer produce a threat. As such prolonged exposure (PE) therapy is utilized to help change the processing of the fearful memory trace (for full description see Section 5.1 in this chapter). In the laboratory, the extinction paradigm is utilized to assess changes in behavior and sleep related to creating a new stronger memory to the previously fearful cue or context. As such, the animals are exposed to the US until they no longer show the CR (typically freezing). We have shown that extinction training is followed by increased REMS (beyond baseline levels) [55]. Furthermore, if the extinction training is unsuccessful, the negative effects on sleep and overt behavior will continue. Work in other laboratories has also found positive correlations between extinction and sleep [16].

3.2. Single prolonged stress (SPS)

SPS has been argued to be an appropriate model for simulating the chronic stress conditions potentially experienced by military personnel. In the SPS model, the animal experiences 2 h of restraint immediately followed by 20 m of forced swim and, after an additional 15 m, exposure to ether until unconsciousness. The SPS model does produce, in animals, increased fast negative feedback of the hypohypothalamic–pituitary–adrenal (HPA) axis [56] and enhanced contextual fear [57] similar to patients with PTSD. Furthermore, following SPS, rats show increased percentage of REMS, increased transitions to REMS, and increased wakefulness during the dark period [58].

Upon subsequent exposure to mild cued fear conditioning, the SPS animals showed impairment to extinction recall compared to the control animals [58, 59]. Unfortunately, sleep alterations associated with fear conditioning and extinction were not recorded, so it is unknown what effect prior SPS and fear conditioning together have on subsequent sleep.

3.3. Immobilization stress

Immobilization stress has been utilized to study processes thought involved in PTSD. Conceptually, immobilization is argued to generate PTSD-like anxiety as it involves the animal (mouse or rat) being restrained for an *unknown* period of time. It can produce both behavioral anxiety and increased negative HPA feedback which are seen in patients with PTSD [60]. Additionally, the timing can be altered from relatively mild (1 h) to extensive (20 h) and acute (1 time) to chronic (across several days) exposure. With a short period of acute immobilization (1–2 h) during the light period, NREMS is increased while REMS may be initially decreased but ultimately increased over the dark period [61–63]. A much more extensive immobilization lasting 20 h a day for 4 days in rats decreased both NREMS and REMS [64]. When the immobilization was conducted for 1 h at the start of the dark period, NREMS and REMS were increased during various phases of the dark period in rats [65–67]. Using rats, Marinesco et al. [68] compared 1, 2, and 4 h immobilization at the beginning of the dark period and found different effects for each duration including no change in sleep following 4 h of restraint. Other authors have also found differences in the effects on sleep depending on when immobilization was experienced [47]. Thus, the duration of immobilization, the acute or chronic nature of the stressor, and the time of the circadian cycle are important for its effects on subsequent sleep. It is not clear which, if any, of the changes in sleep model those occurring in PTSD. Immobilization also does not simulate the situational reminders that often produce symptoms in patients with PTSD.

3.4. Limitation of models

One of the critical problems in studying the effects of stress on sleep in animals with respect to modeling the development of PTSD is the lack of a clear understanding of the nature of the alterations in sleep that are associated with the development of PTSD as opposed to those associated with a normal, and therefore non-pathological, stress response. As noted above, virtually all stressors produce alterations in sleep and it is highly unlikely that all reflect pathological processes. It is also not known whether the initial stress-induced alterations in sleep are the same as those that occur in later stages of PTSD or how they may be modified over time by subsequent life experiences. In addition, work in animals has generally focused on acute stress manipulations and their immediate or near-term effects on sleep. Potential longer-term changes in sleep and their relationship to behaviors indicative of PTSD have received much less attention.

Genetic differences are an important factor in the development of stress-related pathology as approximately 20–30% of individuals who experience traumatic events may develop PTSD [69, 70]. A few attempts to develop animal models that better represent individual differences in clinical populations have included selecting low and high responders to stressors in outbred rat strains [69–71]. However, the potential role of individual differences in resilience and vulnerability has been minimally explored, particularly in studies that involve sleep. The potential differences in sleep among those who develop PTSD and those that adequately cope with significant stress are not known. We have demonstrated that mouse strains that exhibit greater anxiety-like behaviors in response to challenges in wakefulness also show greater and longer duration alterations in sleep after training with inescapable shock and after fearful cues [48] and contexts [72]. Recently, we have also found significant individual differences in stress and conditioned changes in sleep within outbred Wistar strain rats [25].

Thus, significant limitations in animal models of sleep disturbances in PTSD arise from an imperfect understanding of which stressful experiences can lead to persisting psychopathology, how those may interact with individual differences in resilience and vulnerability, and of the role that sleep may play in adaptive coping with stress. These factors suggest that refinement is needed in the way that stress and sleep are studied if truly successful models are to be developed.

4. Neurobiology linking fear and sleep

In order to identify and compare circuitry in normal versus pathological fear responses in humans, cued fear conditioning paradigms are utilized in conjunction with brain imaging. As such, activity within the amygdala, hippocampus, ventromedial prefrontal cortex (vmPFC), and dorsal anterior cingulate cortex (dACC) have been identified as key structures for fear conditioning as well as being central to current concepts of PTSD neurobiology.

4.1. Normal fear circuitry

Amygdala activity is especially important for fear expression and extinction [73–78]. During reversal training, different subnuclei of the amygdala have been implicated related to associational and attentional processes [79]. The hippocampus has been linked to the contextual features associated with fear conditioning and expression and hippocampal activity has been observed during fear behavior in several imaging studies [78, 80–82]. The hippocampus is also implicated in extinction training and recall of extinction [82, 83]. Activity in the vmPFC has been shown to be decreased during acquisition and expression of fear and increased during extinction of fear behavior and recall of extinction [77]. Conversely, dACC is increased during fear acquisition and expression [75, 77, 82]. The amygdala, hippocampus, vmPFC, and dACC are functionally connected during fear expression, whereas just the amygdala, hippocampus, and vmPFC are functionally connected during fear extinction.

It is important to note here that two of the regions involved in the circuitry of normal fear, the amygdala and mPFC, are also involved in modulation of sleep. Neuronal activity of amygdala varies across the sleep-wake states, with increased activity during REMS and less activity during NREMS compared to wakefulness [84, 85]. It is also interconnected with wakefulness promoting and sleep promoting areas throughout the brain. Regions of mPFC also have interconnections with sleep-promoting regions and may be involved in modulation of sleep following fear conditioning. In fact, a recent study found vmPFC activity during fear conditioning was positively correlated with subsequent REMS [86].

4.2. Fear circuitry alterations in patients with PTSD

Imaging studies have found structural abnormalities in fear neurocircuitry, specifically in the dACC, amygdala, and hippocampus in patients with PTSD [87, 88]. Furthermore, this neurocircuitry appears to be activated inappropriately in patients with PTSD. In one study, when asked to recollect traumatic events, PTSD patients had decreased activity in the vmPFC and increased activity in the amygdala compared to controls (reviewed in [89]). This finding was replicated using a task that had presentation of fearful faces [89, 90]. In another experiment, patients with PTSD showed normal extinction learning, but exhibited impaired extinction retention accompanied by increased activation of dACC and decreased activation of hippocampus and vmPFC [83]. It has been suggested that persistent fear in PTSD patients is due to hyperactivation of amygdala and dACC and hypoactivation of vmPFC and hippocampus [83, 91, 92]. This hyperresponsivity of the amygdala to threat-related stimuli may be combined with inadequate top-down governance by the vmPFC leads to hyperarousal and deficits in extinction learning/recall [89].

4.3. Insight from animal models

The amygdala, mPFC, and hippocampus have established roles in fear conditioning and fear extinction (e.g., [37, 93]) as well as being central to current concepts of PTSD (e.g., [94]). Of these regions, the amygdala has a recognized role in regulating fear- and stress-induced alterations in sleep, especially REMS [53, 95, 50] as well as in the acquisition and consolidation of fear conditioning (e.g., [96–102]). In addition to its roles in mediating fear memory and fear responses, the amygdala is important in the regulation of behavioral, physiological, and neuroendocrine responses to stress [103–105] and it appears to be a vital interface between stressful events, stressful memories, and their impact on sleep and arousal.

The amygdala has a strong influence on REMS (e.g., [106–110]), which can be significantly altered by stress [48, 111, 72]. However, there is also evidence that the amygdala can influence all sleep-wakefulness states [107, 109, 110, 112]. This influence most likely involves amygdalar projections to thalamic, hypothalamic, and brainstem target regions [113] that are involved in the control of sleep and arousal. These include direct projections via the central nucleus of the amygdala (CNA; e.g., [114–118]) and the lateral division of the bed nucleus of the stria terminalis (reviewed in [113, 119]), the sources of the major descending outputs of the amygdala to brainstem regions linked to the regulation of REMS.

The functional role of the amygdala in mediating the effects of stress on sleep has been demonstrated. For example, blocking inactivation of the CNA with microinjections of gamma-aminobutyric acid ($GABA_A$) antagonist, bicuculline, immediately following IS can eliminate the reduction in REMS commonly seen following IS [95]. Moreover, blocking inactivation of CNA can alter brain activation, as indicated by c-Fos (a marker of neuronal activity) in a manner consistent with the reduced effect on REMS. That is, there was a reduction in c-Fos activity in the locus coeruleus (LC), an area implicated in the regulation of REMS [120], consistent with enhanced REMS. By comparison, inactivation CNA with microinjections of the $GABA_A$ agonist, muscimol, did not significantly alter the reduction of REMS or c-Fos activation in LC that can be produced by IS.

In addition to its role in the acquisition and consolidation of fear conditioning (e.g., [96–102]), the basolateral nucleus of the amygdala (BLA) also appears to be critical for determining how and whether fear memories impact sleep. For example, the corticotropin-releasing factor antagonist, antalarmin, administered into BLA of rats prior to IS training blocked both IS-induced reductions in REMS and the formation of memories that alter sleep without blocking fear memory as indicated by contextual freezing [53]. By comparison, global inactivation of BLA with microinjections of muscimol prior to IS blocked the post-training reduction in REMS seen in vehicle-treated rats and attenuated contextual freezing and subsequent reductions in REMS [121]. Together, these data indicate that BLA plays a significant role in regulating the initial effects of stress and fear on sleep and in mediating the subsequent effects of fearful memories.

Stressor controllability is an important determinant of the effects of stress and stress-related memories on sleep. The mPFC is a critical region in the perception of control and in mediating the consequences of stress [122–124]. For example, blocking activation of the vmPFC with muscimol in rats presented with escapable shock produced failure in escape learning and greater fear conditioning [124]. By comparison, activation of vmPFC with picrotoxin, a $GABA_A$ antagonist, prior to IS promoted later escape learning in rats provided an opportunity to escape shock in a shuttle box [124].

Unfortunately, the role of the mPFC in mediating the effects of stressor controllability on sleep has not been examined. However, part of the influence of mPFC [124] is enacted through its effects brainstem regions that play roles in modulating REMS [120] as well as in the stress response (reviewed in [125]), thereby providing a potential substrate for regulating the effects of stress on REMS. There also are projections to the BLA and CNA and projections to GABAergic neurons in the intercalated nuclei, which have inhibitory control over CNA output [126]. Thus, projections from the mPFC to brainstem regulatory regions and the amygdala provide a substrate by which stressor controllability could influence REMS.

5. Clinical treatment

Studies of the first-line treatments of PTSD, both psychotherapeutic and pharmacological, have rarely examined the effectiveness of these therapeutic modalities for PTSD-related sleep symptoms. This is especially concerning given the evidence for clinically significant residual sleep problems during and following PTSD treatment [127, 128]. In addition, persistent insomnia and recurrent nightmares can compromise treatment responses to empirically supported PTSD interventions.

5.1. Psychotherapy

The most widely accepted psychotherapies for PTSD are cognitive behavioral treatments (CBTs) and include PE and cognitive processing therapy (CPT) [129]. Galovski and colleagues [130] found that both PE and CPT were effective in reducing global sleep disturbance in adult, female rape survivors; however, sleep impairment remained clinically significant in both groups despite an overall improvement in PTSD symptoms. Gutner and colleagues [128] examined the long-term effects of CPT and PE on sleep disturbance. Similar to previous studies [130, 131], they found significant improvements in waking PTSD symptoms but no remission of the sleep disturbance.

CBT for insomnia (CBT-I) is a brief intervention aimed at improving overall sleep quality [132, 133]. It includes instruction in stimulus control (in order to reduce negative associations with the bed and bedroom) and sleep restriction (in order to increase sleep drive by first limiting, and then gradually raising, the amount of time allowed in bed); cognitive restructuring (to identify and challenge inaccurate beliefs that interfere with sleep); education in sleep hygiene; and relaxation training (to minimize physical and mental tension around sleep onset) [132, 134].

CBT-I may be beneficial for insomnia in PTSD. In a randomized clinical trial (RCT) of CBT-I compared to a waitlist control in a community sample in treatment for PTSD, the CBT-I group had a superior response on measures of sleep amount and quality [135]. However, both groups reported reductions in PTSD symptom severity and post-traumatic nightmares, limiting any conclusions that can be drawn about the therapeutic elements of CBT-I specifically.

Imagery rehearsal (IR) [136–138] is a form of CBT that targets recurrent nightmares. There is evidence that it promotes increased mastery of nightmare content and experience [139]. IR protocols share the following basic steps: choosing a repetitive nightmare, rescripting it during waking, and imaginally rehearsing the new dream script at bedtime. Two recent meta-analyses of predominantly uncontrolled trials of IR reported large effect sizes for nightmare frequency and sleep quality as well as overall PTSD symptomatology [137, 140]. However, a RCT in Vietnam War veterans with chronic, severe PTSD suggested that IR may hold no advantage over a comparison treatment with elements of CBT-I [141]. In a meta-analysis of studies of CBT-I combined with IR, a large gain in sleep quality was reported, but there was no significant improvement in PTSD severity and the nightmare disturbance [140].

5.2. Pharmacotherapies

The selective serotonin reuptake inhibitors (SSRIs) have the strongest evidence base among pharmacotherapies for PTSD [142, 143]. The use of selective norepinephrine-serotonin reuptake inhibitors (SNRIs), in particular venlafaxine, is also supported by clinical guidelines [142]. However, there is little evidence that insomnia and recurrent nightmares in PTSD respond to either the SSRIs or the SNRIs.

The tricyclic antidepressants and monoamine oxidase inhibitors (MAOIs) have not been studied in large RCTs in PTSD [144]. There is only weak support for the usefulness of these classes of psychotropic medication in controlling recurrent nightmares [145]. Considering the prominent REMS suppressant effect of the MAOIs and the evidence that most nightmares emerge from REMS, a methodical investigation of the MAOIs is warranted [145].

The atypical antipsychotic drugs have been minimally studied as a treatment for PTSD. One small placebo-controlled trial of adjunctive olanzapine for combat-related PTSD non-responsive to an SSRI found a greater improvement in sleep, as measured by the Pittsburgh Sleep Quality Index [146]. However, a larger study in veterans showed no significant effect of adjunctive risperidone [147]. There have been no completed RCTs of other medications in this class.

Little is known about the treatment of insomnia in PTSD with benzodiazepines, commonly used to treat other forms of insomnia [148]. Clonazepam, the mainstay of pharmacological treatment for REMS behavior disorder, could have a role in managing excessive movement during sleep in PTSD, a topic for future research. One RCT of the non-benzodiazepine receptor agonist eszopiclone reported greater improvements in PTSD symptoms including sleep disturbance [149].

As noted above, there is strong support for the alpha-1 adrenocepter antagonist prazosin as a treatment for the nightmare disturbance in PTSD. Four placebo-controlled trials of prazosin, two in veterans, one in active-duty US service members, and one in civilians, support its efficacy [12, 150–152]. Prazosin must be administered continuously to avoid the recurrence of

http://dx.doi.org/10.5772/64189

nightmares. It is not known whether there could be a lasting beneficial effect after drug discontinuation.

6. Conclusion

Disturbances of sleep and arousal are significant symptoms of PTSD. Sleep disturbances have also been implicated in the development of PTSD, although, at this time, there is no clear consensus on the role these disturbances may play. As a diagnosis of PTSD may not be determined for several months, there are little data concerning sleep architecture immediately following the precipitating trauma. Thus, the potential role that stress-induced alterations in sleep may play in the development of PTSD is poorly understood and the research questions that could provide answers are inadequately articulated. Problems arise in part because work in animal models, to date, has primarily been descriptive and hypotheses have been based on the effects on sleep arising from experimental stressors that produce diverse effects on subsequent sleep, and can be impacted by a variety of stressor parameters as well as differences in subject vulnerability and resilience. This has led to difficulties in developing hypotheses regarding the potential role of specific sleep states in mediating the outcomes of stress. Thus, improved models of PTSD and improved understanding of the role sleep plays in mediating stress-related psychopathology will be critical for developing more effective treatments for PTSD and sleep symptomatology.

Acknowledgements

Portions of this work were supported by NIH research Grant MH64827 (L.D.S).

Conflict of interest

The views expressed in this article do not represent those of the Department of Veterans Affairs or the US Government

Author details

Laurie L. Wellman[1], Richard J. Ross[2] and Larry D. Sanford[1*]

*Address all correspondence to: sanforld@evms.edu

1 Sleep Research Laboratory, Department of Pathology and Anatomy, Eastern Virginia Medical School, Norfolk, USA

2 Department of Veterans Affairs Medical Center, Philadelphia, USA

References

[1] American Psychiatric Association. Diagnostic and statistical manual of mental disorders (5th ed.): American Psychiatric Publishing: Arlington, VA.; 2013.

[2] Leskin G. A., Woodward S. H., Young H. E., Sheikh J. I. Effects of comorbid diagnoses on sleep disturbance in PTSD. J Psychiatr Res. 2002;36:449–52.

[3] Neylan T. C., Marmar C. R., Metzler T. J., Weiss D. S., Zatzick D. F., Delucchi K. L., et al. Sleep disturbances in the Vietnam generation: findings from a nationally representative sample of male Vietnam veterans. Am J Psychiatry. 1998;155:929–33.

[4] Ohayon M. M., Shapiro C. M. Sleep disturbances and psychiatric disorders associated with posttraumatic stress disorder in the general population. Compr Psychiatry. 2000;41:469–78.

[5] Ross R. J., Ball W. A., Sullivan K. A., Caroff S. N. Sleep disturbance as the hallmark of posttraumatic stress disorder. Am J Psychiatry. 1989;146:697–707.

[6] Breslau N., Roth T., Burduvali E., Kapke A., Schultz L., Roehrs T. Sleep in lifetime posttraumatic stress disorder: a community-based polysomnographic study. Arch Gen Psychiatry. 2004;61:508–16.

[7] Habukawa M., Uchimura N., Maeda M., Kotorii N., Maeda H. Sleep findings in young adult patients with posttraumatic stress disorder. Biol Psychiatry. 2007;62:1179–82.

[8] Hurwitz T. D., Mahowald M. W., Kuskowski M., Engdahl B. E. Polysomnographic sleep is not clinically impaired in Vietnam combat veterans with chronic posttraumatic stress disorder. Biol Psychiatry. 1998;44:1066–73.

[9] Ross R. J., Ball W. A., Dinges D. F., Kribbs N. B., Morrison A. R., Silver S. M., et al. Rapid eye movement sleep disturbance in posttraumatic stress disorder. Biol Psychiatry. 1994;35:195–202.

[10] Mellman T. A., Kobayashi I., Lavela J., Wilson B., Hall Brown T. S. A relationship between REM sleep measures and the duration of posttraumatic stress disorder in a young adult urban minority population. Sleep. 2014;37:1321–6.

[11] Ross R. J. The changing REM sleep signature of posttraumatic stress disorder. Sleep. 2014;37:1281–2.

[12] Taylor F. B., Martin P., Thompson C., Williams J., Mellman T. A., Gross C., et al. Prazosin effects on objective sleep measures and clinical symptoms in civilian trauma posttraumatic stress disorder: a placebo-controlled study. Biol Psychiatry. 2008;63:629–32.

[13] Kobayashi I., Boarts J. M., Delahanty D. L. Polysomnographically measured sleep abnormalities in PTSD: a meta-analytic review. Psychophysiology. 2007;44:660–9.

[14] Rechtschaffen A. The psychophysiology of mental activity during sleep. In: McGuigan FJ, Schoonover RA, editors. The Psychophysiology of Thinking. New York: Academic; 1973.

[15] Ross R. J., Ball W. A., Dinges D. F., Kribbs N. B., Morrison A. R., Silver S. M., et al. Motor dysfunction during sleep in posttraumatic stress disorder. Sleep. 1994;17:723–32.

[16] Datta S., O'Malley M. W. Fear extinction memory consolidation requires potentiation of pontine-wave activity during REM sleep. J Neurosci. 2013;33:4561–9.

[17] Mavanji V., Datta S. Activation of the phasic pontine-wave generator enhances improvement of learning performance: a mechanism for sleep-dependent plasticity. Eur J Neurosci. 2003;17:359–70.

[18] DaSilva J. K., Lei Y., Madan V., Mann G. L., Ross R. J., Tejani-Butt S., et al. Fear conditioning fragments REM sleep in stress-sensitive Wistar-Kyoto, but not Wistar, rats. Prog Neuropsychopharmacol Biol Psychiatry. 2011;35:67–73.

[19] Magruder K. M., Frueh B. C., Knapp R. G., Davis L., Hamner M. B., Martin R. H., et al. Prevalence of posttraumatic stress disorder in Veterans Affairs primary care clinics. Gen Hosp Psychiatry. 2005;27:169–79.

[20] Reynolds C.F., Gillin J.C., Kupfer D.J. Sleep and affective disorders. In: Meltzer HY, editor. Psychopharmacology: the third generation of progress. New York: Raven Press; 1987. pp. 647–54.

[21] Pawlyk A. C., Morrison A. R., Ross R. J., Brennan F. X. Stress-induced changes in sleep in rodents: models and mechanisms. Neurosci Biobehav Rev. 2008;32:99–117.

[22] Chrousos G. P. Stressors, stress, and neuroendocrine integration of the adaptive response. Ann N Y Acad Sci. 1998;851:311–35.

[23] Sanford L. D., Yang L., Wellman L. L., Liu X., Tang X. Differential effects of controllable and uncontrollable footshock stress on sleep in mice. Sleep. 2010;33:621–30.

[24] Yang L., Wellman L.L., Tang, X., Sanford LD. Effects of corticotropin releasing factor (CRF) on increased rapid eye movement sleep and body temperature following controllable footshock stress in mice. Physiol Behav. 2011;104:886–92.

[25] Wellman L. L., Fitzpatrick M. E., Kuzmina O. Y., Sutton A. M., Williams B. L., Sanford L. D. Individual differences in animal stress models: considering resilience, vulnerability and the amygdala in mediating the effects of stress and conditioned fear on sleep. SLEEP. 2016, 39:1293–303.

[26] Bryant R. A., Creamer M., O'Donnell M., Silove D., McFarlane A. C. Sleep disturbance immediately prior to trauma predicts subsequent psychiatric disorder. Sleep. 2010;33:69–74.

[27] Lavie P. Sleep disturbances in the wake of traumatic events. N Engl J Med. 2001;345:1825–32.

[28] Klein E., Koren D., Arnon I., Lavie P. Sleep complaints are not corroborated by objective sleep measures in post-traumatic stress disorder: a 1-year prospective study in survivors of motor vehicle crashes. J Sleep Res. 2003;12:35–41.

[29] Shvil E., Rusch H. L., Sullivan G. M., Neria Y. Neural, psychophysiological, and behavioral markers of fear processing in PTSD: a review of the literature. Curr Psychiatry Rep. 2013;15:358.

[30] Davis M. Animal models of anxiety based on classical conditioning: the conditioned emotional response (CER) and the fear-potentiated startle effect. Pharmacol Ther. 1990;47:147–65.

[31] Davis M. The role of the amygdala in fear and anxiety. Ann Rev Neurosci. 1992;15:353–75.

[32] Davis M. The role of the amygdala in conditioned fear. In: Aggleton J, editor. The Amygdala: Neurobiological Aspects of Emotion, Memory, and Mental Dysfunction. New York: Wiley-Liss, Inc.; 1992. pp. 255–305.

[33] Foa E. B., Zinbarg R., Rothbaum B. O. Uncontrollability and unpredictability in post-traumatic stress disorder: an animal model. Psychol Bull. 1992;112:218–38.

[34] Grillon C., Southwick S. M., Charney D. S. The psychobiological basis of posttraumatic stress disorder. Mol Psychiatry. 1996;1:278–97.

[35] Shalev A. Y., Ragel-Fuchs Y., Pitman R. K. Conditioned fear and psychological trauma. Biol Psychiatry. 1992;31:863–5.

[36] Bouton M. E. Context and behavioral processes in extinction. Learn Mem. 2004;11:485–94.

[37] Myers K. M., Davis M. Mechanisms of fear extinction. Mol Psychiatry. 2007;12:120–50.

[38] Datta S. Avoidance task training potentiates phasic pontine-wave density in the rat: a mechanism for sleep-dependent plasticity. J Neurosci. 2000;20:8607–13.

[39] Smith C., Lapp L. Prolonged increases in both PS and number of REMS following a shuttle avoidance task. Physiol Behav. 1986;36:1053–7.

[40] Smith C., Young J., Young W. Prolonged increases in paradoxical sleep during and after avoidance-task acquisition. Sleep. 1980;3:67–81.

[41] Smith C. Sleep states and learning: a review of the animal literature. Neurosci Biobehav Rev. 1985;9:157–68.

[42] Smith C. Sleep states and memory processes. Behav Brain Res. 1995;69:137–45.

[43] Smith C., Kitahama K., Valatx J. L., Jouvet M. Increased paradoxical sleep in mice during acquisition of a shock avoidance task. Brain Res. 1974;77:221–30.

[44] Adrien J, Dugovic C, Martin P. Sleep-wakefulness patterns in the helpless rat. Physiol Behav. 1991;49:257–62.

[45] Sanford L. D., Fang J., Tang X. Sleep after differing amounts of conditioned fear training in BALB/cJ mice. Behav Brain Res. 2003;147:193–202.

[46] Yang L., Wellman L. L., Ambrozewicz M. A., Sanford L. D. Effects of stressor predictability and controllability on sleep, temperature, and fear behavior in mice. Sleep. 2011;34:759–71.

[47] Machida M., Yang L., Wellman L. L., Sanford L. D. Effects of stressor predictability on escape learning and sleep in mice. Sleep. 2013;36:421–30.

[48] Sanford L. D., Tang X., Ross R. J., Morrison A. R. Influence of shock training and explicit fear-conditioned cues on sleep architecture in mice: strain comparison. Behav Genet. 2003;33:43–58.

[49] Yang L., Tang X., Wellman L. L., Liu X., Sanford L. D. Corticotropin releasing factor (CRF) modulates fear-induced alterations in sleep in mice. Brain Res. 2009;1276:112–22.

[50] Liu X., Wellman L. L., Yang L., Ambrozewicz M. A., Tang X., Sanford L. D. Antagonizing corticotropin-releasing factor in the central nucleus of the amygdala attenuates fear-induced reductions in sleep but not freezing. Sleep. 2011;34:1539–49.

[51] Tang X., Yang L., Sanford L. D. Rat strain differences in freezing and sleep alterations associated with contextual fear. Sleep. 2005;28:1235–44.

[52] Wellman L. L., Fitzpatrick M. E., Machida M., Sanford L. D. The basolateral amygdala determines the effects of fear memory on sleep in an animal model of PTSD. Exp Brain Res. 2014;232:1555–65.

[53] Wellman L. L., Yang L., Ambrozewicz M. A., Machida M., Sanford L. D. Basolateral amygdala and the regulation of fear-conditioned changes in sleep: role of corticotropin-releasing factor. Sleep. 2013;36:471–80.

[54] Pawlyk A. C., Jha S. K., Brennan F. X., Morrison A. R., Ross R. J. A rodent model of sleep disturbances in posttraumatic stress disorder: the role of context after fear conditioning. Biol Psychiatry. 2005;57:268–77.

[55] Wellman L. L., Yang L., Tang X., Sanford L. D. Contextual fear extinction ameliorates sleep disturbances found following fear conditioning in rats. Sleep. 2008;31:1035–42.

[56] Liberzon I., Lopez J. F., Flagel S. B., Vazquez D. M., Young E. A. Differential regulation of hippocampal glucocorticoid receptors mRNA and fast feedback: relevance to post-traumatic stress disorder. J Neuroendocrinol. 1999;11:11–7.

[57] Iwamoto Y., Morinobu S., Takahashi T., Yamawaki S. Single prolonged stress increases contextual freezing and the expression of glycine transporter 1 and vesicle-associated membrane protein 2 mRNA in the hippocampus of rats. Prog Neuropsychopharmacol Biol Psychiatry. 2007;31:642–51.

[58] Vanderheyden W. M., George S. A., Urpa L., Kehoe M., Liberzon I., Poe G. R. Sleep alterations following exposure to stress predict fear-associated memory impairments in a rodent model of PTSD. Exp Brain Res. 2015;233:2335–46.

[59] Knox D., Nault T., Henderson C., Liberzon I. Glucocorticoid receptors and extinction retention deficits in the single prolonged stress model. Neuroscience. 2012;223:163–73.

[60] Neylan T. C., Otte C., Yehuda R., Marmar C. R. Neuroendocrine regulation of sleep disturbances in PTSD. Ann NY Acad Sci. 2006;1071:203–15.

[61] Meerlo P., Easton A., Bergmann B. M., Turek F. W. Restraint increases prolactin and REM sleep in C57BL/6J mice but not in BALB/cJ mice. Am J Physiol Regul Integr Comp Physiol. 2001;281:R846–54.

[62] Vazquez-Palacios G., Velazquez-Moctezuma J. Effect of electric foot shocks, immobilization, and corticosterone administration on the sleep-wake pattern in the rat. Physiol Behav. 2000;71:23–8.

[63] Tiba P. A., Palma B. D., Tufik S., Suchecki D. Effects of early handling on basal and stress-induced sleep parameters in rats. Brain Res. 2003;975:158–66.

[64] Papale L. A., Andersen M. L., Antunes I. B., Alvarenga T. A., Tufik S. Sleep pattern in rats under different stress modalities. Brain Res. 2005;1060:47–54.

[65] Bonnet C., Lger L., Baubet V., Debilly G., Cespuglio R. Influence of a 1 h immobilization stress on sleep states and corticotropin-like intermediate lobe peptide (CLIP or ACTH18-39, Ph-ACTH18-39) brain contents in the rat. Brain Res. 1997;751:54–63.

[66] Koehl M., Bouyer J. J., Darnaudery M., Le Moal M., Mayo W. The effect of restraint stress on paradoxical sleep is influenced by the circadian cycle. Brain Res. 2002;937:45–50.

[67] Dewasmes G., Loos N., Delanaud S., Dewasmes D., Ramadan W. Pattern of rapid-eye movement sleep episode occurrence after an immobilization stress in the rat. Neurosci Lett. 2004;355:17–20.

[68] Marinesco S., Bonnet C., Cespuglio R. Influence of stress duration on the sleep rebound induced by immobilization in the rat: a possible role for corticosterone. Neuroscience. 1999;92:921–33.

[69] Cohen H., Zohar J., Matar M. The relevance of differential response to trauma in an animal model of posttraumatic stress disorder. Biol Psychiatry. 2003;53:463–73.

[70] Kerns J. G., Cohen J. D., MacDonald A. W., 3rd, Cho R. Y., Stenger V. A., Carter C. S. Anterior cingulate conflict monitoring and adjustments in control. Science. 2004;303:1023–6.

[71] Bush D. E., Sotres-Bayon F., LeDoux J. E. Individual differences in fear: isolating fear reactivity and fear recovery phenotypes. J Trauma Stress. 2007;20:413–22.

[72] Sanford L. D., Yang L., Tang X. Influence of contextual fear on sleep in mice: a strain comparison. Sleep. 2003;26:527–40.

[73] Buchel C., Dolan R. J. Classical fear conditioning in functional neuroimaging. Curr Opin Neurobiol. 2000;10:219–23.

[74] LaBar K. S., Gatenby J. C., Gore J. C., LeDoux J. E., Phelps E. A. Human amygdala activation during conditioned fear acquisition and extinction: a mixed-trial fMRI study. Neuron. 1998;20:937–45.

[75] Linnman C., Rougemont-Bucking A., Beucke J. C., Zeffiro T. A., Milad M. R. Unconditioned responses and functional fear networks in human classical conditioning. Behav Brain Res. 2011;221:237–45.

[76] Milad M. R., Quirk G. J., Pitman R. K., Orr S. P., Fischl B., Rauch S. L. A role for the human dorsal anterior cingulate cortex in fear expression. Biol Psychiatry. 2007;62:1191–4.

[77] Phelps E. A., Delgado M. R., Nearing K. I., LeDoux J. E. Extinction learning in humans: role of the amygdala and vmPFC. Neuron. 2004;43:897–905.

[78] Sehlmeyer C., Schoning S., Zwitserlood P., Pfleiderer B., Kircher T., Arolt V., et al. Human fear conditioning and extinction in neuroimaging: a systematic review. PLoS One. 2009;4:e5865.

[79] Boll S., Gamer M., Gluth S., Finsterbusch J., Buchel C. Separate amygdala subregions signal surprise and predictiveness during associative fear learning in humans. Eur J Neurosci. 2013;37:758–67.

[80] Kalisch R., Wiech K., Critchley H. D., Dolan R. J. Levels of appraisal: a medial prefrontal role in high-level appraisal of emotional material. Neuroimage. 2006;30:1458–66.

[81] Knight D. C., Waters N. S., Bandettini P. A. Neural substrates of explicit and implicit fear memory. Neuroimage. 2009;45:208–14.

[82] Milad M. R., Wright C. I., Orr S. P., Pitman R. K., Quirk G. J., Rauch S. L. Recall of fear extinction in humans activates the ventromedial prefrontal cortex and hippocampus in concert. Biol Psychiatry. 2007;62:446–54.

[83] Milad M. R., Pitman R. K., Ellis C. B., Gold A. L., Shin L. M., Lasko N. B., et al. Neurobiological basis of failure to recall extinction memory in posttraumatic stress disorder. Biol Psychiatry. 2009;66:1075–82.

[84] Nofzinger E. A., Buysse D. J., Miewald J. M., Meltzer C. C., Price J. C., Sembrat R. C., et al. Human regional cerebral glucose metabolism during non-rapid eye movement sleep in relation to waking. Brain. 2002;125:1105–15.

[85] Braun A. R., Balkin T. J., Wesenten N. J., Carson R. E., Varga M., Baldwin P., et al. Regional cerebral blood flow throughout the sleep-wake cycle. An H2(15)O PET study. Brain. 1997;120(Pt 7):1173–97.

[86] Spoormaker V. I., Gvozdanovic G. A., Samann P. G., Czisch M. Ventromedial prefrontal cortex activity and rapid eye movement sleep are associated with subsequent fear expression in human subjects. Exp Brain Res. 2014;232:1547–54.

[87] Shin L. M., Rauch S. L., Pitman R. K. Amygdala, medial prefrontal cortex, and hippocampal function in PTSD. Ann NY Acad Sci. 2006;1071:67–79.

[88] Kitayama N., Quinn S., Bremner J. D. Smaller volume of anterior cingulate cortex in abuse-related posttraumatic stress disorder. J Affect Disord. 2006;90(2–3):171–4.

[89] Rauch S. L., Shin L. M., Phelps E. A. Neurocircuitry models of posttraumatic stress disorder and extinction: human neuroimaging research—past, present, and future. Biol Psychiatry. 2006;60:376–82.

[90] Shin L. M., Wright C. I., Cannistraro P. A., Wedig M. M., McMullin K., Martis B., et al. A functional magnetic resonance imaging study of amygdala and medial prefrontal cortex responses to overtly presented fearful faces in posttraumatic stress disorder. Arch Gen Psychiatry. 2005;62:273–81.

[91] Rauch S. L., Whalen P. J., Shin L. M., McInerney S. C., Macklin M. L., Lasko N. B., et al. Exaggerated amygdala response to masked facial stimuli in posttraumatic stress disorder: a functional MRI study. Biol Psychiatry. 2000;47:769–76.

[92] Milad M. R., Quirk G. J. Fear extinction as a model for translational neuroscience: ten years of progress. Annu Rev Psychol. 2012;63:129–51.

[93] Maren S., Phan K. L., Liberzon I. The contextual brain: implications for fear conditioning, extinction and psychopathology. Nat Rev Neurosci. 2013;14:417–28.

[94] Bremner J. D., Vermetten E., Schmahl C., Vaccarino V., Vythilingam M., Afzal N., et al. Positron emission tomographic imaging of neural correlates of a fear acquisition and extinction paradigm in women with childhood sexual-abuse-related post-traumatic stress disorder. Psychol Med. 2005;35:791–806.

[95] Liu X., Yang L., Wellman L. L., Tang X., Sanford L. D. GABAergic antagonism of the central nucleus of the amygdala attenuates reductions in rapid eye movement sleep after inescapable footshock stress. Sleep. 2009;32:888–96.

[96] Cousens G., Otto T. Both pre- and posttraining excitotoxic lesions of the basolateral amygdala abolish the expression of olfactory and contextual fear conditioning. Behav Neurosci. 1998;112:1092–103.

[97] Koo J. W., Han J. S., Kim J. J. Selective neurotoxic lesions of basolateral and central nuclei of the amygdala produce differential effects on fear conditioning. J Neurosci. 2004;24:7654–62.

[98] Maren S. Overtraining does not mitigate contextual fear conditioning deficits produced by neurotoxic lesions of the basolateral amygdala. J Neurosci. 1998;18:3088–97.

[99] Maren S., Aharonov G., Fanselow M. S. Retrograde abolition of conditional fear after excitotoxic lesions in the basolateral amygdala of rats: absence of a temporal gradient. Behav Neurosci. 1996;110:718–26.

[100] Sacchetti B., Lorenzini C. A., Baldi E., Tassoni G., Bucherelli C. Auditory thalamus, dorsal hippocampus, basolateral amygdala, and perirhinal cortex role in the consolidation of conditioned freezing to context and to acoustic conditioned stimulus in the rat. J Neurosci. 1999;19:9570–8.

[101] Helmstetter F. J., Bellgowan P. S. Effects of muscimol applied to the basolateral amygdala on acquisition and expression of contextual fear conditioning in rats. Behav Neurosci. 1994;108:1005–9.

[102] Muller J., Corodimas K. P., Fridel Z., LeDoux J. E. Functional inactivation of the lateral and basal nuclei of the amygdala by muscimol infusion prevents fear conditioning to an explicit conditioned stimulus and to contextual stimuli. Behav Neurosci. 1997;111:683–91.

[103] Bohus B., Koolhaas J. M., Luiten P. G. M., Korte S. M., Roozendaal B, Wiersma A. The neurobiology of the central nucleus of the amygdala in relation to neuroendocrine outflow. Prog Brain Res. 1996;107:447–60.

[104] Roozendaal B, Koolhaus J. M., Bohus B. Attenuated cardiovascular, neuroendocrine, and behavioral responses after a single footshock in central amygdaloid lesioned male rats. Physiol Behav. 1991;50:771–5.

[105] Roozendaal B, Koolhaus J. M., Bohus B. Central amygdala lesions affect behavioral and autonomic balance during stress in rats. Physiol Behav. 1991;50:777–81.

[106] Sanford L. D., Parris B., Tang X. GABAergic regulation of the central nucleus of the amygdala: implications for sleep control. Brain Res. 2002;956:276–84.

[107] Sanford L. D., Tejani-Butt S. M., Ross R. J., Morrison A. R. Amygdaloid control of alerting and behavioral arousal in rats: involvement of serotonergic mechanisms. Arch Ital Biol. 1995;134:81–99.

[108] Calvo J. M., Simón-Arceo K., Fernández-Mas R. Prolonged enhancement of REM sleep produced by carbachol microinjection into the amygdala. Neuro Rep. 1996;7:577–80.

[109] Sanford L. D., Nassar P., Ross R. J., Schulkin J., Morrison A. R. Prolactin microinjections into the amygdalar central nucleus lead to decreased NREM sleep. Sleep Res Online. 1998;1:109–13.

[110] Zhu G. Q., Zhong M. K., Zhang J. X., Zhao L. Z., Ke D. P., Wang M., et al. [Role of basolateral amygdaloid nuclei in sleep and wakeful state regulation]. Sheng Li Xue Bao. 1998;50:688–92.

[111] Jha S. K., Brennan F. X., Pawlyk A. C., Ross R. J., Morrison A. R. REM sleep: a sensitive index of fear conditioning in rats. Eur J Neurosci. 2005;21:1077–80.

[112] Sanford L. D., Yang L., Liu X., Tang X. Effects of tetrodotoxin (TTX) inactivation of the central nucleus of the amygdala (CNA) on dark period sleep and activity. Brain Res. 2006;1084:80–8.

[113] Amaral D. G, Price J. L, Pitkanen A, Carmichael S. T. Anatomical organization of the primate amydaloid complex. In: Aggleton J, editor. The Amygdala: Neurobiological Aspects of Emotion, Memory, and Mental Dysfunction. New York: Wiley-Liss, Inc.; 1992. p. 1–66.

[114] Krettek J. E., Price J. L. Amygdaloid projections to subcortical structures within the basal forebrain and brainstem in the rat and cat. J Comp Neurol. 1978;178:225–54.

[115] Peyron C., Petit J. M., Rampon C., Jouvet M., Luppi P. H. Forebrain afferents to the rat dorsal raphe nucleus demonstrated by retrograde and anterograde tracing methods. Neuroscience. 1998;82:443–68.

[116] Price J. L, Russchen F. T, Amaral D. G. The limbic region. II: The amygdaloid complex. In: Swanson L, editor. Handbook of chemical neuroanatomy Integrated systems of the CNA, Part I. New York: Elsevier; 1987. p. 279–375.

[117] Semba K., Fibiger H. C. Afferent connections of the laterodorsal and the pedunculopontine tegmental nuclei in the rat: a retro- and antero-grade transport and immunohistochemical study. J Comp Neurol. 1992;323:387–410.

[118] Inagaki S., Kawai Y., Matsuzaki T., Shiosaka S., Tohyama M. Precise terminal fields of the descending somatostatinergic neuron system from the amygdaloid complex of the rat. J Hirnforsch. 1983;24:345–56.

[119] Davis M., Whalen P. J. The amygdala: vigilance and emotion. Mol Psychiatry. 2001;6:13–34.

[120] Steriade M, McCarley R.W Brainstem Control of Wakefulness and Sleep. New York: Plenum Press; 1990.

[121] Falls W. A., Carlson S., Turner J. G., Willott J. F. Fear-potentiated startle in two strains of inbred mice. Behav Neurosci. 1997;111:855–61.

[122] Smith S. M., Vale W. W. The role of the hypothalamic-pituitary-adrenal axis in neuroendocrine responses to stress. Dialogues Clin Neurosci. 2006;8:383–95.

[123] Irit Akirav and Mouna Maroun, "The Role of the Medial Prefrontal Cortex-Amygdala Circuit in Stress Effects on the Extinction of Fear," Neural Plasticity, vol. 2007, Article ID 30873, 11 pages, 2007. doi:10.1155/2007/30873

[124] Maier S. F., Amat J., Baratta M. V., Paul E., Watkins L. R. Behavioral control, the medial prefrontal cortex, and resilience. Dialogues Clin Neurosci. 2006;8:397–406.

[125] Sanford L. D., Suchecki D., Meerlo P. Stress, arousal, and sleep. Curr Top Behav Neurosci. 2015;25:379–410.

[126] Vertes R. P. Differential projections of the infralimbic and prelimbic cortex in the rat. Synapse. 2004;51:32–58.

[127] Belleville G., Guay S., Marchand A. Persistence of sleep disturbances following cognitive-behavior therapy for posttraumatic stress disorder. J Psychosom Res. 2011;70:318–27.

[128] Gutner C. A., Casement M. D., Stavitsky Gilbert K., Resick P. A. Change in sleep symptoms across cognitive processing therapy and prolonged exposure: a longitudinal perspective. Behav Res Ther. 2013;51:817–22.

[129] Jonas D. E., Cusack K., Forneris C. A., Wilkins T. M., Sonis J., Middleton J. C., et al. Psychological and Pharmacological Treatments for Adults With Posttraumatic Stress Disorder (PTSD). Rockville (MD): Agency for Healthcare Research and Quality (US); 2013 Apr. Report No.: 13-EHC011-EF.2013.

[130] Galovski T. E., Monson C., Bruce S. E., Resick P. A. Does cognitive-behavioral therapy for PTSD improve perceived health and sleep impairment? J Trauma Stress. 2009;22:197–204.

[131] Zayfert C., DeViva J. C. Residual insomnia following cognitive behavioral therapy for PTSD. J Traum Stress. 2004;17:69–73.

[132] Morin C.M., Espie C.A. Insomnia: a clinical guide to assessment and treatment. New York: Kluwer Academic/Plenum Publisher; 2003.

[133] Morin C. M., Benca R. Chronic insomnia. Lancet. 2012;379:1129–41.

[134] Siebern A. T., Manber R. New developments in cognitive behavioral therapy as the first-line treatment of insomnia. Psychol Res Behav Manag. 2011;4:21–8.

[135] Talbot L. S., Maguen S., Metzler T. J., Schmitz M., McCaslin S. E., Richards A., et al. Cognitive behavioral therapy for insomnia in posttraumatic stress disorder: a randomized controlled trial. Sleep. 2014;37:327–41.

[136] Cooper N. A., Clum G. A. Imaginal flooding as a supplementary treatment for PTSD in combat veterans: a controlled study. Behav Ther. 1989;20:381–91.

[137] Hansen K., Hofling V., Kroner-Borowik T., Stangier U., Steil R. Efficacy of psychological interventions aiming to reduce chronic nightmares: a meta-analysis. Clin Psychol Rev. 2013;33:146–55.

[138] Nappi C. M., Drummond S. P., Hall J. M. Treating nightmares and insomnia in posttraumatic stress disorder: a review of current evidence. Neuropharmacology. 2012;62:576–85.

[139] Germain A., Krakow B., Faucher B., Zadra A., Nielsen T., Hollifield M., et al. Increased mastery elements associated with imagery rehearsal treatment for nightmares in sexual assault survivors with PTSD. Dreaming. 2004;14:195–206.

[140] Casement M. D., Swanson L. M. A meta-analysis of imagery rehearsal for post-trauma nightmares: effects on nightmare frequency, sleep quality, and posttraumatic stress. Clin Psychol Rev. 2012;32:566–74.

[141] Cook J. M., Harb G. C., Gehrman P. R., Cary M. S., Gamble G. M., Forbes D., et al. Imagery rehearsal for posttraumatic nightmares: a randomized controlled trial. J Trauma Stress. 2010;23:553–63.

[142] Institute of Medicine. Treatment of posttraumatic stress disorder in military and veteran populations: final assessment. Washington, DC.: National Academies Press; 2014.

[143] Watts B. V., Schnurr P. P., Mayo L., Young-Xu Y., Weeks W. B., Friedman M. J. Meta-analysis of the efficacy of treatments for posttraumatic stress disorder. J Clin Psychiatry. 2013;74:e541–50.

[144] Ravindran L. N., Stein M. B. Pharmacotherapy of PTSD: premises, principles, and priorities. Brain Res. 2009;1293:24–39.

[145] Aurora R. N., Zak R. S., Auerbach S. H., Casey K. R., Chowdhuri S., Karippot A., et al. Best practice guide for the treatment of nightmare disorder in adults. J Clin Sleep Med. 2010;6:389–401.

[146] Stein M. B., Kline N. A., Matloff J. L. Adjunctive olanzapine for SSRI-resistant combat-related PTSD: a double-blind, placebo-controlled study. Am J Psychiatry. 2002;159:1777–9.

[147] Han C., Pae C. U., Wang S. M., Lee S. J., Patkar A. A., Masand P. S., et al. The potential role of atypical antipsychotics for the treatment of posttraumatic stress disorder. J Psychiatr Res. 2014;56:72–81.

[148] Schutte-Rodin S., Broch L., Buysse D., Dorsey C., Sateia M. Clinical guideline for the evaluation and management of chronic insomnia in adults. J Clin Sleep Med. 2008;4:487–504.

[149] Pollack M. H., Hoge E. A., Worthington J. J., Moshier S. J., Wechsler R. S., Brandes M., et al. Eszopiclone for the treatment of posttraumatic stress disorder and associated insomnia: a randomized, double-blind, placebo-controlled trial. J Clin Psychiatry. 2011;72:892–7.

[150] Raskind M. A., Peterson K., Williams T., Hoff D. J., Hart K., Holmes H., et al. A trial of prazosin for combat trauma PTSD with nightmares in active-duty soldiers returned from Iraq and Afghanistan. Am J Psychiatry. 2013;170:1003–10.

[151] Raskind M. A., Peskind E. R., Kanter E. D., Petrie E. C., Radant A., Thompson C. E., et al. Reduction of nightmares and other PTSD symptoms in combat veterans by prazosin: a placebo-controlled study. Am J Psychiatry. 2003;160:371–3.

[152] Raskind M. A., Peskind E. R., Hoff D. J., Hart K. L., Holmes H. A., Warren D., et al. A parallel group placebo controlled study of prazosin for trauma nightmares and sleep disturbance in combat veterans with post-traumatic stress disorder. Biol Psychiatry. 2007;61:928–34.

Chapter 3

Disruption of Bradycardia During Vigilance: Autonomic Cardiac Dysregulation is Prelude to Disinhibition, Hyperarousal, and Attention Bias in Combat Veterans with PTSD

Jay P. Ginsberg and Madan Nagpal

Additional information is available at the end of the chapter

http://dx.doi.org/10.5772/64492

Abstract

We propose a model to account for the post-traumatic stress disorder (PTSD) symptoms of disinhibition, hyperarousal, and attention bias. We review the background literature which is the foundation on which our model rests, present key results of our ongoing research, and suggest testable hypotheses for further research. Our laboratory is in a Veterans Affairs (VA) Medical Center, where we began our work with a search for the significant causes and predictors of hyperarousal in combat veterans with PTSD using eyeblink and autonomic conditioning protocols. We believe our studies will lead to integration of a treatment intervention for war veterans (and equally as well for treatment of the traumatically stressed in the general population). Our research has begun to show strong associations between lowered heart rate variability (HRV) and PTSD. Loss of bradycardia during normal vigilance is the cause of lowered HRV, which impairs appraisal of threat value of environmental stimulation, thereby leading to disinhibition, hyperarousal, and attention bias toward and away from threat. The next steps of research we plan are outlined and designed to elucidate how HRV biofeedback is a promising intervention to increase HRV during vigilance of stimuli and restore cognitive appraisal and response selection, thereby reducing PTSD symptoms and normalizing behavior.

Keywords: autonomic cardiac regulation, PTSD, combat veteran, orienting, attention bias

1. Introduction

Brain-based hypersensitivity to environmental stimulation underlies pathological states that have been defined as "disorders of arousal" [1]. "Autonomic tuning" is the term that was historically used to describe the process of normally balanced sympathetic and parasympathetic branches of the autonomic nervous system (ANS), in contrast to the disorders of arousal which are characterized by ANS dysfunction, affective lability, anxiety, stress, and emotional disorders:

> It is a matter of everyday experience that a person's reaction to a given situation depends very much upon his own mental physical, and emotional state. One might be said to be "set" to respond in a given manner ... the autonomic response to a given stimulus may at one time be predominantly sympathetic and may at another time be pre-dominantly parasympathetic.([2], pp. 90–91; quoted in [3], p. 179)

ANS dysregulation impacts on both physical (increasing cardiovascular risk) and mental (compromising psychological well-being) health at multiple levels. Loss of regulation of normal autonomic control of cardiac adjustment to environmental stressors leads to negative impacts on physiological function affecting arterial blood pressure, heart rate and rhythm, and vagal afference. Allostatic load is a term that has been used for decades to describe "the wear and tear on the body" which grows over time when the individual is exposed to repeated or chronic stress [4]. Allostatic load is the physiological consequence of chronic exposure to fluctuating or heightened neural or neuroendocrine response that results from repeated or chronic stress. Thus, it is that chronic autonomic imbalance finally leads to allostasis of affective, cognitive, and behavioral level of function. The effect of heart rate variability (HRV) biofeedback (HRVB) is to manipulate peripheral autonomic state feedback to the central nervous system circuits regulating emotional, cognitive, and sensorimotor activity. The study of HRV and effects of HRVB provide important insights into the mechanisms of autonomic arousal in normal, successful adaptation and pathological states such as PTSD.

2. Key concepts

The chapter is organized into several sections. In Section 3, the role of HRV in autonomic cardiac control as it is found in normal adaptation is described. The specific topic headings in this section are: *Autonomic cardiac regulation; HRV and HRV coherence; Neurophysiological basis of HRV: polyvagal and neurovisceral; HRV and orienting; Executive control of attention and defense;* and *Autonomic cardiac regulation and fear.* In Section 4, the topic headings *Autonomic cardiac dysregulation in PTSD* and *PTSD and attention bias* discuss the derangement of normal ANS cardiac control by PTSD. Section 5 has only one topic heading titled *Applied psychophysiological therapy for PTSD and attention bias: HRV biofeedback* which presents the case that application of the HRVB intervention is intuitively and theoretically sound. In Section 6, *Models of Autonomic Dysregulation in PTSD* is a graphic representation of our ideas of how HRV influences orienting in normal and in the PTSD phenotype. In Section 7, the topic heading *Completed Research on HRVB and PTSD* and *Planned Research on HRVB and PTSD: The Action Cascade* details the work that has been done in our laboratory and the direction we are taking to further this important line of clinical research.

3. Theories

3.1. Autonomic cardiac regulation

The ANS controls how the individual appraises the valence of environmental stimuli and the responses selection consequent to the appraisal (e.g., maintenance of resting homeostasis, mobilization of defensive response, task performance, tonic immobilization, and/or affiliation) by interplay between sympathetic (accelerative) and parasympathetic (decelerative) influences on the heart. This model of adaptive behavior integrates polyvagal theory [5–8]. Thus, cardiac adjustments to environmental stimuli affect the internal physiological and emotional state of the individual as well as the quality of information processing that the individual can perform during the stimulus appraisal stage of the orienting response. Bradycardia is adaptive in early stages of orientation to novel or potential threat, while greater HRV power serves to facilitate self-regulation, stimulus information processing and appraisal, and appropriate response selection [9–11]. As we have previously modeled, this process occurs during the initial stage of the stimulus orienting response (OR), and it can lead to autonomic and somatic-motor conditioning [12].

3.2. HRV and HRV coherence

The number of studies of the relevance of the ANS to stress and mental disorder has increased markedly in the past 20 years [13, 14]. HRV is the quantification of the variance of inter-beat intervals (ibi) between cardiac pulses. HRV can be measured by electrocardiogram (ECG), fingertip pulse photoplethysmograph (ppg), or beat-to-beat (continuous) changes in arterial blood pressure. *Instantaneous heart rate* in beats per minute (bpm) can be calculated from a single ibi (with unit of seconds) as HR (bpm) = (60 s/min) × (1/ibi) = 60/ibi. On the other hand, neither ibi nor HRV can be calculated from HR in bpm because bpm is an averaged value. We have been studying and recoding HR and HRV in combat veterans for several years.

Quantification of HRV is accomplished in several different ways. The two most common types of HRV variables, and the most easily understood and physiologically interpretable, are the *time-domain* and *frequency-domain* variables [14, 15]. In the time domain, variance of ibi's, or power, across a recording time period is simply derived from the time intervals of either consecutive heartbeats (standard deviation of all N-N intervals, SDNN) or the differences between consecutive intervals (square root of the mean of the sum of squares of differences between adjacent N-N intervals, RMSSD. More variance = more power. In the frequency domain, power in units of ms^2/Hz is derived as the integral (area) under the curve of a given frequency range. Frequency-domain measures are computed with power spectral density (PSD) analysis using fast Fourier transform of the tachygram of HR against time. The PSD graphically represents how variance or power is distributed as a function of frequency. Three main spectral components are distinguished: very low frequency (VLF, 0.003–0.05 Hz), low frequency (LF, 0.05–0.15 Hz), and high frequency (HF, 0.15–0.50 Hz). There is also an ultra-low frequency (ULF) band of HRV cycle frequency recognized between 0.00001 and 0.003 Hz—that is, a period of months—that has been receiving some attention in recent years. **Table 1** indicates how frequency ranges can be associated with physiologically and behaviorally relevant time periods.

Sec/cycle (Period)	86400	600	300	60	15	10	6	5	4	1	.75
Cycles/s (Hz)	0.00001	0.002	0.003	0.017	0.067	0.100	0.167	0.200	0.250	1.000	1.33
Minutes/cycle	1440.0	10.00	5.00	1.00	0.25	0.17	0.1	8	0.07	0.02	0.01
Cycles/min	0.0007	0.1	0.2	1	4	6	10	12	15	60	80
Function	24 h					RFB and BR	Normal respiration				Normal HR

RFB, resonant frequency breathing, BR, baroreflex.

Table 1. Correspondences of period, cycle, and physiological and behavioral functions in the HRV power spectrum.

There is general agreement that efferent parasympathetic output from the vagus cranial nerve is the major contributor to the HF component. HF HRV power is an indicator of respiratory sinus arrhythmia (RSA), the breath-to-breath heart rate fluctuation due to cardiac modulation by vagal parasympathetic output associated with respiration; in the normal state, heart rate accelerates on inspiration and decelerates on expiration during each respiratory cycle. Vagal parasympathetic output results in cardiac deceleration and higher HF HRV power. Although the mediation of HF HRV is complex, the primary source of HF HRV is mediated through the vagus nerve, such that blocking vagal activity removes virtually all HF HRV [16]. RSA results from interaction between lung and brainstem. Lung inflation activates afferent stretch receptors which results in inhibition of vagal parasympathetic cardiac outflow and increased HR; during expiration, the stretch is reduced and vagal inhibition removed leading to reduced HR. The term "vagal tone" has been used to refer to HF HRV although parasympathetic influence on cardiovascular function and HRV, through the baroreflex, extends into the LF range as well.

LF HRV power is a mixture of activity of sympathetic and parasympathetic cardiac efference and afference in feedback loops between heart and brain that control short-term arterial blood pressure changes. "This discrepancy is due to the fact that in some conditions associated with sympathetic excitation, a decrease in the absolute power of the LF component is observed. It is important to recall that during sympathetic activation the resulting tachycardia is usually accompanied by a marked reduction in total power, whereas the reverse occurs during vagal activation" [17]. Furthermore, after reporting complete abolition of the HF and the LF 0.1 Hz peaks as a result of parasympathetic blockade, Akselrod concluded that "our data indicate that

http://dx.doi.org/10.5772/64492

the parasympathetic nervous system (PNS) mediates heart rate fluctuations at frequencies corresponding to the low- and high-frequency peaks of the power spectrum" [16].

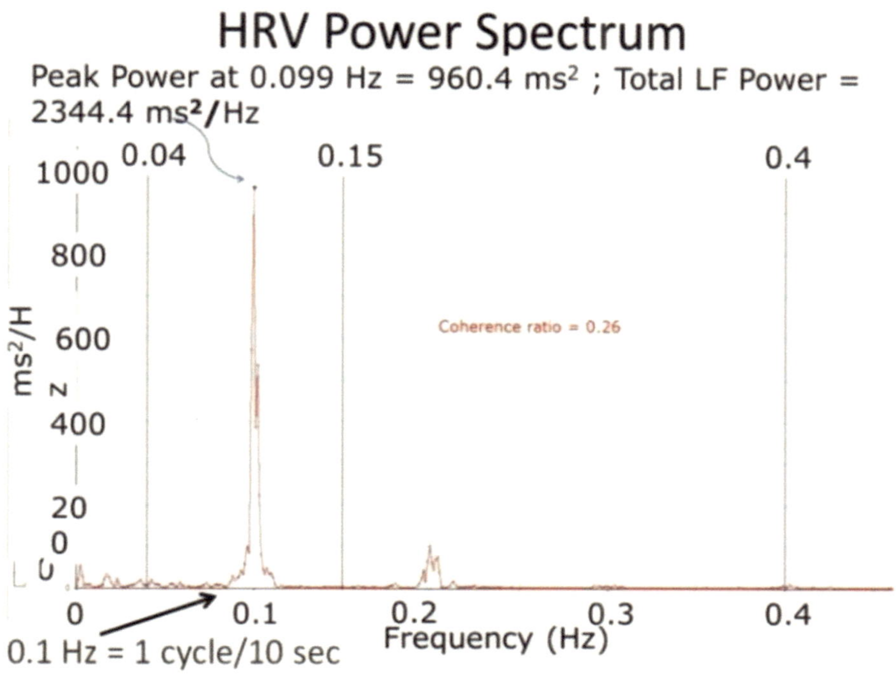

Figure 1. Example of an HRV spectrum showing HRV coherence.

HRV coherence is a physiological state of the individual that is produced when *resonance* occurs in the cardiovascular feedback systems controlling heart rate, arterial blood pressure (baroreflex), and vasomotor tone. When resonance occurs, the difference between the highest and the lowest instantaneous heart rate within one respiratory cycle is maximized [18]. It can easily be seen then that HRV coherence means that HRV of the individual is maximized. HRV coherence is operationalized as the frequency spectrum of a sine wave-like heart rate tachygram that has a narrow, high-amplitude peak in the LF region of the HRV power spectrum, around 0.1 Hz, with no other major peaks in the VLF or HF regions [19, 20]. An example of HRV coherence from our own recording is shown in **Figure 1**. Although there are different ways to calculate a value from the PSD that reflects HRV coherence, one well-known method of calculating a "coherence ratio" is to (1) identify the maximum peak in the 0.04–0.26 Hz range of the HRV power spectrum (which represents parasympathetic function) and calculate the integral in a 0.030-Hz-wide window centered on the highest peak in that region, (2) calculate the total power of the entire spectrum, and (3) divide the parasympathetic power by (total power minus parasympathetic power) [21]. In many if not most individuals who are free from cardiovascular disease, HRV coherence can be reliably produced by diaphragmatic breathing around the 0.1 Hz cycle (six breaths per minute), which is called resonant frequency breathing

(RFB) because that is the frequency when resonance of the cardiovascular system occurs. RFB is integral to the practice of HRVB (see below for more detail). HRV coherence is associated with increased emotional self-regulation and mental alertness [20].

3.3. Neurophysiological basis of HRV: polyvagal and neurovisceral

The polyvagal theory of Porges [7, 22–25] describes the neurophysiological basis of the interface of autonomic state and behavior. Polyvagal theory presents the hierarchical relation among three subsystems of the autonomic nervous system supporting adaptive behaviors in response to the particular features of safety, danger, and life threat in environmental stimulation. The name of the theory "polyvagal" denotes that two vagal pathways operate in mammals. One of the vagal circuits is a vestige of an evolutionarily primordial circuit that associated with defensive responding to threat; the other vagal circuit is a relatively recent evolutionary development, one that is not observed in other animals than mammals. This newer vagal circuit produces physiological states associated with safety and affiliation, and it is crucial for social engagement. Thus, when an individual feels safe the somatic or vegetative conditions are supportive of growth and restoration ("trophotropic" [26, 27]). This newer vagal circuit is characterized by *myelinated* vagal efferent pathways, including the cardiac pacemaker to cause heart rate deceleration and inhibit the fight-flight mechanism of the sympathetic nervous system. The stress response of the hypothalamic-pituitary-adrenal (HPA) axis ("ergotrophic") is dampened, and inflammation is reduced through modulation of cytokine and other immune reactions. Second, integration of nuclei in the brainstem that regulate myelinated vagus with nuclei controlling muscles of the face and head used in facial expressions occurs. As a result, neural pathways are created that enable a social engagement system with bidirectional coupling of bodily states and social behaviors such as facial expressions and prosodic vocalizations [8].

The neurovisceral integration model (NvIM) suggests that vagally mediated HRV (vmHRV) represents a psychophysiological index of cognitive inhibitory control and thus is associated with emotion regulation capacity [25, 28, 29]. Executive brain areas located in prefrontal cortex exert inhibitory influence on subcortical structures, importantly the amygdala, allowing the individual to adaptively respond to demands from the environment and organize responses effectively [30–32]. Thus, at rest, active cortical brain areas are indicative of greater inhibitory and emotion regulation. The NvIM proposes that individual differences in vagal function, as indexed by HRV at rest, reflect the activity of this flexible and integrative neural network which enables effective integration of basic responses (behavioral, cognitive, and emotional) that support goal-directed behavior. The NvIM is founded upon a complex interplay between cortical and subcortical regions of the brain that are grouped under the collective term "central autonomic network" (CAN; [33]). The CAN links the ANS to a higher-order cognitive functioning, especially the prefrontal cortex. Many specific brain nuclei and structures are included and reciprocally interconnected in the CAN: the ventromedial prefrontal cortices, the central nucleus of the amygdala, the anterior cingulate, the insula, the paraventricular nuclei of the hypothalamus, the periaquaductual gray matter, the nucleus of the solitary tract (NST), the nucleus ambiguus, and the medullary tegmental field. Output of the widespread CAN circuitry extends to autonomic inputs to the heart, including the vagus nerve. By exerting inhibitory control over subcortical pathways, prefrontal cortex functions to enable the individual to perceive and adapt to environmental challenges through higher levels of HRV (i.e., greater vagal tone) at rest.

Converging evidence suggests that these core sets of neural structures are responsible for not only inhibition but also the regulation of the ANS activity and reactivity. The heart and other peripheral organs are under tonic inhibitory control by the ANS. More specifically, this influence is characterized by a relative dominance of the parasympathetic nervous system (PNS) over influences of the sympathetic nervous system (SNS). Vagal parasympathetic control represents the major descending inhibitory pathway (DIP), adaptively regulating physiological functions shaped by psychological processes including emotion regulation. The NvIM posits that vagally mediated HRV may be more than just a simple index of healthy heart function, and also serves as readily available measure and index of the degree to which the brain's integrative system for adaptive regulation provides flexible control over the periphery.

3.4. HRV and orienting

Autonomic cardiac adjustments to environmental stimulation are an integral part of the orienting response (OR) to stimulation in the environment. Deceleration of HR is identifiable during the OR, while acceleration of HR reflects response selection of a defense response after a stimulus is cognitively appraised to be dangerous or threatening. The direction of attention (externally toward environmental information vs internally for information processing) and change in heart rate (deceleration vs acceleration, respectively) are linked. Lacey and Lacey [34, 35] put forward the "intake-rejection hypothesis", proposing that attention to cognitive tasks can be directed toward the environment (intake of the environment) or it can be directed toward internal processing (rejection of the environment). Cardiac deceleration occurs during externally directed tasks (e.g., visual attention and search, empathic listening) due to activation of the parasympathetic branch of the autonomic nervous system. Cardiac acceleration occurs during internally directed tasks (e.g., mental arithmetic or imagery, response selection and output or performance) due to activation of the sympathetic branch of autonomic nervous system via release of norepinephrine from locus coeruleus to stellate ganglion of the heart [36].

Autonomic cardiac adjustments to environmental stimulation are furthermore and more basically an integral part of the OR. Orienting is the enhancement of stimulus reception by information processing and appraisal. Early work in this area determined that a deceleration of HR is identifiable during the orienting response, while HR acceleration reflects selection of a behavioral defense response (DR) after stimulus information appraisal indicated the need for it [37, 38]. The history of theory and research on the OR and DR (defense response) includes the role of general psychophysiological measures and phasic cardiac responses in both humans and animals. Obrist called this "cardiovascular learning" [39, 40]. Autonomic substrates of cardiac responding have behavioral significance for the OR and DR, and reveal that cardiac deceleration is necessary for stimulus appraisal after vigilance in orienting, and cardiac acceleration is necessary for defensive response selection [41, 42].

Currently, however, the construct of attention is considerably more complex than is described by intake-rejection hypothesis. Although attention is being defined and measured using varied behavioral tasks, such as spatial cueing, sustained vigilance, and selective focus, the many different types of attention have been grouped into three basic categories, labeled as "alerting," "orienting," and "executive" [43]. Critically, the basic premise that cardiac deceleration is necessary for successful externally directed attention has held up and found new life in the widely accepted practice of employing HRVB for optimal performance enhancement, notably sports preperformance preparation (e.g., [44]).

3.5. Executive control of attention and defense

The human brain is equipped with various executive functions such as selective attention to deal with the vast amount of information flow from the external world in a seemingly effortless manner [45]. Emotional stimuli with their perceptual properties and biological significance must have attentional prioritization in order for adaptation to occur. For example, a dot-probe task was used to investigate whether task-irrelevant auditory emotional information can provide cues for orientation of auditory spatial attention [46]. In this experiment, participants were significantly faster to locate a target when it replaced the negative cue compared to when it replaced the neutral cue, while the positive cues did not produce a clear attentional bias. The results indicate that negative affect can provide cues for the orientation of spatial attention in the auditory domain. By way of possible mechanism for this effect, it has been shown that negative emotion induced by visual stimuli can affect auditory event-related potentials (ERPs) as early as 20 ms after stimulus onset [47], and more generally that scalp potentials are associated reflect autonomic activity associated with behavioral responding [48].

The pressures of evolution have hardwired in humans a set of inborn and automatically activated defense behaviors, termed "the defense cascade." The first step in the defense cascade is arousal; if danger or threat is then perceived, the next step is activation of flight or fight, while freezing is an alternate response at this stage, a "flight-or-fight response put on hold." Tonic, collapsed, or passive immobility (also called fear bradycardia) is the response of last resort, when active fight or flight defense responses have failed and the threat to survival is imminent and inescapable. Each of these defense reactions has a distinctive autonomic pattern mediated by neural pathways. Freezing differs importantly from immobility in the cardiac state: accelerated heart rate characterizes freezing and decelerated heart rate characterizes immobility. The defense cascade is known to activate neural structures that are also central to the CAN: the extended amygdala, hypothalamus, periaqueductal gray (PAG), ventral pontine tegmentum, ventral and dorsal medulla, vagal and sympathetic nuclei, and spinal cord [49].

The hypothalamus (paraventricular nucleus) plays a major role in arousal by increasing sympathetic visceremotor tone and in striated muscles of the somatomotor nervous system. The body becomes prepared for action by vasoconstriction of blood vessels to the salivary glands (dry mouth) and tension one in the laryngeal muscles of the back. Smooth and striated muscles contract, heart rate and respiration accelerate, and posture is stabilized [49].

3.6. Autonomic cardiac regulation and fear

Fear is an emotion caused by the cognition that a stimulus perceived in the environment is dangerous, threatening, or likely to cause pain. Fear causes a change in brain and autonomic system, and ultimately a change in behavior, such as running away, hiding, or freezing.

Heart rate (HR) conditioning in rabbits (*Oryctolagus cuniculus*) is a widely used model of classical Pavlovian fear conditioning of autonomic responding. Acquisition and retention of conditioned bradycardia (deceleration of heart rate) in the rabbit is useful because the rabbit is a species considered by many as an ideal intact preparation for the study of neural mechanisms of associative learning, and in particular, cardiovascular conditioning. The neural mechanisms underlying HR conditioning have been widely researched in rabbits and other species including humans, with studies concentrating on vagal-mediated, parasympathetic cardiovascular changes, sympathetic-mediated changes, emotional/affective learning components involving the amygdala and prefrontal cortex and extrapyramidal system including some but not all cerebellar structures [50].

Up until his death in 2011, Donald A. Powell was for decades a leading researcher in classical (Pavlovian) conditioning of autonomic and somatomotor function and the founder of our laboratory. His major findings (summarized below) continue to guide the work in our laboratory at the present time. A fear conditioning paradigm was used to concomitantly condition autonomic (cardiac adjustments) and somatic (eyeblink) function [51]. This approach was applied to a classical conditioning model of PTSD in veterans and a parallel translational lesion model of conditioning in rabbits [52, 53]. Dr. Powell's research elucidated two separable neural circuits with different fear conditioning parameters: the cortico-limbic circuit controlling autonomic conditioning and an extrapyramidal neural circuit controlling skeletal, or somatomotor, conditioning.

Lesions of substantia nigra prevented acquisition of the eyeblink conditioned response and had no effect on conditioned bradycardia [54, 55]. While medial prefrontal cortex (mPFC) is not critical for acquisition of somatomotor conditioning [56], post-training lesioning of mPFC impaired performance of the conditioned eyeblink response [57–59]. Moreover, while deep nuclei of the cerebellum are understood to be necessary for eyeblink conditioning [60], manipulation of this extrapyramidal substrate does not affect heart rate conditioning [61].

In contrast, lesion studies demonstrated that conditioning of autonomic cardiovascular control requires intact function of a cortico-limbic circuit [62, 63]. Acquisition of conditioned bradycardia in the rabbit is dependent on a prefrontal-amygdala pathway, and the major structures in this pathway are medial prefrontal cortex [64–66] and central nucleus of the amygdala. Interestingly, subiculum of the hippocampus was not found to be necessary for acquisition of conditioned bradycardia in this paradigm [67]. Furthermore, autonomic cardiac conditioning is rapid compared to somatomotor eyeblink conditioning. In animals, conditioned slowing of heart rate was shown to occur within the first 3–5 conditioning trials, whereas eyeblink conditioning requires many more trials, in the range of 50–60 [68]. Similarly, heart rate conditioning in humans was more quickly acquired with shorter interstimulus interval than eyeblink [69]. At the single neuron recording level, mPFC processing of stimulus information appears to be driving decelerative heart rate-conditioned responding [70].

Since the same set of stimulus contingencies will classically condition both autonomic function and somatomotor behavior, the existence of a process that integrates the two would be expected. The septo-hippocampal system may be the brain circuit that performs this activity. Extinction of classically conditioned bradycardia is delayed by vasopressin, which increases peripheral vascular resistance and arterial blood pressure, a result that seemingly increases the autonomic conditioning cortico-limbic circuit to include hypothalamus and pituitary [71]. Intraseptal injection of the antimuscarinic anticholinergic scopolamine in the concomitant autonomic and somatomotor conditioning paradigm enhanced cardiac deceleration and impaired eyeblink conditioning [72]. Thus, there may be a central border zone cardiac-somatic linkage [39] that couples and uncouples cortico-limbic (stimulus registration and appraisal) from neostriatal (response selection) activities [73]. More research is needed in this area to integrate these crucially important past and current constructs of arousal, attention, and behavior.

4. Clinical implications

4.1. Autonomic cardiac dysregulation in PTSD

Unlike animals, which generally are able to restore their standard mode of functioning once a fear-provoking stimulus is past, humans often are not, and they may find themselves stuck in the autonomic profile associated with response that was tied to the original danger or trauma. This is traumatization of the nervous system. When the nervous system is traumatized, current environmental stimuli, or associatively conditioned reminders of the original danger, repetitively trigger the behavioral response to past fearful events. A simple working definition of PTSD then, apart from the formal clinical diagnostic criteria, is that the ANS of the traumatized individual has become stuck in, or is easily shifted into, a state of ergotropic behavioral response to fear, dominated by sympathetic outflow and its accelerative effects on cardiac adjustment. As a result, PTSD influences on autonomic control of heart rate and HRV impact orienting and stimulus appraisal [9].

The effect of PTSD on HRV has been studied since the late 1990s. Our own meta-analysis assessed all available studies of sympathetic and parasympathetic influences on HRV to determine effect sizes and the utility of HRV as a potential psychophysiological indicator of PTSD, summarized below [74]. Using keywords "PTSD" and ("heart rate or HRV or vagal or autonomic nervous system"), 453 potentially relevant studies were identified; after inclusion criteria were added, 39 studies were considered; exclusion criteria reduced the study sample to 19, all of which were then included in the meta-analysis. The meta-analysis was performed according to PRISMA (Preferred Reporting Items for Systematic Reviews and Meta-Analyses) and Cochrane Handbook guidelines, using Comprehensive Meta-analysis Software, ver. 2.0. We calculated the Hedges' g effect size with 95% confidence interval (CI), statistical significance (*p*), and heterogeneity for each effect size estimate. Several HRV variables were considered, and for each an individual, meta-analysis was performed. Heart rate (HR) was significantly elevated in PTSD patients. The available scientific literature clearly showed that reductions in SDNN, RMSSD, and HF power, and increased LF/HF ratio, have utility as indicators of autonomic effects of PTSD, which can be associated with impaired vagal activity. The positive LF/HF effect size indicates increase in sympatho-vagal function under PTSD as compared with controls, and also reflects, we believe, non-linearity in co-occurring shifts in LF and HF power with proportionately greater reduction in HF than LF [74].

HRV has been shown to be significantly correlated with eyeblink conditioning in normal adults [11, 69]; in combat veterans with and without PTSD (PTSD+ and PTSD-, respectively), EB conditioning was associated with resting HRV. In the PTSD+ veterans, frequency and amplitude of eyeblinks, HRV, and immediate memory on a verbal learning test were all lower than in the control group [12]. Factor analysis revealed four separable factors corresponding to (1) eyeblink amplitude, (2) HRV, (3) immediate memory, and (4) self-report of mood state (depression and anxiety), and eyeblink frequency was significantly predicted by HRV and immediate memory. Furthermore, and importantly, in this study reduced HRV was also shown to be associated with poorer performance on the immediate verbal memory test [12]. Further analysis revealed the effects of eyeblink conditioning on heart rate responding in the same study [10]. In this paradigm, which was discriminative conditioning, a light signal was presented for 5 s followed by a tone conditioning stimulus (CS) that was paired with either an eyepuff (CS+) or no eyepuff (CS-). Thus, there was a 5-s vigilance period before onset of the tone CS. A linear HR deceleration from baseline during the 5-s vigilance period before onset of the tone CS was found in the PTSD- subgroup but was not present in the PTSD+ subgroup. This is strong evidence that PTSD disrupts bradycardia during vigilance.

4.2. PTSD and attention bias

Healthy adaptation requires people to allocate attention to genuine threats in the environment while ignoring other similar stimuli. Traumatic events offset this delicate balance and induce cognitive biases that give rise to threat avoidance and threat-related hypervigilance, among other clinical symptoms. Attentional problems are a common complaint of patients with a PTSD diagnosis, and clinical research data support this. Vietnam veterans with PTSD were found to be significantly worse on controls without PTSD on tasks measuring focused and sustained attention [75]. Using the attentional network test [43], PTSD participants were found to be impaired in inhibiting irrelevant information, a function of the executive attentional network [76].

PTSD may be associated with hypervigilance to salient and threat-related stimuli, but results of attention bias studies in PTSD have found biases both toward and away from threat. Hypervigilance manifest as attention biased toward threat cues while avoidance of threat-related stimuli. Attention bias indexes the degree to which attention fluctuates between vigilance and avoidance and is based on reaction time data derived from variants of the classic dot-probe task. In this task, pairs of threat and neutral (or positive) stimuli are simultaneously presented across repeated trials. Each stimulus pair is followed by a target probe appearing at the location of either the threat stimulus (congruent trials) or the neutral stimulus (incongruent trials). An attention bias score is calculated as the difference between the mean reaction times of these two types of trials.

Attentional bias toward threat in PTSD could reflect either difficulty disengaging from threat-related stimuli or facilitated engagement of such stimuli, although there is some evidence that attentional bias toward threat in PTSD reflects difficulty disengaging as opposed to facilitated engagement [77]. Early dot probe studies in PTSD in adults and children reported mixed findings. Some studies found bias toward trauma or threat-elated stimuli in PTSD [78–82], while others reported an association between PTSD and a bias away from trauma or threat [83, 84]. Still others have failed to find significant attentional bias differences between PTSD and control groups, consisting of healthy individuals and a group of recent trauma survivors that included individuals both with and without acute stress disorder [85, 86]. Difficulty disengaging from threatening stimuli has been associated with the 5-HTTLPR serotonin transporter gene polymorphism [87], although the significance of this finding has not been explained.

Iacoviello [88] derived a measure of attention bias by grouping, or "binning," consecutive 20-trial sequences on the dot-probe task and calculating a bias score for each bin. The standard deviation of the bias scores across bins was then divided by the participant's mean reaction time to generate the measure of attention bias for each subject throughout the session. Results of this study revealed greater attention bias in participants with PTSD than in trauma-exposed participants without PTSD and nonexposed healthy participants. Attention bias was also positively correlated with PTSD symptom severity.

Different selective attentional orienting mechanisms underlying anxiety-related attentional bias have been identified, such as engagement and disengagement of attention [89]. These mechanisms are thought to contribute to the onset and maintenance of general anxiety disorders and have relevance for the study of attention bias in PTSD. General anxiety seems to be associated with a preferential bias for negativity. The measure of attention bias has recently been refined by employing a moving average technique, rather than the previously employed binning method, to generate a more stable index that is influenced less by the number of trials in any particular study [90]. However, attention bias is still something of a novel measure, and we know of no reports of test-retest reliability. Overall, attention bias may be best conceptualized as reflecting natural plasticity built into the threat-monitoring system that is influenced by different contexts and situations, rather than indexing a stable trait.

Attentional training (sometimes called attention bias modification, ABM) is aimed at reducing symptoms and behaviors associated with anxiety by systematically reducing negative attentional biases and training selective attention to orient away, or to disengage, from threat [91]. Attention control training, but not attention bias modification, was found to significantly reduce attention bias and reduce PTSD symptoms [92]. Thus, further study of treatment efficacy for attention bias, and its underlying neurocognitive mechanisms, seems warranted.

5. Applied psychophysiological therapy for PTSD and attention bias: HRV biofeedback

The scientific and clinical data supporting the facts of diminished vagal and increased sympathetic activity in PTSD increased notably in the past decade and continue to mount [13]. In developing a treatment intervention, it is important to understand the signature patterns of normal and deranged stimulus processing and appraisal, and response output type, whether immobility, defense, or affiliative. Effective interventions aim to activate, deactivate, or modify one or more components of the abnormal cardiac adjustment pattern. Because the process of treatment intervention pertains to humans, we may speak of an intervention that shifts the response pattern of cardiac adjustment as being a "mind-body intervention."

In our clinical research, we use HRVB as a psychophysiological intervention to study the effects of psychological trauma and its potential amelioration. HRVB is a very well-tolerated, easy-to-use, and effective mind-body technique that appears to have achieved acceptance as an integrative health procedure for routine healthcare. HRVB training teaches the practitioner to self-regulate his or her own HRV by monitoring visual feedback indicating whether or not HRV coherence is attained, and then associating that feedback with self-regulation of emotional state. With practice, the individual learns how to voluntarily and quickly produce HRV coherence using RFB, focused attention, and conscious voluntary positive emotional state. HRVB is an interactive procedure that uses hardware/software systems to monitor and display the individual's HRV patterns in real time. Visual feedback of HRV (either quantitative display or animated challenge games) is provided as participants practice techniques of attention focusing (such as mindfulness), RFB, and induction of a positive emotional state. Acquisition of the skill of self-regulation of HRV coherence takes anywhere from 1 to 6 weekly sessions of about 45 min each. Summaries of the evidence for the efficacy of HRVB in reducing mental and physical symptom burden are available [93–95].

6. Models of autonomic dysregulation and treatment of PTSD

Figure 2 is a model of HRV, orienting, and PTSD. The process begins in the upper left corner of the figure, when a stimulus in the environment is registered A normal OR is initiated in less than a second, and proceeds (blue arrow) to appraisal through cortical processing with an output of cardiac adjustment that depends on the appraisal: stimulus is not further perceived with return to baseline vigilance *or* appraisal of life threat with no escape (immobilization) *or* appraisal of affiliative engagement *or* appraisal of danger with freeze, fight, or flight response. Each of the latter appraisal outcomes is associated with an autonomic state, respectively: return to preregistration baseline, bradycardia modulated by dorsal vagal nucleus, bradycardia modulated by ventral vagus and nucleus ambiguus, cardiac acceleration modulated by withdrawal of rostroventral lateral medulla, and activation of sympathetic nervous system. This process is shown in schematized and highly simplified form in the right upper portion of **Figure 2** (for more detail of the vagal afferent and efferent neural circuits controlling cardiac function, see [19, 31]; see [96] for a thorough discussion of the centrally key role of the paraventricular nucleus of the hypothalamus in autonomic dysfunction). In the individual with PTSD, however, cortical appraisal is short-circuited (red arrows) with repetitive activation of sympathetic nervous system and freeze of fight/flight. We propose that the beneficial effects of HRVB on PTSD symptoms, including attention bias, occur according to the model shown in **Figure 3**.

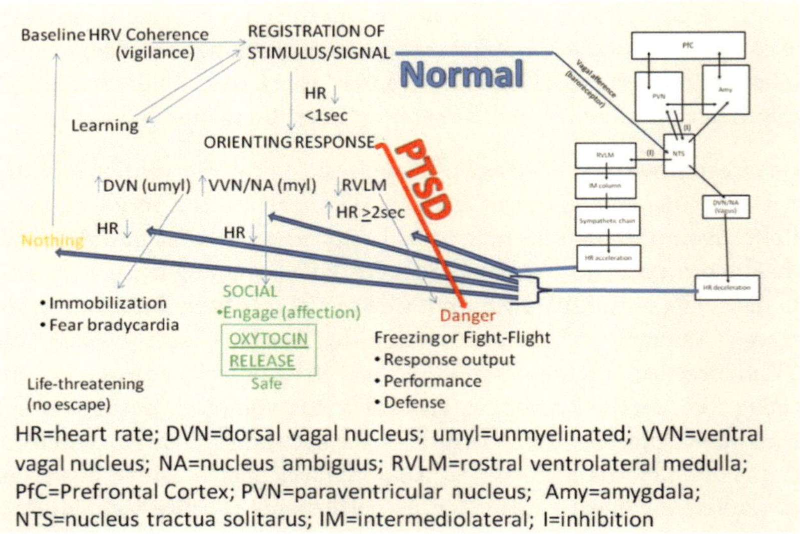

Figure 2. Model of HRV, orienting, and PTSD.

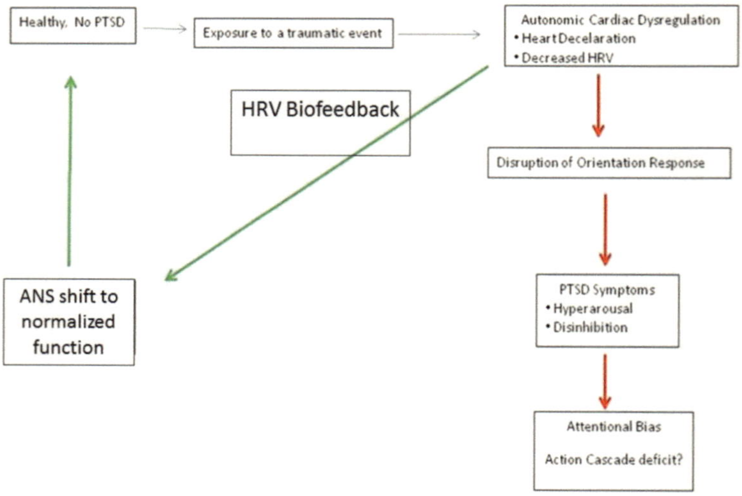

Figure 3. Dysregulation of heart rate deceleraton by PTSD and reduction if PTSD symptoms by HRVB.

7. Research

7.1. Completed research on HRVB and PTSD

In our meta-analysis of PTSD and HRV [74], we also examined the effects of treatment of PTSD on various HRV parameters. The first finding was that very few controlled studies examining changes in HRV variables pre- and posttreatment on PTSD have been published [97–100]. However, all of these studies employed some form of HRV biofeedback as the treatment intervention. The study by Lande [98] was excluded because HRV data were not included in the study report. Using conservative random effect modeling for the meta-analysis, a significant increase in RMSSD could be discerned and a decrease in HR was nearly significant (p 1-tailed = 0.08).

Our small-scale controlled study of the co-occurrence of reduction in HRV parameters and sustained attention in Iraq combat veterans with and without PTSD. We [97] tested the effects of HRVB using as outcomes HRV coherence and a small battery of attentional tests patterned on Mirsky's model of attention [101]. Veterans met with an HRVB professional once weekly for 4 weeks for HRVB. HRV coherence was achieved in all participants, and the increase in coherence ratio was significant post-HRVB training. Furthermore, significant improvements were observed as increased digit span backwards and fewer commission errors on continuous performance testing, with a significant interaction of training with PTSD on word list learning that demonstrated combat veterans with PTSD were able to benefit from HRVB to a greater degree than veterans without PTSD.

Based on the findings of that small-scale study, we recently performed a 3-year study of HRV and HRVB in combat veterans with PTSD, funded by the US Department of Defense. Below are some of the key findings from that study which have not been previously published anywhere else. Operation Iraqi Freedom (OIF)/Operation Enduring Freedom (OEF) veterans 21–45 years old with and without PTSD were recruited from our veterans' hospital outpatient population. PTSD+ veterans receiving standard of care for PTSD were assigned to one of two treatment groups: active HRVB training and sham HRVB training. PTSD- veterans served as a baseline control group only and did not receive any HRVB training. The length of training was 6 weekly sessions. A follow-up assessment was made 8 weeks post-training to test for persistence of effects (no HRVB was administered during the 8-week period post-training until follow-up). Pre-training (baseline), post-training, and follow-up PTSD symptom levels were assessed by licensed clinical psychologist raters using the Clinician Administered PTSD Scale (CAPS). Raters were blind to the training assignment groups. The study used DSM-IV-TR criteria, not DSM-5 criteria, because the latter were not in existence at that time. Enrollment was planned for 30 PTSD+ veterans in each of the two HRVB groups (active and sham), and 15–20 PTSD- veterans in the control group; final results included 29 and 32 PTSD+ combat veterans in the active and sham HRVB subgroups, respectively, and 12 PTSD- combat veterans in the control group.

Some of the important findings from this study are summarized here and are being prepared for submission as a research article elsewhere. HRV coherence was quantified as log10 of the peak LF power, thus the measures of HRV analyzed were SDNN, RMSSD, log10 HF, and log10 peak LF. Nonparametric statistical tests revealed that all four pre-training HRV measures were significantly intercorrelated; overall, SDNN was most strongly correlated to the other three HRV variables, and the largest correlation coefficient with log10 peak LF was SDNN (rho = 0.765, p(1-tailed)<0.001). Pre-training SDNN, RMSSD, and log HF were all significantly lower in the PTSD+ compared to the PTSD- subgroup (Mann-Whitney U, all *ps* < 0.020); however, SDNN discriminated best between groups with and without PTSD.

Data showing correlations between HRV variables and measures of PTSD in a sample this size have not, to the best of our knowledge, been previously published. When the four pre-training HRV variables were tested for associations with pre-training PTSD, we found that Log10 HF power was most closely correlated with severity of PTSD measured as total CAPS score (p = -0.370, p(1-tailed) = 0.001); HF power is a traditional measure of parasympathetic activity and consistent with the research hypotheses, the correlation between parasympathetic activity (which indicates vagal tone) was negative. Thus, as vagal tone increased, total PTSD severity decreased. Closer examination revealed that the pre-training HRV variables associated differentially with the three pre-training CAPS clusters: intrusive thoughts (e.g., nightmares, daytime memories), avoidance/numbing (e.g., depression, avoidance behaviors), and arousal (e.g., irritability, exaggerated startle). Log10 HF power was also the only HRV variable to significantly correlate with all three clusters (p(1-tailed) < 0.05, all correlations negative). The time-domain HRV variables SDNN and RMSSD were both significantly negatively correlated with the arousal cluster. The intrusive thoughts cluster was negatively correlated with log10 HF power, yet was not correlated with either of the time domain variables. The pre-training coherence indicator, log10 peak LF, did not correlate significantly with CAPS total or any of the clusters, presumably because none of the subjects had received any training at that point in time.

With respect to differences between the active and sham HRVB subgroups, whereas pre-training differences in the two HRVB subgroups were nonsignificant (p = 0.913), the post-training active HRVB active group had significantly higher coherence compared to the Sham group (p = 0.007). This is strong evidence that active HRVB training produced coherence in those veterans who received it.

Active HRVB produced increased HRV SDNN and RMSSD post-training, and reduced PTSD, while sham HRVB produced little or no change. Results showed that the interaction of group (Sham vs HRVB+) x time period of assessment (pre-, post-, follow-up) interaction effect was significant, with clinically significant improvements in PTSD severity in the active HRVB subgroup relative to the sham HRVB subgroup. The mean CAPS score of PTSD+ subgroup receiving active HRVB training improved from 79.4 to 57.3. Within the active HRVB group, the mean PTSD severity did rebound between post-training and follow-up 8 weeks later to 60.8, but this increase was not statistically different from the post-training mean, and at follow-up, the PTSD severity mean was statistically lower and clinically improved relative to the pre-training mean. Within the sham HRVB group, there were no statistical or clinical improvements in the mean PTSD severity score post-training or at follow-up.

7.2. Planned research on HRVB and PTSD: the action cascade

The basic results presented above provide evidence that HRVB reduces formal DSM-IV symptoms, yet there remains a gap in our understanding of stimulus appraisal, attention, and orienting aspects of PTSD. The orienting reflex could facilitate attention and perception toward a stimulus on one hand, whereas it could bias attention away from the percept on the other hand. Our planned research on the autonomic stages of the OR in combat veterans with PTSD uses the action cascade, a software program of our own creation. The action cascade is a computerized test that presents the subject with stimulus trials that produce an experimental analog of the naturalistic stages of orienting and response: Rest, Alert, Vigilance, Orienting and Appraisal, and Response Selection and Output. Each trial lasts about 25 s (**Figure 4**). Heart rate and HRV are recorded continuously and simultaneously with task performance on the action cascade by linking the physiological recorder to the computer stimulus presentation program.

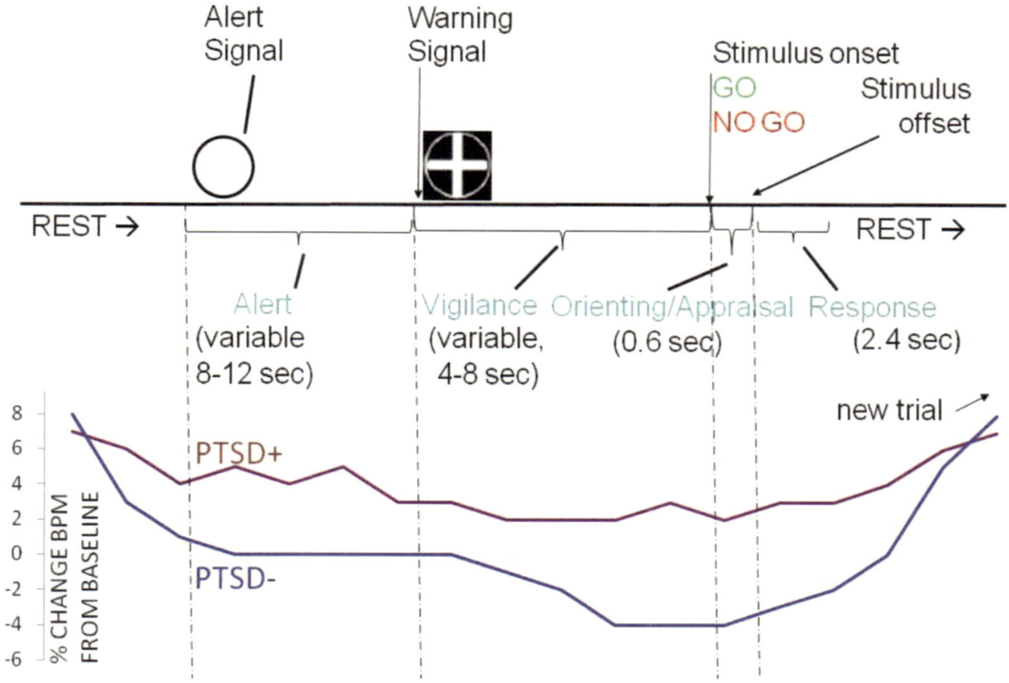

Figure 4. Action cascade: HRV during stages of rest, alert, vigilance, stimulus orienting/appraisal and response.

We have developed HRV Cascade Action Software to measure HRV during the stages of Rest, Alert, Vigilance, Orienting/Appraisal and Response. Durations of the Rest, Alert, and Vigilance stages vary to reduce the anticipatory predictability of the task. The action cascade is a close analog of the defense cascade paradigm, but modified stimulus valence (e.g., pleasant, unpleasant or fear-provoking)—which would provoke emotionally laden ANS responding—to be instead only informational (Go, No Go) and thereby guiding the action of stimulus appraisal into the cortical (mPFC) portion of the cortico-limbic circuit controlling autonomic cardiac regulation. The action cascade protocol is in preliminary data collection stage at this time. The working hypothesis, illustrated in **Figure 4**, is that cardiac deceleration will be absent or at least attenuated in the PTSD+ subjects pre-training HRVB, and this deficit will be normalized or at least improved post-training HRVB. Results may bridge the gap in understanding the role that ANS dysfunction plays in the adverse effects of PTSD on arousal, attention, and response disinhibition.

8. Summary and conclusions

Our chapter has reviewed evidence underlying the theory that ANS control of cardiac adjustments to environmental stimulation is a central factor in the symptom complex of PTSD. HRV is measured and quantified in terms of power (variance) and the coherence ratio of parasympathetic to total variance in the tachygram. Understanding of vagus nerve as the major control point of responsivity to environmental stimulation, with inputs and outputs affecting emotions, cognition, and behavior, fits into the evolutionary framework that includes the range of response outputs—fight or flight, freezing, tonic immobility, and affiliation. The neurovisceral integration model specifies the neuroanatomical networks of vagal afference and efference which control the rhythm of cardiac acceleration and deceleration. The entire system of ANS-regulated defense cascade is due to the executive ability of prefrontal cortex. Fear is a normal and adaptively healthy aspect of the defense cascade, well-understood and modeled by translational models. Dysregulation of the normal fear response by traumatization deranges the ANS and its control of HRV and subsequent defense cascade. As a result, attentional bias both toward and away from reminders and fear-provoking stimulation occurs. HRVB is theoretically and intuitively beneficial in the restoration of ANS function to adaptive parasympathetic and sympathetic levels. While these complex relations can be heuristically modeled, the reader is cautioned that PTSD is a very heterogeneous and multifactorial disorder and numerous other approaches to modeling and treatment (epigenetic, neuro-inflammatory, cognitive-behavioral, to name a few) are certain to add to our understanding and successful treatment outcomes. Our research provides preliminary evidence that HRVB improves HRV and reduces PTSD symptoms, and we intend to further develop our model with an experimental paradigm.

Author details

Jay P. Ginsberg* and Madan Nagpal

*Address all correspondence to: jay.ginsberg@va.gov

Dorn VA Medical Center and Dorn Research Institute, Columbia, SC, USA

References

[1] Gellhorn E. Central nervous system tuning and its implications for neuropsychiatry. J Nerv Mental Dis. 1968;147(2):148–62.

[2] Gellhorn E, Loofburrow G. Emotions and emotional disorders. New York, NY: Harper & Row; 1963. pp. 90–91.

[3] Everly Jr GS, Lating JM. A clinical guide to the treatment of the human stress response (3rd ed.). New York, NY: Springer; 2012.

[4] McEwen BS, Stellar E. Stress and the individual. Mechanisms leading to disease. Arch Intern Med. 1993;153(18):2093–101.

[5] Beauchaine T. Vagal tone, development, and Gray's motivational theory: toward an integrated model of autonomic nervous system functioning in psychopathology. Dev Psychopathol. 2001;13(2):183–214.

[6] Porges SW. Autonomic regulation and attention. In: Campbell BA, Hayne H, Richardson R, editors. Attention and information processing in infants and adults. Hillside, NJ: Erlbaum; 1992. p. 201–23.

[7] Porges SW. The polyvagal theory: new insights into adaptive reactions of the autonomic nervous system. Cleve Clin J Med. 2009;76 Suppl 2:S86–90.

[8] Porges S. The polyvagal theory: neurophysiological foundations of emotions, attachment, communication, and self-regulation. New York, NY: W.W. Norton and Company; 2011.

[9] Ginsberg JP. Autonomic control of heart rate and heart rate variability: influences on orienting and information processing in combat veterans with PTSD. In: Powell DA, editor. Central nervous system control of learned autonomic adjustments. Kerala, India: Research Signposts; 2009. p. 79–114.

[10] Ginsberg JP, Ayers E, Burriss L, Powell DA. Disruption of bradycardia associated with discriminative conditioning in combat veterans with PTSD. Neuropsychiatr Dis Treat. 2008;4(3):635–46.

[11] Tapp W, Servatius R, Hunt J, Powell DA. Vagal activity predicts eyeblink conditioning in human subjects. Neuroreport. 1997;8(5):1203–7.

[12] Ginsberg J, Ayers E, Burriss L, Powell D. Discriminative delay Pavlovian eyeblink conditioning in veterans with and without posttraumatic stress disorder. J Anxiety Disord. 2008;22:809–23.

[13] Agorastos, A., Kellner, M., Baker, D. G., & Stiedl, O. (2015). Diminished Vagal and/or Increased Sympathetic Activity in Post-Traumatic Stress Disorder. In C. R. Martin, V. R. Preedy, & V. B. Patel (Eds.), *Comprehensive Guide to Post-Traumatic Stress Disorder* (Vol.

DOI 10.1007/978-3-319-08613-2_30-1, pp. 1–15). Switzerland: Springer INternational Publishing.

[14] Quintana DS, Alvares GA, Heathers JA. Guidelines for reporting articles on psychiatry and heart rate variability (GRAPH): recommendations to advance research communication. Transl Psychiatry. 2016;6:e803.

[15] Electrophysiology TFotESoCatNASoPa. Heart rate variability: standards of measurement, physiological interpretation, and clinical use. Circulation 1996;93:1043–65.

[16] Akselrod S, Gordon D, Ubel FA, Shannon DC, Berger A, Cohen RJ. Power spectrum analysis of heart rate fluctuation: a quantitative probe of beat-to-beat cardiovascular control. Science. 1981;213(4504):220–2.

[17] Camm A, Malik M, Bigger J, Breithardt G, Cerutti S, Cohen R, et al. Heart rate variability: standards of measurement, physiological interpretation and clinical use. Task Force of the European Society of Cardiology and the North American Society of Pacing and Electrophysiology. Circulation. 1996;93(5):1043–65.

[18] Lehrer PM, Vaschillo E, Vaschillo B. Resonant frequency biofeedback training to increase cardiac variability: rationale and manual for training. Appl Psychophysiol Biofeedback. 2000;25(3):177–91.

[19] McCraty R, Childre D. Coherence: bridging personal, social, and global health. Altern Ther Health Med. 2010;16(4):10–24.

[20] Shaffer FB, McCraty R, Zerr CL. A healthy heart is not a metronome: An integrative review of the heart's anatomy and heart rate variability. Psychol Clinic Settings. 2014;5:1040.

[21] McCraty R, Atkinson M, Tomasino D, Bradley RT. The coherent heart: heart-brain interactions, psychophysiological coherence, and the emergence of system-wide order. Integral Review. 2009;5(2):10–115.

[22] Porges S. A phylogenetic journey through the vague and ambiguous Xth cranial nerve: a commentary on contemporary heart rate variability research. Biol Psychol. 2007;74:301–7.

[23] Porges SW. The polyvagal theory: phylogenetic substrates of a social nervous system. Int J Psychophysiol: Off J Int Org Psychophysiol. 2001;42(2):123–46.

[24] Porges S. Orienting in a defensive world: mammalian modification of our evolutionary heritage. a polyvagal theory. Psychophysiology. 1995;32:301–18.

[25] Williamson JB, Porges EC, Lamb DG, Porges SW. Maladaptive autonomic regulation in PTSD accelerates physiological aging. Front Psychol. 2014;5:1571.

[26] Hess, W. R. (1981). Function and neural regulation of internal organs. In *Biological Order and Brain Organization* (pp. 17–32). Springer Berlin Heidelberg.

[27] Akert K. Walter Rudolf Hess (1881–1973) and his contribution to neuroscience. J Hist Neurosci. 1999;8(3):248–63.

[28] Gillie BL, Thayer JF. Individual differences in resting heart rate variability and cognitive control in posttraumatic stress disorder. Front Psychol. 2014;5.

[29] Gillie BL, Vasey MW, Thayer JF. Heart rate variability predicts control over memory retrieval. Psychol Sci. 2014;25(2):458–65.

[30] Thayer JF AF, Fredrikson M, Sollers JJ 3rd, Wager TD. A meta-analysis of heart rate variability and neuroimaging studies: implications for heart rate variability as a marker of stress and health. Neurosci Biobehav Rev. 2012;36: 747–56.

[31] Thayer JF, Hansen AL, Saus-Rose E, Johnsen BH. Heart rate variability, prefrontal neural function, and cognitive performance: the neurovisceral integration perspective on self-regulation, adaptation, and health. Ann Behav Med: a publication of the Society of Behavioral Medicine. 2009;37(2):141–53.

[32] Thayer JF, Lane RD. A model of neurovisceral integration in emotion regulation and dysregulation. J Affect Disord. 2000;61(3):201–16.

[33] Benarroch, E. E. (1993). *The central autonomic network: functional organization, dysfunction, and perspective*. Paper presented at the Mayo Clinic Proceedings, Amsterdam.

[34] Lacey BC, Lacey JI. Presidential address, 1979. Cognitive modulation of time-dependent primary bradycardia. Psychophysiology. 1980;17(3):209–21.

[35] Lacey BC, Lacey JI. Two-way communication between the heart and the brain. Significance of time within the cardiac cycle. Am Psychol. 1978;33(2):99–113.

[36] Coles M. Cardiac and respiratory activity during visual search. J Exp Psychol. 1972;96(2):371.

[37] Graham FK, Clifton RK. Heart-rate change as a component of the orienting response. Psychol Bull. 1966;65(5):305.

[38] Sokolov EN, Cacioppo J. Orienting and defense reflexes: vector coding the cardiac response. In: Lang PJ, Simons RF, Balaban MT, editors. Attention and orienting: sensory and motivational processes. Mahwah, NJ: LEA Publishers; 1997. p. 1–22.

[39] Obrist, P. A. (1981). *Cardiovascular Psychophysiology*. New York, NY: Springer Science and Business Media.

[40] Cohen DH, Obrist PA. Interactions between behavior and the cardiovascular system. Circ Res. 1975;37:693–706.

[41] Vila J GP, Muñoz MA, et al. Cardiac defense: from attention to action. J Psychophysiol. 2007;66:169–82.

[42] Fernandez MC, Vila J. Cognitive versus motivational significance of the cardiac response to intense auditory stimulation. Int J Psychophysiol. 1989;8(1):49–59.

[43] Fan J, McCandliss BD, Fossella J, Flombaum JI, Posner MI. The activation of attentional networks. NeuroImage. 2005;26(2):471–9.

[44] Cottyn J, De Clercq D, Crombez G, Lenoir M. The role of preparatory heart rate deceleration on balance beam performance. J Sport Exerc Psychol. 2008;30(2):159–70.

[45] Driver J. A selective review of selective attention research from the past century. Br J Psychol. 2001;92(1):53–78.

[46] Asutay E, Västfjäll D. Negative emotion provides cues for orienting auditory spatial attention. Front Psychol. 2015;6.

[47] Wang J, Nicol T, Skoe E, Sams M, Kraus N. Emotion modulates early auditory response to speech. J Cogn Neurosci. 2009;21(11):2121–8.

[48] Yu X, Zhang J, Xie D, Wang J, Zhang C. Relationship between scalp potential and autonomic nervous activity during a mental arithmetic task. Auton Neurosci. 2009;146:81–6.

[49] Kozlowska K, Walker P, McLean L, Carrive P. Fear and the defense cascade: clinical implications and management. Harv Rev Psychiatry. 2015;23(4):263.

[50] Supple WF, Jr., Kapp BS. The anterior cerebellar vermis: essential involvement in classically conditioned bradycardia in the rabbit. J Neurosci. 1993;13(9):3705–11.

[51] Powell DA, Mankowski D, Buchanan S. Concomitant heart rate and corneoretinal potential conditioning in the rabbit (*Oryctolagus cuniculus*): effects of caudate lesions. Physiol Behav. 1978;20(2):143–50.

[52] Albiniak BA, Powell DA. Peripheral autonomic mechanisms and Pavlovian conditioning in the rabbit (*Oryctolagus cuniculus*). J Comp Physiol Psychol. 1980;94(6):1101–13.

[53] Ayers ED, White J, Powell DA. Pavlovian eyeblink conditioning in combat veterans with and without post-traumatic stress disorder. Integr Physiol Behav Sci. 2003;38(3): 230–47.

[54] Kao K, Powell DA. Lesions of substantia nigra retard Pavlovian somatomotor learning but do not affect autonomic conditioning. Neurosci Lett. 1986;64(1):1–6.

[55] Kao KT, Powell DA. Lesions of the substantia nigra retard Pavlovian eye-blink but not heart rate conditioning in the rabbit. Behav Neurosci. 1988;102(4):515–25.

[56] Powell DA, McLaughlin J, Chachich M. Classical conditioning of autonomic and somatomotor responses and their central nervous system substrates. In: Steinmetz JE, Woodruff-Pak DS, editors. Eyeblink classical conditioning volume 2: animal models. Boston, MA: Kluwer Academic Publishers; 2000. p. 257–86.

[57] Chachich M, Powell DA. Both medial prefrontal and amygdala central nucleus lesions abolish heart rate classical conditioning, but only prefrontal lesions impair reversal of eyeblink differential conditioning. Neurosci Lett. 1998;257(3):151–4.

[58] Powell DA, Skaggs H, Churchwell J, McLaughlin J. Posttraining lesions of the medial prefrontal cortex impair performance of Pavlovian eyeblink conditioning but have no effect on concomitant heart rate changes in rabbits (*Oryctolagus cuniculus*). Behav Neurosci. 2001;115(5):1029–38.

[59] McLaughlin J, Powell DA. Posttraining prefrontal lesions impair jaw movement conditioning performance, but have no effect on accompanying heart rate changes. Neurobiol Learn Mem. 2002;78(2):279–93.

[60] McCormick DA, Thompson RF. Cerebellum: essential involvement in the classically conditioned eyelid response. Science. 1984;223(4633):296–9.

[61] Lavond DG, Lincoln JS, McCormick DA, Thompson RF. Effect of bilateral lesions of the dentate and interpositus cerebellar nuclei on conditioning of heart-rate and nictitating membrane/eyelid responses in the rabbit. Brain research. 1984;305(2):323–30.

[62] Buchanan SL, Powell DA. Cingulate cortex: its role in Pavlovian conditioning. J Comp Physiol Psychol. 1982;96(5):755–74.

[63] Buchanan SL, Powell DA. Cingulate damage attenuates conditioned bradycardia. Neurosci Lett. 1982;29(3):261–8.

[64] Buchanan SL, Valentine J, Powell DA. Autonomic responses are elicited by electrical stimulation of the medial but not lateral frontal cortex in rabbits. Behav Brain Res. 1985;18(1):51–62.

[65] Powell DA, Watson K, Maxwell B. Involvement of subdivisions of the medial prefrontal cortex in learned cardiac adjustments in rabbits. Behav Neurosci. 1994;108(2):294–307.

[66] Powell DA, Chachich M, Murphy V, McLaughlin J, Tebbutt D, Buchanan SL. Amygdala-prefrontal interactions and conditioned bradycardia in the rabbit. Behav Neurosci. 1997;111(5):1056–74.

[67] Chachich M, Penney J, Powell DA. Subicular lesions disrupt but do not abolish classically conditioned bradycardia in rabbits. Behav Neurosci. 1996;110(4):707–17.

[68] Powell DA. Rapid associative learning: conditioned bradycardia and its central nervous system substrates. Integr Physiol Behav Sci. 1994;29(2):109–33.

[69] Prescott L, Durkin M, Furchtgott E, Powell DA. Concomitant heart rate and eyeblink Pavlovian conditioning in human subjects as a function of interstimulus interval. Psychophysiology. 1992;29(6):646–56.

[70] Powell DA, Ginsberg JP. Single unit activity in the medial prefrontal cortex during Pavlovian heart rate conditioning: effects of peripheral autonomic blockade. Neurobiol Learn Mem. 2005;84(3):200–13.

[71] Hernandez LL, Powell DA. Vasopressin analog delays extinction of classically conditioned bradycardia. Peptides. 1983;4(1):37–41.

[72] Powell DA, Hernandez L, Buchanan SL. Intraseptal scopolamine has differential effects on Pavlovian eye blink and heart rate conditioning. Behav Neurosci. 1985;99(1):75–87.

[73] Pribram KH, McGuinness D. Arousal, activation, and effort in the control of attention. Psychol Rev. 1975;82(2):116–49.

[74] Nagpal M, Gleichauf K, Ginsberg J. Meta-analysis of heart rate variability as a psychophysiological indicator of posttraumatic stress disorder. J Trauma Treat. 2013;3:182. doi: 10.4172/2167-1222.1000182.

[75] Vasterling JJ, Brailey K, Constans JI, Sutker PB. Attention and memory dysfunction in posttraumatic stress disorder. Neuropsychology. 1998;12(1):125–33.

[76] Leskin LP, White PM. Attentional networks reveal executive function deficits in posttraumatic stress disorder. Neuropsychology. 2007;21(3):275–84.

[77] Bardeen JR, Orcutt HK. Attentional control as a moderator of the relationship between posttraumatic stress symptoms and attentional threat bias. J Anxiety Disord. 2011;25(8): 1008–18.

[78] Bryant RA, Harvey AG. Attentional bias in posttraumatic stress disorder. J Trauma Stress. 1997;10(4):635–44.

[79] Dalgleish T, Taghavi R, Neshat-Doost H, Moradi A, Canterbury R, Yule W. Patterns of processing bias for emotional information across clinical disorders: a comparison of attention, memory, and prospective cognition in children and adolescents with depression, generalized anxiety, and posttraumatic stress disorder. J Clin Child Adolesc Psychol. 2003;32(1):10–21.

[80] Dalgleish T, Moradi A, Taghavi M, Neshat-Doost H, Yule W. An experimental investigation of hypervigilance for threat in children and adolescents with post-traumatic stress disorder. Psychol Med. 2001;31(03):541–7.

[81] Fani N, Tone EB, Phifer J, Norrholm SD, Bradley B, Ressler KJ, et al. Attention bias toward threat is associated with exaggerated fear expression and impaired extinction in PTSD. Psychol Med. 2012;42(03):533–43.

[82] Fani N, Jovanovic T, Ely TD, Bradley B, Gutman D, Tone EB, et al. Neural correlates of attention bias to threat in post-traumatic stress disorder. Biol Psychol. 2012;90(2):134–42.

[83] Pine, D. S., Mogg, K., Bradley, B. P., Montgomery, L., Monk, C. S., McClure, E., ... & Kaufman, J. (2005). Attention bias to threat in maltreated children: Implications for vulnerability to stress-related psychopathology. *American Journal of Psychiatry*, 162(2), 291–296.

[84] Fani N, Bradley-Davino B, Ressler KJ, McClure-Tone EB. Attention bias in adult survivors of childhood maltreatment with and without posttraumatic stress disorder. Cognit Ther Res. 2011;35(1):57–67.

[85] Elsesser K, Sartory G, Tackenberg A. Attention, heart rate, and startle response during exposure to trauma-relevant pictures: a comparison of recent trauma victims and patients with posttraumatic stress disorder. J Abnorm Psychol. 2004;113(2):289.

[86] Elsesser K, Sartory G, Tackenberg A. Initial symptoms and reactions to trauma-related stimuli and the development of posttraumatic stress disorder. Depress Anxiety. 2005;21(2):61–70.

[87] Beevers CG, Wells TT, Ellis AJ, McGeary JE. Association of the serotonin transporter gene promoter region (5-HTTLPR) polymorphism with biased attention for emotional stimuli. J Abnorm Psychol. 2009;118(3):670.

[88] Iacoviello BM, Wu G, Abend R, Murrough JW, Feder A, Fruchter E, et al. Attention bias variability and symptoms of posttraumatic stress disorder. J Trauma Stress. 2014;27(2): 232–9.

[89] Yiend J, Mathews A, Cowan N. Selective Attention Tasks in Clinical and Cognitive Research. In: Rubin AWDC, editor. Cognitive methods and their application to clinical research. Washington, DC, USA: American Psychological Association; 2005. p. 65–71.

[90] Naim R, Abend R, Wald I, Eldar S, Levi O, Fruchter E, et al. Threat- related attention bias variability and posttraumatic stress. Am J Psychiatry. 2015;172(12):1242–50.

[91] Koster EH, De Raedt R, Leyman L, De Lissnyder E. Mood-congruent attention and memory bias in dysphoria: Exploring the coherence among information-processing biases. Behav Res Ther. 2010;48(3):219–25.

[92] Badura-Brack AS, Naim R, Ryan TJ, Levy O, Abend R, Khanna MM, et al. Effect of attention training on attention bias variability and PTSD symptoms: randomized controlled trials in Israeli and US combat veterans. Am J Psychiatry. 2015;172(12):1233–41.

[93] Schwartz, M. S., & Andrasik, F. E. (2003). *Biofeedback: A practitioner's guide*. New York, NY: Guilford Press.

[94] Khazan, I. Z. (2013). *The clinical handbook of biofeedback: A step-by-step guide for training and practice with mindfulness*. Hoboken, NJ: John Wiley & Sons.

[95] Yucha C, Montgomery D. Evidence-based practice in biofeedback and neurofeedback. Wheat Ridge, CO: AAPB; 2008.

[96] Ferguson AV, Latchford KJ, Samson WK. The paraventricular nucleus of the hypothalamus—a potential target for integrative treatment of autonomic dysfunction. Expert Opin Ther Targets. 2008;12(6):717–27.

[97] Ginsberg JP, Berry ME, Powell DA. Cardiac coherence and posttraumatic stress disorder in combat veterans. Altern Ther Health Med. 2010;16(4):52–60.

[98] Lande RG, Williams LB, Francis JL, Gragnani C, Morin ML. Efficacy of biofeedback for post-traumatic stress disorder. Complement Ther Med. 2010;18(6):256–9.

[99] Tan G, Dao TK, Farmer L, Sutherland RJ, Gevirtz R. Heart rate variability (HRV) and posttraumatic stress disorder (PTSD): a pilot study. Appl Psychophysiol Biofeedback. 2011;36(1):27–35.

[100] Zucker T, Samuelson K, Muench F, Greenberg M, Gevirtz R. The effects of respiratorysinus arrhythmia biofeedback on heart rate variability and posttraumatic stress disorder symptoms: a pilot study. Appl Psychophysiol Biofeedback. 2009;34(2):135–43.

[101] Vasterling JJ, Duke LM, Brailey K, Constans JI, Allain AN, Sutker PB. Attention, learning, and memory performances and intellectual resources in Vietnam veterans: PTSD and no disorder comparisons. Neuropsychology. 2002;16(1):5.

Section 2

Clinical and Methodological Perspectives

Chapter 4

Childhood Interpersonal Trauma and its Repercussions in Adulthood: An Analysis of Psychological and Interpersonal Sequelae

Caroline Dugal, Noémie Bigras,
Natacha Godbout and Claude Bélanger

Additional information is available at the end of the chapter

http://dx.doi.org/10.5772/64476

Abstract

Despite decades of prevention campaigns and research, childhood interpersonal trauma (i.e., psychological, physical and sexual abuse, psychological and physical neglect, witnessing interparental violence) remains an endemic problem with longstanding and deleterious negative effects on adult psycho-relational functioning. This chapter aims to present a comprehensive literature review of the repercussions associated with exposure to childhood interpersonal trauma. First, the nature and various forms of childhood interpersonal trauma are described. Subsequently, a review of the studies documenting disruptions in psychological and interpersonal functioning and the mechanisms explaining the development of each of these repercussions is unraveled. These repercussions include posttraumatic stress disorder, anxiety disorders, depression, personality disorders, affect dysregulation, substance use disorders, eating disorders, suicidal behaviors, alterations in attention and consciousness, disruptions in attributions, attachment, sexuality and violence in intimate relationships. Finally, suggestions for future research and intervention guidelines with childhood interpersonal trauma survivors are discussed.

Keywords: childhood interpersonal trauma, psychological repercussions, interpersonal repercussions

1. Introduction

Childhood exposure to maltreatment, or early interpersonal trauma, is considered as an endemic health issue with tragic personal, social and economic repercussions [1, 2]. Recent international and US national studies show its alarming prevalence [3, 4], with 61% of children who have experienced at least one type of interpersonal trauma and more than one-third who report two or more additional types of interpersonal violence. Moreover, numerous studies have shown that exposure to interpersonal trauma during childhood can chronically and pervasively alter social, psychological, and cognitive development [5, 6]. Indeed, childhood interpersonal trauma is associated with a plethora of serious short-term [7, 8] and life-long consequences [9] such as impaired physical and mental health, increased incidence of affect dysregulation, alterations in attention and consciousness, identity impairments, and interpersonal difficulties [10, 1, 4]. In the past few years, this area of research has expanded from depictions of the prevalence of interpersonal trauma in various populations to the documentation of its possible repercussions, and identification of risk and protective factors that contribute to adaptation or lack thereof in the wake of early interpersonal trauma [11].

This chapter aims to present a comprehensive narrative literature review of the repercussions associated with exposure to childhood interpersonal trauma. First, the nature and different forms of childhood maltreatment will be described. Subsequently, a review of the studies documenting disruptions in psychological and interpersonal functioning and the mechanisms explaining the development of each of these repercussions will be unraveled. This review was conducted using two different strategies. First, pertinent keywords in various combinations (e.g., "childhood interpersonal trauma" AND "effects" OR "repercussions"; "child interpersonal maltreatment" AND "personality disorders" OR "psychological disorders" OR "post-traumatic stress disorder"; "childhood maltreatment" AND "interpersonal relationships"; "child abuse" AND "attachment") were used to search PsycINFO and PubMed databases, up to January 2016, for relevant English or French language peer-reviewed articles and books. Subsequently, the references of the identified articles and chapters were examined to find additional pertinent papers. In accordance with the results of the research conducted, the childhood interpersonal trauma aftereffects that will be addressed in this chapter include posttraumatic stress disorder, anxiety disorders, depression, personality disorders, affect dysregulation, substance use disorders, eating disorders, suicidal behaviors, alterations in attention and consciousness, disruptions in attributions, attachment, sexuality and violence in intimate relationships.

2. Childhood interpersonal trauma

Psychological, physical, and sexual abuse, neglect, and witnessing interparental violence before 18 years of age consist of different forms of childhood interpersonal trauma as they result in actual or potential harm to a child's health, survival, development, or dignity in the context of a relationship of responsibility, trust, or power [4]. According to Briere [12], childhood interpersonal trauma can be divided into two categories: acts of omission and acts of commission. Acts of omission refer to the incapacity or refusal of caregivers to adopt interpersonal behaviors essential to the development of a child, such as sustained responsiveness and availability, so that he or she is deprived of care, support, and psychological stimulation [12, 13]. Acts of omission include both psychological and physical neglect. Psychological neglect is defined as the experience of having been ignored or not felt loved nor understood by a caregiver. Physical neglect is defined as not having received regular meals, baths, clean clothes, needed medical attention or having been confined in a room alone for extended periods of time [14]. According to a recent meta-analysis [15], psychological neglect is reported by 18% of the general population and physical neglect by 16%.

Unlike acts of omission, acts of commission involve abusive behaviors such as psychological, physical, or sexual abuse directed toward the child [12]. Psychological abuse describes the repeated experience of humiliation, blame, criticism, rejection, threats, or insults from the caregiver [16]. This form of abuse affects 36–46% of the general population [17, 18]. Physical abuse refers to the experience of physical contacts or constraints perpetrated with the intention of injuring the child. These abusive acts include punching, kicking, slapping, shoving, pushing, and beating with an object [19]. In the general population, 31–42% of men and 21–33% of women report having sustained physical abuse during childhood [17, 18]. According to Canada's legal dispositions, sexual abuse is defined as any sexual contact between a child under 16 years of age and a person at least 5 years older [20]. North American prevalence rates for childhood sexual abuse exhibit considerable variability across studies but tend to confirm that 10% of men and 20% of women report this type of interpersonal trauma [21]. Another form of childhood interpersonal trauma is being exposed to interparental violence. In 2007, according to the *Youth Protection Act*, exposure to interparental violence has been added to the reasons compromising a child's development [22]. Specifically, exposure to this kind of violence is defined as the observation, between the parents or parental figures, of physical aggression, sexual coercion, psychological harassment, or more general constraint or coercion [23]. Data from the *Canadian Incidence Study of Reported Child Abuse and Neglect* indicate that up to 26% of children are exposed to psychological or physical interparental violence [22].

Interestingly, early interpersonal trauma not only produces compelling and long-lasting psychological and relational maladjustment, but it is also related to a greater probability of sustaining additional interpersonal trauma during childhood and later in life. This vulnerability is referred to as *revictimization* [24, 25]. Substantial evidence suggests that individuals exposed to one category of interpersonal trauma during childhood are also likely to have experienced other types of victimization [26]. Research increasingly points to the experience of multiple types of interpersonal trauma, referred to as polyvictimization [3, 27, 28] and cumulative trauma [29]. Some researchers also refer to this phenomenon as complex childhood trauma since it encompasses exposure to multiple, often prolonged or extended developmentally adverse traumatic events that occur early in life [5, 24, 30]. Typically, these constructs refer to the experience of some combination of psychological, physical, and sexual abuse, psychological and physical neglect, and exposure to interparental violence and are operationalized as the total number of different types of interpersonal victimization experienced by a given individual [8, 17, 10, 31].

Studies are generally consistent in finding that experiencing multiple types of childhood interpersonal trauma may be particularly detrimental since it is related to more severe and complex psychological and relational consequences, both in childhood and adulthood, when compared to exposure to a single type of interpersonal trauma [8, 10, 32–34]. Indeed, cumulative or complex interpersonal trauma not only increases the risk of posttraumatic stress symptoms but can also result in an intricate pattern of psycho-relational symptoms [24].

3. Repercussions of childhood interpersonal trauma

Childhood interpersonal trauma can have a detrimental impact on a child's development, especially regarding psychological and interpersonal functioning [35, 36]. Their potentially adverse consequences on the psychological sphere are manifold: increased risk of depression, anxiety, posttraumatic stress symptoms, aggression, dissociation, substance use, risky sexual behaviors, as well as borderline, antisocial, schizotypal, avoidant, and schizoid personality disorders [37–41]. In the long run, these psychological repercussions may take a chronic course and lead to high rates of suicidality and low levels of social functioning [42, 43].

3.1. Psychological repercussions of childhood interpersonal trauma

Research has consistently shown that some traumatic events are more symptom-producing and cause greater distress and posttraumatic aftereffects than others [10]. For instance, childhood interpersonal trauma, especially cumulative trauma, is the form of traumatic event that is the most strongly associated with later difficulties because of its effects on psycho-relational health and child development [10, 13, 24]. Indeed, childhood interpersonal trauma is associated with increased risk of mental health problems throughout the lifespan [44], including posttraumatic stress, eating disorders [45], depression, anxiety, suicidality, and substance use [24, 46]. Ultimately, these psychological problems may take a chronic course and lead to low levels of relational and professional functioning, higher rates of suicidality and less active social participation [40, 42, 43]. Moreover, there appears to be a cumulative effect of exposure to trauma during childhood with the risk of psychological, physical, and relational health problems increasing as the number of different types of victimization experienced increases [31, 44, 47, 48]. Thereby, a clear understanding of the most common forms of psychological impairment in adult survivors of early interpersonal trauma is deemed necessary.

3.1.1. Posttraumatic stress disorder

Posttraumatic stress disorder is highly prevalent in adult survivors of childhood interpersonal trauma [40, 49–52] especially since interpersonal trauma represents the form of traumatic experiences that induces the highest rates of posttraumatic symptoms [44, 53].

According to several authors [12, 40, 50, 53], the propensity to develop posttraumatic stress symptoms depends on many factors such as one's temperament, the number of different types of interpersonal trauma experienced, pre-existing psychological difficulties, biological vulnerabilities to stress, or exposure to previous traumatic events. For instance, gender, age, socioeconomic status, the presence of psychological dysfunctions or disorders, family dysfunctions or psychopathology history, previous trauma exposure, peritraumatic dissociation, and the interaction between genetic predispositions and environmental stress may influence a victim's risk of developing posttraumatic symptoms [24]. According to Briere [12], an individual's reaction to a traumatic event would thus be contingent on the degree to which the stressor overwhelms this person' ability to manage its repercussions. Yet, characteristics specific to the traumatic events can also shape a victim's trajectory from early interpersonal trauma to posttraumatic stress symptoms such as the presence of life threat, sexual victimization, physical injury, or trauma of longer duration or greater frequency [24].

Researchers have highlighted a significant proportion of survivors who present complex posttraumatic stress, which describes difficulties arising from severe, profound, and repeated interpersonal trauma beginning in childhood [24]. Thus, early interpersonal trauma survivors tend to present more complex psychological difficulties that might not only involve posttraumatic stress symptoms, but also disturbances in self-organization [54], borderline personality disorder [55], major depression, substance abuse/dependence, simple phobia, social phobia, and agoraphobia [56]. Indeed, posttraumatic stress disorder rarely occurs alone, with up to 80% of those diagnosed with this disorder also presenting at least one other psychological disorder [56].

3.1.2. Anxiety disorders

Anxiety disorders are the most common category of diagnoses. Approximately 29% of the US population is estimated to have or to have had one or more diagnosable anxiety disorders at some point in their lives (see [57]). Empirical results reveal that childhood interpersonal trauma is associated with the presence and severity of anxiety disorders (for a review see [58–60]). Indeed, results of a longitudinal study conducted in New Zealand revealed that generalized anxiety disorder was associated with physical abuse and sexual abuse during childhood [61].

Contemporary theories and empirical research provide interesting developmental models of anxiety disorders in adulthood. According to learning theories, early experiences act as vulnerability factors that can considerably affect the psychological consequences of traumatic life events often implicated in the origins of anxiety disorders [62]. Such early learning, along with temperamental vulnerabilities, can serve as diatheses that make certain individuals more susceptible to adverse and stressful experiences that sometimes lead to the development of anxiety disorders. That is, people who have a history of uncontrollable and unpredictable life stressors (e.g., childhood interpersonal trauma) are more likely to develop anxiety disorders [62]. Certain cognitions and behaviors may serve as an attempt to suppress, control, or avoid trauma-related anxiety, but those avoidance mechanisms may lead to more negative intrusive thoughts or perceptions of uncontrollability, which are, in turn, associated with greater anxiety, leading to a vicious cycle [62, 63].

Childhood interpersonal trauma has also been linked to an increased likelihood of developing social phobia [64, 65] and panic disorder [66]. Conditioning theory is a useful model to understand the onset of social phobias. Indeed, several features of conditioning events themselves have a strong impact on how much fear is acquired. For example, having control over a traumatic event (such as being able to escape) has a major impact on how much fear is conditioned to the trauma-related stimuli. Far less fear is conditioned when the aversive event is escapable than when it is inescapable [62]. When it comes to childhood interpersonal trauma, the possibility to escape is lessened since the perpetrator is often a caregiver. This specificity might have a crucial impact on how much fear is experienced, acquired, or maintained over time and to what extent, over the long haul, people, places, and situations reminiscent of the trauma will be avoided by the survivor. In the same vein, prior learning experiences that lead to perceptions of lack of control and helplessness such as interpersonal trauma may serve as psychological vulnerability factors influencing the development of panic disorder and agoraphobia [67].

3.1.3. Depression

Substantial evidence from both cross-sectional and prospective studies indicates that childhood interpersonal trauma is a robust predictor of the development of clinical depression in different samples of adults [68–73]. Indeed, those who have been exposed to trauma are at risk of developing major depressive disorder, especially since depression is one of the most common comorbid disorders for posttraumatic stress disorder [53, 74]. Moreover, research shows a strong association between the number of traumatic events experienced during childhood and mental health problems, including depression, in adulthood [75, 76]. For example, results indicate that childhood interpersonal trauma survivors are two to four times more at risk for depression when compared to non-survivors [48, 77]. Finally, a recent meta-analysis on the associations between different childhood experiences of interpersonal trauma and major depression reveals that psychological abuse is the strongest predictor for later depression compared to other forms of interpersonal trauma [78].

3.1.4. Personality disorders

According to the DSM-5 [79], personality disorders are defined as inflexible, pervasive, and enduring patterns of inner experience and behavior that lead to clinically significant distress or impairment in social, occupational, or other important areas of functioning. Despite the lack of knowledge as to the precise development of personality disorders, there is a consensus in the actual scientific literature that personality disorders result from the combination of a variety of biological, temperamental, developmental, and environmental influences [80]. For instance, according to the diathesis-stress model [81], antisocial personality disorder would arise from certain genetic vulnerabilities, which lead to problematic behaviors in childhood that are aggravated by high-risk environments [82, 83]. As such, early environmental factors such as childhood interpersonal trauma, disrupted family bonds, and externalizing behavioral problems (including aggression and bullying) could act as risk factors for antisocial personality disorder [82, 84].

Borderline personality disorder would also emanate from a combination of biological and environmental mechanisms, the latter of which would include social and attachment-related disturbances [85]. In her biosocial model, Linehan [86] puts forward a transactional approach to borderline personality disorder, which is conceptualized as the result of an individual's biological predisposition to emotion regulation difficulties and an invalidating rearing environment. Therefore, the development of borderline personality disorder would be due to lack of responsiveness and proximity from relevant caregivers, which would subsequently disrupt the ability to effectively regulate emotions [85, 87]. As it happens, such caregiving shortcomings commonly characterize early interpersonal trauma survivors [85]. Consistent with these theoretical perspectives, there is a robust body of literature indicating an association between borderline personality disorder and a history of neglect, and of physical, sexual and psychological abuse as well as the cumulative experience of several forms of childhood interpersonal trauma [55]. Precisely, between 30 and 90% of individuals diagnosed with borderline personality disorder report having sustained childhood sexual, physical, or psychological abuse [88–90].

Although the association between childhood interpersonal trauma and borderline personality disorder is quite substantial, less attention has been paid to other types of personality disorders in trauma survivors [91], even though clinical and populational studies have both shown personality disorders to be more prevalent among adults who have experienced childhood interpersonal trauma than among those who have not [92–95]. In addition, the scientific knowledge on the links between trauma types and specific personality disorders is compounded due to the frequent co-occurrence of different types of early interpersonal trauma and the high comorbidity between personality disorders [41]. As of now, only a few researchers have tried to pinpoint these trauma-personality disorder associations. In a recent study, Lobbestael et al. [94] investigated the relationships between five types of childhood interpersonal trauma and 10 personality disorders as described in the DSM-IV. According to the results of this study, sexual abuse was associated with paranoid, schizoid, borderline, and avoidant personality disorders; physical abuse was related to antisocial personality disorder; psychological abuse showed significant associations with paranoid, schizotypal, borderline, avoidant, dependent, and obsessive-compulsive personality disorders; and psychological neglect was associated with histrionic and borderline personality disorders. Similarly, in a psychiatric sample, Cohen et al. [93] provided support for independent relationships between physical abuse and antisocial traits; psychological abuse and avoidant, dependent, and obsessive-compulsive personality disorders; and neglect and paranoid, schizoid, and schizotypal personality disorders. Finally, Waxman et al. [41] identified specific associations between borderline and schizotypal personality disorders with a history of child sexual abuse (CSA), antisocial personality disorder with child physical abuse. They also found an association between avoidant and schizoid personality disorders and psychological neglect.

Nonetheless, even if studies are consistent in finding that interpersonal trauma commonly increases the risk for adult personality disorders, the specific associations between different types of interpersonal trauma and personality disorders still remain poorly understood. Future studies should thus pursue the exploration of distinct trauma-personality disorder associations as well as relationships between the co-occurrence of multiples types of early interpersonal trauma and subsequent personality disorders.

3.1.5. Affect dysregulation

An overarching negative repercussion of childhood interpersonal trauma is affect dysregulation. Affect regulation refers to an individual's capacity to control and tolerate strong and negative emotions without resorting to avoidance strategies that distract, soothe, or draw attention away from emotional distress [12]. Specifically, affect regulation can be conceptualized as a multidimensional construct [96], comprised of a cognitive and a behavioral dimension [97]. The cognitive dimension of emotion regulation is based on the regulation of affects and refers to the inhibition of mood swings or of the expression of anger. The behavioral dimension of emotion regulation is reflected by the ability to refrain from externalizing negative emotions through avoidance or dysfunctional behaviors [98]. These behavioral strategies manifest as tension reduction behaviors, the most common of which are self-destructive behaviors, binge/purge eating, impulsivity, as well as aggressive and risky sexual behaviors [98]. Indeed, up to 79% of those who self-harm report histories of childhood interpersonal trauma [99].

Researchers have suggested that, by its premature and severe nature, childhood interpersonal trauma would not only interrupt normal child development and associate negative affect to trauma-related stimuli, but would also interfere with the development of essential regulation skills [10]. As such, the experience of interpersonal trauma during childhood may impede the development of adaptive affect regulation by exposing children to overwhelming or extreme emotional demands while simultaneously failing to teach them how to regulate emotional arousal, to control their behaviors in the context of emotional arousal or to tolerate emotional distress [100]. Consequently, when faced with insufficient affect regulation skills or overwhelming negative emotions, adult survivors of childhood interpersonal trauma are often unable to cope and tend to resort to avoidance strategies to numb or reduce the impact and duration of experienced negative affect [101]. Moreover, when faced with trauma-related affects, memories, or cognitions, survivors might experience overwhelming distress and be constrained to use avoidance as a way to deal with these negative affects. Despite its alleviating effect on the negative emotions associated with trauma-related intrusive and distressing memories, avoidance may also disrupt psychological well-being and further development of regulation skills, both of which are essential to adult functioning [10, 63]. Thus, empirical data have provided support for these theoretical propositions by showing that adult survivors of childhood interpersonal trauma tend to exhibit affect dysregulation as reflected by emotional instability, a tendency to overreact to negative or stressful events, problems in inhibiting the expression of strong affects, and the use of tension reduction behaviors [10, 64, 102–104].

3.1.6. Substance use disorders

Substance use disorders are relatively common among individuals who were exposed to traumatic events, especially those who have experienced interpersonal trauma [64, 105, 106]. Results from the Adverse Childhood Experiences (ACE) study showed a strong graded association between the risk of drug initiation from early adolescence into adulthood and problems with drug use, drug addiction, and parenteral use. Results also showed that, compared to individuals with no ACEs or no experience of childhood interpersonal trauma, those with more than five ACEs were 7–10 times more likely to report illicit drug use problems, addiction to illicit drugs, and parenteral drug use [107].

Resorting to alcohol and drugs could be well understood along the lines of Briere's Self-Trauma Model under the spectrum of insufficiently developed affect regulation [108]. In contrast to the positive and caring environment within which a child generally develops, chronically abused or neglected children may have been exposed to insurmountable affective obstacles, such as emotionally intolerable physical or sexual abuse, or persistent, invasive psychological abuse. Without a basic safe environment for the development of optimal skills, victims may become experts at using more powerful avoidance strategies such as substance abuse, allowing them to "function" despite their otherwise overwhelming distress [12, 109]. Based on clinical experience with substance-using survivors, Briere and Scott [24] also suggest that insufficiently processed trauma-related distress may motivate the use of drugs and alcohol in an attempt to "self-medicate." Thus, drugs and alcohol use would contribute to decreased environmental awareness and at the same time, involvement in risky behaviors. Unfortunately, those circumstances increase the likelihood of erratic behaviors and additional trauma, and associated posttraumatic stress, ultimately leading to greater distress and substance abuse [10].

3.1.7. Eating disorders

Mixed findings are observed regarding eating disorders in childhood interpersonal trauma survivors. Documented in children and adolescent survivors, eating disorders are also known to persist in adulthood [110]. A recent study using a representative sample of men and women across the United States [111] found that the vast majority of women and men with anorexia nervosa, bulimia nervosa, and binge eating disorder reported a history of childhood interpersonal trauma. Even though sexual abuse is more often identified as a potential risk factor for eating psychopathology, recent findings demonstrate the role of different types of childhood interpersonal trauma (i.e., childhood psychological and physical abuse, childhood psychological and physical neglect) in the etiology of eating psychopathology [112].

According to some researchers, childhood interpersonal trauma might contribute to poor self-esteem or even self-hatred, which might result in binge eating as a way to punish one's own body or to use dissociative coping strategies. Childhood interpersonal trauma might also make the survivors feel as if their life is out of control, contributing to a need to re-exert control through self-starvation (see [113]). Other theoretical avenues suggest that the link between childhood interpersonal trauma and eating disorders may lie on emotion regulation difficulties arising from poor parental models of distress regulation and tolerance, which result in a limited repertoire of emotion regulation strategies in the lifespan [114]. For instance, impulsivity and compulsivity in childhood interpersonal trauma survivors might manifest as disordered eating behavior, such as binge eating and compensatory behaviors (e.g., purging, laxative use), used to cope with trauma [115].

3.1.8. Suicidal behaviors

Among the wide range of repercussions observed in the aftermath of childhood interpersonal trauma, one of the most troubling is the development of suicidal thoughts and behaviors [116]. Several studies suggest that psychological, physical, and sexual abuse is related to later suicidal ideation, threats or attempts [117, 118]. More precisely, survivors of childhood interpersonal trauma are 2–5 times more likely to manifest suicidal thoughts or behaviors when compared to non-victims [119, 120]. Although no definite consensus prevails pertaining to the type of childhood interpersonal trauma that is most associated with suicidality, numerous theories have been proposed to explain this relationship.

Suicide-focused theories support the potential role of childhood interpersonal trauma as an etiological factor for suicidal behaviors. Based on the Suicidal Mode Theory [121] and the Interpersonal-Psychological Theory of Suicide [122, 123], childhood interpersonal trauma may lead to feelings of social alienation and produce emotions and cognitions (e.g., involving helplessness and hopelessness) that leave survivors with a persisting vulnerability for suicidal ideation and behaviors. Other authors have also hypothesized that suicidality might result from a desperate search to avoid or reduce abuse-related affective states and posttraumatic stress [10, 124].

3.1.9. Alterations in attention and consciousness

Alterations in attention and consciousness can take multiple forms including dissociation, depersonalization, memory disturbances, concentration difficulties, and disrupted executive functioning [1, 125]. Dissociation is a common response to traumatic events, including childhood interpersonal trauma [24, 126, 127]. According to the *DSM-5*, dissociation is "a disruption of and/or discontinuity in the normal integration of consciousness, memory, identity, emotion, perception, body representation, motor control and behaviour" (p. 291). Dissociation is often viewed by clinicians and researchers as an avoidance strategy used to temporarily numb, distract, or forestall negative experiences, thereby redirecting attention away from otherwise overwhelming emotions [10]. Several studies have documented the role of childhood physical abuse as a predictor of dissociation; yet, Haferkamp et al. [38] showed that emotional components of trauma such as psychological abuse were also correlated with dissociative symptoms in adulthood. Moreover, the experience of different types of childhood trauma (e.g., cumulative trauma) is increasingly documented as being associated with dissociation. For example, the total number of different types of interpersonal trauma is associated with dysfunctional avoidance and symptom complexity in adults, including dissociation [10, 76].

Liotti's model [128] suggests that the primary function and etiology of dissociation is as a defense against trauma. While the tendency to use avoidance to cope with negative emotional states caused by memories of the abuse may, at first, provide relief from trauma-related stress, avoidance has been identified as an important risk factor for subsequent psychological problems in trauma survivors [129]. Over the long haul, avoidance can generate negative outcomes because it reinforces fear beliefs [130], prevents the survivor from the opportunity to create new structures of associations [131] and paradoxically, tends to exacerbate initial distress (see the Pain Paradox [24]). The use of dissociation in trauma survivors would also be maintained by a conditioned behavioral response (e.g., negative reinforcement) within which suffering and distress are temporary alleviated. As such, the effectiveness with which avoidance strategies quickly relieve survivors' distress keeps them in a behavioral loop [132].

Also observed in interpersonal trauma survivors is "other-directedness" attention [12]. Early abuse typically pulls the child's attention away from internal experiences toward the environment because that is where potential danger exists and it must be gauged. This ongoing "other-directed" attention prevents the child from developing a coherent sense of self and impedes optimal psychological functioning in adulthood since it precludes from internal self-monitoring and self-awareness [102]. Attentional difficulties in the aftermath of a traumatic event such as childhood interpersonal trauma are well documented, with general consensus that these attentional disturbances are due to posttraumatic stress [133, 134].

3.1.10. Attributions

Attribution theory states that individuals have a vital need and tendency to explain the cause of events, especially when they are unexpected, unwanted or unusual, such as traumatic events [135]. To explain trauma, an individual may thus attribute its cause to either external or internal factors [136].

When traumatic events are attributed to external factors, individuals may believe that the traumatic experience and its related effects result of chance or the actions of others rather than by their own actions. In contrast, those who attribute such events to internal factors believe they are responsible for the trauma and its repercussions [136]. Attributional styles are associated with how one will respond to an event, either by alleviating or exacerbating the psychological sequelae and distress associated with trauma [136, 137]. For instance, children who have sustained interpersonal trauma often exhibit distorted attributions about themselves and the world that might set the stage for generalized shame and guilt, poor self-efficacy, and external locus of control [138, 1]. Self-blame, shame, and guilt are common sequelae of childhood interpersonal trauma and may lead survivors to hold themselves accountable for the victimization and even think they « asked for it » or « deserved it » [139, 140]. In addition, since early interpersonal trauma experiences are likely to occur within the caregiving system, the child may be cautioned or threatened to conceal the abuse, creating even more guilt, greater sense of betrayal, and a continual state of anxiety and hypervigilance [141].

In the long run, internal attributions of blame for childhood interpersonal trauma are generally associated with greater psychological distress and more depressive, anxious, and intrusive symptomatology [136, 137]. In addition, childhood interpersonal trauma survivors are prone to low self-esteem, and overestimation of danger, more commonly when they have experienced chronic trauma, as a result of which they develop a sense of having little power to affect future potentially negative events [24]. Taken together, these cognitive repercussions might generate pervasive predicaments in understanding others' behaviors and taking responsibility for one's own behavior and experiences in childhood trauma survivors [1].

3.2. Interpersonal repercussions of childhood interpersonal trauma

The peculiarity of childhood interpersonal trauma lies in its relational context. Indeed, interpersonal trauma includes elements of malevolence, betrayal, and disregard, which lead to feelings of insecurity about the trustworthiness of others [142, 143]. As such, when faced with an abusive caregiver, a child tends to develop disruptive styles of coping and relating to others and to oneself [12, 144] as well as enduring cognitive models about the self, others, the world, and the future known to generate hardships in subsequent interpersonal relationships [24, 145]. Survivors would thus experience interpersonal traumatic events as more "traumatizing" than non-interpersonal trauma (such as natural disasters) [53, 109, 146]. Hence, compared to impersonal traumatic stressors, such as natural disasters or motor vehicle accidents, interpersonal trauma during childhood is presumed to cause more detrimental and severe outcomes due to its deliberate nature [13, 147].

Several theoretical perspectives (e.g., social learning, object relations, attachment) suggest that individuals build expectations about others and relationships based on their interactions with significant others, especially in childhood [148–150]. In the context of early interpersonal trauma, survivors may develop negative schemas, beliefs, cognitions, and behaviors that impact the formation and maintenance of positive interpersonal relationships across the lifespan [151, 152]. Consistent with this assumption, recent studies have highlighted that childhood interpersonal trauma impairs the development and maintenance of adaptive relationships in childhood and beyond [35, 153]. For instance, early interpersonal trauma has been associated with poor social functioning and conflict resolution skills, problematic adult relationships and sexual adjustment [145, 151, 154], as well as beliefs that others are not trustworthy or will not provide adequate support when called upon [145]. In response to these convictions, survivors tend to exhibit lower social support [155], higher social isolation [156], domineering and controlling behavior [145], as well as distance in interpersonal relationships [157].

Romantic relationships generally represent the most important, yet challenging, interactions for a majority of adults, especially for survivors of childhood interpersonal trauma. As such, commitment to a romantic partner can be difficult [151] and survivors' disruptions in the formation and maintenance of interpersonal relationships would be especially salient in romantic relationships [158]. The development of commitment and intimacy may increase feelings of vulnerability and trigger unresolved issues, emotions, and cognitions associated with past traumatic experiences [159]. A review of the theoretical, clinical, and empirical literature also suggests that, once these relationships are formed, childhood interpersonal trauma survivors are more likely than non-survivors to report dissatisfaction, separation, or divorce [151]. Thus, even when survivors are able to commit to a romantic partner, their relationships are generally more dysfunctional, exhibit lack in closeness, feelings of affection, and personal disclosure [160] and show greater couple and sexual dissatisfaction [17, 154].

Studies are generally consistent with life course perspectives, whereby some of the repercussions associated with childhood interpersonal trauma are exacerbated by the relational nature of the couple relationship [13, 161]. The following sections provide an overview of some of the most documented relational posttraumatic repercussions of early interpersonal trauma: dysfunctional attachment patterns, sexuality and violence in intimate relationships.

3.2.1. *Attachment*

Several skills that are required for optimal relational functioning in adulthood are developed during infancy and childhood within caring and responsive bonds with primary caregivers [12, 149, 162, 163]. According to Bowlby's attachment theory [149, 162, 163], children are motivated to seek proximity to a caregiver or an attachment figure when faced with emotional distress or threats. When caregivers are able to provide comfort and reassurance, it allows the child to pursue nonattachment goals in a safe environment with the belief that they will be available if needed [164]. On the contrary, violent or abusive parents reduce the caregiver's capacity to attend to a child's needs and may challenge the child's confidence in the parents' availability and responsiveness [12, 165]. Children who are exposed to parental violence are less likely to have their basic need for available and consistently responsive caregivers fulfilled, thus preventing the development of a core sense of security in relationships [166]. Consequently, an abusive or neglectful relational context with a primary caregiver, in which a child experiences harm, or is neglected by an attachment figure, is likely to produce long-lasting relational difficulties through attachment insecurities [17, 165], particularly since children exposed to interpersonal trauma must deal with their attachment figures as potential sources of danger [167]. Indeed, attachment insecurities are overrepresented in adults who have been neglected, physically abused, or sexually abused during their childhood [168–170].

In adulthood, since the romantic partner often becomes the person toward which a distressed individual turns to for comfort and reassurance [171, 172], researchers have suggested that early attachment bonds share similar attachments features with the romantic partner's relationship [173, 174]. According to Brassard and Lussier [175], attachment insecurities in romantic relationships are shaped along two dimensions: abandonment anxiety and avoidance of intimacy. Abandonment anxiety refers to the extent to which one holds a negative or positive model of oneself and a perception of being worthy and loved. Interpersonal trauma survivors generally present a hyperactivation of this attachment system represented by intense demands of affection, a sensitivity to perceived or real threats of rejection by the partner, a certain control over the partner's behaviors, or an excessive dependence toward the partner in reaction to the perception that the other is insufficiently available to answer one's own needs of love and protection. Avoidance of intimacy depicts individuals who are uncomfortable in intimate contexts especially within close relationships and who see others as being untrustworthy or unavailable [164].

According to Godbout et al. [176], childhood interpersonal trauma hinder one's opportunities to develop the interpersonal skills that are essential to satisfactory intimate relationships such as the ability to trust others and understand the mental states that underlie their behaviors. In essence, the violent dynamics in which a survivor's first interpersonal encounters take place might shape dysfunctional interaction patterns that will be repeated in subsequent relationships. For example, abusive or neglectful experiences can produce fear of intimacy, which, in conjunction with the need for connection, leads to ambivalent, chaotic, or transient intimate relationships [176]. Hence, when lack of mutuality prevails in couple interactions, a survivor's perceived vulnerability might trigger power responses, used to protect oneself, further diminishing the already compromised relational processes of the couple [177].

In certain cases, parents who are not able to provide a safe haven for their children offer them frightening or unpredictable caregiving. As a result, children fail to organize a coherent strategy for ensuring protective access to their caregiver and tend to develop insecure representation of themselves, others, and the world [178]. Recent studies have referred to these difficulties as disorganized attachment [179–181]. Arising from the inability to deal with distress in the caregiver's presence [182, 183], disorganized attachment depicts a set of both approach and avoidance strategies [167] that persist across the lifespan [184]. In adulthood, survivors with a disorganized attachment style are known to have the most acrimonious romantic relationships [185].

3.2.2. Sexuality

A growing body of research shows that childhood interpersonal trauma, especially child sexual abuse (CSA), is associated with the presence of sexual difficulties in adulthood (e.g., [161, 186, 187]). Childhood interpersonal trauma often involves a malicious intent from the abuser, or betrayal from an attachment figure [143]. This betrayal feeling is likely to be reactivated in the context of adult close relationships and to generate difficulties in the sexual sphere. Sexual intimacy is a context in which the individual is vulnerable and where relational issues are likely to be re-evoked. This is especially difficult and anxiety-provoking for childhood interpersonal trauma survivors with trust issues, breakage boundaries, feelings of helplessness and betrayal.

According to Finkelhor and Browne's [188] traumagenic dynamics model, the impact of childhood interpersonal trauma on sexuality can be understood through four dynamics: *betrayal, traumatic sexualization, stigmatization, and powerlessness*, which are believed to "alter children's cognitive and emotional orientation to the world, and create trauma by distorting children's self-concept, world view, and affective capacities" (p. 531). Scientific literature highlights two trajectories within which sexual outcomes of CSA can be classified: sexual avoidance and sexual compulsivity [189, 190]. Sexual aversion, negative sexual attitudes, a wide range of sexual dysfunctions including vulvodynia, lack of interest in sex, orgasmic difficulties (see [191–194]), and lower sexual self-esteem [195] are examples of avoidance-related outcomes of CSA. In contrast, sexual compulsivity manifests as excessive sexual concerns, initiation to sex at an early age, an elevated number of sexual partners, risky sexual behaviors, and extradyadic sexual involvement [159, 196–198].

Regardless of the related trajectory, avoidant and compulsive sexual behaviors are conceptualized as dysfunctional coping mechanisms used to soothe, reduce, or distance from suffering traumatic memories, or to reinforce self-esteem as it was shattered by the experience of childhood interpersonal trauma [199, 200]. Yet, clinical and empirical observations reveal that those sexual outcomes are not necessarily exclusive and that mixed behaviors of avoidance and compulsivity are often present, underlying some sort of sexual ambivalence [190]. Multiple experiences of childhood interpersonal trauma are also found to predict lower levels of sexual satisfaction [29, 201]. Indeed, sexual repercussions of childhood interpersonal trauma not only pertain to CSA: increased risk of sexually transmitted diseases and risky sexual behaviors (i.e., sex with uncommitted partners, unprotected sex, impulsive sex, or risky anal sex) have also been observed in survivors of neglect, psychological and physical abuse [39, 202, 203]. Although research in this direction is still at an early stage, recent results suggest that childhood interpersonal trauma hinders sexual fulfillment and pleasure and the perception of living a satisfying sexuality [161, 204, 205].

3.2.3. *Violence in intimate relationships*

A large body of literature has reported an association between childhood interpersonal trauma and an increased risk of sustaining [52, 206] and of perpetrating [165, 207] intimate partner violence (IPV) in adulthood. Indeed, most victims of IPV [208], the majority of convicted batterers [209] and individuals from clinical samples who report having experienced IPV [69, 210] disclose high rates of childhood interpersonal trauma, ranging from 30 to 80% [209]. In the scientific literature, this phenomenon is referred to as the intergenerational transmission of IPV [211, 212]. According to those studies, growing up in a violent home would increase the probability of experiencing IPV in adulthood by 2–4 times [213]. However, not all victims of childhood interpersonal trauma become IPV perpetrators nor are revictimized [212, 214].

One of the most prominent theoretical explanations for the intergenerational transmission of IPV has its roots in the social learning theory [215], which posits that through behavioral conditioning, modeling, and observational learning, children raised with violence will come to consider violence as an appropriate response to conflict [211]. Indeed, by seeing the use of violence being reinforced (the resulting control of the partner or of the situation) or normalized, survivors of childhood interpersonal trauma would learn to use violent rather than nonviolent methods to resolve disputes or conflicts, thus integrating positive attitudes toward violence [216, 217]. Still, social learning theory does not sufficiently describe the association between early interpersonal trauma and IPV since it does not explain why some survivors of childhood interpersonal trauma experience later IPV while others do not. In addition, in a recent meta-analysis, Smith-Marek et al. [211] found a weak-to-moderate association between childhood interpersonal trauma and later IPV, with an overall effect size of 0.25 for perpetration and 0.21 for victimization across 124 studies. The high proportion of unexplained variance suggests that other possible factors might interact with the experience of early interpersonal trauma over the course of a survivor's life and contribute to later IPV.

In response to these shortcomings, researchers have suggested that children who grow up with violence, through social learning mechanisms and the influence of temperament or personality factors, may be more prone to develop an aggressive interpersonal style that is related to violence in intimate relationships [218, 219]. According to the bioecological perspective [220], individuals biologically inherit traits and tendencies that are strengthened or weakened by their relational experiences. This suggests that although early victimization continues to have an impact on adult functioning, this influence will be partly explained by other relational risk and protective factors that interact with the experience of early interpersonal trauma [216]. Consequently, a number of researchers have examined situational factors, usually pertaining to communication or conflicts that set the stage for violent interactions between romantic partners [216, 221, 222]. By combining these theoretical perspectives, IPV can thus be considered as a dynamic process that emerges as a result of early and situational relational experiences, learning processes, and biological affective dispositions [216]. Nevertheless, the fact that the strength of the relationship between early interpersonal trauma and adult IPV varies across studies calls for further studies exploring the mechanisms that might explain why some survivors of childhood interpersonal trauma experience IPV during adulthood while others do not [97]. For instance, Arata et al. [223] have suggested that the experience of multiple types of childhood interpersonal trauma, known to generate more important and complex repercussions than a single type of interpersonal trauma, could partly explain these different trajectories.

4. Conclusion

This chapter aimed to provide an overview of the long-term repercussions of childhood interpersonal trauma that persist in adulthood. This literature review demonstrates the extent to which childhood interpersonal trauma impacts multiple spheres of adult functioning, ranging from classic posttraumatic stress to violence in intimate relationships or sexual dissatisfaction. These outcomes, often considered as direct consequences of early interpersonal trauma, might also be causal mechanisms that trigger or exacerbate the onset of a series of psychological and relational difficulties in adulthood.

As such, trauma-related symptoms often extend beyond posttraumatic stress in an array of complex symptoms including depression, self-destructive behaviors, dissociation, substance abuse, somatic symptoms, and high comorbidity with other psychological disorders [31, 51, 53, 68]. For instance, affect regulation difficulties and posttraumatic stress following childhood interpersonal trauma might enhance the risk of experiencing IPV in adult survivors [52, 100, 210]. Interferences in the sense of attachment security may also preclude maintenance or reestablishment of emotional equanimity during and following trauma, thereby contributing to the formation of posttraumatic stress symptoms [166]. In contrast, if internal or external sources of support can be mobilized during or after a traumatic event, attachment security could act, at least to some extent, as a protective shield against the development of emotional problems following trauma, including posttraumatic stress symptoms [166]. Another example of the intermediate role of childhood interpersonal trauma repercussions to explain posttraumatic stress is the presence of peritraumatic dissociation that occurs during or immediately after a traumatic experience that appears to be strongly and consistently related to the presence of posttraumatic stress symptoms in adulthood [224].

However, following decades of research and prevention campaigns and despite dreadful consequences and economic effects (15M per year in judicial, health, education, employment, and personal costs in Canada [225]), early interpersonal trauma remains an understudied phenomenon, especially with regard to the identification of protective factors, such as partner support or certain personality traits, that might temper its effects on psychological and relational adult functioning. In addition, early relationships are a crucial part of the psycho-social scaffolding on which adult psycho-relational health rests yet, since personal history, relational experiences, and psychological adjustment are interrelated, future studies must consider multiple variables [13]. The challenges associated with the development of such studies lie in the plethora of intrapersonal, environmental, and interpersonal variables that must be examined but are better studied using longitudinal and systemic research protocols. As such, future studies should aim at following childhood interpersonal trauma survivors throughout as many years as possible, while assessing specific variables in the survivor's close relationships (e.g., parental, social and partner support). Integrative models, including both psychological and relational variables should also be examined in order to better understand the survivor's psychological and social development following childhood interpersonal trauma.

Also, given the substantial proportion of individuals who report any experience of childhood interpersonal trauma, health professionals are likely to encounter patients with trauma history. In this regard, they must acknowledge how these early experiences can shape both psychological and interpersonal functioning in order to properly evaluate and provide a treatment that is well-suited to survivors' needs and capacities. By recognizing the lasting and pernicious effects of childhood interpersonal trauma, therapists will be more able to validate the survivor's traumatic experience. Moreover, with the assistance of a secure and sincere therapeutic alliance, therapists who work with trauma survivors should be able to provide a warm, safe, and empathic environment that will help survivors in cultivating a new conception of interpersonal relationships. Thus, by providing a space to create new representations of the self and of others, therapists will grant survivors with a sense of hope and a feeling that their traumatic experience or actual symptoms do not define who they are.

Being aware that childhood interpersonal trauma survivors may lack self-regulatory or relational skills might also give therapists a sense of the importance of gradual exposure that will allow the survivor to develop new abilities and experiences [24]. In cases where a survivor's romantic relationship is characterized by emotional depth, relationship satisfaction, and adjustment, this particular relationship can also participate in a powerful healing experience. Indeed, healthy romantic relationships can foster a survivor's adjustment by facilitating a reorganization of dysfunctional schemes and cognitive processes that were developed in the context of childhood interpersonal trauma. In the same way as a sincere therapeutic alliance, romantic relationships can provide a space to explore new healthy relationship dynamics that will foster the survivor's psychosocial adjustment through the promotion of positive representations of self, others, and the outside world [176].

Author details

Caroline Dugal[1,2], Noémie Bigras[1,2], Natacha Godbout[2,3] and Claude Bélanger[1,2,4*]

*Address all correspondence to: belanger.claude@uqam.ca

1 Department of Psychology, University of Quebec in Montreal, Montreal, Canada

2 CRIPCAS, The Interdisciplinary Research Centre on Intimate Relationship Problems and Sexual Abuse, Montreal, Canada

3 Department of Sexology, University of Quebec in Montreal, Montreal, Canada

4 Department of Psychiatry, McGill University, Montreal, Canada

References

[1] D'Andrea, W., Ford, J., Stolbach, B., Spinazzola, J., & van der Kolk, B. A. (2012). Understanding interpersonal trauma in children: why we need a developmentally appropriate trauma diagnosis. American Journal of Orthopsychiatry, 82(2), 187–200.

[2] Kaffman, A. (2009). The silent epidemic of neurodevelopmental injuries. Biological Psychiatry, 66(7), 624–626. doi:10.1016/j.biopsych.2009.08.002

[3] Finkelhor, D., Turner, H., Ormrod, R., & Hamby, S. L. (2009). Violence, abuse, and crime exposure in a national sample of children and youth. Pediatrics, 124(5), 1411–1423.

[4] World Health Organization. (2015). Violence and Injury Prevention: Child Maltreatment (« child abuse »). Retrieved from http://www.who.int/violence_injury_prevention/violence/child/en/

[5] Cook, A., Spinazzola, J., Ford, J., Lanktree, C., Blaustein, M., Cloitre, M., van der Kolk, B. (2005). Complex trauma in children and adolescents. Psychiatric Annals, 35(5), 390–398.

[6] Godbout, N., Lussier, Y., & Sabourin, S. (2014). Childhood sexual abuse and subsequent psychological and interpersonal distress: the role of parental support. Child Abuse and Neglect, 38, 317–325. doi:10.1016/j.chiabu.2013.10.001

[7] Danielson, C. K., Ruggiero, K. J., Daughters, S. B., & Lejuez, C. W. (2010). Distress tolerance, risk-taking propensity, and PTSD symptoms in trauma-exposed youth: pilot study. The Behavior Therapist, 33(2), 28–34.

[8] Hodges, M., Godbout, N., Briere, J., Lanktree, C., Gilbert, A., & Kletzka, N. T. (2013). Cumulative trauma and symptom complexity in children: a path analysis. Child Abuse & Neglect, 37(11), 891–898. doi:10.1016/j.chiabu.2013.04.001.

[9] Irish, L., Kobayashi, I., & Delahanty, D. L. (2010). Long-term physical health consequences of childhood sexual abuse: a meta-analytic review. Journal of Pediatric Psychology, 35(5), 450–461. doi:10.1093/jpepsy/jsp118

[10] Briere, J., Hodges, M., & Godbout, N. (2010). Traumatic stress, affect dysregulation, and dysfunctional avoidance: a structural equation model. Journal of Traumatic Stress, 23(6), 767–774. doi:10.1002/jts.20578.

[11] Cicchetti, D., & Valentino, K. (2006). An ecological transactional perspective on child maltreatment: failure of the average expectable environment and its influence upon child development. In D. Cicchetti & D. J. Cohen (Eds.), Developmental Psychopathology (2nd ed., Vol. 3, pp. 129–201). New York: Wiley.

[12] Briere, J. (2002). Treating adult survivors of severe childhood abuse and neglect: further development of an integrative model. In J. E. B. Myers, L. Berliner, J. Briere, C. T. Hendrix, T. Reid & C. Jenny (Eds.), The APSAC Handbook on Child Maltreatment (2nd ed.). Newbury Park, CA: SAGE Publications.

[13] Godbout, N., Bigras, N., Runtz, M., & Briere, J. (In press). Traumas dans l'enfance et les relations de couple. In Y. Lussier, S. Sabourin, & C. Bélanger (Eds.). Fondements de la psychologie du couple. Québec, QC: Presses de l'Université du Québec (PUQ).

[14] Higgins, D. J., & McCabe, M. P. (2001). The development of the comprehensive child maltreatment scale. Journal of Family Studies, 7(1), 7–28.

[15] Stoltenborgh, M., Bakermans-Kranenburg, M. J., Alink, L. R. A., & van Ijzendoorn, M. H. (2012). The universality of childhood emotional abuse: a metaanalysis of worldwide prevalence. Journal of Aggression, Maltreatment & Trauma, 21(8), 870–890. doi: 10.1080/10926771.2012.708014.

[16] Canadian Red Cross. (2015). Emotional and Physical Abuse and Neglect. Retrieved from http://www.redcross.ca/how-we-help/violence--bullying-and-abuse-prevention/youth/emotional-and-physical-abuse-and-neglect?lang=en-ca&_ga=1.168347169.162162899.1456000882

[17] Godbout, N., Lussier, Y., & Sabourin, S. (2006). Early abuse experiences and subsequent gender differences in couple adjustment. Violence and Victims, 21(6), 744–760. doi: 10.1891/vvv21i6a005.

[18] Stoltenborgh, M., Bakermans-Kranenburg, M. J., Alink, L. R. A., & van Ijzendoorn, M. H. (2015). The prevalence of child maltreatment across the globe: review of a series of meta-analyses. Child Abuse Review, 24(1), 37–50. doi:10.1002/car.2353.

[19] Bremner, J. D., Bolus, R., & Mayer, E. A. (2007). Psychometric properties of the early trauma inventory-self report. Journal of Nervous and Mental Disease, 195, 211–218.

[20] Criminal Code, R.S.C. 1985, c.34, s.150(1).

[21] Hébert, M., Cyr, M., & Tourigny, M. (2011). L'agression sexuelle envers les enfants, Tome I. Ste-Foy: Presses de l'Université du Québec.

[22] Trocmé, N., Fallon, B., MacLaurin, B., Sinha, V., Black, T., Fast, E.,…Holroyd, J. (2010). Étude canadienne sur l'incidence des signalements de cas de violence et de neégligence envers les enfants - donneées principales Retrieved from http://www.phac-aspc.gc.ca/cm-vee/public-fra.php.

[23] World Health Organization. (2002). World Report on Violence and Health: Summary. World Health Organization, Geneva.

[24] Briere, J., & Scott, C. (2015). Principles of Trauma Therapy: A Guide to Symptoms, Evaluation, and Treatment (2nd ed., DSM-5 update). Thousand Oaks, CA: Sage Publications.

[25] Duckworth, M. P., & Follette, V. M. (2012). Retraumatization: Assessment, Treatment, and Prevention. New York: Routledge/Taylor & Francis Group.

[26] Elliott, A. N., Alexander, A. A., Pierce, T. W., Aspelmeier, J. E., & Richmond, J. M. (2009). Childhood victimization, poly-victimization, and adjustment to college in women. Child Maltreatment, 14(4), 330–343. doi:10.1177/1077559509332262

[27] Cyr, K., Chamberland, C., Clément, M.-É., Lessard, G., Wemmers, J.-A., Collin-Vézina, D., Damant, D. (2013). Polyvictimization and victimization of children and youth: results from a populational survey. Child Abuse & Neglect, 37(10), 814–820. doi: 10.1016/j.chiabu.2013.03.009

[28] Pereda, N., Guilera, G., & Abad, J. (2014). Victimization and polyvictimization of Spanish children and youth: results from a community sample. Child Abuse & Neglect, 38(4), 640–649. doi:10.1016/j.chiabu.2014.01.019

[29] Bigras, N., Daspe, M-E, Godbout, N, Sabourin, S, & Briere, J. (2016). Cumulative childhood trauma and adult sexual satisfaction: mediation by affect dysregulation and sexual anxiety in men and women. Journal of Sex & Marital Therapy. [Epub ahead of print]

[30] Gallegos, R. A., & Hillbrand, M. (2016). Integrative treatment of complex trauma: integrating behavioral, dynamic, and attribution models. Journal of Psychotherapy Integration. Advance online publication. doi:10.1037/a0040043

[31] Cloitre, M., Stolbach, B. C., Herman, J. L., van der Kolk, B., Pynoos, R., Wang, J., et al. (2009). A developmental approach to complex PTSD: childhood and adult cumulative

trauma as predictors of symptom complexity. Journal of Traumatic Stress, 22, 399–408. doi:10.1002/jts.20444.

[32] Álvarez-Lister, M. S., Pereda, N., Abad, J., Guilera, G., & GReVIA. (2014). Polyvictimization and its relationship to symptoms of psychopathology in a southern European sample of adolescent outpatients. Child Abuse & Neglect, 38(4), 747–756. doi:10.1016/j.chiabu.2013.09.005

[33] Finkelhor, D., Hamby, S. L., Ormrod, R., & Turner, H. (2005). The juvenile victimization questionnaire: reliability, validity, and national norms. Child Abuse & Neglect, 29, 383–412. doi:10.1016/j.chiabu.2004.11.001

[34] Putnam, K. T., Harris, W. W., & Putnam, F. W. (2013). Synergistic childhood adversities and complex adult psychopathology. Journal of Traumatic Stress, 26(4), 435–442. doi: 10.1002/jts.21833

[35] Dodge Reyome, N. (2010) Childhood emotional maltreatment and later intimate relationships: themes from the empirical literature, Journal of Aggression, Maltreatment & Trauma, 19(2), 224–242, doi: 10.1080/10926770903539664.

[36] Schury, K., Kolassa, I. T. (2012). Biological memory of childhood maltreatment: current knowledge and recommendations for future research. Annals of the New York Academy of Sciences, 1262, 93–100.

[37] Godbout, N., & Briere, J. (2012). Psychological responses to trauma. In C. R. Figley (Ed.), Encyclopedia of Trauma, An Interdisciplinary Guide (pp. 485–489). Thousand Oaks, CA: Sage Publications. ISBN: 9781412978798.

[38] Haferkamp, L., Bebermeier, A., Möllering, A., & Neuner, F. (2015). Dissociation is associated with emotional maltreatment in a sample of traumatized women with a history of child abuse. Journal of Trauma & Dissociation, 16(1), 86–99. doi: 10.1080/15299732.2014.959149

[39] Norman, R. E., Byambaa, M., De, R., Butchart, A., Scott, J., & Vos, T. (2012). The long-term health consequences of child physical abuse, emotional abuse, and neglect: a systematic review and meta-analysis. PLoS Med, 9(11): e1001349. doi:10.1371/journal.pmed.1001349

[40] Ramo-Fernández, L., Schneider, A., Wilker, S., & Kolassa, I.-T. (2015). Epigenetic alterations associated with war trauma and childhood maltreatment. Behavioral Sciences & the Law, 33(5), 701–721. doi:10.1002/bsl.2200

[41] Waxman, R., Fenton, M. C., Skodol, A. E., Grant, B. F., & Hasin, D. (2014). Childhood maltreatment and personality disorders in the USA: specificity of effects and the impact of gender. Personality and Mental Health, 8(1), 30–41. doi:10.1002/pmh.1239

[42] Sareen, J., Cox, B. J., Afifi, T. O., de Graaf, R., Asmundson, G. J. G., ten Have, M., & Stein, M. B. (2005). Anxiety disorders and risk for suicidal ideation and suicide attempts. Archives on General Psychiatry, 62(11), 1249–1257.

[43] Stansfeld, S. A., Clark, C., Rodgers, B., Caldwell, T., & Power, C. (2010). Repeated exposure to socioeconomic disadvantage and health selection as life course pathways to mid-life depressive and anxiety disorders. Social Psychiatry and Psychiatric Epidemiology, 46(7), 549–558.

[44] Greene, C. A., Ford, J. D., Wakefield, D. B., & Barry, L. C. (2014). Posttraumatic stress mediates the relationship between childhood victimization and current mental health burden in newly incarcerated adults. Child Abuse & Neglect, 38(10), 1569–1580. doi: 10.1016/j.chiabu.2014.07.006

[45] Copeland, W. E., Bulik, C. M., Zucker, N., Wolke, D., Lereya, S. T., & Costello, E. J. (2015). Does childhood bullying predict eating disorder symptoms? A prospective, longitudinal analysis. International Journal of Eating Disorders. Advance online publication. doi:10.1002/eat.22459

[46] Maniglio, R. (2009). The impact of child sexual abuse on health: a systematic review of reviews. Clinical Psychology Review, 29, 647–657. doi:10.1016/j.cpr.2009.08.003

[47] Anda, R. F., Felitti, V. J., Bremner, J. D., Walker, J. D., Whitfield, C., Perry, B. D., Dube, S. R., & Giles, W. H. (2006). The enduring effects of abuse and related adverse experiences in childhood. European Archives of Psychiatry and Clinical Neuroscience, 256, 174–186.

[48] Edwards, V., Holden, G. W., Felitti, V. J., & Anda, R. F. (2003). Relationship between multiple forms of childhood maltreatment and adult mental health in community respondents: results from the adverse childhood experiences study. American Journal of Psychiatry, 160, 1453–1460.

[49] Becker, K. D., Stuewig, J., & McCloskey, L. A. (2010). Traumatic stress symptoms of women exposed to different forms of childhood victimization and intimate partner violence. Journal of Interpersonal Violence, 25(9), 1699–1715. doi: 10.1177/0886260509354578

[50] Briere, J., Agee, E., & Dietrich, A. (2016). Cumulative trauma and current posttraumatic stress disorder status in general population and inmate samples. Psychological Trauma: Theory, Research, Practice, and Policy. Advance online publication. doi:10.1037/tra0000107

[51] Ehring, T., Welboren, R., Morina, N., Wicherts, J. M., Freitag, J., & Emmelkamp, P. M. G. (2014). Meta-analysis of psychological treatments for posttraumatic stress disorder in adult survivors of childhood abuse. Clinical Psychology Review, 34(8), 645–657. doi: 10.1016/j.cpr.2014.10.004

[52] Messing, J. T., La Flair, L., Cavanaugh, C. E., Kanga, M. R., & Campbell, J. C. (2012) Testing posttraumatic stress as a mediator of childhood trauma and adult intimate partner violence victimization. Journal of Aggression, Maltreatment & Trauma, 21(7), 792–811, doi:10.1080/10926771.2012.686963.

[53] Brillon, P. (2013). Comment aider les victims souffrant de stress post-traumatique (5e édition). Montréal: Éditions Québec-Livre.

[54] Cloitre, M., Garvert, D. W., Brewin, C. R., Bryant, R. A., & Maercker, A. (2013). Evidence for proposed ICD-11 PTSD and complex PTSD: a latent profile analysis. European Journal of Psychotraumatology, 4, 20706, doi:10.3402/ejpt.v4i0.20706

[55] MacIntosh, H., Godbout, N., & Dubash, N. (2015). Borderline personality disorder: disorder of trauma or personality, a review of the empirical literature. Canadian Psychology, 56(2), 227–241. doi:10.1037/cap0000028.

[56] Spinazzola, J., Blaustein, M., & van der Kolk, B. A. (2005). Posttraumatic stress disorder treatment outcome research: the study of unrepresentative samples? Journal of Traumatic Stress, 18(5), 425–436. doi:10.1002/jts.20050.

[57] Kessler, R. C., Berglund, P., Demler, O., Jin, R., & Walters, E. E. (2005). Lifetime prevalence and age-of-onset distributions of DSM–IV disorders in the National Comorbidity Survey Replication. Archives of General Psychiatry, 62, 593–602.

[58] Carr, C. P., Severi, C. M., Stingel, A. M., Lemgruber, V. B., Juruena, M. F. (2013). The role of early life stress in adult psychiatric disorders: a systematic review according to childhood trauma subtypes. Journal of Nervous and Mental Disease, 201, 1007–1020. doi:10.1097/NMD.0000000000000049

[59] Fergusson, D., & Mullen, P. (1999). Childhood Sexual Abuse: An Evidence based Perspective. Thousand Oaks: Sage Publications, Inc.

[60] Green, J. G., McLaughlin, K. A., Berglund, P. A., Gruber, M. J., Sampson, N. A., Zaslavsky, A. M., et al. (2010). Childhood adversities and adult psychiatric dis- orders in the national comorbidity survey replication I: associations with first onset of DSM-IV disorders. Archives of General Psychiatry, 67, 113–123, doi :10.1001/archgenpsychiatry.2009.186.

[61] Moffit, E. T., Caspi, A., Harrington, H., Milne, B. J., Melchior, M., Goldberg, D., & Poulton, R. (2007). Generalized anxiety disorder and depression: childhood risk factors in a birth cohort followed to age 32. Psychological Medicine, 37, 441–452. doi:10.1017/S0033291706009640

[62] Mineka, S., & Zinbarg, R. (2006). A contemporary learning theory perspective on the etiology of anxiety disorders. American Psychologist, 61, 10–26. doi:10.1037/0003-066X.61.1.10

[63] Godbout, N., Bigras, N., & Dion, J. (2016). Présence attentive et traumas interpersonnels subis durant l'enfance. Dans S. Grégoire, L. Lachance et L. Richer (Eds.), La présence attentive, Mindfulness: État des connaissances théoriques, empiriques et pratiques (pp. 229–246). Québec, Qc : Presses de l'Université du Québec (PUQ).

[64] Banducci, A. N., Hoffman, E., Lejuez, C. W., & Koenen, K. C. (2014). The relationship between child abuse and negative outcomes among substance users: Psychopathology, health, and comorbidities. Addictive Behaviors, 39, 1522–1527.

[65] Cougle, J. R., Timpano, K. R., Sachs-Ericsson, N., Keough, M. E., & Riccardi, C. J. (2010). Examining the unique relationships between anxiety disorders and childhood physical and sexual abuse in the National Comorbidity Survey-Replication. Psychiatry Research, 177(1), 150–155. doi:10.1016/j.psychres.2009.03.008

[66] Spinhoven, P., Elzinga, B. M., Hovens, J. G., Roelofs, K., Zitman, F. G., van Oppen, P., Penninx, B. (2010). The specificity of childhood adversities and negative life events across the life span to anxiety and depressive disorders. Journal of Affective Disorders, 126, 103–112. doi:10.1016/j.jad.2010.02.132

[67] Bouton, M., Mineka, S., & Barlow, D. H. (2001). A contemporary learning theory perspective on the etiology of panic disorder. Psychological Review, 108, 4–32.

[68] Abela, J., Skitch, S., 2007. Dysfunctional attitudes, self-esteem, and hassles: cognitive vulnerability to depression in children of affectively ill parents. Behaviour Research and Therapy, 45(6), 1127–1140. doi:10.1016/j.brat.2006.09.011

[69] Berthelot, N., Hébert, M., Godbout, N., Goulet, M., Bergeron, S., & Boucher, S. (2014). Childhood maltreatment increases the risk of intimate partner violence via PTSD and anger personality traits in individuals consulting for sexual problems. Journal of Aggression, Maltreatment & Trauma, 23(9), 982–998. doi: 10.1080/10926771.2014.960631.

[70] Bifulco, A., Brown, G. W., Moran, P., Ball, C., & Campbell, C. (1998). Predicting depression in women: the role of past and present vulnerability. Psychological Medicine, 28, 39–50.

[71] Gibb, B. E., Alloy, A., & Abramson, L., (2001). History of childhood maltreatment, depressogenic cognitive style, and episodes of depression in adulthood. Cognitive Therapy and Research, 25(4), 425–446.

[72] MacMillan, H. L., Fleming, J. E., Streiner, D. L., Lin, E., Boyle, M. H., Jamieson, E., Duku, E. K., Walsh, C. A., Wong, M. Y., & Beardslee, W. R. (2001). Childhood abuse and lifetime psychopathology in a community sample. The American Journal of Psychiatry, 158(11), 1878–1883.

[73] Widom, C. S., DuMont, K., & Czaja, S. J. (2007). A prospective investigation of major depressive disorder and comorbidity in abused and neglected children grown up. Archives of General Psychiatry, 64(1), 49–56. doi:10.1001/archpsyc.64.1.49.

[74] Kessler, R. C., Sonnega, A., Bromet, E., Hughes, M., & Nelson, C. B. (1995). Posttraumatic stress disorder in the National Comorbidity Survey. Archives of General Psychiatry, 52(12), 1048–60.

[75] Bolduc, R., Bigras, N., Daspe, M-E., Godbout, N., & Hébert, M. (2015). The Role of Mindfulness and Dissociation in the Relation Between Cumulative Trauma and

Depression: A Conceptual Model. Poster presented at the 76th Annual Canadian Psychological Association (CPA) Convention, June 4-6 2015, Ottawa, Ontario.

[76] Briere, J., Kaltman, S., & Green, B. L. (2008). Accumulated childhood trauma and symptom complexity. Journal of Traumatic Stress, 21, 223–226. doi:10.1002/jts. 20317.

[77] Chapman D. P., Whitfield, C. L., Felitti, V. J., Dube, S. R., Edwards, V. J., & Anda, R. F. (2004). Adverse childhood experiences and the risk of depressive disorders in adulthood. Journal of Affective Disorders, 82(2), 217–25.

[78] Infurna, M. R., Reichl, C., Parzer, P., Schimmenti, A., Bifulco, A., & Kaess, M. (2016). Associations between depression and specific childhood experiences of abuse and neglect: a meta-analysis. Journal of Affective Disorders, 190, 47–55. doi:10.1016/j.jad. 2015.09.006.

[79] American Psychiatric Association. (2013). Diagnostic and Statistical Manual of Mental Disorders (5th ed.). Washington, DC: Author.

[80] Joyce, P. R., McKenzie, J. M., Luty, S. E., Mulder, R. T., Carter, J. D., Sullivan, P. F., & Cloninger, C. R. (2003). Temperament, childhood environment and psychopathology as risk factors for avoidant and borderline personality disorders. Australian and New Zealand Journal of Psychiatry, 37(6), 756–764. doi:10.1111/j.1440-1614.2003.01263.x

[81] Gunderson, J. G., Lyons-Ruth, K. (2008). BPD's interpersonal hypersensitivity phenotype: a gene–environment–developmental model. Journal of Personality Disorders, 22(22–41).

[82] Krastins, A., Francis, A. J. P., Field, A. M., & Carr, S. N. (2014). Childhood predictors of adulthood antisocial personality disorder symptomatology. Australian Psychologist, 49(3), 142–150. doi:10.1111/ap.12048

[83] Moffit, E. T., Caspi, A., Harrington, H., & Milne, J. B. (2002). Males on the life-course persistent and adolescence-limited antisocial pathways: follow-up at 26 years. Development and Psychopathology, 14, 179–207. doi:10.1017/ S0954579402001104.

[84] Semiz, B. U., Basoglu, C., Ebrinc, S., & Cetin, M. (2007). Childhood trauma history and dissociative experiences among Turkish men diagnosed with antisocial personality disorder. Social Psychiatry and Psychiatric Epidemiology, 42, 865–873. doi:10.1007/ s00127-007-0248-2

[85] Kuo, J. R., Khoury, J. E., Metcalfe, R., Fitzpatrick, S., & Goodwill, A. (2015). An examination of the relationship between childhood emotional abuse and borderline personality disorder features: the role of difficulties with emotion regulation. Child Abuse & Neglect, 39, 147–155. doi:10.1016/j.chiabu.2014.08.008

[86] Linehan, M. M. (1993). Cognitive-Behavioral Treatment of Borderline Personality Disorder. New York: Guilford Press.

[87] Hughes, A. E., Crowell, S. E., Uyeji, L., & Coan, J. A. (2012). A developmental neuroscience of borderline pathology: emotion dysregulation and social baseline theory. Journal of Abnormal Child Psychology, 40(1), 21–33. doi:10.1007/s10802-011-9555-x

[88] Ball, J. S., & Links, P. S. (2009). Borderline personality disorder and childhood trauma: evidence for a causal relationship. Current Psychiatry Reports, 11, 63–68. doi:10.1007/s11920-009-00104

[89] Bornovalova, M. A., Gratz, K. L., Delany-Brumsey, A., Paulson, A., & Lejuez, C. W. (2006). Temperamental and environmental risk factors for borderline personality disorder among inner-city substance users in residential treatment. Journal of Personality Disorders, 20(3), 218–231. doi:10.1521/pedi.2006.20.3.218

[90] Zanarini, M. C. (2000). Childhood experiences associated with the development of borderline personality disorder. Psychiatric Clinics of North America, 23(1), 89–101. doi:10.1016/S0193-953X(05)70145-3

[91] Battle, C. L., Shea, M. T., Johnson, D. M., Yen, S., Zlotnick, C., Zanarini, M. C., Morey, L. C. (2004). Childhood maltreatment associated with adult personality disorders: findings from the collaborative longitudinal personality disorders study. Journal of Personality Disorders, 18(2), 193–211. doi:10.1521/pedi.18.2.193.32777

[92] Afifi, T. O., Mather, A., Boman, J., Fleisher, W., Enns, M. W., MacMillan, H., & Sareen, J. (2011). Childhood adversity and personality disorders: results from a nationally representative population-based study. Journal of Psychiatric Research, 45(6), 814–822. doi:10.1016/j.jpsychires.2010.11.008

[93] Cohen, L. J., Tanis, T., Bhattacharjee, R., Nesci, C., Halmi, W., & Galynker, I. (2014). Are there differential relationships between different types of childhood maltreatment and different types of adult personality pathology? Psychiatry Research, 215(1), 192–201. doi:10.1016/j.psychres.2013.10.036

[94] Lobbestael, J., Arntz, A., & Berstein, D. P. (2010). Disentangling the relationship between different types of childhood maltreatment and personality disorders. Journal of Personality Disorders, 24(3), 285–295. doi:10.1521/pedi.2010.24.3.285

[95] Tyrka, A. R., Wyche, M. C., Kelly, M. M., Price, L. H., Carpenter, L. L. (2009). Childhood maltreatment and adult personality disorder symptoms: influence of maltreatment type. Psychiatry Research, 165, 281–287.

[96] Gratz, K. L., & Roemer, L. (2004). Multidimensional assessment of emotion regulation and dysregulation: development, factor structure, and initial validation of the difficulties in emotion regulation scale. Journal of Psychopathology and Behavioral Assessment, 26(1), 41–54. doi:10.1023/B:JOBA.0000007455.08539.94

[97] Berzenski, S. R., & Yates, T. M. (2010). Research on intimate partner violence: a developmental process analysis of the contribution of childhood emotional abuse to

relationship violence. Journal of Aggression, Maltreatment & Trauma, 19(2), 180–203. doi:10.1080/10926770903539474.

[98] Briere, J., & Runtz, M. (2002). The Inventory of Altered Self-Capacities (IASC): a standardized measure of identity, affect regulation, and relationship disturbance. Assessment, 9(3), 230–239. doi:10.1177/1073191102009003002.

[99] Arens, A. M., Gaher, R. M., & Simons, J. S. (2012). Child maltreatment and deliberate self-harm among college students: testing mediation and moderation models for impulsivity. American Journal of Orthopsychiatry, 82(3), doi:10.1111/j.1939-0025.2012.01165.x.

[100] Gratz, K. L., Paulson, A., Jakupcak, M., & Tull, M. T. (2009). Exploring the relationship between childhood maltreatment and intimate partner abuse: gender differences in the mediating role of emotion dysregulation. Violence and Victims, 24, 68–82. doi: 10.1891/0886-6708.24.1.68.

[101] Briere, J., & Lanktree, C. B. (2008). Integrative Treatment of Complex Trauma for Children (ITCT-C): A Guide for the Treatment of Multiply-Traumatized Children Aged Eigth to Twelve Years. Long Beach, CA: MCAVIC-USC Child and Adolescent Trauma Program National Child Traumatic Stress Network WEB: http://www.johnbriere.com).

[102] Briere, J., & Rickards, S. (2007). Self-awareness, affect regulation, and relatedness: differential sequels of childhood versus adult victimization experiences. Journal of Nervous and Mental Disease, 195(6), 497–503. doi:10.1097/NMD.0b013e31803044e2.

[103] Green, B. L., Krupnick, J. L., Stockton, P., Goodman, L., Corcoran, C., & Petty, R. (2005). Effects of adolescent trauma exposure on risky behavior in college women. Psychiatry, 68, 363–376.

[104] Shackman, J. E., & Pollak, S. D. (2014). Impact of physical maltreatment on the regulation of negative affect and aggression. Development and Psychopathology, 26(4), 1021–1033. doi:10.1017/S0954579414000546

[105] Hedtke, K. A., Ruggiero, K. J., Fitzgerald, M. M., Zinzow, H. M., Saunders, B. E., Resnick, H. S., & Kilpatrick, D. G. (2008). A longitudinal investigation of interpersonal violence in relation to mental health and substance abuse. Journal of Consulting and Clinical Psychology, 76, 633–647.

[106] Ouimette, P., & Brown, P. J. (2003) Trauma and Substance Abuse: Causes, Consequences, and Treatment of Comorbid Disorders. Washington, DC: American Psychological Association.

[107] Dube, S. R., Felitti, V. J., Dong, M., Chapman, D. P., Giles, W. H., & Anda, R. F. (2003). Childhood abuse, neglect, and household dysfunction and the risk of illicit drug use: the adverse childhood experiences study. Pediatrics, 111, 564–572. doi:10.1542/peds.111.3.564

[108] Pearlman, L. (1998). Trauma and the self: a theoretical and clinical perspective. Journal of Emotional Abuse, 1, 7–25.

[109] Briere, J., & Scott, C. (2006). Principles of Trauma Therapy: A Guide to Symptoms, Evaluation, and Treatment. Thousand Oaks, CA: Sage.

[110] Brewerton, T. D. (2015). Stress, trauma, and adversity as risk factors in the development of eating disorders. In Smolak, L., & Levine, M. P. (Eds.), The Wiley Handbook of Eating Disorders. West Sussex, UK: John Wiley & Sons.

[111] Mitchell, K. S., Mazzeo, S. E., Schlesinger, M. R., Brewerton, T. D., & Smith, B. N. (2012). Comorbidity of partial and subthreshold PTSD among men and women with eating disorders in the national comorbidity survey-replication study. International Journal of Eating Disorders, 45(3), 307–15. doi:10.1002/eat.20965.

[112] Moulton, S. J., Newman, E., Power, K., Swanson, V., & Day, K. (2015). Childhood trauma and eating psychopathology: a mediating role for dissociation and emotion dysregulation? Child Abuse & Neglect, 39, 167–174. doi:10.1016/j.chiabu.2014.07.003

[113] Smolak, L., & Murnen, S. K. (2002). A meta-analytic examination of the relationship between child sexual abuse and eating disorders. International Journal of Eating Disorders, 31, 136–150. doi:10.1002/eat.10008

[114] Morris, A. S., Silk, J. S., Steinberg, L., Myers, S. S., & Robinson, L. R. (2007). The role of the family context in the development of emotion regulation. Social Development, 16, 361– 388.

[115] Dworkin, E., Javdani, S., Verona, E., & Campbell, R. (2014). Child sexual abuse and disordered eating: the mediating role of impulsive and compulsive tendencies. Psychology of Violence, 4(1), 21–36. doi:10.1037/a0031779

[116] Briere, J., Madni, L. A., & Godbout, N. (2015). Recent suicidality in the general population: multivariate association with childhood maltreatment and adult victimization. Journal of Interpersonal Violence, 1–17. doi: 10.1177/0886260515584339

[117] Brodsky, B., & Stanley, B. (2008). Adverse childhood experiences and suicidal behavior. Psychiatric Clinics of North America, 31, 223–235.

[118] Mironova, P., Rhodes, A. E., Bethell, J. M., Tonmyr, L., Boyle, M. H., Wekerle, C., Leslie, B. (2011). Childhood physical abuse and suicide-related behavior: a systematic review. Vulnerable Children and Youth Studies, 6, 1–7.

[119] Briere, J., Godbout, N., & Dias, C. (2015). Cumulative trauma, hyperarousal, and suicidality in the general population: a path analysis. Journal of Trauma & Dissociation, 16(2), 153–169. doi:10.1080/15299732.2014.970265

[120] Dube, S. R., Anda, R. F., Felitti, V. J., Chapman, D. P., Williamson, D. F., & Giles, W. H. (2001). Childhood abuse, household dysfunction, and the risk of attempted suicide

throughout the life span: findings from the Adverse Childhood Experiences study. Journal of the American Medical Association, 286, 3089–3096.

[121] Rudd, M. D. (2006). Fluid vulnerability theory: a cognitive approach to understanding the process of acute and chronic suicide risk. In T. Ellis (Ed.), Cognition and Suicide: Theory, Research, and Therapy (pp. 355–368). Washington, DC: American Psychological Association.

[122] Joiner, T. E. (2005). Why People Die by Suicide. Cambridge, MA: Harvard University Press.

[123] Van Orden, K. A., Witte, T. K., Cukrowicz, K. C., Braithwaite, S. R., Selby, E. A., & Joiner, T. E., Jr. (2010). The interpersonal theory of suicide. Psychological Review, 117, 575–600.

[124] Wilcox, H. C., Storr, C. L., & Breslau, N. (2009). Posttraumatic stress disorder and suicide attempts in a community sample of urban American young adults. Archives of General Psychiatry, 66, 305–311.

[125] Lanius, R. A. (2015). Trauma-related dissociation and altered states of consciousness: a call for clinical, treatment, and neuroscience research. European Journal of Psychotraumatology, 6. Published online. doi:10.3402/ejpt.v6.27905

[126] Briere, J., & Runtz, M. (2015). Dissociation in individuals denying trauma exposure: findings from two samples. Journal of Nervous and Mental Disease, 203(6), 439–442. doi:10.1097/NMD.0000000000000303

[127] Dalenberg, C. J., & Palesh, O. G. (2004). Relationship between child abuse history, trauma, and dissociation in Russian college students. Child Abuse & Neglect, 28, 461–474. doi:10.1016/j.chiabu.2003.11.020

[128] Liotti, G. (1992). Disorganized/disoriented attachment in the etiology of the dissociative disorders. Dissociation, 5(4), 196–204.

[129] Holtforth, M. G. (2008). Avoidance motivation in psychological problems and psychotherapy. Psychotherapy Research, 18, 147–159.

[130] Elliot, A. J. (2006). The hierarchical model of approach-avoidance motivation. Motivation and Emotion, 30, 111–116.

[131] Foa, E. B., Steketee, G., & Rothbaum, B. O. (1989). Behavioral-cognitive conceptualizations of post-traumatic stress disorder. Behavior Therapy, 20, 155–176.

[132] Hayes, S. C., & Gifford, E. V. (1997). The trouble with language: experiential avoidance, rules, and the nature of verbal events. Psychological Science, 8(3), 170–173.

[133] Kimble, M. O., Fleming, L., Bandy, C. (2010). Attention to novel and target stimuli in trauma survivors. Psychiatry Research, 178(3), 501–506. doi:10.1016/j.psychres.2009.10.009.

[134] Vasterling, J. J., Duke, L. M., Brailey, K., Constans, J. I., Allain, A. N., Sutkey, P. B. (2002). Attention, learning, and memory performance and intellectual resources in Vietnam

veterans: PTSD and no disorder comparisons. Neuropsychology. 16, 5–14. [PubMed: 11853357]

[135] Weiner, B. (1986). Spontaneous causal thinking. Psychological Bulletin, 97, 74–84.

[136] Barker-Collo, S. L. (2001). Adult reports of child and adult attributions of blame for childhood sexual abuse: predicting adult adjustment and suicidal behaviors in females. Child Abuse & Neglect, 25(10), 1329–1341. doi:10.1016/S0145-2134(01)00278-2

[137] Steel, J., Sanna, L., Hammond, B., Whipple, J., & Cross, H. (2004). Psychological sequelae of childhood sexual abuse: abuse-related characteristics, coping strategies, and attributional style. Child Abuse & Neglect, 28(7), 785–801. doi:10.1016/j.chiabu.2003.12.004

[138] Daigneault, I., Hébert, M., & Tourigny, M. (2006). Attributions and coping in sexually abused adolescents referred for group treatment. Journal of Child Sexual Abuse, 15(3), 35–59.

[139] van Loon, A. M., & Kralik, D. (2005). Facilitating Transition after Child Sexual Abuse. SA: RDNS Research Unit.

[140] Walker, L. (1994). Abused Women and Survivor Therapy: A Practical Guide for the Psychotherapist. Washington DC: American Psychological Association

[141] Lawson, D. M., & Quinn, J. (2013). Complex trauma in children and adolescents: evidence-based practice in clinical settings. Journal of Clinical Psychology: In Session, 69(5), 497–509. doi: 10.1002/jclp.21990

[142] Courtois, C. A. (n.d.). Understanding Complex Trauma, Complex Reactions, and Treatment Approaches. Retrieved from: http://www.giftfromwithin.org/pdf/Understanding-CPTSD.pdf.

[143] Freyd, J. J. (1996). Betrayal Trauma: The Logic of Forgetting Childhood Abuse. Cambridge, MA: Harvard University Press.

[144] Putnam, F. W. (1997). Dissociation in Children and Adolescents: A Developmental Perspective. New York: Guilford Press.

[145] Messman-Moore, T. L., & Coates, A. A. (2007) The impact of childhood psychological abuse on adult interpersonal conflict. Journal of Emotional Abuse, 7(2), 75–92, doi: 10.1300/J135v07n02_05.

[146] Freyd, J. J., Klest, B., & Allard, C. B. (2005). Betrayal trauma: relationship to physical health, psychological distress, and a written disclosure intervention. Journal of Trauma and Dissociation, 6, 83–104.

[147] Pearlman, L. A., & Courtois, C. A. (2005). Clinical applications of the attachment framework: relational treatment of complex trauma. Journal of Traumatic Stress, 18(5), 449–459. doi:10.1002/jts.20052

[148] Bandura, A. (1977). Social Learning Theory. Englewood Cliffs, NJ: Prentice Hall.

[149] Bowlby, J. (1969). Attachment and Loss (Vol. 1. Attachment). New York: Basic Books.

[150] Fairbairn, W. R. D. (1952). Psychological Studies of the Personality. London: Routledge & Kegan Paul.

[151] Colman, R. A., & Widom, C. S. (2004). Childhood abuse and neglect and adult intimate relationships: a prospective study. Child Abuse and Neglect, 28(11), 1133–1151. doi: 10.1016/j.chiabu.2004.02.005

[152] Young, J. E., Klosko, J. S., & Weishaar, M. E. (2003). Schema Therapy: A Practitioner's Guide. New York: Guilford Press.

[153] Taussig, H. N., & Culhane, S. E. (2010). Emotional maltreatment and psychosocial functioning in preadolescent youth placed in out-of-home care. Journal of Aggression, Maltreatment and Trauma, 19(1), 52–74.

[154] Bigras, N., Godbout, N., Hébert, M., Runtz, M., & Daspe, M.-È. (2015). Identity and relatedness as mediators between child emotional abuse and adult couple adjustment in women. Child Abuse & Neglect, 50, 85–93. doi:10.1016/j.chiabu.2015.07.009

[155] Muller, R. T., Gragtmans, K., & Baker, R. (2008). Childhood physical abuse, attachment, and adult social support: test of a mediational model. Canadian Journal of Behavioural Science/Revue canadienne des sciences du comportement, 40(2), 80–89. doi: 10.1037/0008-400X.40.2.80

[156] Berlin, L. J., Appleyard, K., & Dodge, K. A. (2011). Intergenerational continuity in child maltreatment: mediating mechanisms and implications for prevention. Child Development, 82(1), 162–176. doi:10.1111/j.1467-8624.2010.01547.x.

[157] Drapeau, M., & Perry, J. (2004). Childhood trauma and adult interpersonal functioning: a study using the Core Conflictual Relationship Theme Method (CCRT). Child Abuse and Neglect, 28, 1049–1066.

[158] Liang, B., Williams, L. M., et Siegel, J. A. (2006). Relational outcomes of childhood sexual trauma in female survivors: a longitudinal study. Journal of Interpersonal Violence, 21, 42–57.

[159] Vaillancourt-Morel, M.-P., Godbout, N., Sabourin, S., Briere, J., Lussier, Y., & Runtz, M. (2016). Adult sexual outcomes of child sexual abuse vary according to relationship status. Journal of Marital and Family Therapy. Advance online publication. doi:10.1111/jmft.12154

[160] DiLillo, D., Lewis, T., & Di Loreto-Colgan, A. (2007). Child maltreatment history and subsequent romantic relationships: exploring a psychological route to dyadic difficulties. Journal of Aggression, Maltreatment & Trauma, 15(1), 19–36. doi:10.1300/J146v15n01_02.

[161] Rellini, A. H. (2014). Sexual abuse and sexual function. In G. Corona, E. A. Jannini, & M. Maggi (Eds.), Emotional, Physical and Sexual Abuse. Impact in Children and Social Minorities (pp. 61–70). Cham, Switzerland: Springer.

[162] Bowlby, J. (1973). Attachment and Loss: Separation: Anxiety and Anger. New York: Basic Books.

[163] Bowlby, J. (1984). Violence in the family as a disorder of the attachment and caregiving systems. American Journal of Psychoanalysis, 44, 9–27.

[164] Mikulincer, M., & Shaver, P. R. (2007). Attachment in Adulthood: Structure, Dynamics, and Change. New York: Guilford Publications.

[165] Godbout, N., Dutton, D. G., Lussier, Y., & Sabourin, S. (2009). Early exposure to violence, domestic violence, attachment representations, and marital adjustment. Personal Relationships, 16(3), 365–384. doi:10.1111/j.1475-6811.2009.01228.x.

[166] Mikulincer, M., Shaver, P. R., & Solomon, Z. (2015). An attachment perspective on traumatic and posttraumatic reactions. In M. P. Safir, H. S. Wallach, & A. S. Rizzo (Eds.), Future Directions in Post-traumatic Stress Disorder: Prevention, Diagnosis, and Treatment (pp. 79–96). New York: Springer. doi:10.1007/978-1-4899-7522-5_4

[167] Hesse, E., & Main, M. (2006). Frightened, threatening, and dissociative parental behavior in low-risk samples: Description, discussion, and interpretations. Development and Psychopathology, 18, 309–343. doi:10.10170S0954579406060172

[168] Carlson, V., Cicchetti, D., Barnett, D., & Braunwald, K. (1989). Disorganized/disoriented attachment relationships in maltreated infants. Developmental Psychology, 25, 525–531.

[169] Egeland, B., & Sroufe, L. A. (1981). Developmental sequelae of maltreatment in infancy. In R. Rizley & D. Cicchetti (Eds.), New Directions for Child Development: Developmental Perspectives in Child Maltreatment. San Francisco, CA: Jossey-Bass.

[170] Roche, D. N., Runtz, M., & Hunter, M. A. (1999). Adult attachment: a mediator between child sexual abuse and later psychological adjustment. Journal of Interpersonal Violence, 14(2), 184–207.

[171] Kiecolt-Glaser, J. K., & Newton, T. L. (2001). Marriage and health: his and hers. Psychological Bulletin, 127(4), 472–503.

[172] Slatcher, R. B. (2010). Marital functioning and physical health: implications for social and personality psychology. Social and Personality Psychology Compass, 4(7), 455–469. doi:10.1111/j.1751-9004.2010.00273.x

[173] Hazan, C., & Shaver, P. (1987). Romantic love conceptualized as an attachment process. Journal of Personality and Social Psychology, 52(3), 511–524. doi: 10.1037/0022-3514.52.3.511

[174] Shaver, P. R., & Hazan, C. (1988). A biased overview of the study of love. Journal of Social and Personal Relationships, 5, 473–501.

[175] Brassard, A., & Lussier, Y. (2009). L'attachement dans les relations de couple: fonctions et enjeux cliniques. Psychologie Québec, 26(3), 24–26.

[176] Godbout, N., Runtz, M., MacIntosh, H., & Briere, J., (2013). Traumas interpersonnels vécus en enfance et relations de couple: comprendre les répercussions afin d'intervenir efficacement. Psychologie, 3(2), 14–18.

[177] Wells, M. A., & Kuhn, V. P. (2015). Couple therapy with adult survivors of child abuse: Gender, power, and trust. In C. Knudson-Martin, M. A. Wells, & S. K. Samman (Eds.), AFTA Springer Briefs in Family Therapy. Socio-emotional Relationship Therapy: Bridging Emotion, Societal Context, and Couple Interaction (pp. 107–119). doi: 10.1007/978-3-319-13398-0_9.

[178] Solomon, J., & George, C. (Eds.) (2011). Disorganized Attachment and Caregiving. NY: Guilford Press.

[179] Bigras, N., Runtz, M., Godbout, N., & Briere, J. (June, 2016). Long term effects of dysfunctional caregiving on sexual disturbances partially explained by disorganized attachment. 77th Annual Meeting of the Canadian Psychological Association (CPA), Victoria, Canada.

[180] Cyr, C., Euser, E. M.., Bakermans-Kranenburg, M. J., & Van Ijzendoorn, M. H. (2010). Attachment security and disorganization in maltreating and high-risk families: a series of meta-analyses. Development and Psychopathology, 22, 87–108.

[181] Runtz, M., Godbout, N., Briere, J., & Eadie, E. (2014). Development of a new measure of adult relational attachment and its links with interpersonal trauma. 75th Convention of the Canadian Psychological Association (CPA), Vancouver, Canada.

[182] Main, M., & Solomon, J. (1990). Procedures for identifying infants as disorganized/ disoriented during the Ainsworth Strange Situation. In M. T. Greenberg, D. Cicchetti & E. M. Cummings (Eds.), Attachment in the Preschool Years: Theory, Research and Intervention (pp. 121–160). Chicago: University of Chicago Press.

[183] IOM (Institute of Medicine) and NRC (National Research Council). (2014). New Directions in Child Abuse and Neglect Research. Washington, DC: The National Academies Press.

[184] Paetzold, R. L., Rholes, W. S., & Kohn, J. L. (2015). Disorganized attachment in adulthood: theory, measurement, and implications for romantic relationships. Review of General Psychology, 19(2), 146–156

[185] Crowell, J. A., Treboux, D., & Waters, E. (2002). Stability of attachment representations: the transition to marriage. Developmental Psychology, 38(4), 467–479.

[186] Bigras, N., Godbout, N., & Briere, J. (2015). Childhood sexual abuse, sexual anxiety, and sexual satisfaction: the role of self-capacities. Journal of Child Sexual Abuse, 24(5), 464–483. doi:10.1080/10538712.2015.1042184.

[187] Vaillancourt-Morel, M.-P., Godbout, N., Sabourin, S., Péloquin, K., & Wright, J. (2014). Les séquelles conjugales d'une agression sexuelle vécue à l'enfance ou à l'adolescence. Carnet de notes sur les maltraitances infantiles, 3, 21–41.

[188] Finkelhor, D., & Browne, A. (1985). The traumatic impact of child sexual abuse: a conceptualization. American Journal of Orthopsychiatry, 55(4), 530–541. doi:10.1111/j.1939-0025.1985.tb02703.x

[189] Aaron, M. (2012). The pathways of problematic sexual behavior: a literature review of factors affecting adult sexual behavior in survivors of childhood sexual abuse. Sexual Addiction & Compulsivity: The Journal of Treatment & Prevention, 19(3), 199–218.

[190] Vaillancourt-Morel, M.-P., Godbout, N., Labadie, C., Runtz, M., Lussier, Y., & Sabourin, S. (2015). Avoidant and compulsive sexual behaviors in male and female survivors of childhood sexual abuse. Child Abuse & Neglect, 40, 48–59. doi:10.1016/j.chiabu.2014.10.024.

[191] Bergeron, S., Likes, W. M., Steben, M. (2014). Psychosexual aspects of vulvovaginal pain. Best Practice & Research Clinical Obstetrics and Gynaecology, 28(7), 991–999. doi:10.1016/j.bpobgyn.2014.07.007.

[192] Dennerstein, L., Guthrie, J. R., & Alford, S. (2004). Childhood abuse and its association with mid-aged women's sexual functioning. Journal of Sex and Marital Therapy, 30(4), 225–34.

[193] Najman, J. M., Dunne, M. P., Purdie, D. M., Boyle, F. M., & Coxeter, P. D. (2005). Sexual abuse in childhood and sexual dysfunction in adulthood: an Australian population-based study. Archives of Sexual behavior, 34(5), 517–526. doi:10.1007/s10508-005-6277

[194] Staples, J., Rellini, A. H., & Roberts, S. P. (2012). Avoiding experiences: sexual dysfunction in women with a history of sexual abuse in childhood and adolescence. Archives of Sexual behavior, 41(2), 341–350. doi:10.1007/s10508-011-9773-x

[195] Van Bruggen L., K., Runtz, M., & Kadlec, H. (2006). Sexual revictimization: the role of sexual self-esteem and dysfunctional sexual behaviors. Child Maltreatment, 11, 131–145.

[196] Fernet, M., Hébert, M., Gascon, S., & Lacelle, C. (2012). Agression sexuelle et comportements sexuels à risque à l'adolescence. Dans : Hébert M, Cyr M, Tourigny M, éditeurs. L'agression sexuelle envers les enfants, Tome II. Québec: Presses de l'Université du Québec, p. 131–70.

[197] Noll, J. G., Trickett, P. K., & Putnam, F. W. (2003). A prospective investigation of the impact of childhood sexual abuse on the development of sexuality. Journal of Consulting and Clinical Psychology, 71, 575–86.

[198] Vaillancourt-Morel, M-P., Dugal, C., Poirier Stewart, R., Godbout, N., Sabourin, S., Lussier, Y., Briere, J. (2015). Extradyadic sexual involvement and sexual compulsivity in male and female sexual abuse survivors. Journal of Sex Research, 1–12 [Epub ahead of print]

[199] Blain, L. M., Muench, F., Morgenstern, J., & Parsons, J. T. (2012). Exploring the role of child sexual abuse and posttraumatic stress disorder symptoms in gay and bisexual men reporting compulsive sexual behavior. Child Abuse & Neglect, 36(5):413–22.

[200] Lemieux, S. R., & Byers, S. E. (2008). The sexual well-being of women who have experienced child sexual abuse. Psychology of Women Quartely, 32, 126–44.

[201] Rellini, A. H., Vujanovic, A. A., Gilbert, M., & Zvolensky, M. J. (2012). Childhood maltreatment and difficulties in emotion regulation: associations with sexual and relationship satisfaction among young adult women. Journal of Sex Research, 49(5), 434–442. doi:10.1080/00224499.2011.565430

[202] Voisin, D. R., Hotton, A., & Schneider, J. (2014). Exposure to verbal parental aggression and sexual activity among low income African American youth. Journal of Child and Family Studies, 23(2), 285–292. doi:10.1007/s10826-013-9720-7

[203] Walsh, K., Latzman, N. E., & Latzman, R. D. (2014). Pathway from child sexual and physical abuse to risky sex among emerging adults: the role of trauma-related intrusions and alcohol problems. Journal of Adolescent Health, 54(4), 442–448. doi:10.1016/j.jadohealth.2013.09.020

[204] Leonard, Iverson, K. M., & Follette, V. M. (2008). Sexual functioning and sexual satisfaction among women who report a history of childhood and/or adolescent sexual abuse. Journal of Sex & Marital Therapy, 34(5), 375–384. doi:10.1080/00926230802156202

[205] Rellini, A. H., & Meston, C. M. (2007). Sexual function and satisfaction in adults based on the definition of child sexual abuse. The Journal of Sexual Medicine, 4(5), 1312–1321.

[206] Lilly, M. M., London, M. J., & Bridgett, D. J. (2014). Using SEM to examine emotion regulation and revictimization in predicting PTSD symptoms among childhood abuse survivors. Psychological Trauma: Theory, Research, Practice, and Policy, 6(6), 644–651. doi:10.1037/a0036460.

[207] Daisy, N. V., & Hien, D. A. (2014). The role of dissociation in the cycle of violence. Journal of Family Violence, 29(2), 99–107. doi :10.1007/s10896-013

[208] Desai, S., Arias, I., Thompson, M. P., & Basile, K. C. (2002). Childhood victimization and subsequent adult revictimization assessed in a nationally representative sample of women and men. Violence and Victims, 17, 639–653. doi:10.1891/vivi.17.6.639.33725.

[209] Lee, R. D., Walters, M. L., Hall, J. E., & Basile, K. C. (2013). Behavioral and attitudinal factors differentiating male intimate partner violence perpetrators with and without a history of childhood family violence. Journal of Family Violence, 28(1), 85–94. doi: 10.1007/s10896-012-9475-8.

[210] Dugal, C., Godbout, N., Bigras, N., & Bélanger, C. (November 2015). The Impact of Child Abuse and Neglect on Psychological Violence in Intimate Relationships. Oral presentation at the ISTSS Annual Meeting. New Orleans, LA, USA.

[211] Smith-Marek, E. N., Cafferky, B., Dharnidharka, P., Mallory, A. B., Dominguez, M., High, J., Stith, S. M., & Mendez, M. (2015). Effects of childhood experiences of family violence on adult partner violence: a meta-analytic review. Journal of Family Theory & Review, 7, 498–519. doi:10.1111/jftr.12113.

[212] Stith, S. M., Rosen, K. H., Middleton, K. A., Busch, A. L., Lundeberg, K., & Carlton, R. P. (2000). The intergenerational transmission of spouse abuse: a meta-analysis. Journal of Marriage and the Family, 62, 640–654. doi:10.1111/j.1741-3737.2000.00640.

[213] Iverson, K. M., Jimenez, S., Harrington, K. M., & Resick, P. A. (2011). The contribution of childhood family violence on later intimate partner violence among robbery victims. Violence and Victims, 26(1), 73–87. doi:10.1891/0886-6708.26.1.73

[214] Capaldi, D. M., Knoble, N. B., Shortt, J. W., & Kim, H. K. (2012). A systematic review of risk factors for intimate partner violence. Partner Abuse, 3(2), 231–280. doi: 10.1891/1946- 6560.3.2.231.

[215] Bandura, A., Ross, D., & Ross, S. A. (1961). Transmission of aggression through imitation of aggressive models. Journal of Abnormal and Social Psychology, 63(3), 575–582. doi:10.1037/h0045925

[216] Busby, D. M., Holman, T. B., & Walker, E. (2008). Pathways to relationship aggression between adult partners. Family Relations, 57(1), 72–83. doi:10.1111/j. 1741-3729.2007.00484.x

[217] Holtzworth-Munroe, A., & Stuart, G. L. (1994). Typologies of male batterers: three subtypes and the differences among them. Psychological Bulletin, 116(3), 476–497. doi: 10.1037/0033-2909.116.3.476.

[218] Bevan, E., & Higgins, D. J. (2002). Is domestic violence learned? The contribution of five forms of child maltreatment to men's violence and adjustment. Journal of Family Violence, 17, 223–245.

[219] Capaldi, D. M., & Gorman-Smith, D. (2003). The development of aggression in young male/female couples. In P. Florsheim (Ed.), Adolescent Romantic Relations and Sexual Behavior: Theory, Research, and Practical Implications (pp. 243–278). Mahwah, NJ: Erlbaum.

[220] Bronfenbrenner, U. (Ed.). (2005). Making Human Beings Human: Bioecological Perspectives on Human Development. Thousand Oaks, CA: Sage Publications.

[221] Johnson, M. P., & Ferraro, K. J. (2000). Research on domestic violence in the 1990s: making distinctions. Journal of Marriage and the Family, 62, 948–963.

[222] Riggs, D. S., & O'Leary, K. D. (1996). Aggression between heterosexual dating partners: an examination of a causal model of courtship aggression. Journal of Interpersonal Violence, 11, 519–540.

[223] Arata, C. M., Langhinrichsen-Rohling, J., Bowers, D., & O'Farrill-Swails, L. (2005). Single versus multitype maltreatment: an examination of the long-term effects of child abuse. Journal of Aggression, Maltreatment & Trauma, 11(4), 29–52. doi:10.1300/J146v11n04_02.

[224] Hetzel, M. D., & McCanne, T. R. (2005). The roles of peritraumatic dissociation, child physical abuse, and child sexual abuse in the development of posttraumatic stress disorder and adult victimization. Child Abuse & Neglect, 29(8), 915–930. doi:10.1016/j.chiabu.2004.11.008

[225] Bowlus, A., McKenna, K., Day, T., & Wright, D. (2003). The Economic Costs and Consequences of Child Abuse in Canada: Report to the Law Commission of Canada. Ottawa: Law Commission of Canada.

Chapter 5

Childhood Traumatic Experiences and Post-Traumatic Stress Disorder in Female Adults: Which is the Role Played by Romantic Attachment?

Alessandra Simonelli and Chiara Sacchi

Additional information is available at the end of the chapter

http://dx.doi.org/10.5772/65367

Abstract

Childhood traumatic experiences are known to have strong and durable effects on physical, mental and reproductive health. One of the most studied consequences of childhood trauma is the post-traumatic stress disorder (PTSD). The present study aims to investigate in a community sample of Italian female students: (1) the prevalence of PTSD; (2) the association between reported childhood traumatic experiences and the presence of PTSD in adulthood and the role played by the romantic attachment (*anxiety*, *avoidance*) on the relationship between childhood traumatic experiences and PTSD symptoms. Three hundred and twenty-seven female Italian students (mean age = 23.09 years; SD = 2.98) of the University of Padova participated in the study. Participants have been tested on childhood traumatic experiences (Childhood Trauma Questionnaire-Short Form, CTQ-SF); romantic attachment (Experience in Close Relationship-Revised, ECR-R) and post-traumatic stress disorder (Post-traumatic Stress Disorder Checklist for DSM-5, PCL-5). Results show that PTSD symptoms are significantly predicted by the experiences of emotional abuse and neglect. Moreover, anxiety and avoidance play a significant role in the relationship between the emotional forms of traumatic experiences and the current presence of PTSD symptoms. Clinical implications for the treatment of PTSD patients with history of interpersonal trauma are discussed.

Keywords: childhood traumatic experiences, romantic attachment, post-traumatic stress disorder, mediating effect, moderating effect

1. Introduction

Childhood traumatic experiences are known to have strong and lasting consequences on the physical, mental and reproductive health of victims as well as confining them to low mental health in adulthood [1]. A body of researches largely documented the severe and long-lasting effects of the adverse childhood experiences (ACEs) on the biological and psychological development of victims [1, 2], highlighting severe impairments in stress regulation and socio-emotional development. Indeed, early interpersonal traumas expose victims to attachment disorganization and progressive deterioration in the self-worth from the first and most vulnerable stages of a child's development [3].

Moreover, studies reported a significant odd-ratio for psychiatric disorders in adulthood, including major depression, panic disorder and bulimia nervosa in sexually abused victims [4]. Adults' at-risk behaviors, such as substance abuse and dependence, are twice as common among victims, compared to the general population [5], and a major risk for sexual behaviors as well as for re-victimization is also largely documented [6–8].

Complex trauma, referring to children's experiences of multiple traumatic events that occur within the caregiving system [9], has significant long-lasting effects on brain maturation. Structural and functional abnormalities are reported in abused children, namely reduction in the volume of the orbitofrontal cortex and over reactivity of the amygdala [10]. Both areas are of fundamental importance in emotional and stress responses, which display atypical functioning in abused children from the earliest stages of life [11].

Child maltreatment and adverse childhood experiences are a common occurrence. In 2013, 9.1 per 1000 children in the USA known to child protective services (CPS) had been victims of abuse and neglect experiences [12]. In Europe, more than 18 million children are estimated to suffer from maltreatment, as reported by the World Health Organization [13]. In particular, a prevalence of 9.6% for sexual abuse, 22.9% for physical abuse and 29.1% for mental or emotional abuse is reported. In Italy, around 9.5% per 1000 children and adolescents are subject to some form of violence in childhood [14]; the data support the international portrait.

One of the most studied effects of traumatic experiences in childhood is post-traumatic stress disorder (PTSD). Post-traumatic stress disorder is classified as a "trauma and stress-related disorder" in the new Diagnostic and Statistical Manual of Mental Disorders 5 (American Psychological Association, 2013). PTSD represents the most frequent consequence of interpersonal trauma histories [15], with 48–85% of childhood abuse survivors developing PTSD symptoms across life [16, 17].

Despite the fact that studies have mainly analyzed only the stress-related consequences of physical and sexual traumatic experiences, emotional abuse and neglect have also been shown to be associated with the development of PTSD symptoms [18].

The exposure to traumatic experiences is a necessary but not sufficient condition for the development of PTSD. According to Van der Kolk, to consider a linear relationship between early traumatic experiences and adult psychiatric disorders represents an oversimplification

[19]; underlying mechanisms and victims' characteristics involved in the association between traumatic experiences and adult psychopathology is still a matter of on-going study.

Different studies report that psychopathological outcomes of childhood abuse are related to the quality of early attachment relationship. Around 80% of physical and emotional abuses during childhood are perpetrated by parents or close relatives [20], whom are supposed to be the primary and the first external source of emotion and stress regulation. Indeed, the parent-child relationship represents a key feature for the long-term ability of auto-regulation and social support [19, 21].

According to the attachment theory, the quality of early interactions between the caregiver and his/her child determines the child's immediate emotional response to stress and plays a decisive and lasting role in the latter's emotion-regulation ability [22–26]. Through the daily over-repetition of the interactive exchanges, a set of internal working models (IWMs) develops and becomes internalized as a patrimony of personal schema of self and of the other. The internal working models enable people to regulate emotions in interactions and to cope with stressful interpersonal situations across the life. These personal schemas are entirely developed during the first years of a child's life and become relatively stable across the life span. As a consequence, they represent a personal guide influencing interactions and relationships in adulthood [27].

Childhood experiences of abuse and maltreatment constitute a fearful and dangerous developmental environment, in which the intimacy and proximity with the caregiver produce a sense of fear instead of a feeling of "felt security," thus provoking a disorganization of the attachment system. Indeed, child abuse victims show significantly higher rates of attachment insecurity (70–100%) compared to the general population (30%) [28]. In addition, fearful and angry-dismissive patterns are the most associated with interpersonal traumatic experiences [29].

Furthermore, neglectful caregiving, even in the absence of physical and sexual abuse, denies the child the needed coherent external support. Through the inconsistent and neglectful responses of the caregiver, children develop interpersonal strategies characterized by anxious and/or avoidant behaviors [30].

As a consequence, the adverse childhood experiences shape the interpersonal strategies characterizing adult relationships. In particular, high levels of dependency or avoidance in social relationship as well as insecurity, suspiciousness, isolation, emotional distress and low intimacy in close relationships are reported as a consequence of traumatic experiences [19, 31, 32]. Indeed, the core concept of the attachment theory is that childhood attachment quality constitutes the paradigm for forming the adult romantic relationship [33]. Romantic attachment represents a personal system of beliefs and expectations on the availability and the responsiveness of the partner. It is based on the childhood experiences of being loved and felt security in the relationship with the caregiver [33], and it guides the interactive exchanges between partners. People differently experience and manage intimacy with the partner according to their own early experiences of caregiver's proximity and responsiveness. In particular, insecure adults are worried of being abandoned or being too close to and dependent on the partner [33]. According to Hazan and Shaver [33], a lack of self-worth and a negative model of self tend to produce anxiety for not being loved and being abandoned; in contrast, a negative view of the other leads to mistrust feelings, expressed by avoidant behaviors and fear of intimacy.

Adult and adolescent victims of abuse have higher attachment insecurity and display more anxiety and/or avoidance in close relationships [15, 34]. In particular, 70% of female victims of sexual abuse have insecure romantic attachments [35]. Lower satisfaction and couple adjustment are also reported in female victims compared to the women who were not abused [34, 36, 37]. In addition, high levels of insecurity in adult attachments and romantic attachments are reported to be associated with increased distress and psychopathology, in particular depression, anxiety, substance abuse and post-traumatic stress disorder [35, 38, 39].

The attachment patterns characterized by insecure or negative IWMs seem to increase the risk of a post-traumatic stress disorder and promote post-traumatic symptoms [38, 40]. In contrast, secure attachment is reported to be a protective factor in adult trauma survivors, moderating the relationship between a traumatic event and the development of PTSD.

Different studies confirm that insecure schema of self and the other generate interpretation biases in interpersonal stressful situations. This mechanism leads to dysfunctional responses characterized by hyper-activation or deactivation of emotion regulation [30, 41]. In particular, the attachment patterns characterized by high levels of anxiety are likely to display hyper-activation of emotional and behavioral response to stress, causing an exaggerated seeking of proximity. In contrast, people with avoidant attachment deactivate the interpersonal strategies of stress response and suppress the search for support [42]. As a consequence, attachment serves as a regulatory system for the stress response; a mental representation of the other's unresponsiveness during stressful situations can be the mechanism responsible for the increased vulnerability to post-traumatic symptoms [42].

In both PTSD and insecure attachments, there is a lack of security in social and interpersonal contexts. Indeed, people suffering from PTSD report feelings of distrust and a state of anxious apprehension which impedes them from having satisfying interpersonal relationships [43].

As a consequence, both the difficulties in emotion regulation and the lack of interpersonal security represent key variables in association with insecure romantic attachment and post-traumatic stress disorder in victims of childhood traumatic experiences.

Up until now, there are only a few studies investigating the relationship between romantic attachment and the PTSD symptoms in childhood trauma victims. Hence, further studies are needed in order to examine the role played by anxiety and avoidance on the development and the severity of the post-traumatic stress disorder in adult victims of interpersonal traumatic experiences.

Available studies in this field suggest mediating or moderating role for social support, emotion regulation and coping strategies [30]. Few studies showed that romantic attachment styles characterized by high levels of anxiety and avoidance influence the relationship between early traumatic experiences and the development of psychopathology, including post-traumatic stress disorder [44–46]. Another study [47] observed that insecure attachment mediated the relationship between childhood trauma and somatization in adulthood. Other studies [48, 49] reported that adult attachment moderates the association between childhood experiences of abuse and depressive symptoms as well as PTSD in adulthood.

Yet, in other studies [20, 50] it was established that an association between insecure attachment and greater number of PTSD in adult women victims of child sexual abuse exists. Moreover, the ability to maintain closeness in intimate relationships is found to mediate the association between child sexual trauma and global psychological functioning [38].

Finally, all these studies have investigated romantic attachment in clinical samples, while no research has studied the contribution of attachment style to the association between post-traumatic stress disorder and childhood traumatic experiences in a general population [51]. This shortcoming of the available literature represents the starting point for our study.

2. Aims

The present study aims to investigate a nonclinical sample of female students: (1) the prevalence of PTSD in adulthood; (2) the association between reported childhood traumatic experiences and the presence of post-traumatic stress disorders in adulthood and the role played by romantic attachment.

3. Method

The sample is composed by 327 female students from different faculties of the University of Padova: 58.4% from Psychology, 17.1% from Educational Sciences, 9.5% from International Economy, 6.7% from Social Services, 5.2% from Human Rights and Multi-Governance, 1.5% from Communication Strategies, and 1.5% from Engineering.

Complete demographics of the sample are displayed in **Table 1**.

The participants were recruited on a voluntary basis and were part of a broader study on early traumatic experiences and adult psychological outcomes. All participants signed a consent form and no compensation was given for participation.

3.1. Measures

Participants completed the Childhood Trauma Questionnaire-Short Form, CTQ-SF, [52] in order to assess the presence and severity of childhood traumatic experiences; the Experience in Close Relationship-Revised, ECR-R, [53] for the evaluation of the romantic attachment; and the Post-traumatic Checklist for DSM-5, PCL-5 [54] for the post-traumatic stress disorder diagnosis.

The *Childhood Trauma Questionnaire-Short Form* (CTQ-SF; Bernstein et al. [52]) is a self-report questionnaire used to assess retrospectively the frequency and severity of different childhood experiences of abuse (emotional, physical, sexual) and neglect (emotional, physical). The short form consists of 28 items, scored on a 5-point (Never True-Very Often True, when growing up) Likert scale. Twenty-five items are equally distributed among five clinical scales: Physical Abuse, Emotional Abuse, Sexual Abuse, Physical Neglect and Emotional Neglect. Three items assess the tendencies of responders to minimize or deny negative childhood experiences, composing the minimization/denial scale. In the present study, the Italian version of CTQ-SF, translated by Petrone and colleagues [55], was administered. The original study of Bernstein [52] demonstrated good internal consistency reliability for each of the CTQ-SF scales, across four heterogeneous clinical and not clinical samples. Cronbach's α ranged respectively from 0.83 to 0.86 for Physical Abuse, 0.84 to 0.89 for Emotional Abuse, 0.92 to 0.95 for Sexual Abuse; 0.61 to 0.78 for Physical Neglect and 0.85 to 0.91 for Emotional Neglect. In particular, in the community sample the reliability ranged from $\alpha = 0.61$ for the Physical Neglect to $\alpha = 0.92$ for the Sexual Abuse. For the Italian version, the CTQ-SF showed reliable psychometrics, with good reliability and confirmed structure validity (Sacchi, Simonelli, in preparation). In the present study, the Cronbach's α ranged from 0.51 for Physical Neglect to 0.90 for the Sexual Abuse, confirming that Physical Neglect represents the less reliable scale of the self-report.

Age	23.09 (2.98)
Ethnicity	
Italian	311 (96.3%)
Marital status	
Single	101 (31.1%)
Involved	202 (62.2%)
Living together	15 (4.6%)
Married	6 (1.8%)
Separated/divorced	1 (0.3%)
Widow	0%
Education	
College	58 (17.8%)
Professional high school	7 (2.1%)
Bachelor degree	254 (77.9%)
Master degree	4 (1.2%)
Postgraduate degree	2 (0.6%)
PhD	1 (0.3%)

Table 1. Demographics of the sample ($N = 327$).

The *Experiences in Close Relationships Scale-Revised* (ECR-R; Fraley et al. [53]; Italian version Calvo, 2008) is a 36-item questionnaire that measures the adult romantic attachment style.

Respondents are given a description of a possible attitude toward relationships and asked to rate them on a 7-point Likert scale, ranging from "strongly disagree" to "strongly agree." The ECR-R contains two subscales that measure orthogonal dimensions of adult romantic attachment: attachment avoidance and attachment anxiety; each dimension is measured by summing 18 items. The ECR-R presented excellent psychometric properties in its Italian version. In the cross-cultural study of Calvo [56], the Cronbach's α was 0.93 for the avoidance and 0.88 for the anxiety. In the present study, the internal consistency reliability of the ECR-R was $\alpha = 0.93$ for the attachment avoidance scale and $\alpha = 0.90$ for the attachment anxiety scale.

The *Post-traumatic Stress Disorder Checklist* for DSM-5 (PCL-5; Weathers et al. [54]) is a 20-item self-report for the assessment of current post-traumatic stress disorder symptoms. The PCL-5 is developed from the PCL, and the 20 items correspond to the 20 symptoms describing the diagnosis of PTSD in the Diagnostic and Statistical Manual for Mental Disorders V version [57]. Since no Italian version for the PCL-5 is currently available, in the present study the original version was translated, using the back-translation method [58]. The 20 items belong to four sub-scales representing different clusters of the diagnosis of post-traumatic stress disorder. The severity of each class of symptoms is obtained by the sum of the scores within each cluster. For a provisional PTSD diagnosis and in order to have cutoff scores for the evaluation of symptoms' severity, items score 2 (moderately) or higher are considered as symptoms. In particular, the PCL-5 diagnosis requires at least: 1 B item, 1 C item, 2 D items and 2 E items score 2 or higher. Preliminary validation work proposes the overall cutoff point of 38 for the PTSD diagnosis, as "reasonable" http://www.ptsd.va.gov/. The PCL was largely examined, demonstrating excellent psychometric properties [59], while less information is available on PCL-5. Two recent studies demonstrate high internal consistency, with Cronbach's α of 0.94 and 0.95. In the present study, the internal consistency reliability result scored high for each cluster and for the overall measure. In particular, the overall Cronbach's α was 0.93.

4. Data analyses

First, means, standard deviations and percentile ranks have been calculated for the distribution of PCL-5 scores, in order to attest the rate of Italian female young students showing current PTSD symptoms above the cutoff point. The PCL-5 provisional diagnosis for PTSD was established following the indication of the National Centre for PTSD **http://www.ptsd.va.gov/**. Namely, it reflects the DSM-5 diagnostic rules according to which are required: at least 1 item in Cluster B scored above 2 point; at least 1 item in Cluster C above 2; at least 2 items above 2 in Cluster D; and 2 items above 2 in Cluster E.

Second, in order to examine the relationship between childhood traumatic experiences, romantic attachment and current post-traumatic symptoms, correlation analyses have been preliminary done on all dimensions and scales of the three measures. Then, moderation and mediation effects have been studied. The hypotheses are displayed in **Figures 1** and **2**.

In order to study moderation effects, a hierarchical regression analysis was built, in accordance with Baron and Kenny recommendations [60]. The interaction between predictors and moderators was created by multiplying CTQ-SF five scales and the two dimensions of ECR-R. In the Step 1, predictors (childhood traumatic experiences) and moderators (avoidance and anxiety) were entered for direct effects analyses; in Step 2, variables of the previous step were considered along with the ten interaction variables for moderating effects, as suggested by Frazier and Barron [61].

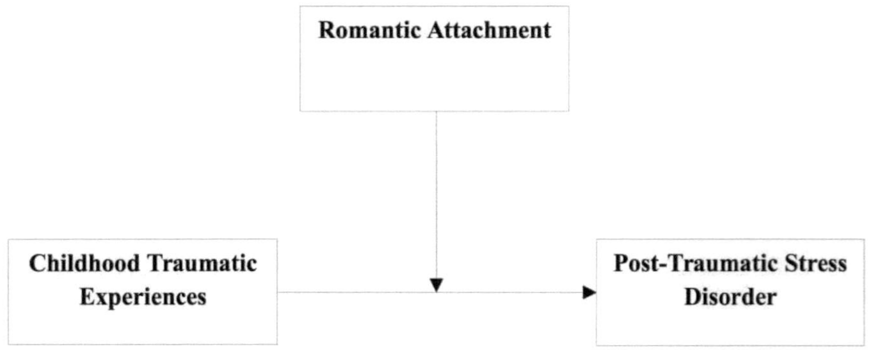

Figure 1. Moderation model of childhood traumatic experiences, romantic attachment and PTSD.

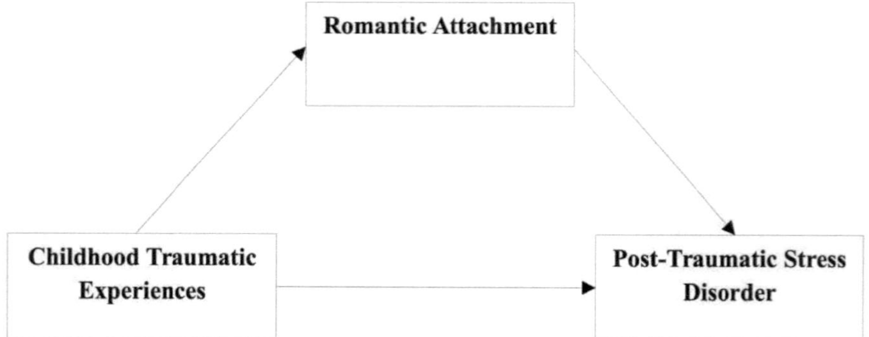

Figure 2. Mediation model of childhood traumatic experiences, romantic attachment and PTSD.

For the mediation effect hypothesized, a path analysis was performed using LISREL 8.8 [62]. PCL-5 total score has been used as dependent variable and the five scales of the CTQ-SF as independent variables. Avoidance and anxiety in romantic attachment have been considered as mediator variables. In a first saturated model, all the five scales of the CTQ-SF were supposed to have both direct and mediated effects on the post-traumatic symptoms. Secondly, from first results, a second model has been performed including the clinical scales of CTQ-SF presenting significant direct and/or mediated effects in the first model.

http://dx.doi.org/10.5772/65367

5. Results

Descriptive statistics of the variables are presented in **Table 2**.

Measures	Means	Standard deviation	Min	Max
Childhood Trauma Questionnaire-Short Form (CTQ-SF)				
Emotional Abuse	6.62	2.601	5	22
Physical Abuse	5.42	1.490	5	19
Sexual Abuse	5.29	1.423	5	17
Emotional Neglect	8.92	3.829	5	24
Physical Neglect	5.67	1.393	5	16
Experience in Close Relationship-Revised(ECR-R)				
Avoidance	42.13	18.181	8	99
Anxiety	54.09	18.832	19	118
Post-traumatic Checklist for DSM-5 DSM-5 (PCL-5)				
Total PTSD score	18.21	13.699	0	66

Table 2. *Descriptive statistics of CTQ-SF, ECR-R, PCL-5 (N = 327).*

5.1. Prevalence of PTSD symptoms

Table 3 shows percentile ranks of PCL-5 and the rate of subjects exceeding cutoff point for the overall PTSD measure.

Measure (C.O.)	% above C.O.	25th percentile	50th percentile	75th percentile	90th percentile
PCL-5 total score (38)	9.5	7	15	27	37
Provisional diagnosis (DSM V*)	34.9%				

C.O., cutoff.
*The provisional diagnosis is calculated considering: at least 1 item of Cluster B scored above 2 point; at least 1 item of Cluster C above 2;, at least 2 items above 2 in Cluster D and 2 items above 2 in Cluster E.

Table 3. PCL-5 percentile scores.

5.2. Moderating role of romantic attachment

Table 4 presents the hierarchical regression analyses results.

Results from the hierarchical regression analyses showed that PTSD symptoms are significantly predicted using childhood traumatic experiences.

In particular, in the Model 1, both the Emotional Abuse (β = 0.198; p = 0.01) and Emotional Neglect (β = 0.148; p = 0.03) show significant direct effects on PTSD symptoms; moreover, the physical categories of traumatic experiences (abuse and neglect), display negative effects on PTSD, respectively, with β = −0.136; p = 0.03 and β = −0.170; p = 0.01.

As regards the romantic attachment, anxiety shows a direct effect on the post-traumatic stress symptoms, β = 0.286; p = 0.00, while no effects have been found for the avoidance. Globally, the R^2 of the first model indicates that childhood traumatic experiences and the romantic attachment account for the 22.7% of PTSD variance.

Measures	Model 1		Model 2	
	β	SE	B	SE
Step 1				
Emotional Abuse	0.198**	0.390	0.262**	0.434
Physical Abuse	−0.136*	0.576	−0.147*	0.649
Sexual Abuse	0.087	0.530	0.083	0.706
Emotional Neglect	0.148*	0.245	0.133	0.257
Physical Neglect	−0.170**	0.631	−0.178**	0.671
Avoidance	0.105	0.044	0.124*	0.046
Anxiety	0.286**	0.042	0.265***	0.044
Step 2				
Emotional Abuse × Anxiety			−0.150	1.109
Emotional Abuse × Avoidance			0.058	1.051
Physical Abuse × Anxiety			0.104	1.042
Physical Abuse × Avoidance			−0.025	1.383
Sexual Abuse × Anxiety			0.079	0.964
Sexual Abuse × Avoidance			−0.103	1.287
Emotional Neglect × Anxiety			−0.019	0.972
Emotional Neglect × Avoidance			−0.032	0.989
Physical Neglect × Anxiety			0.094	1.148
Physical Neglect × Avoidance			−0.027	1.174
Intercept	3.835	3.971	3.655	5.110
R^2	0.227		0.253	

*p < 0.05; **p < 0.01; ****p < 0.001.

Table 4. Hierarchical regression analyses: direct and moderating effect on PTSD symptoms.

In the Model 2, results show no moderating effects of anxiety and avoidance dimensions, with interaction variables presenting no significant weights. Among childhood traumatic experiences, Emotional Abuse (β = 0.262; p = 0.00), Physical Abuse (β = −0.147; p = 0.04) and Physical

Neglect (β = −0.178; p = 0.01) remain significant predictors, while Emotional Abuse shows no significant association with post-traumatic symptoms. In particular, Emotional Abuse has a positive effect, while Physical Abuse and Neglects present negative influences. With regard to romantic attachment, in the second model, both anxiety and avoidance display direct significant effects on PTSD overall symptoms, respectively, β = 0.265; p = 0.00 for anxiety and β = −0.124; p = 0.04 for avoidance. The R^2 shows that Model 2 accounted a small (2.6%) nonsignificant percentage of additional variance of PTSD.

5.3. Mediating role of romantic attachment

Results of the first saturated model tested show the childhood traumatic experiences to have mainly direct effects on PTSD symptoms' severity.

From the results of the first model, a second path analysis was performed, removing Sexual Abuse and testing the direct effects of Emotional Abuse, Emotional and Physical Neglect. Moreover, in the second model, the effect of Physical Abuse and Emotional Neglect on avoidance and the effect of Physical Neglect on anxiety were tested.

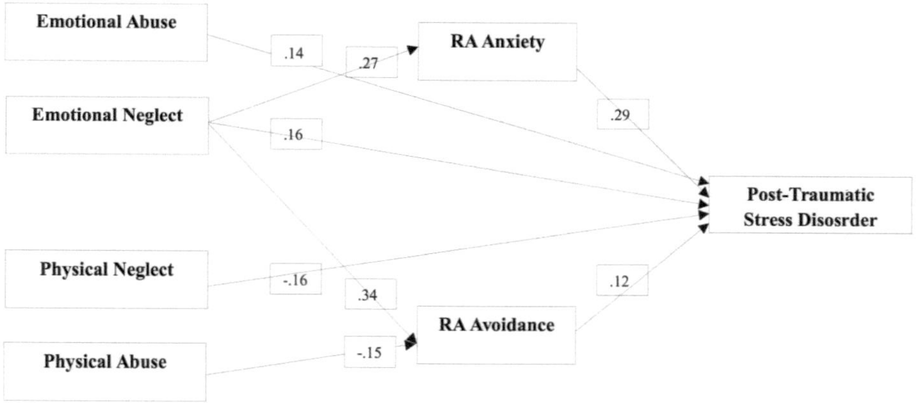

Figure 3. Results of mediation analyses.

For both models, the overall fit was provided by different goodness-of-fit indices, while the path coefficients estimated the relative effect of one variable on another. The goodness-of-fit indices, following Schermelleh and colleagues [63] recommendations, were: the Non-normed Fit Index (NNFI) and the Comparative Fit Index (CFI), both ranging from 0 to 1 with values close to 1 indicating good fit. The root mean square error of approximation (RMSEA) was considered, following Browne and Cudec [64] indications, that is: ≤0.05 considered as a good fit, between 0.05 and 0.08 as an adequate fit, and between 0.08 and 0.10 as a mediocre fit, whereas values >0.10 are considered not acceptable.

Chi-square of the second model was 6.84 df = 6; p = 0.34. Considering the definition of fit, all indices show a good fit, with NNFI and CFI equal to 1 and RMSEA 0.021.

Path coefficients indicate significant direct and mediating effects. In particular, in the second model, anxiety and avoidance mediate the effect of Emotional Neglect on PTSD ($\beta = 0.12$) and avoidance shows a tending to significance mediation of Physical Abuse on PTSD ($\beta = -0.02$; $p = 0.091$).

For the direct effects, Emotional Abuse shows significant direct effect ($\beta = 0.14$) on PTSD; Physical Abuse shows no direct influence on PTSD, but a significant negative effect on avoidance ($\beta = -0.15$). Emotional Neglect has direct effect on PTSD as well as on avoidance and anxiety, respectively 0.16, 0.34 and 0.27. The Physical Neglect only fits negatively to PTSD symptoms (−0.16).

Results of the mediation analyses are presented in **Figure 3**.

6. Discussion

The first aim of this study was to explore preliminary descriptive data on the presence of significant post-traumatic symptoms in nonclinical female students attending courses at the University of Padova. Moreover, the purpose of the present study was to analyze the relationship between childhood experiences of interpersonal traumas and the presence of current post-traumatic stress disorder symptoms in an Italian sample of students. More precisely, this study tested whether romantic attachment is a significant moderator and/or mediator in the relationship between traumatic experiences and current PTSD symptoms.

6.1. PTSD prevalence

The first objective of the study was to provide preliminary descriptive data on PTSD in Italian female students. Although university students are considered high functioning samples, results highlight that around 10% of female students attending courses at the University of Padova exceed the cutoff point indicating a potential for the presence of post-traumatic symptoms. A high percentage of them, 34.9%, satisfy DSM-5 criteria for a provisional clinical diagnosis of post-traumatic stress disorder. This result supports the on-going investigations to assess long-term effects of childhood adverse experiences as well as other factors influencing post-traumatic manifestations.

6.2. Moderating effect

With regard to the study of a moderating effect played by anxiety and avoidance, the aim of the study was to observe whether the long-term effects of childhood traumatic experiences can be altered, namely increased, under two different conditions: higher levels of anxiety in close relationship and higher levels of avoidance of intimacy. Our results do not support this hypothesis.

In the hierarchical regression, no interaction between traumas and romantic attachment significantly predicted the severity of post-traumatic symptoms. As a consequence, the present

http://dx.doi.org/10.5772/65367

study suggests that romantic attachment is not a significant moderator in the association between childhood traumatic experiences and PTSD in adulthood. This result is in line with a recent study on the moderating role of partner emotional support and negative interaction [65], in which authors found no moderation and observed that the stress buffering theory does not explain the role of social support in distress. Our results may confirm that couple attachment does not buffer the effect of childhood trauma on post-traumatic symptoms in adulthood. However, the authors [65] suggest that further investigations should run both moderation and mediation analyses in order to have different functional understanding on the role of social support variables.

A previous study [50] found a moderation of the quality of romantic relationship on the association between sexual abuse experience and depression. However, methodological limitations linked to sampling and measure may account for the absence of the same result in our study.

Direct effects show that both anxiety and avoidance represent significant predictors of PTSD. Moreover, when all conditions are controlled, students with higher levels of emotional abuse present higher PTSD symptoms, confirming the centrality of the emotion dysregulation in the expression of post-traumatic symptoms.

The physical abuse and neglect both show direct negative effects on PTSD. This result is not immediate to understand and claims for further analyses. As a consequence, functional approaches overcome the limit of descriptive interpretations of results. Finally, the variance explained by predictors and moderators suggests that other variables could be involved as independent predictors as well as significant moderators.

6.3. Mediating effect

Results of the path analyses show that different forms of childhood traumatic experiences present different relationship with current post-traumatic symptoms: some forms of trauma show a direct influence on PTSD, while others are independent or have a combination of direct and indirect effects.

First, our results highlight that the inability to manage intimacy and closeness in romantic relationships leads to a severity of emotional neglect and ultimately, the development of post-traumatic symptoms in adulthood. Moreover, emotional abuse and emotional neglect display direct influences on PTSD.

These results allow two considerations. First, emotional components of trauma appear to have the greatest direct and mediated influences on PTSD. In particular, a possible explanation is that emotional traumas damage or compromise the development of affect regulation in infancy; such early impairment lasts into adulthood and exposes victims to a major risk of maladaptive response in stressful situations. Moreover, the emotional abuse appears to impede interpersonal affect regulation, with victims presenting higher levels of anxiety and avoidance in romantic attachment and then greater PTSD.

Emotional abuse and neglect experiences are mainly expressed in chronic familiar contexts, including ignoring the child, being constantly absent, blaming, humiliating and constantly criticizing the child. These repeated experiences produce a negative self-worth and a sense of guilt which are symptoms of complex PTSD. Moreover, emotional neglect involves showing no emotions in interactive exchanges with the child which leads to extreme difficulties in recognizing self- and other-emotions. This mechanism damages the development of reliable internal model of self and other, making victims more vulnerable to high levels of anxiety and avoidance in intimate relationship.

Second, the mediation of the relationship between emotional neglect and PTSD is provided by both anxiety and avoidance in romantic attachments. It is possible to suppose that previous levels of stress, due to traumatic repetitive experiences, like the inaccessibility of emotional support, can be reactivated by the vulnerability in the relationship, such as a perceived threat of abandonment. As a consequence, this mechanism might encourage people to read interpersonal minor stressors, quarrel and separations as trigger for high levels of stress, which, on the other hand, exposes hidden PTSD symptomatology. According to Van der Kolk [21], abused and maltreated children may show biases in the interpretation of interpersonal situations, quickly seeing the changes in voice tone and facial expression as a threat; consequently, they rapidly shift from the stimuli to a defensive reaction. In adulthood, this consolidated experience produces the internal perception of stress, even in neutral situation of fight or discussion in close relationships. The repetition of such mechanism produces dysregulation of emotion and hyper-arousal, characteristics of PTSD, as a response to non-stressing stimulus. A previous study shows that adult victims of childhood traumatic experiences are more likely to react with a deeper affective and physiological dysregulation to a harmless situation, compared to adult victims of a traumatic experience in adulthood [20].

A more controversial result is given by the negative influence of both physical abuse and neglect on post-traumatic stress disorder. Other investigations previously attested the ambiguous role of the dismissing pattern of attachment (characterized by greater avoidance) in association with PTSD. Moreover, this pattern appears to be less frequent in female samples. The two elements related to our study may affect the results. However, a possible interpretation of the results may also include that the negative emotions characterizing avoidance in romantic attachment may result in increase in emotional forms of trauma; physical abuse and neglect may have different long-terms effects, less connected with emotion regulation and PTSD. Physically abused subjects may have developed different defensive mechanisms reducing avoidance and PTSD. Further studies in this field are needed to reach a clearer interpretation.

Finally, the present study suggests that further investigations should consider the role of other independent predictors and other possible mediators, reported by literature, in the expression of post-traumatic symptoms and in the long-terms effects of physical interpersonal traumatic experiences.

6.4. Limitations

The present study has some limitations. First, for a broader and more complete understanding of the variables involved in the relationship between childhood traumas and post-traumatic symptoms, the measures of childhood experiences, attachment and psychological outcomes should include interviews and different kinds of assessment. Indeed, the present results are totally produced based on self-report measures. Second, the measure of traumatic experiences is retrospective and participants are female students; further studies should be done with clinical subjects to evaluate, in clinical or high risk groups, the role of attachment on their symptomatology. Moreover, participants were all Italians; hence, the external validity is so far limited. Another limit is due to the lack of other psychopathological outcomes which might impact on the different roles played by anxiety and/or avoidance on different psychopathologies.

However, even if methodological shortcomings of the present results do not allow clear interpretations on the role that romantic attachment may play in determining adult post-traumatic symptomatology, one of the strength of the study lays in the opportunity to describe, in a functional framework, the relationship between childhood experiences and adult post-traumatic symptomatology. Indeed, the study of both moderation and mediation overcome limits linked with descriptive models.

7. Conclusion

In conclusion, the present study provides interesting results on the relationship between childhood traumatic experiences, romantic attachment and post-traumatic stress disorder, considering both the limited number of investigations involving nonclinical samples and the novelty of the application of a functional approach.

In particular, the results of the present study point out the role of emotional forms of trauma in later psychopathology and well-being, evidencing the role of severe impairment of early emotional regulation on stress and socio-emotional development.

The present results might be considered in a clinical framework, pointing to some aspects which should be included and focused on in the intervention with adults experiencing post-traumatic stress disorder as a result of the connection with a childhood history of abuse. From this study, we discover the role of anxiety and avoidance in close relationship as features to include in the clinical work with female victims presenting PTSD in adulthood.

In particular, programs of intervention should consider focusing on affect and interpersonal regulatory skills and implement strategies addressing the work on fear of abandonment as well as on avoidance of intimacy, in order to boost more adaptive coping skills to face stressful situations. Namely, reducing the negative self-believes and/or other-believes which lead to dependence on or avoidance of the other people may reduce their hyper sensibility to stressful situation and their avoidance of negative emotion. Both features characterize affect dysregulation, interpersonal disturbance and negative self-concept typical of complex PTSD. Finally, results about the presence of PTSD among female students suggest the need for further studies and screening in general populations.

Author details

Alessandra Simonelli* and Chiara Sacchi

*Address all correspondence to: alessandra.simonelli@unipd.it

Department of Developmental Psychology and Socialization, University of Padova, Padova, Italy

References

[1] Cicchetti D, Toth SL. Child maltreatment. Annual Review of Clinical Psychology. 2005;1:409–438. doi:10.1146/annurev.clinpsy.1.102803.144029

[2] Caldij C, Hellstrom IC, Zhang TY, Diorio J, Meaney MJ. Environmental regulation of the neural epigenome. FEBS Letters. 2011;585:2049–2058. doi:10.1016/j.febslet.2011.03.032

[3] Carbone-Lopez K, Esbensen FA, Brick BT. Correlates and consequences of peer victimization: gender differences in direct and indirect forms of bullying. Youth Violence and Juvenile Justice. 2010;8:332–350. doi:10.1177/1541204010362954

[4] Cashmore J, Shackel R. The long-term effects of child sexual abuse. Melbourne: Australian Institute of Family Studies. 2013.

[5] Sideli L, Mule A, La Barbera D, Murray RM. Do child abuse and maltreatment increase risk of schizophrenia? Psychiatry investigation. 2010:9(2):87–99.

[6] Molnar BE, Buka SL, Kessler RC. Child sexual abuse and subsequent psychopathology: results from the National Comorbidity Survey. American Journal of Public Health. 2001;91:753–760. doi:10.2105/ajph.91.5.753

[7] Repetti RL, Taylor SE, Seeman TE. Risky families: family social environments and the mental and physical health of offspring. Psychological Bulletin. 2002;128:330–366. doi: 10.1037/0033-2909.128.2.330

[8] Bierer LM, Yehuda R, Schmeidler J, Mitropoulou V, New AS, Silverman JM, et al. Abuse and neglect in childhood: relationship to personality disorder diagnoses. CNS Spectrums. 2003;8:737–754. doi:10.1017/S1092852900019118

[9] Cook A, Blaustein M, Spinazzola J, van der Kolk B. Complex trauma in children and adolescents. National Child Traumatic Stress Network. 2003. Available From: http://www.NCTSNet.org

[10] Hanson JL, Chung MK, Avants BB, Shirtcliff EA, Gee JC, Davidson RJ, Pollak SD. Early stress is associated with alterations in the orbitofrontal cortex: a tensor-based morphometry investigation of brain structure and behavioral risk. The Journal of Neuroscience. 2010;30(22):7466–7472.

[11] Ha T, Granger DA. Family relations, stress, and vulnerability: biobehavioral implications for prevention and practice. Family Relations. 2016:65(1):9–23.

[12] Child maltreatment 2013. Children's Bureau (Administration on Children, Youth and Families, Administration for Children and Families) of the U.S. Department of Health and Human Services. 2015. Available from: http://www.acf.hhs.gov/programs/cb/research-data-technology/statistics-research/child-maltreatment.

[13] Sethi D. European report on preventing child maltreatment. Copenhagen: World Health Organization, Regional Office for Europe. 2013.

[14] Bollini A, Giannotta F, Angeli A. Children maltreatment: How many victims in Italy? First National investigation of children maltreatment (Maltrattamento sui bambini. Quante le vittime in Italia? Prima Indagine nazionale quali-quantitativa sul maltrattamento a danno dei bambini). Terre des hommes, CISMAI. 2013.

[15] Elwood LS, Williams NL. PTSD-related cognitions and romantic attachment style as moderators of psychological symptoms in victims of interpersonal trauma. Journal of Social and Clinical Psychology. 2007;26:1189–1209. doi:10.1521/jscp.2007.26.10.1189

[16] Yehuda R, Spertus IL, Golier JA. Relationship between childhood traumatic experiences and PTSD in adults. PTSD in children and adolescents. Review of Psychiatry. 2001;20,17–158.

[17] Kessler RC, Chiu WT, Demier O, Walters EE. Prevalence, severity, and comorbidity of 12-month DSM-IV disorders in the National Comorbidity Survey Replication. Archives of General Psychiatry. 2005;62:617–627. doi:10.1001/archpsyc.62.6.617

[18] Yehuda R, Halligan SL, Grossman R. Childhood trauma and risk for PTSD: relationship to intergenerational effects of trauma, parental PTSD, and cortisol excretion. Development and Psychopathology. 2001;13:733–753. doi:10.1017/S0954579401003170

[19] Van der Kolk BA. Developmental trauma disorder: towards a rational diagnosis for chronically traumatized children. Praxis Der Kinderpsychologie Und Kinderpsychiatrie, 2008;58:572–586. doi:10.1037/e517302011-025

[20] Busuito A, Huth-Bocks A, Puro E. Romantic attachment as a moderator of the association between childhood abuse and posttraumatic stress disorder symptoms. Journal of Family Violence. 2014;29:567–577. doi:10.1007/s10896-014-9611-8

[21] Van Der Kolk B. The body keeps the score: brain, mind, and body in the healing of trauma. London: Penguin. 2014.

[22] Bowlby J. Attachment and loss: retrospect and prospect. American Journal of Orthopsychiatry. 1982;52:664–678. doi:10.1111/j.1939-0025.1982.tb01456.x

[23] Bartholomew K, Horowitz LM. Attachment styles among young adults: a test of a four-category model. Journal of Personality and Social Psychology. 1991;61:226–244. doi: 10.1037/0022-3514.61.2.226

[24] Schore AN. Affect Regulation and the Origin of the Self: The Neurobiology of Emotional Development. Mahwah, NJ: Erlbaum. 1994.

[25] Schore AN. Attachment and the regulation of the right brain. Attachment and Human Development. 2000;2:23–47. doi:10.1080/146167300361309

[26] Schore JR, Schore AN. Modern attachment theory: the central role of affect regulation in development and treatment. Clinical Social Work Journal. 2008;36:9–20. doi:10.1007/s10615-007-0111-7

[27] Main M, Kaplan N, Cassidy J. Security in infancy, childhood, and adulthood: a move to the level of representation. Monographs of the Society for Research in Child Development. 1985;50:66–104. doi:10.2307/3333827

[28] Baer JC, Martinez CD. Child maltreatment and insecure attachment: a meta-analysis. Journal of Reproductive and Infant Psychology. 2006;24:187–197. doi: 10.1080/02646830600821231

[29] Bifulco A, Kwon J, Jacobs C, Moran PM, Bunn A, Beer N. Adult attachment style as mediator between childhood neglect/abuse and adult depression and anxiety. Social Psychiatry and Psychiatric Epidemiology. 2006;41:796–805. doi:10.1007/s00127-006-0101-z

[30] Woodhouse S, Ayers S, Field AP. The relationship between adult attachment style and post-traumatic stress symptoms: a meta-analysis. Journal of Anxiety Disorders. 2015;35:103–117. doi:10.1016/j.janxdis.2015.07.002

[31] Cole PM, Putnam FW. Effect of incest on self and social functioning: a developmental psychopathology perspective. Journal of Consulting and Clinical Psychology. 1992;60:174–184. doi:10.1037/0022-006X.60.2.174

[32] Shields A, Cicchetti D. Parental maltreatment and emotion dysregulation as risk factors for bullying and victimization in middle childhood. Journal of Clinical Child Psychology. 2001;30:349–363. doi:10.1207/S15374424JCCP3003_7

[33] Hazan C, Shaver P. Romantic love conceptualized as an attachment process. Journal of Personality and Social Psychology. 1987;52:511–524. doi: 10.1037/0022-3514.52.3.511

[34] Riggs SA. Childhood emotional abuse and the attachment system across the life cycle: what theory and research tell us. Journal of Aggression, Maltreatment and Trauma. 2010;19:5–51. doi:10.1080/10926770903475968

[35] Muller RT, Sicoli LA, Lemieux KE. Relationship between attachment style and posttraumatic stress symptomatology among adults who report the experience of childhood abuse. Journal of Traumatic Stress. 2000;13:321–332. doi:10.1023/A: 1007752719557

[36] Rumstein-McKean O, Hunsley J. Interpersonal and family functioning of female survivors of childhood sexual abuse. Clinical Psychology Review. 2001;21:471–490. doi: 10.1016/S0272-7358(99)00069-0

[37] Testa M, Van Zile-Tamsen C, Livingston JA. Childhood sexual abuse, relationship satisfaction, and sexual risk taking in a community sample of women. Psychology of Women Quarterly. 2005;29:345–352. doi:10.1037/0022-006X. 73.6.1116

[38] Muller RT, Lemieux KE. Social support, attachment, and psychopathology in high risk formerly maltreated adults. Child Abuse and Neglect. 2000;24:883–900. doi:10.1016/ S0145-2134(00)00150-2

[39] Fowler JC, Allen JG, Oldham JM, Frueh BC. Exposure to interpersonal trauma, attachment insecurity, and depression severity. Journal of Affective Disorders. 2013;149:313–318. doi:10.1016/j.jad.2013.01.045

[40] Declercq F, Palmans V. Two subjective factors as moderators between critical incidents and the occurrence of post traumatic stress disorders: adult attachment and perception of social support. Psychology and Psychotherapy: Theory, Research and Practice. 2006;79:323–333. doi:10.1348/147608305X53684

[41] Mikulincer M, Florian V. The relationship between adult attachment styles and emotional and cognitive reactions to stressful events. In: Simpson JA, Rholes WS, editors. Attachment Theory and Close Relationships. New York, US: Guilford Press; 1998. p. 143–165.

[42] Chris Fraley R, Niedenthal PM, Marks M, Brumbaugh C, Vicary A. Adult attachment and the perception of emotional expressions: probing the hyperactivating strategies underlying anxious attachment. Journal of Personality. 2006;74:1163–1190. doi:10.1111/ j.1467-6494.2006.00406.x

[43] Stewart SH. Alcohol abuse in individuals exposed to trauma: a critical review. Psychological Bulletin. 1996;120:83–112. doi:10.1037/0033-2909.120.1.83

[44] Roche DN, Runtz MG, Hunter MA. Adult attachment a mediator between child sexual abuse and later psychological adjustment. Journal of Interpersonal Violence. 1999;14:184–207. doi:10.1177/088626099014002006

[45] Shapiro DL, Levendosky AA. Adolescent survivors of childhood sexual abuse: the mediating role of attachment style and coping in psychological and interpersonal functioning. Child Abuse and Neglect. 1999;23:1175–1191. doi:10.1016/S0145-2134(99)00085-X

[46] Twaite JA, Rodriguez-Srednicki O. Childhood sexual and physical abuse and adult vulnerability to PTSD: the mediating effects of attachment and dissociation. Journal of Child Sexual Abuse. 2004;13:17–38. doi:10.1300/J070v13n01_02

[47] Waldinger RJ, Schulz MS, Barsky AJ, Ahern DK. Mapping the road from childhood trauma to adult somatization: the role of attachment. Psychosomatic Medicine. 2006;68:129–135. doi:10.1097/01.psy.0000195834.37094.a4

[48] Allanson S, Astbury J. Attachment style and broken attachments: violence, pregnancy, and abortion. Australian Journal of Psychology. 2001;53:146–151. doi: 10.1080/00049530108255137

[49] Anderson CL, Alexander PC. The relationship between attachment and dissociation in adult survivors of incest. Psychiatry: Interpersonal and Biological Processes. 1996;59:240–254. doi:10.1521/00332747.1996.11024765

[50] Whiffen VE, Judd ME, Aube JA. Intimate relationships moderate the association between childhood sexual abuse and depression. Journal of Interpersonal Violence. 1999;14:940–954. doi:10.1177/088626099014009002

[51] O'Connor M, Elklit A. Attachment styles, traumatic events, and PTSD: a cross-sectional investigation of adult attachment and trauma. Attachment and Human Development. 2008;10:59–71. doi:10.1080/14616730701868597

[52] Bernstein DP, Stein JA, Newcomb MD, Walker E, Pogge D, Ahluvalia T, et al. Development and validation of a brief screening version of the Childhood Trauma Questionnaire. Child Abuse and Neglect. 2003;27:169–190. doi:10.1016/S0145-2134(02)00541-0

[53] Fraley RC, Waller NG, Brennan KA. The experience in Close Relationships-Revised (ECR-R) Questionnaire. 2000. Available from: http://www.psych.uiuc.edu/~rcfraley/measures/ecrritems.htm.

[54] Weathers FW, Litz BT, Keane TM, Palmieri PA, Marx BP, Schnurr PP. The PTSD checklist for DSM-5 (LEC-5). 2013. Available from: www.ptsd.va.gov.

[55] Petrone L, Manca M, Pedon A, Ricci S. Maltreatment or malteratments? Preliminary data of the Childhood Trauma Questionnaire Short-Form italian adaptation (Maltrattamento o maltrattamenti? Dati preliminari dell'adattamento italiano del Childhood

Trauma Questionnaire Short Form). International Journal of Developmental and Educational Psychology. 2012;1:199–204.

[56] Calvo V. The ECR-R questionnaire: validation of the Italian Version (Il questionario ECR-R: aspetti di validazione della versione italiana dello strumento). X National Congress of the Italian Association of Psychology (AIP), Clinical Dynamic Section. Padua 12–14 September. 2008: 275–279.

[57] American Psychiatric Association. Diagnostic and Statistical Manual of Mental Disorders (DSM-5®). Washington, DC: American Psychiatric Pub. 2013.

[58] Brislin RW. (1980). Translation and Content Analysis of Oral and Written Material. Handbook of Cross-Cultural Psychology, 2(2), 349–444.

[59] Blevins CA, Weathers FW, Davis MT, Witte TK, Domino JL. The posttraumatic stress disorder checklist for DSM-5 (PCL-5): development and initial psychometric evaluation. Journal of Traumatic Stress. 2015;28:489–498. doi:10.1002/jts.22059

[60] Baron RM, Kenny DA. The moderator-mediator variable distinction in social psychological research: conceptual, strategic, and statistical considerations. Journal of Personality and Social Psychology. 1986;51:1173–1182. doi:10.1037/0022-3514.51.6.1173

[61] Frazier PA, Tix AP, Barron KE. Testing moderator and mediator effects in counseling psychology research. Journal of Counseling Psychology. 2004;51:115–134. doi: 10.1037/0022-0167.51.1.115

[62] Joreskong KG, Sorbom D. LISREL 8: user's Reference Guide. Chicago: Scientific Software International. 1996.

[63] Schermelleh-engel K, Moosbrugger H, Müller H. Evaluating the fit of structural equation models: tests of significance and descriptive goodness-of-fit measures. Methods of Psychological Research Online. 2003;8:23–74.

[64] Browne MW, Cudeck R. Alternative ways of assessing model fit. Sociological Methods & Research. 1992;21:230–258. doi:10.1177/0049124192021002005.

[65] Cox DW, Buhr EE, Owen JJ, Davidson E. Linking partner emotional support, partner negative interaction, and trauma with psychological distress direct and moderating effects. Journal of Social and Personal Relationships. 2016;33(3):303–319.

Chapter 6

Acute Stress Disorder Diagnosis, Clusters, and Symptoms as Predictors of Posttraumatic Stress Disorder, and Gender Differences in Victims of Violent Crimes

Stéphane Guay , Myra Gravel-Crevier ,
Richard Boyer and André Marchand

Additional information is available at the end of the chapter

http://dx.doi.org/10.5772/64900

Abstract

Violent crimes represent a societal problem, and victims, namely women, often develop posttraumatic stress disorder (PTSD). Previous studies have identified acute stress disorder (ASD) as a predictor of PTSD, as well as dissociation. However, there are some inconsistencies regarding which cluster or symptom has better predictive power, and the impact of gender is still unknown in victims of violent crimes. The aim of this study was to determine the predictive power of full and partial ASD diagnosis, clusters, and symptoms according to gender. To do so, 39 women and 36 men were evaluated using validated semi-structured clinical interviews within 30 days post crime for ASD and 2 months later for PTSD. Results showed that 52% of individuals had full ASD and 20% has partial ASD, 40% had full PTSD and 17% had partial PTSD. Both full and partial ASD diagnoses, as well as all clusters, and most symptoms, were good predictors of PTSD. No gender differences were observed concerning the predictive power of ASD clusters and symptoms. The decreased emphasis on dissociative reactions in the Diagnostic and Statistical Manual of Mental Disorders, Fifth Edition (DSM 5) to establish an ASD diagnosis appears relevant to better identify women and men at risk of PTSD after a violent crime, and to deliver appropriate early preventive interventions.

Keywords: violent crime, acute stress disorder, PTSD, predictors, gender

1. Introduction

1.1. Victims of violent crimes

Criminal acts are the most common traumatic events to which the general population is exposed [1]. According to Canada's General Social Survey [2], 6% of the population reported having been a victim of a violent crime in the last 12 months (e.g., sexual assault, armed robbery, and physical assault). Interpersonal violence represents a significant societal problem and has a detrimental impact on victims' health. Studies have shown that victims of violent crimes usually report important impairment to their functioning and psychological difficulties. Up to 20–21% subsequently develop posttraumatic stress disorder (PTSD) that might become chronic without intervention [3, 4], and this is all the more true for women [5, 6]. Indeed, lifetime prevalence rates of PTSD are twice as high in women as in men (10.4 vs. 5%) and women are four times more likely to develop PTSD when exposed to the same trauma. Thus, it appears important to identify victims at risk of developing subsequent PTSD, and to better understand gender differences regarding this risk.

The acute stress disorder (ASD) diagnosis was first introduced into the 4th edition of Diagnostic and Statistical Manual of Mental Disorders (DSM-IV) [7] to recognize stress reactions within the first month following a traumatic event and to identify victims at risk of developing PTSD [8]. To meet criteria for ASD in DSM-IV, the individual must have experienced, witnessed, or been confronted to a traumatic event that triggered fear, helplessness, or horror (criteria A1 and A2). Moreover, the individual has to report symptoms from four clusters: three dissociative symptoms (criterion B), one reexperiencing symptom (criterion C), one avoidance symptom (criterion D), and one arousal symptom (criterion E). Symptoms have to cause distress or impairment (criterion F), and persist for at least 2 days, but no longer than 4 weeks (criterion G). However, in the recent DSM-5 [9], no dissociative reaction is mandatory to establish an ASD diagnosis. According to Bryant [10], people who are at high risk for PTSD may not have met ASD criteria in the DSM-IV because of the requirement of dissociative symptoms. Other studies suggest that the impact of dissociation may vanish on long-term adjustment [11, 12]. In the DSM-5, the individual must report nine symptoms out of 14, with onset or exacerbation occurring after the traumatic event. Symptoms for ASD in the DSM-5 include intrusion (4), negative mood (1), dissociation (2), avoidance (2), and arousal (5). Hence, it appears relevant to comment on the DSM-5 decisions in the hope of better detecting victims at risk for PTSD.

The predictive ability of ASD to predict PTSD is evaluated through the concept of predictive power. *Positive predictive power* refers to the probability of developing PTSD when an ASD symptom is present, while *negative predictive power* represents the probability of not developing PTSD when an ASD symptom is absent. To date, some studies have examined the positive and negative predictive power of ASD diagnosis, clusters, and/or symptoms on subsequent PTSD, and found inconsistent results [13]. A review has observed variability in the predictive ability of ASD, which could be explained by the diversity of trauma samples studied [14]. Most included studies focused on victims of major vehicle accidents (MVAs). Victims of major vehicle accidents and violent crimes differ in particular in terms of the interpersonal nature of

http://dx.doi.org/10.5772/64900

the act. Victims of violence can struggle with feelings of injustice and betrayal as they attempt to come to terms with the fact that another human being is responsible for such reprehensive behavior [15]. A comparison study between MVA victims and violent crime victims revealed differences, such as lower positive predictive power in victims of violent crimes [8, 16]. In the literature, higher rates of PTSD are associated with intentionally inflicted violence [17]. Thus, these samples appear distinctive, which reinforces the importance of examining specific studies regarding victims of violent crimes.

1.2. ASD diagnosis, clusters, and symptoms as predictors of PTSD

To date, four studies have examined the prevalence of ASD, the incidence of PTSD, and the predictive power of ASD diagnosis and clusters between 48 h and 6 weeks after a violent crime (i.e., physical assault, rape, and bank robbery) on PTSD 3–6 months later [4, 18–20]. Full ASD diagnosis was found in 12–59% of victims, and partial ASD (i.e., meeting all criteria except for dissociation symptoms) in 7–21%. Subsequently, 7–35% met full PTSD criteria and 22% for partial PTSD (i.e., at least one severe symptom in each symptom category plus reported impairment from these symptoms). The highest percentages were found in victims of rape, which were all women. ASD diagnosis had the best PTSD classification compared to each cluster (i.e., 62–90% of correct classification). For each cluster, negative predictive power was high, while positive predictive power was low. Two studies reported dissociation as the best predictive cluster (i.e., between 49 and 80% of correct classification). However, in these studies, ASD and PTSD symptoms were self-reported.

Regarding all types of trauma, only two studies (MVA and burn victims) have examined the predictive ability of ASD symptoms [8, 21, 22]. Results have shown that all symptoms were predictors, ranging from low to high positive predictive power (i.e., 0.12–1.00) and moderate to high negative predictive power (i.e., 0.78–1.00). Difede et al. [21] found that victims of burn injuries who developed PTSD reported recurrent images or thoughts, distress on exposure, avoidance of thoughts and activities, difficulty sleeping, irritability, poor concentration, motor restlessness, reduced awareness, and derealization more often than did individuals without PTSD. However, the generalization of these results to victims of violent crimes, who generally report more PTSD symptoms than victims of accidents, may be limited [23].

1.3. Gender differences in the predictive power of ASD

A study on victims of MVA showed that ASD was a better predictor of PTSD in women [24]. The authors suggested that this result was attributable to dissociation being a greater risk factor of PTSD in women. Moreover, positive predictive power was higher in women while negative predictive power was higher in men. Another study on MVA victims found that women were at greater risk for PTSD, and also more likely to report arousal symptoms, avoidance, and numbing symptoms and some reexperiencing symptoms [25]. In this study, women with dissociation were more at risk of developing PTSD. Thus, studies suggested a better predictive power of ASD for PTSD in women mainly because of gender differences in dissociative reactions.

Globally, studies on victims of violent crimes have supported the relevance of ASD diagnosis to predict PTSD. Predictive ability of partial ASD has only been documented in one study. Overall, all ASD clusters have shown high negative predictive power and low positive predictive power. However, it remains unclear which cluster better predicts PTSD diagnosis. The predictive power of each ASD symptom has not been examined in victims of violent crimes. Moreover, the differential predictive power of ASD clusters and symptoms according to gender has not been studied in these victims. Finally, previous studies have used self-report measures to evaluate ASD and PTSD, which suggests that responses were influenced by the victims' perceptions.

Moreover, it is well known that women are twice as likely as men to develop PTSD, but the reasons underlying this discrepancy remain unclear [5]. If ASD is considered a predictor of PTSD, it appears pertinent to determine to what extent ASD clusters and symptoms predict PTSD according to gender.

2. The current study

The purpose of the present study was to determine the predictive power of ASD diagnosis, clusters, and symptoms on PTSD diagnosis based on semi-structured interviews according to gender in victims of violent crimes. To do so, four operational objectives were defined. The first objective was to assess the percentage of individuals with or without ASD (i.e., full, partial, or no diagnosis) who will have developed PTSD (i.e., full and partial) 2 months after a violent crime. The second objective was to assess the predictive power of overall ASD diagnosis and each ASD cluster (i.e., B, C, D, and E) on PTSD diagnosis (full or partial compared to no diagnosis). Moreover, we predicted that dissociation would better classify PTSD compared to other clusters. The third objective was to evaluate the predictive power of each ASD symptom on PTSD diagnosis. The fourth objective was to examine the predictive power of each ASD cluster and symptom according to gender.

2.1. Method

2.1.1. Participants and procedure

The study was part of a larger longitudinal study that aimed to examine the evolution of distress and well-being after a violent crime, as well as predictive factors of PTSD. Individuals were recruited between 2009 and 2014 through the Trauma Studies Center (TSC) with the collaboration of the Montreal Crime Assistance Center (CAC). The inclusion criteria were the following: (a) being exposed to a violent crime (e. g., physical or sexual aggression and armed robbery) during the previous 30 days (i.e., the timeframe to screen for ASD), (b) being aged between 18 and 65 years old, and (c) being able to communicate in French or English. Exclusion criteria included a past or present psychotic episode, bipolar disorder, traumatic brain injury, an organic mental disorder or active suicidal ideations requiring an intervention.

Individuals were informed of the project by the CAC up to 30 days post crime. Interested individuals contacted the coordinator to clarify the circumstances of the crime and to be screened according to the research criteria. Then, symptoms of individuals admitted to the study were assessed with a semi-structured clinical interview (T0) conducted by a trained assistant to evaluate the ASD diagnosis and to fill out questionnaires. Individuals were reassessed for PTSD diagnosis after 2 months (T1) and questionnaires were sent by mail to be completed at home. For each completed assessment, individuals received a 20$ compensation. For the present subset of the larger study, only quantitative information of semi-structured interviews was used (i.e., ASD diagnosis, clusters, and symptoms at T0 and PTSD diagnosis at T1). In total, 69% of individuals completed both assessments.

2.2. Sociodemographic characteristics at baseline

Table 1 presents the sociodemographic characteristics of individuals. In total, 39 female and 36 male victims of violent crimes participated in the study. The mean age was 35 years old for women and 42 years old for men. Most participants were Caucasians. Twenty-three percent of women and 38% of men were currently in a relationship. Thirty-nine percent of women and 50% of men were employed. Most often, women and men reported having been victims of a physical assault (i.e., 77 and 84%, respectively).

Variable	Men (n = 36)	Women (n = 39)
Age (mean)	41.9 (15.9)	35.1 (13.8)
Relationship status (% with partner)	37.8	22.5
Occupational status (%)		
Employed	50.0	38.9
Temporary Break from Work	33.3	41.7
Not working (retired or by choice)	16.7	19.4
Type of trauma (%)		
Physical assault	83.8	76.9
Sexual assault	2.8	5.1
Threats	13.9	10.2
Witness in others' events	0.0	2.6
Other	16.7	20.5
Time since trauma (# days)	28.3 (10.8)	24.7 (9.3)

Table 1. Sociodemographic characteristics at baseline.

2.3. Measurement

The acute stress disorder interview (ASDI) [26] is a semi-structured interview administered at T0 that assesses ASD symptoms according to the DSM-IV. Individuals meeting all criteria were classified as having full ASD. Partial ASD was diagnosed when individuals met all criteria except for criteria B, for which only one out of three dissociative symptoms was required [18]. The ASDI has shown good internal consistency ($\alpha = 0.90$), temporal stability ($r = 0.90$), sensibility (91%), and specificity (93%) based on clinicians' judgment [26].

The structured clinical interview for DSM-IV axis I disorders (SCID-I) [27] was used at T1 to assess the presence or absence of PTSD (i.e., full, partial, or no diagnosis) and other axis I diagnoses. Partial PTSD was diagnosed when individuals met all criteria for each cluster except one (i.e., B, C, or D) [18]. This semi-structured interview showed good convergent validity according to clinicians' judgment ($k = 0.69$), as well as an inter-rater reliability ranging from 0.77 to 0.92 [28].

3. Results

3.1. ASD cases and incidence of PTSD

Table 2 presents the percentage of individuals who met criteria for ASD and PTSD diagnoses. At the initial assessment (T0), 39 victims of violent crimes (52%) met criteria for full ASD, and 15 victims (20%) for partial ASD. These 15 individuals did not meet criteria for dissociation (i.e., fewer than the three symptoms required). At the 2-month post-trauma assessment (T1), 21 victims (40%) met full criteria for PTSD and nine victims (17%) met criteria for partial PTSD. Partial diagnoses were due to individuals not meeting criteria for avoidance (i.e., $n = 9$, fewer than the three symptoms required).

ASD (T0)			**PTSD (T1)**			
Criteria	N	%	**# contacted**	**Criteria**	N	%
Full	39	52.0	25	Full	15	60.0
				Partial	6	24.0
				None	4	16.0
Partial	15	20.0	11	Full	6	54.5
				Partial	2	18.2
				None	3	27.3
None	21	26.9	16	Full	0	0.0
				Partial	1	6.3
				None	15	93.8
Total	75		52			

Table 2. Percentages of individuals with full, partial, and no ASD diagnoses who met criteria for full, partial, and no PTSD.

http://dx.doi.org/10.5772/64900

Among individuals who completed both assessments, 15 (60%) of those who had received a diagnosis of full ASD met full criteria for PTSD at the 2-month follow-up. Of those with a partial ASD diagnosis, six victims (55%) met full criteria for PTSD and two victims (18%) met partial criteria for PTSD. The 55% within the partial ASD group that met full criteria for PTSD consisted of individuals who did not meet criteria for dissociation.

3.2. Predictive power of ASD diagnosis and clusters on PTSD

Table 3 presents positive and negative predictive power of ASD clusters on PTSD. Positive predictive power was calculated by dividing the number of individuals who reported each ASD cluster and who later developed PTSD (i.e., full and partial diagnoses combined) by the total number of individuals who reported each ASD cluster. Negative predictive power was calculated by dividing the number of individuals who did not report each ASD cluster and who later did not develop PTSD (full and partial combined) by the total number of those who did not report the cluster.

Cluster	Positive predictive power[a]	Negative predictive power[b]	% of correct PTSD classification
B: Dissociation	0.59	0.67	65.4
C: Reexperiencing	0.60	0.50	82.7
D: Avoidance	0.65	0.50	82.4
E: Arousal	0.66	0.55	84.3
ASD diagnosis[c]	0.58	0.94	84.6

[a] The probability of the presence of PTSD when the criteria for the cluster were met.
[b] The probability of the absence of PTSD when the criteria for the cluster were not met.
[c] Full and partial diagnoses combined.

Table 3. Positive and negative predictive power for PTSD of each ASD cluster.

Results show that both negative and positive predictive power were moderate for all clusters (i.e., 0.50–0.67) and negative predictive power was high for ASD diagnosis (i.e., 0.94) according to Cohen (0.2 for low, 0.5 for moderate, and 0.8 for high [23]). A logistic regression analysis with PTSD diagnosis as the dependant variable (i.e., full and partial combined compared to no diagnosis) and each individual cluster (i.e., B, C, D, and E) and overall ASD diagnosis (i.e., full and partial) as independent variables were performed to determine the percentage of correct PTSD classification. Dissociation provided the lowest score compared to clusters C, D, E, and ASD diagnosis. However, no significant differences emerged based on Cochran's *Q*-test.

3.3. Predictive power of ASD symptoms on PTSD

Table 4 presents the percentage of individuals who reported each ASD symptom as a function of their PTSD diagnostic status at 2 months post trauma. Full PTSD and partial PTSD diagnoses were grouped together for the purpose of these analyses. Chi-squared analyses of individuals with and without PTSD were subjected to a Bonferroni adjustment in which the alpha level was set at 0.002. The presence of several ASD symptoms was significantly associated with a greater probability of having PTSD, recurrent images or thoughts, nightmares, distress on exposure, avoidance of thoughts, places and people, difficulty sleeping, poor concentration, exaggerated startle response, and motor restlessness. Individuals diagnosed with PTSD reported the abovementioned symptoms more often than individuals without a diagnosis of PTSD.

ASD symptom	Full and partial PTSD	No PTSD	χ^2,1, n = 52	Positive predictive power[a]	Negative predictive power[b]
Hurt/death	96.7	86.4	1.90	0.60	0.75
Fear	96.7	90.9	0.77	0.59	0.67
Helplessness	83.3	77.3	0.30	0.60	0.50
Numbing	56.7	40.9	1.26	0.65	0.50
Reduced awareness	70.0	50.0	2.15	0.66	0.55
Derealization	86.7	68.2	2.60	0.63	0.64
Depersonalization	23.3	13.6	0.77	0.70	0.63
Dissociative amnesia	63.3	54.5	1.65	0.66	0.52
Recurrent images or thoughts	93.3	50.0	12.71**	0.72	0.85
Nightmares	76.7	72.7	12.55**	0.79	0.70
Sense of reliving experience	26.7	90.9	2.52	0.80	0.48
Distress on exposure	93.3	59.1	17.00**	0.76	0.87
Avoidance of thoughts	100.0	54.5	21.27**	0.75	1.00
Avoidance of discussions	60.0	77.3	7.148	0.78	0.59
Avoidance of places	93.3	45.5	10.76*	0.70	0.83
Avoidance of people	93.1	72.7	23.74**	0.82	0.89
Difficulty sleeping	96.7	63.6	22.49**	0.78	0.93
Irritability	76.7	59.1	6.86	0.72	0.65
Poor concentration	86.7	50.0	8.314*	0.70	0.73
Hypervigilance	93.3	18.2	1.649	0.61	0.67
Exaggerated startle response	90.0	77.3	24.27**	0.84	0.85
Motor restlessness	90.0	61.9	15.46	0.77	0.81

[a] The probability of the presence of PTSD when the symptom is present.
[b] The probability of the absence of PTSD when the symptom is absent.
* $p < 0.002$.
** $p < 0.0001$.

Table 4. Percentages of each ASD symptom on the basis of their PTSD diagnostic status (full and partial or no PTSD) and positive and negative predictive power of each symptom.

Both positive and negative predictive powers were moderate according to Cohen [29] for the following symptoms: afraid, hurt/death, helplessness, numbing, reduced awareness, derealization, depersonalization, dissociative amnesia, nightmares, avoidance of discussions, irritability, poor concentration, and hypervigilance. Negative predictive power was high while positive predictive power was moderate for recurrent thoughts or images, distress on exposure, avoidance of thoughts, avoidance of places, difficulty sleeping, and motor restlessness. Positive predictive power was high while negative predictive power was low for sense of reliving. Finally, both positive and negative predictive powers were high for avoidance of people and exaggerated startle response.

3.4. Gender differences in the positive and negative predictive power of ASD clusters and symptoms on PTSD

Table 5 presents the proportion of women and men who reported each ASD symptom and cluster. Chi-squared analyses were conducted with a Bonferroni adjustment, $p < 0.002$. There were no significant differences in the presence of ASD symptoms and clusters between men and women. **Table 5** shows the positive and negative predictive power of each ASD symptom and cluster for men and women as a function of PTSD diagnostic status post trauma. Positive and negative predictive powers were similar for men and women for all clusters and symptoms.

ASD symptom	Individuals meeting symptom/criterion		χ^2 (df = 1)	Positive predictive power[a]		Negative predictive power[b]	
	Male (n = 36)	Female (n = 39)		Male	Female	Male	Female
Cluster A: exposure to trauma	94.4	94.9	0.01	0.61	0.62	1.00	1.00
Hurt/death	94.4	89.7	0.56	0.61	0.60	1.00	0.67
Fear	88.9	97.4	2.20	0.59	0.59	0.50	1.00
Helplessness	77.8	87.2	1.16	0.56	0.63	0.67	0.75
Cluster B: dissociation	58.3	66.7	0.56	0.77	0.63	0.64	0.56
Numbing	52.8	43.6	0.63	0.67	0.64	0.50	0.50
Reduced awareness	55.6	69.2	1.50	0.77	0.58	0.64	0.44
Derealization	72.2	82.1	1.03	0.64	0.63	0.57	0.75
Depersonalization	19.4	20.5	0.01	0.75	0.67	0.45	0.45
Dissociative amnesia	52.8	51.3	0.02	0.64	0.67	0.50	0.54
Cluster C: reexperiencing	86.1	92.3	0.75	0.74	0.62	1.00	1.00
Recurrent images/thoughts	66.7	87.2	4.49	0.86	0.64	0.80	1.00
Nightmares	55.6	59.0	0.09	0.79	0.80	0.70	0.69
Sense of reliving experience	25.0	15.4	1.08	0.60	1.00	0.42	0.52
Distress on exposure	63.9	76.9	1.53	0.87	0.68	0.89	0.83
Cluster D: avoidance	86.1	87.2	0.02	0.67	0.70	1.00	1.00
Avoidance of thoughts	66.7	82.1	2.34	0.78	0.73	1.00	1.00
Avoidance of discussions	44.4	51.3	0.35	0.75	0.82	0.58	0.59

ASD symptom	Individuals meeting symptom/criterion		χ^2 (df = 1)	Positive predictive power[a]		Negative predictive power[b]	
	Male (n = 36)	Female (n = 39)		Male	Female	Male	Female
Avoidance of places	77.8	71.8	0.35	0.65	0.75	0.75	0.88
Avoidance of people	65.7	64.1	0.02	0.80	0.83	0.88	0.90
Cluster E: arousal	91.7	94.9	0.31	0.64	0.59	1.00	1.00
Difficulty sleeping	72.2	76.9	0.22	0.82	0.75	1.00	0.88
Irritability	63.9	61.5	0.04	0.75	0.69	0.75	0.58
Poor concentration	69.4	79.5	1.00	0.75	0.67	0.75	0.71
Hypervigilance	88.9	87.2	0.05	0.64	0.58	1.00	0.50
Exaggerated startle response	58.3	69.2	0.97	0.92	0.79	0.81	0.88
Motor restlessness	77.8	60.5	2.57	0.74	0.81	1.00	0.73

[a] The probability of the presence of PTSD when the symptom is present.
[b] The probability of the absence of PTSD when the symptom is absent.

Table 5. Proportion of women and men reporting symptoms and predictive power of each ASD clusters and symptoms and gender differences.

4. Discussion

To our knowledge, this is the first study to examine the predictive power of full and partial ASD diagnosis, clusters, and symptoms according to gender in victims of violent crimes. Results showed that 52% of victims met criteria for full ASD and 20% for partial ASD, while 40% met criteria for full PTSD and 17% for partial PTSD. Both full and partial ASD diagnoses, as well as all symptom clusters, and most symptoms, were predictive of PTSD. No gender differences were observed concerning the predictive power of ASD clusters and symptoms.

4.1. ASD cases and incidence of PTSD

In the present study, 60% of the participants who had a full diagnosis of ASD met full criteria for PTSD and 24% received a partial diagnosis of PTSD, compared to 89 and 11% in the Elklit and Brink study [18]. Of those with a partial ASD diagnosis, 55% met full criteria for PTSD and 18% met partial criteria for PTSD, compared to 51 and 46% in the previous study. Differences in the results could be attributable to the traumatic event experienced (i.e., bank robbery compared to violent crimes in our study) and the methodology used (i.e., questionnaires compared to clinical interviews in our study). Globally, these results showed that both full and partial ASD diagnoses are useful in predicting PTSD among victims of violent crimes. In both studies, partial ASD was attributed because cluster B for dissociation was not fulfilled. However, this situation is no longer an issue considering the decreased emphasis on dissociation in the DSM-5. Indeed, the fact that partial ASD is as good as full ASD to predict PTSD supports changes made in the DSM-5 not to require dissociative symptoms to meet criteria of PTSD.

4.2. Predictive power of ASD diagnosis, clusters, and symptoms

In line with previous studies, ASD diagnosis showed the highest correct PTSD classification compared to each cluster. However, both positive and negative predictive powers were generally moderate, and each cluster was a relatively good predictor. Previous studies on victims of violent crimes found high negative predictive power (i.e., between 0.82 and 1.00) and low positive predictive power (i.e., between 0.22 and 0.39) for each cluster [4, 18–20]. Thus, the absence of a specific cluster (i.e., true negative) was more relevant in the prediction of PTSD diagnosis than the presence of that cluster (i.e., true positive). However, our results support the importance of both the presence and the absence of ASD clusters in predicting PTSD. The likelihood of developing PTSD without ASD seems weaker than when a victim is diagnosed with ASD. In the absence of acute stress reactions in the first days following trauma, it seems unlikely that posttraumatic stress symptoms appear. However, a partial or complete presence of ASD does not seem to systematically turn into PTSD, particularly due to the fact that coping strategies (e.g., seeking social support) set up by the victims following the violent crime may alter the psychopathological path of the individual.

Second, dissociation was not a better predictor compared to other clusters. These results may reflect differences between samples of victims of violent crimes and MVA. Indeed, a comparison study suggested that dissociation has a higher positive predictive power in samples of MVA compared to violent crimes (i.e., 0.71 and 0.61 compared with 0.33) [8]. MVA may induce more threatening stimuli (e.g., the sound of broken windows, risk of explosion, numerous smells), which may increase the risk of peritraumatic dissociation. Moreover, MVA occurs rapidly and suddenly, and victims may not have the time to react and to fully realize what is occurring, which may facilitate the onset of dissociative reactions. In studies on MVA, dissociation appears as an independent predictor of PTSD.

Contrary to previous studies on victims of MVA and burn injury [8, 21, 22], in our sample most symptoms had moderate to high positive and negative predictive powers, and were relatively good predictors of PTSD. As for clusters, our results support the pertinence of considering both the presence and the absence of ASD symptoms. Our findings on the predictive ability of ASD symptoms were similar to the ones obtained by Difede et al. [21] with the exception of nightmares and startle responses, which are more discriminative in victims of violent crimes, and reduced awareness, derealization, and irritability, which are more predictive of PTSD in burn victims. Similar to MVA, burn victims may be more at risk for dissociative reactions because of the rapid nature of the event and elevated risk of severe injury. They may also feel more irritable because of physical pain and the visibility of their burns.

4.3. Gender differences in the predictive power of ASD clusters and symptoms

Contrary to previous studies on MVA samples, our results revealed no gender differences in the predictive power of ASD on PTSD. Moreover, positive and negative predictive powers were similar for gender across all clusters and symptoms. Several factors could explain this absence of gender differences. In our sample, women and men reported similar percentages of ASD diagnosis (i.e., 51.3 and 52.8%, respectively) contrary to Bryant and Harvey [24] for MVA (i.e., 23 and 8%, respectively). In addition, in studies on MVA, dissociation was a better predictor in women, [8], but not in our study on victims of violent crimes. Indeed, a study found that dissociation was a better predictor for PTSD in women after an accidental traumatic event, but not after a violent crime [30]. Again, these findings highlight the potential indirect association between dissociation and PTSD in interpersonal traumatic events. Other factors may better explain gender differences in the prevalence of PTSD in victims of violent crimes. For instance, social support has been identified as a strongest effect size among several types of risk factors of PTSD ($d = 0.28$ and 0.40 [8, 24]). A study found that negative social interactions after a violent crime mediated the relation between gender and PTSD symptoms [3]. Hence, greater PTSD symptoms found in women were explained by more frequent negative social interactions.

4.4. Research implications

This study comprises several strengths, such as the examination of the positive and negative predictive powers of full and partial ASD diagnosis, clusters, and symptoms according to gender in victims of crimes. Moreover, ASD and PTSD were evaluated with validated semi-structured interviews by trained assistants. Our results revealed that both full and partial ASD diagnoses are useful in predicting subsequent PTSD. Hence, our findings support the decision of the DSM-5 to decrease the emphasis on dissociative reactions to establish the ASD diagnosis. The prevalence of ASD was possibly underestimated in the DSM-IV because of the required dissociative symptoms [10], which were overly restrictive. As the decision to remove the dissociation requirement is the DSM-5 was not only based on ASD's power to predict PTSD, it remains to be seen whether this change could affect the prediction of PTSD. Henceforth, future studies could determine the ability of ASD to predict PTSD, with both diagnoses based on the new formulation of the DSM-5. Furthermore, findings indicate the usefulness of evaluating both the presence and the absence of each ASD cluster and most symptoms to better detect victims at risk for PTSD.

Interestingly, dissociation did not appear to be a better predictor of PTSD, in contradiction to studies on victims of MVA. Hence, future studies could examine the role of peritraumatic dissociation (i.e., during the trauma) compared to acute dissociation (i.e., within the first month following the trauma) in the prediction of PTSD. Persistent dissociation may imply ongoing dissociation reactions which negatively impact on the emotional processing of the traumatic experience [31], and may be more predictive of ASD and PTSD [32]. In fact, the restricted awareness aspect of acute dissociation was demonstrated to be the only significant predictor of PTSD variance [18]. In the same line, future studies could test the relation between persistent dissociation, PTSD, and risk factors such as childhood traumatic experiences. Moreover, contrary to studies on MVA victims, no gender differences were found in the predictive ability of ASD cluster and symptoms. Future studies could examine gender dimensions. Gender is culturally understood as a socially prescribed and experienced dimension of femaleness and

http://dx.doi.org/10.5772/64900

maleness in a society, exemplified by gender roles [33]. Future studies could explore the relation between adherence to feminine and masculine characteristics and the expression of distress, symptoms, and the way individuals seek help after a traumatic event, using the Bem Sex Inventory [34]. Finally, future studies should examine the relation between ASD, PTSD, gender dimensions, and social support to better explain women's greater vulnerability for PTSD.

4.5. Limitations

The results of this study should be considered along with their limitations. It should be noted that our moderate sample size was associated with limited statistical power to detect significant effects, specifically for gender differences. Moreover, 31% of individuals did not complete both assessments. Victims were recruited within the 30 days following the crime, but the mean of 24 days is close to the maximum of 30 days allowed for establishing an ASD diagnosis and the minimum required for a PTSD diagnosis. In addition, a selection bias was possible because individuals referred to the research project may have been experiencing more difficulties and distress than usual. This fact may have decreased the potential of specific clusters of symptoms, such as dissociation, to predict PTSD.

4.6. Clinical and policy implications

The changes made to the diagnosis of ASD in the DSM-5 should allow for more distressed individuals, specifically those that previously had a partial ASD because of insufficient dissociative symptoms, to have access to mental health services. In spite of the fact that women are twice as likely as men to develop PTSD, our results suggest that screening both men and women for ASD after a violent crime is judicious. Moreover, some ASD symptoms were more predictive of PTSD. Thus, it seems relevant for clinicians to target these symptoms throughout the treatment to prevent the development of PTSD. Furthermore, it would be important to facilitate the access to psychological services, and to offer training to mental health providers in order to adequately screen for ASD using the DSM-5. Also, it would be pertinent to deliver evidence-based interventions. Indeed, trauma-focused cognitive behavioral therapy (CBT) for individuals with PTSD has been shown to be an efficient treatment to reduce PTSD symptoms [6]. Thus, it would be pertinent to test the effectiveness of an early brief preventive CBT for victims of crimes with ASD to prevent PTSD. This intervention has been shown to be efficient in female rape victims [35] but less so among victims of different violent crimes at long term [36].

5. Conclusion

The present study highlights the importance of preventing PTSD in victims of violent crimes. Results indicate that ASD diagnosis, clusters, and symptoms appear pertinent to predict PTSD. Globally, findings support the DSM-5 decision regarding the decreased emphasis on dissociative reactions for an ASD diagnosis to better identify women and men at risk for PTSD.

Hence, screening for ASD after a violent crime appears to be an appropriate measure to detect at-risk victims, and subsequently to deliver appropriate interventions in order to prevent the development of PTSD.

Author details

Stéphane Guay[1,2*], Myra Gravel-Crevier[2,3], Richard Boyer[2,4] and André Marchand[2,3]

*Address all correspondence to: stephane.guay@umontreal.ca

1 School of Criminology, University of Montreal, Montreal, Canada

2 Trauma Studies Centre, Mental Health University Institute, Montreal, Canada

3 Department of Psychology, University of Quebec in Montreal, Montreal, Canada

4 Department of Psychiatry, University of Montreal, Montreal, Canada

References

[1] Breslau, N., et al., Trauma and posttraumatic stress disorder in the community: The 1996 Detroit Area Survey of Trauma. Archives of General Psychiatry, 1998. 55(7): p. 626–632.

[2] Statistique Canada., Criminal victimization in Canada. General Social Survey 2009. Juristat, 2010. 30(2): p. 1–41.

[3] Brewin, C.R., Andrews, B., and Rose S., Diagnostic overlap between acute stress disorder and PTSD in victims of violent crime. American Journal of Psychiatry, 2003. 160(4): p. 783–785.

[4] Brewin, C.R., et al., Acute stress disorder and posttraumatic stress disorder in victims of violent crime. American Journal of Psychiatry, 1999. 156(3): p. 360–366.

[5] Tolin, D.F. and Foa E.B., Sex differences in trauma and posttraumatic stress disorder: a quantitative review of 25 years of research. Psychological Bulletin, 2006. 132(6): p. 959–992.

[6] Foa, E.B., et al., Effective treatments for PTSD: practice guidelines from the International Society for Traumatic Stress Studies. 2008, New York, NY: Guilford Press.

[7] American Psychiatric Association, Diagnostic and statistical manual of mental disorders DSM-IV-TR fourth edition (text revision). 2000, Washington, DC: American Psychiatric Association.

[8] Harvey, A.G. and Bryant, R.A., Acute stress disorder: a synthesis and critique. Psychological Bulletin, 2002. 128(6): p. 886.

[9] American Psychiatric Association, Diagnostic and statistical manual of mental disorders (DSM-5®). 2013, Washington, DC: American Psychiatric Association.

[10] Bryant, R.A., Early predictors of posttraumatic stress disorder. Biological Psychiatry, 2003. 53(9): p. 789–795.

[11] Holen, A., A long-term outcome study of survivors from a disaster: The Alexander L. Kielland disaster in perspective. 1990: Department of Psychiatry, University of Oslo.

[12] Freedman, S.A., et al., Predictors of chronic post-traumatic stress disorder. A prospective study. The British Journal of Psychiatry, 1999. 174(4): p. 353–359.

[13] Bryant, R.A., et al., A review of acute stress disorder in DSM-5. Depression and Anxiety, 2011. 28(9): p. 802–817.

[14] Bryant, R.A., Acute stress disorder as a predictor of posttraumatic stress disorder: A systematic review. The Journal of Clinical Psychiatry, 2010. 72(2): p. 233–239.

[15] Green, B.L., Identifying survivors at risk: Trauma and stressors across events., in The Plenum Series on Stress and Coping, Raphael, J.P.W.B., Editor. 1993, Plenum Press: New York, NY, USA. p. 138–144.

[16] Demarble, J., et al. Gender differences in peritraumatic dissociation and distress among victims of violent crimes. Poster presented at the International Society for Traumatic Stress Studies (ISTSS). November 2014. Miami, FL, USA.

[17] Mellman, T.A., et al., Predictors of post-traumatic stress disorder following severe injury. Depression and Anxiety, 2001. 14(4): p. 226–231.

[18] Elklit, A. and O. Brink, Acute stress disorder as a predictor of post-traumatic stress disorder in physical assault victims. Journal of Interpersonal Violence, 2004. 19(6): p. 709–726.

[19] Elklit, A. and Christiansen D.M., ASD and PTSD in rape victims. Journal of Interpersonal Violence, 2010. 25(8): p. 1470–1488.

[20] Hansen, M. and Elklit, A., Does acute stress disorder predict posttraumatic stress disorder following bank robbery? Journal of Interpersonal Violence, 2012. 28(1): p. 25–44.

[21] Difede, J., et al., Acute stress disorder after burn injury: a predictor of posttraumatic stress disorder? Psychosomatic Medicine, 2002. 64(5): p. 826–834.

[22] Harvey, A.G. and Bryant, R.A., Two-year prospective evaluation of the relationship between acute stress disorder and posttraumatic stress disorder following mild traumatic brain injury. American Journal of Psychiatry, 2000. 157(4): p. 626–628.

[23] Nickerson, A., et al., Accidental and intentional perpetration of serious injury or death: Correlates and relationship to trauma exposure. Journal of Trauma and Acute Care Surgery, 2011. 71(6): p. 1821–1828.

[24] Bryant, R.A. and Harvey, A.G., Gender differences in the relationship between acute stress disorder and posttraumatic stress disorder following motor vehicle accidents. Australian and New Zealand Journal of Psychiatry, 2003. 37(2): p. 226–229.

[25] Fullerton, C.S., et al., Gender differences in posttraumatic stress disorder after motor vehicle accidents. American Journal of Psychiatry, 2001. 158(9): p. 1486–1491.

[26] Bryant, R.A., et al., Assessing acute stress disorder: Psychometric properties of a structured clinical interview. Psychological Assessment, 1998. 10(3): p. 215–220.

[27] Michael, B., et al., Structured Clinical Interview for DSM-IV Axis I Disorders Clinician Version (SCID-CV). 1996, American Psychiatric Press: Washington, DC.

[28] Summerfeldt, L.J. and Antony, M.M., Structured and semistructured diagnostic interviews, in Handbook of assessment and treatment planning for psychological disorders, Antony M.M. and Barlow D.H., Editors. 2002, Guilford Press: New York, NY. p. 3–37.

[29] Cohen, J., Statistical power analysis for the behavior science. 1988, Hillsdale: Lawrence Erlbaum Association.

[30] Christiansen, D.M. and Elklit, A., Risk factors predict post-traumatic stress disorder differently in men and women. Annals of General Psychiatry, 2008. 7(1).

[31] Bryant, R.A., Does dissociation further our understanding of PTSD? Journal of Anxiety Disorders, 2007. 21(2): p. 183–191.

[32] Briere, J., Scott, C., and Weathers, F., Peritraumatic and persistent dissociation in the presumed etiology of PTSD. American Journal of Psychiatry, 2005. 162(12): p. 2295–2301.

[33] Johnson, J.L., Greaves, L., and Repta, R., Better science with sex and gender: Facilitating the use of a sex and gender-based analysis in health research. International Journal for Equity in Health, 2009. 8(14).

[34] Bem, S.L., The measurement of psychological androgyny. Journal of Consulting and Clinical Psychology, 1974. 42(2): p. 155–162.

[35] Foa, E.B., Zoellner, L.A., and Feeny, N.C., An evaluation of three brief programs for facilitating recovery after assault. Journal of Traumatic Stress, 2006. 19(1): p. 29–43.

[36] Sijbrandij, M., et al., Treatment of acute posttraumatic stress disorder with brief cognitive behavioral therapy: A randomized controlled trial. American Journal of Psychiatry, 2007. 164(1): p. 82–90.

Chapter 7

Personality Traits and Coping Strategies for Contrasting the Occurrence of Traumatic Reactions in Emergency Rescuers

Anna Maria Giannini, Laura Piccardi,
Pierluigi Cordellieri, Francesca Baralla,
Roberto Sgalla, Umberto Guidoni,
Emanuela Tizzani and Sandro Vedovi

Additional information is available at the end of the chapter

http://dx.doi.org/10.5772/64547

Abstract

We investigated personality traits, coping strategies, and social factors among emergency rescuers of three different catastrophic events that occurred in 2009 and 2013. These events were natural disasters, two of which were caused by human negligence. We used the cognitive interview (CI) protocol to interview witnesses and investigate their memory of the event. A qualitative analysis using the ATLAS.ti software was performed to subdivide the type of verbal production in the number of scenes recollected, negative emotions, vivid mental images, and self-experience of the event. All participants were also assessed using the Trauma Symptom Inventory for the presence of traumatic reactions at the time of the interview and tests (from December 2015 until January 2016) and 6 months before the interview to exclude the presence of further Traumatic job-related events. Personality traits (Big Five Questionnaire), coping strategies (Coping Inventory for Stressful Situations-Adult), and other social factors (the Post-Traumatic Growth Inventory) have been assessed. The aim of the study is to identify individual factors contributing to the development of post-traumatic stress disorder (PTSD) in emergency rescuers. We found that some personality traits, social factors, and specific cognitive strategies may act as protective factors to traumatic reactions.

Keywords: PTSD, traumatic events, coping style, personality traits, emergency rescuers

1. Introduction

In the early morning of 6 April 2009, a 6.9-Richter-magnitude earthquake struck L'Aquila (Abruzzo, Italy) and affected more than 45 towns and small villages, killing 309 people, injuring 1,600 people, and forcing more than 80,000 inhabitants to leave their homes. Police officers at the scene were among the first to assist in communicating to those trapped under the ruins and organizing rescue efforts in L'Aquila and the surrounding areas.

Two and a half months later, on 29 June 2009, a derailment of a freight train and subsequent fire in the railway station in Viareggio (Tuscany, Italy) occurred, which also involved a derailed wagon that crashed into a number of houses. A large area of Viareggio was damaged in the fires caused by the wagons, which were carrying liquefied petroleum and caused explosions. Thirty-three people were killed in the explosions and from collapsing houses. The deaths occurred at the time of the explosion and in the following days due to the severity of the injuries. Twenty-five people were injured, and 100 were left homeless. Police officers were among the first to intervene at the scene to secure the area and assist other rescuers.

Approximately 4 years later, on 28 July 2013, a coach with 48 people on board that was traveling to Naples from Telese Terme following a pilgrimage hit several vehicles before breaching a barrier and falling down a 30-m slope near the town of Avellino (Campania, Italy). This coach crash is considered the country's worst road accident. Forty people died, and 10 were severely injured.

Disasters can strike at any time and place. First responders, such as police officers, are repeatedly exposed to traumatic events as part of their daily routine. A discussion on the seriousness of a traumatic experience, which can trigger post-traumatic stress reactions, is still active [1]. One question thus concerns when one can pass from acceptable reactions, though they are occasionally imbued with suffering, to reactions that have a greater psychopathological meaning.

Stress is a pervasive experience that occurs when one's perceived demands outweigh one's perceived resources [2]. Although low to moderate levels of acute stress can be adaptive, the accumulated effects of chronic exposure to stress can lead to negative outcomes, including exhaustion, cognitive dysfunction, avoidance behavior, poor health behaviors, depressive symptoms, and negative social relationships [3]. It must be emphasized that traumatic stress reactions can differ according to the experienced event: In cases of technological or natural disasters or major terrorist attacks, the tendency is to increase mutual contact and look for reassurance in others [4]. This is also in line with neuroimaging studies in which specific networks of brain areas underpin post-traumatic stress disorder (PTSD) after various traumatic events [5, 6].

Over 85% of emergency personnel involved in traumatic incidents have experienced a traumatic stress reaction at some point [7]. Events that are considered stressful include being shot at, being physically threatened, having one's family threatened, working with victims who have been badly beaten [8–10], and experiencing the death of a fellow officer and physical attacks [11, 12]. Collins and Gibbs [9] report that stressors that are most frequently identified

http://dx.doi.org/10.5772/64547

among police officers are most likely to involve organizational issues such as work demands, lack of control over the workload, lack of communication, and inadequate support. Several studies on first rescuers reported low levels of PTSD symptoms e.g., [13–18], although Levy-Gigi et al. [19] highlighted the hidden consequences of being repeatedly exposed to traumatic experiences. Specifically, the presence of an impaired reversal learning has emerged [20] in individuals who were not diagnosed with PTSD but were repeatedly exposed to traumatic events in the line of duty; these individuals fail to encode traumatic associations in the appropriate context [19]. Furthermore, Levy-Gigi and colleagues [19] found that the specific type of impairment may vary due to the function of the occupation; specifically, they observed differences between firefighters and crime-scene investigation police officers. One interpretation of these differences was related to the different roles that they play in an event. Generally speaking, these first responders arrive at the scene at different times: Firefighters arrive at the scene soon after the occurrence, followed by the police. Firefighters rescue people and properties, whereas the police collect and provide evidence that may be useful in court in the event of prosecution. For this reason, firefighters' actions result in immediate positive or negative feedback according to the severity of the event, but police actions do not immediately affect the event or its outcome [19]. Some studies suggest that these differences may have a role in self-perception and the subsequent development of PTSD symptoms [21].

Factors that mitigate post-traumatic stress or post-traumatic growth have not yet been established. In particular, individual differences in post-trauma outcomes and the way in which certain putative key workplace, social support, and coping variables may combine to influence these outcomes are still open to debate [22]. Coping with stress requires subjective appraisal and reappraisal of the situation [23].

The selection process for police officers includes a measurement of personality traits, and potential recruits undergo strict screening procedures prior to their acceptance into the department. Several studies empirically suggest the existence of a "police personality" [24, 25], hypothesizing that this personality is a dynamic process that is affected by life experiences and recognizes the extraordinary job experiences that are unique to police work (see [25]). Specifically, the police personality is a characteristic or a set of characteristics that are acquired by individuals after they become officers and are illustrative of the personality attributes possessed solely by police officers. These personality characteristics may be common to police officers but may not necessarily be exclusively so [25]. Personality traits are considered significant predictors of police performance [26–28], with higher levels of conscientiousness and lower levels of neuroticism identified as the most significant predictors of police membership and performance [28, 29]. In general, people who score high in conscientiousness have also been characterized by the use of active coping skills and refrain from the use of passive coping skills [30]. The term *coping* refers to cognitive and behavioral efforts that are used to manage specific external and/or internal demands that are appraised as stressful or exceeding one's personal resources [31]. Coping strategies may be either problem focused or emotion focused [32]. Problem-focused coping refers to responses that are aimed at directly altering or resolving a stressful situation, whereas emotion-focused coping refers to responses aimed at managing and regulating one's emotional reactions to the stressful situation [33]. In general, problem-focused coping strategies are more useful than emotion-focused coping strategies [34, 35]. The ability to cope with stress is considered a crucial factor within police settings. Anshel [36] individuates poor coping skills as significant predictors of high-level stress in police work. Grubb et al.'s [37] findings suggested the existence of a "police personality/profile" and linked good coping skills with the tendency to use fewer maladaptive cognitive strategies to regulate their emotions and cope with stress.

In the present study, we investigated the role of personal traits and coping strategies in developing or being resilient to post-traumatic stress disorder as well as in predicting post-traumatic growth. For this reason, we interviewed police officers who responded to three different catastrophic events that occurred in 2009 and 2013. We asked to the respondents to freely recall and imagine the event, as well as imagining that the perspective changed. We then analyzed the number of memories reported, emotions, and personal experiences as part of the three instructions in the modified cognitive interview (CI).

We also analyzed the three groups to investigate the differences related to the specific event in which they participated.

We hypothesized the following observations: (1) proactive coping strategies are seen more often than maladaptive strategies, and the type of coping style may be associated with the presence of trauma symptoms; (2) the observation of specific personality traits are not observed because of the homogeneous sample, that is, we compared police officers involved in different types of disasters but not different types of rescuers; and (3) differences are found only for L'Aquila earthquake event because only in this event did rescuers experience the stress of being both primary and secondary victims.

2. Method

2.1. Participants

We recruited 15 police officers (14 men). These officers ranged from 43 to 61 years old; their educational level ranged from 8 to 18 years of schooling; and the group comprised officers who were involved in three different catastrophic events (six police officers were involved in L'Aquila earthquake, four police officers were involved in the Viareggio train derailment, and five police officers were involved in the Avellino coach crash).

To exclude the presence of traumatic job-related events that occurred in the 6 months prior to the time of the testing, all participants completed the Trauma Symptom Inventory (TSI) ([38] Italian Version: [39]). We also asked them to complete the Maslach Burnout Inventory (MBI) ([40, 41]; Italian Version: [42]) to exclude the presence of burnout. None of the participants showed the presence of PTSD or burnout.

Furthermore, all participants completed an initial form that requested information about the respondents' age and level of education, gender, area of work, grade, training, supervisory responsibilities, partnership status and number of children, and length of time in the occupation. The confidentiality and anonymity of the data were emphasized. In **Tables 1** and **2**, the means and standard deviations of the respondents' information are shown.

Groups	Number of participants in the event	Age (years)	Education (years)	Professional experience (years)
L'Aquila earthquake	6	51.2 (6.8)	15 (2.74)	31 (7.75)
Viareggio derailment	4	53.3 (5.23)	13 (0)	30.5 (3.63)
Avellino coach crash	5	52.6 (5.64)	15 (2.97)	30.67 (4.98)

Table 1. Means and (standard deviations) are reported.

Participants	Other Traumatic events experienced	Coping strategies adopted during the event		Sleep disturbances	Reexperiencing (includes flashbacks, intrusive memories, dreams)	General health disorders	Habitual fatigue
		Task-oriented and emotional disengagement	Peer support				
AV01	Yes	Yes	No	Yes	Yes	Yes	Yes
AV02	Yes	Yes	Yes	No	Yes	No	No
AV03	Yes	Yes	Yes	Yes	Yes	No	No
AV04	Yes	Yes	Yes	No	No	No	No
AV05	No	Yes	Yes	Yes	No	No	Yes
VI01	Yes	Yes	No	No	No	Yes	Yes
VI02	Yes	Yes	Yes	No	Yes	No	No
VI03	Yes	Yes	No	Yes	Yes	No	Yes
VI04	Yes	Yes	Yes	No	No	No	No
AQ01	Yes	Yes	No	Yes	Yes	Yes	No
AQ02	No	Yes	No	Yes	Yes	Yes	No
AQ03	Yes	Yes	No	Yes	Yes	Yes	No
AQ04	Yes	Yes	No	Yes	Yes	Yes	No
AQ05	No	Yes	Yes	No	Yes	No	No
AQ06	Yes	Yes	Yes	Yes	Yes	No	Yes

Table 2. Information related to the traumatic event (presence/absence).

2.2. Measures

Big Five Questionnaire (BFQ) (Italian version: [43, 44]) is a 132-item self-reporting inventory in its original extended form and it is commonly used to assess personality traits. The BFQ is based on the five-factor model (FFM), a widely known theory that describes personality within five broad dimensions [45]. The five factors have been defined as openness to experience, conscientiousness, extraversion/vivaciousness, agreeableness, and emotional stability. The reliability of the five dimensions of the Italian version of the BFQ (Cronbach's alpha) is within the range of 0.73–0.90, while reliability of the 10 subdimensions ranges from 0.68 to 0.86.

The respondents indicate agreement with the extent to which each item describes them on a five-point scale, ranging from complete disagreement (1 = extremely false for me) to complete agreement (5 = extremely true for me).

Coping Inventory for Stressful Situations-Adult (CISS) ([46]; Italian Version: [47]). This is a self-reporting inventory composed of 48 items that investigated the way the respondents react in stressful and demanding situations. The CISS measures three types of coping styles: task-orientated, emotion-orientated, and avoidance coping. It also identifies two types of avoidance patterns: distraction and social diversion. In particular, (1) the task-oriented coping style involves active and offensive coping styles, stressing proactive responses to the stressors (e.g., "I focus on the problem and see how I can solve it"); (2) emotion-oriented coping style concerns coping styles directed at altering negative emotional responses to stressors, such as negative thinking (e.g., "My efforts will surely fail"), decreased self-confidence (e.g., "I cannot handle this problem") or poor self-image (e.g., "I am useless"); and (3) the avoidance coping style represents withdrawal behaviors and the redirection of personal resources toward different activities, such as sports and leisure time (e.g., "I buy something"). The Cronbach's alpha estimates for the CISS dimensions were good (emotion-oriented coping 0.82) or acceptable (task-oriented coping 0.75, outreach-oriented coping 0.72, treat oneself-oriented coping 0.72) [48].

The respondents were asked to rate each item on a five-point scale, ranging from (1) "not at all" to (5) "very much."

The Post-Traumatic Growth Inventory (PTGI) ([49]; Italian Version: [50]) measures the positive outcomes reported by people who have experienced traumatic events. This scale is composed of 21 self-statements including the components of new possibilities, relating to others, personal strength, spiritual change, and appreciation of life. The respondents were asked to indicate for each statement the degree to which the change listed occurred in his/her life as the result of the crisis on a six-point Likert scale, which ranged from 0 ("I did not experience this change as a result of my crisis") to 5 ("I experienced this change to very great degree as a result of my crisis"). The intermediate scores and the changes experienced were the following: 1, a very small degree of change experienced; 2, a small degree of change experienced; (3, a moderate degree of change experienced; and 4, a great degree of change experienced. At the beginning of the inventory, the respondents were given space to indicate the difficult life event that occurred (e.g., bereavement, injury-producing accidents, separation or divorce of parents, relationship break-up, criminal victimization, illness, retirement, disaster, vehicular accident, and other events) and when it occurred. In the Italian version, the internal reliability of this instrument is Cronbach's alpha = 0.93, while the reliability of the five dimensions of the Italian version of the PTGI (Cronbach's alpha) is within the range of 0.42–0.73 [50].

The Trauma Symptom Inventory (TSI). The Italian version of the TSI [39] was a translation of the original questionnaire [38] with exactly the same item numbering.

The TSI includes 100 self-statements that are subdivided into 3 validity scales (inconsistent response, response level, and atypical response scales) and 10 clinical scales. The validity scales are designed to detect conflicting, underreporting and overreporting response sets, respectively [38]. The clinical scales measure the extent to which the responder endorses the four categories of distress. Specifically, anxious arousal (AA), depression (D), and anger/irritability (AI) represent the dysphoric mood states that are often encountered by those experiencing significant psychological trauma. The scales of intrusive experiences (IE), defensive avoidance (DA), and dissociation (DIS) are designed to measure the re-experiencing and avoidance symptoms of PTSD. The sexual concerns (SC) and dysfunctional sexual behavior (DSB) scales measure attitudes and feelings regarding sex as well as sexual problems, respectively. The impaired self-reference (ISR) and tension-reduction behavior (TRB) scales tap into difficulties with the self and affect regulation, including the outward behavior manifestations that are used to manage negative effects, such as self-mutilation [38]. The internal consistency reliabilities of the Italian version of the TSI ranged from 0.71 to 0.83 for the validity scales and from 0.70 to 0.90 for the clinical scales across the samples [39]. The respondents are asked to rate the items on a four-point Likert scale, with "0" representing no experience of the symptom and "3" representing frequent occurrences over the past 6 months.

The Maslach Burnout Inventory (MBI) ([40, 41]; Italian Version: [42]) measures the outcome of chronic stress. This scale is composed of 22 items that rated on a frequency and intensity scale and measures three dimensions: emotional exhaustion (EE), depersonalization (D), and personal accomplishment (PA). The Cronbach's alpha estimates for the Italian version of the MBI dimensions were 0.88 for EE, 0.70 for D, and 0.83 for PA [51]. The frequency scale ranges from 0 (never) to 6 (every day), while the intensity scale ranges from 1 (never) to 6 (very strong).

Modified Cognitive Interview (CI) protocol for investigating the traumatic event. We used three of the four techniques used to interview the eyewitnesses in the CI; we specifically considered the context reinstatement and asked them about free recall, mental images, and the changed perspective. We did not ask participants to perform the changed order, in which the interviewees are asked to report as many details as they could in reverse order, starting with the last scene remembered. We also asked participants about the presence/absence of other events that they considered traumatic and the most traumatic event they had ever experienced, coping strategies adopted during the event, the event aftermath, the presence/absence of sleep disorders, intrusive memories of the event, health disorders, and useful suggestions they would provide to select law enforcement recruits.

In general, the procedure for the CI involved several steps. The researchers first ensured that the participant was comfortable and then asked him/her to imagine into the mood he/she experienced during the event and concentrate (if needed, he/she could also close his/her eyes for 10 s to think). Later, the researchers gave the participant the mental reinstatement of the context instruction to encourage him/her to report all information that he/she could accurately remember.

Specifically, the CI began with this recommendation: "I want that you tell me everything you can remember, every little detail you can remember, even if you think it is not important or if you are not sure about it." Four different instructions were then given. (1) The "free recall" technique [52] asked the participants to report as many as details as they could to accurately recreate the scene. This technique has been shown to be one of the most valuable components of the CI (e.g., [53]). (2) We also modified the "image" technique because we asked the participants to report as many as details as they could regarding the first and the most emotionally impactful images of the event. (3) A modified "changed perspective" technique was used, in which we asked the participants to try to observe the scene above from a bird's-eye view and report as many details as they could, in addition to the emotion experienced.

2.3. Coding and scoring

All CI were audio-recorded and transcribed verbatim. Later, the CIs were scored to evaluate each unit of information recalled by the participants. The units of information or details were categorized according to whether they were reported in the free recall, image, or changed perspective instructions. Two different coders (psychology post-doc students) scored the interviews; only when an agreement between them was reached were the audiotape details coded.

For all the three techniques, we extracted and analyzed the number of scenes recreated, negative emotions, vividness of mental images, and self-experiences. We also used ATLAS.ti for the analysis and coding of the interviews.

3. Statistical analyses

We performed a descriptive analysis concerning the demographic data for years of experience. We also reported the presence/absence of traumatic events experienced, the coping strategies adopted during the emergency, sleep disorders, intrusive memories of the event, and general health disorders (see **Table 2**).

To evaluate the factors that predict post-traumatic stress and the post-traumatic growth, we performed separate stepwise regression analyses loading personality traits and coping strategies as independent variables.

To examine the possible differences between the groups due to the exposure to the three different events, we performed an analysis of variance (ANOVA) with the group (Avellino, Viareggio, and L'Aquila) and the number of memories, emotions and experiences that emerged from the modified cognitive interview in the three different instructions sections (free recall, mental image, and changed perspective).

http://dx.doi.org/10.5772/64547

4. Results

4.1. Regression analyses

To evaluate the personality traits and coping strategies that predict the traumatic effects in a critical event, we performed separate stepwise regression analyses considering the scores of the CISS and the BFQ as the independent variables and the scores in TSI and PTGI as the dependent variables. None of the sociodemographic variables correlated with any of the dependent variables, hence we did not have to control for any in the regression model.

4.2. CISS vs. TSI

The stepwise regression analysis revealed a significant effect for the factor *emotion oriented* on TSI AA (*scale of dysphoric mood states;* $\beta = 0.691$, $t = 3.582$, $p < 0.01$), TSI AI (*anger/irritability;* $\beta = 0.716$, $t = 3.836$, $p < 0.01$), TSI DIS (*dissociation;* $\beta = 0.786$, $t = 4.763$, $p < 0.001$), and TSI TRB (*tension-reduction behavior;* $\beta = 0.611$, $t = 2.889$, $p < 0.05$).

4.3. BFQ vs. TSI

The stepwise regression revealed a significant effect only for the *emotional stability* factor of BFQ on TSI DIS (*dissociation;* $\beta = -0.580$; $t = 2.568$, $p < 0.05$), and the *conscientiousness* factor on TSI TRB (*tension-reduction behavior;* $\beta = -0.658$; $t = 3.152$, $p < 0.01$). No other factor was statistically significant.

4.4. CISS vs. PTGI

No CISS factors showed significant effects.

4.5. BFQ vs. PTGI

The stepwise regression performed on the PTGI scores showed a significant effect of *emotional stability* and *conscientiousness* as predictors of *new line possibilities* (respectively, $\beta = -0.683$; $t = -3.803$, $p < 0.01$, and $\beta = 0.549$; $t = 3.056$, $p < 0.01$), the factors of *conscientiousness and extraversion/vivaciousness on personal strength growth* (respectively, $\beta = 889$; $t = 4.405$, $p < 0.001$ and $\beta = -530$; $t = -2.653$, $p < 0.05$). Finally, the *emotional stability* factor also showed a significant effect on *spiritual change* ($\beta = -0.533$; $t = 2.270$, $p < 0.05$).

4.6. ANOVAs

To investigate the presence of significant differences between the three groups interviewed through CI, we performed separate ANOVAs for the three techniques (free recall, mental image, and change perspective) of the CI considering the group (L'Aquila earthquake, Viareggio derailment, and Avellino coach crash) as the independent variable and the verbal production in free recall/mental images and change perspective (number of scenes recreated, negative emotions, vividness of the mental image, and self-experience) as the dependent variables. The statistical power is 0.06. Hence, all nonsignificant results from the ANOVA cannot be interpreted to avoid making type II errors. We however report them for transparency reasons only. From the ANOVA performed on the free recall, only a main effect of the group with respect to the self-experience was seen ($F_{(2,14)} = 3.993$; $p = 0.04$; see **Figure 1A**). All other differences were not significant most probably because of low power: the number of scenes recreated ($F_{(2,14)} = 0.985$; $p = 0.40$), negative emotions ($F_{(2,14)} = 0.635$; $p = 0.54$), and the vividness of mental images ($F_{(2,14)} = 1.495$; $p = 0.26$). In the mental image section, the three groups differed in terms of the self-experience reported ($F_{(2,14)} = 3.993$; $p < 0.05$) and of the number of scenes recreated ($F_{(2,14)} = 5.48$; $p = 0.02$), but the other types of verbal production differences were not significant most probably because of low power ($Fs_{(2,14)}$ = from 3.993 to 0.635; *ps* = n.s.; see **Figure 1B**). No significant differences emerged from the change perspective technique in the verbal production of the three groups ($Fs_{(2,14)}$ = from 1.919 to 0.181; *ps* = n.s.; see **Figure 1C**).

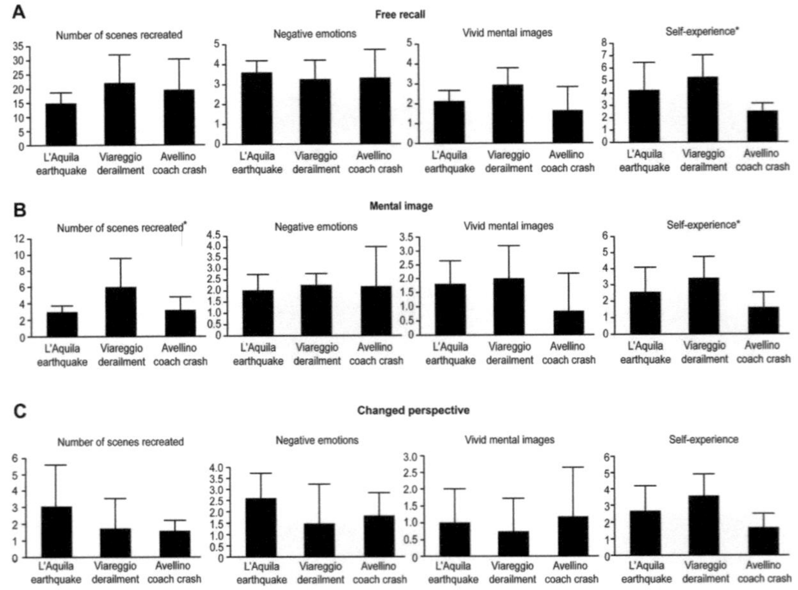

Figure 1. (A) Means of verbal production (number of scenes recreated, negative emotions, vividness of mental image, and self-experience) of the three groups in the free recall of CI; (B) means of verbal production (number of scenes recreated, negative emotions, vividness of mental image, and self-experience) of the three groups in the mental image of CI; (C) means of verbal production (number of scenes recreated, negative emotions, vividness of mental image, and self-experience) of the three groups in the change perspective of CI.

5. Discussion

Studies on traumatic reactions in first responders suggest that stress symptoms can continue over a significant period of time [54] and may include guilt, anxiety, depression, sleep disturbances, flashbacks (e.g., intrusive thoughts), and excessive anger [55]. This is one of the reasons we decided to investigate this aspect 3 and 7 years from the three different catastrophic events that occurred in Italy in which the police officers interviewed had an important role in the protection and preservation of life, property, and the environment. They were on the front lines of these three events, and they also worked hard in the aftermath, which lasted several months. In particular, in one of these disasters (i.e., L'Aquila), the long-lasting effects of the traumatic experience are currently manifested mainly by feeling "on edge" in addition to with hyperarousal and sleeping problems. Indeed, we observed significant differences between the self-experience and the number of scenes recreated by the police officers who responded. Both in the L'Aquila earthquake and in the Viareggio derailment, the first-responders were exposed to hazardous environmental conditions. In the L'Aquila event, the main shock (Richter magnitude 6.9) was followed by several thousands of aftershocks (30 of which had a Richter magnitude of greater than 3.5), which made the rescue difficult. Conversely, in the Viareggio train derailment, there was the tangible risk of further wagon explosions due to the high temperature emitted by the first wagon transporting liquefied petroleum gas (LPG) that had already exploded and destroyed houses alongside the railway line. Separately, in the Avellino coach crash, the first police officers arrived at the crash epicenter without knowing the severity of the situation because the initial information received from the operations room was not alarming. In some cases, the officers were able to rescue injured people in the upper part of the viaduct but were unable to reach the people trapped in the crashed coach approximately 100 ft under the viaduct.

Furthermore, only in L'Aquila earthquake scenario did the double condition of the victims (i.e., all lived in L'Aquila and in the earthquake-affected areas) and rescuers emerge. Indeed, the L'Aquila interviews are characterized by the reenactment of the rescue experiences that occurred later; many operators were at home with their families during the earthquake. As is well-known, police officers consider situations in which their own family is threatened especially stressful [10]. During the interview, their concerns for the safety of their families, friends, and peers who were not in the line of duty at the time of the earthquake emerged frequently. Moreover, all experienced the death of a fellow officer due to the collapse of the officer's house. This double experience as victims and rescuers in this group produced self-experiences that were significantly different from those produced in the other groups. Although the sample observed is small and the result must be considered with caution, we maintain that it may provide some useful guidelines for emergency rescuers in long-term stress management when rescuers have the double role of being direct and indirect victims.

Concerning the absence of significant difference in negative emotions and the vividness of the mental images recalled, no conclusions or explanations can be drawn because of the lack of statistical power.

Although the three groups are different in their experiences, all participants have been exposed to a traumatic experience, and 12 out of 15 participants reported other traumatic experience related to their job activity. Among the most traumatic experiences on the job included fatal accidents involving children or adolescents and self-perceived errors in death notifications. According to Colwell et al. [56], these types of traumatic experiences are reported in 27.2 and

1.3% of their sample, respectively, and in some way can be considered part of the risk of the job.

We found interesting results when investigating personality traits and coping strategies with respect to TSI and post-traumatic growth.

Specifically, we found that some coping strategies, such as emotion-oriented ones, predict the result in some TSI scales. In particular, emotion-oriented strategies predict performance with respect to the anxious/arousal scale, a scale of dysphoric mood states; the anger/irritability scale, a scale strictly related to the experience of psychological trauma; dissociation, a scale concerns the reexperiencing of the traumatic event; and tension-reduction behavior, a scale that examines difficulties with oneself and affects regulation.

Generally speaking, emotion-oriented strategies are considered proactive, and studies on coping associate these strategies with better adjustment, higher self-rated coping effectiveness, and lower levels of depression (e.g., [57, 58]). Indeed, when an individual adopts this type of coping style, he/she contrasts negative emotional responses with the stressors. Considering the time from the traumatic event (3 or 7 years), this type of coping strategy is surely more functional than problem-focused strategies, which were used by all rescuers during the emergency, as reported from the CI. Folkman and Lazarus [59], in introducing the functions of coping strategies, highlight that individuals use these strategies to manage problems causing stress and to govern emotions relating to the stressors. In the light of this definition, several studies consider a situation stressful whenever the individual perceives a lower ability to cope with the situation. Furthermore, the adopted coping strategies are strictly related to the way in which a stressor is evaluated, which means that a stressor that is perceived as controllable tends to elicit more proactive coping mechanisms [60], while a stressor perceived as uncontrollable tends elicit more avoidance strategies (e.g., [2, 61]).

The few studies on coping strategies among police officers seem to suggest that police officers have the tendency to use maladaptive emotion-focused behaviors for immediate stress reduction (e.g., [62]), while the avoidance coping strategy been more frequently associated with psychological stress [63]. In contrast, Ortega and colleagues [64] found that only personality and tenure were significantly related to coping strategy and the management of the occupational stress. In a recent study, Grubb et al. [37] found that the UK police officers use fewer maladaptive cognitive strategies to regulate their emotions and cope with stress, suggesting that they are adept at avoiding strategies that are negative and dysfunctional. Here, we found that only proactive coping strategies allowed the respondents to cope with the traumatic experience. We also found that only emotional stability for personality traits is a predictor of dissociation as evaluated by the TSI scales; this is in line with the proactive emotional coping strategies used in this research. Moreover, the conscientiousness of personality traits predicts the tension-reduction behaviors of TSI.

Another interesting result was that personality traits predict post-traumatic growth. In particular, we found that emotional stability and conscientiousness predicts new line possibilities; the conscientiousness and extraversion/energetic factor predict personal strength growth (specifically, extraversion/vivaciousness predicts growth in the negative direction);

and emotional stability predicts spiritual changes. These findings are of interest because the process of healing may consume mental and emotional energy, which could explain the negative prediction of the extraversion/vivaciousness trait. Indeed, people with a tendency toward being energetic may experience the reduction of the available resources more than others. Conversely, emotional stability may help in the building of new relationships and consolidating strong personal ties. In the same direction, individuals with conscientiousness traits are well organized, methodical, and thorough; this trait fosters the growth of personal strength as well as new life possibilities.

Our results seem to suggest that in the coping process, the traumatic event is important, both in terms of personality and methods of coping with the event. In some ways, coping strategies have an important function in protecting the individual and promoting his/her resilience. Personality has an important role in the meaning that the individual gives to his/her post-traumatic life and his/her capability to cope with the trauma. This an important result that takes into account the fact that police officers, as a consequence of their job, are not able to avoid future situations that are similar to the traumatic event or other potentially traumatic events. In this sense, they may be vulnerable to re-victimization; moreover, the exposure to new stressors may make spontaneous recovery more demanding because they would over-burden an already overloaded system [11, 36]. For this reason, a goal of future studies should be to better investigate the role of all protective factors that may help rescuers in terms of resiliency and enhancing their capability for post-traumatic growth.

In conclusion, we believe that our results—above all, those related to the role of emotional coping strategies as a protective factor in the prevention of post-traumatic stress disorders—may have important implications in terms of training new police officers. Indeed, preventive measure could be implemented to enhance the adaptive and proactive coping strategies in the management of stress. The evidence that personality traits may play an important role in not developing traumatic symptoms as well as in positive post-traumatic growth is information of interest that may have an impact in terms of recruitment. Furthermore, the use of structured cognitive interviews for investigating traumatic events could become a useful tool for supporting and reducing stress reactions. Moreover, one of the innovations of this study is related to the long amount of time that elapsed from the traumatic event exposure and the structured cognitive interviews. For example, a previous study by Marchand et al. [65] involved interviews of police officers at between 5 and 15 days and at 1 month, 3 months, and 12 months after the event. Our study is the first to investigate the psychological long-term effects of the exposure to a traumatic experience. From this perspective, the data in this study show that emotion-coping strategies and some positive emotional and mental personality traits appear to be beneficial for police officers. In this vein, our study suggests that through a modified cognitive interview, veteran police officers may share their experiences with cadets during academic training to help them avoid being overwhelmed from unexpected emotions and job-related experience.

It is also important to highlight that, even if our sample is small, which can be perceived as a limitation, interviewing police officers about a severe traumatic event may be very difficult because they are often prone to underestimating the magnitude of their distress. Moreover, the events investigated occurred several years ago, and the rescuers who intervened at that time are now at different police stations throughout Italy. However, we managed to interview all police officers who intervened as first rescuers who are now retired; all participants understood the implications of their contributions in terms of the academic training of cadets. This collective participation should be more appreciated in consideration of the "virility" culture [66], which prevents officers from expressing their emotions and feelings. This culture can force police officers into the role of superheroes, an idea that is supported by both the citizens and the police officers themselves. "Virility" can be considered a defensive mechanism strategy and may have an important role in protecting police officers from a high level of anxiety that could prevent them from doing their job. The embodiment of the "virility" culture does not allow displays of weakness and traumatic reactions. To offset risk, police officers can become risk takers. Police officers are generally perceived by citizens as superheroes and they, in line with this image, attempt to not fail such expectations by displaying "weaknesses" such as traumatic reactions or the long-term effects of trauma. For this reason, they generally never show any effects of the trauma exposure and tend to minimize their distress.

The participation of policemen in this study is a signal that knowledge and scientific results are changing the minds and culture in the direction of more effective attitudes toward the prevention and promotion of health.

6. Conclusion

The present study shows that emotion-coping strategies and some positive emotional and mental personality traits appear to play an important role as a protective factor for the development of post-traumatic stress disorder, as well as for the post-traumatic growth.

Moreover, it explores the possibility to use a modified cognitive interview to allow veteran police officers to share their experiences with cadets during academic training to help them avoid being overwhelmed from unexpected emotions and job-related experience. In spite of its limitations (the small number of participants for traumatic event and lack of statistical power for some analyses), the results seem to suggest the importance to use systematic measurements of coping strategies adopted as well as debriefing in the immediate aftermath (for small and large emergencies) and over the course of the following years (for large emergencies).

Acknowledgements

The authors wish to thank the study participants. This work was supported by the ANIA Foundation.

Author details

Anna Maria Giannini[1], Laura Piccardi[2,3*], Pierluigi Cordellieri[1], Francesca Baralla[1], Roberto Sgalla[4], Umberto Guidoni[5], Emanuela Tizzani[4] and Sandro Vedovi[5]

*Address all correspondence to: laura.piccardi@cc.univaq.it

1 Psychology Department, University Sapienza of Rome, Italy

2 Department of Life, Health and Environmental Sciences, L'Aquila University, L'Aquila, Italy

3 Neuropsychology Unit, IRCCS Fondazione Santa Lucia, Rome, Italy

4 Ministry of Interior, Department of Public Security, Rome, Italy

5 ANIA Foundation, Rome, Italy

References

[1] Chung H, Breslau N: The latent structure of post-traumatic stress disorder: tests of invariance by gender and trauma type. Psychol Med. 2008; 38: 563–573. DOI: 10.1017/S0033291707002589.

[2] Lazarus RS, Folkman S: Stress appraisal and coping. New York: Springer; 1984.

[3] Juster RP, McEwen BS, Lupien SJ: Allostatic load biomarkers of chronic stress and impact on health and cognition. Neurosci Biobehav Rev. 2010; 35: 2–16. DOI: 10.1016/j.neubiorev.2009.10.002.

[4] Schuster MA, Stein BD, Jaycox L, Collins RL, Marshall GN, Elliott MN, Zhou AJ, Kanouse DE, Morrison JL, Berry SH: A national survey of stress reactions after the September 11, 2001, terrorist attacks. N Engl J Med. 2001; 345: 1507–1512. DOI: 10.1056/NEJM200111153452024.

[5] Boccia M, D'Amico S, Bianchini F, Marano A, Giannini AM, Piccardi L: Different neural modifications underpin PTSD after different traumatic events: an fMRI meta-analytic study. Brain Imaging Behav. 2016; 10: 226–237. DOI: 10.1007/s11682-015-9387-3.

[6] Piccardi L, Boccia M, Colangeli S, Bianchini F, Marano A, Giannini AM, Palmiero M, D'Amico S: Neuro-functional alterations due to PTSD after environmental disasters: fMRI evidence and clinical suggestions. J Psychopathol. 2016; accepted.

[7] Mitchell JT, Bray GP: Emergency service stress. Englewood Cliffs, NJ: Prentice Hall; 1990.

[8] Martin LA, McKean HE, Veltkamp LJ: Posttraumatic stress disorder in police and working with victims: a pilot study. J Police Sci Adm. 1986; 14: 98–101.

[9] Collins PA, Gibbs ACC: Stress in police officers: a study of the origins, prevalence and severity of stress-related symptoms within a county police force. Occ Med. 2003; 53: 256–264. DOI: 10.1093/occmed/kqg061.

[10] Addis N, Stephens C: An evaluation of a police debriefing programme: outcomes for police officers five years after a police shooting. Int J Police Sci Manag. 2008; 10: 361–373. DOI: 10.1350/ijps.2008.10.4.092.

[11] Violanti JM: Trauma stress and police work. In Paton D, Violanti J, editors: Traumatic stress in critical occupations: recognition, consequences and treatment. Springfield, IL: Charles C. Thomas; 1996, p. 87–112.

[12] Conn SM: Stress in policing. In Fink G, editor: Stress: concepts, cognition, emotion, and behavior. Handbook of Stress Series, Volume 1. Elsevier, Academic Press; 2016, p. 393–398.

[13] Pole N, Neylan TC, Otte C, Henn-Hasse C, Metzler TJ, Marmar CR: Prospective prediction of posttraumatic stress disorder symptoms using fear potentiated auditory startle responses. Biol Psychiatry. 2009; 65: 235–240. DOI: 10.1016/j.biopsych.2008.07.015.

[14] Soo J, Webber MP, Gustave J, Lee R, Hall CB, Cohen HW, Kelly KJ, Prezant DJ: Trends in probable PTSD in firefighters exposed to the world trade center disaster, 2001–2010. Disaster Med Public Health. 2011; 5(Suppl. 2): 197–203. DOI: 10.1001/dmp.2011.48.

[15] Fushimi M: Posttraumatic stress in professional firefighters in Japan: rescue efforts after the Great East Japan Earthquake (Higashi Nihon Dai-Shinsai). Prehosp Disaster Med. 2012; 27: 416–418. DOI: 10.1017/S1049023X12001070.

[16] Meyer EC, Zimering R, Daly E, Knight J, Kamholz BW, Gulliver SB: Predictors of posttraumatic stress disorder and other psychological symptoms in trauma-exposed firefighters. Psychol Serv. 2012; 9: 1–15. DOI: 10.1037/a0026414.

[17] Orr SP, Lasko NB, Macklin ML, Pineles SL, Chang Y, Pitman RK: Predicting post-trauma stress symptoms from pre-trauma psychophysiologic reactivity, personality traits and measures of psychopathology. Biol Mood Anxiety Disord. 2012; 2: 1–12. http://www.biolmoodanxietydisord.com/content/2/1/8.

[18] Admon R, Leykin D, Lubin G, Engert V, Andrews J, Pruessner J, Hendler T: Stress-induced reduction in hippocampal volume and connectivity with the ventromedial prefrontal cortex are related to maladaptive responses to stressful military service. Hum Brain Mapp. 2013; 34: 2808–2816. DOI: 10.1002/hbm.22100.

[19] Levy-Gigi E, Richter-Levin G, Kéri S: The hidden price of repeated traumatic exposure: different cognitive deficits in different first-responders. Frontiers Behav Neurosc. 2014; 8(281): 1–10. DOI: 10.3389/fnbeh.2014.00281.

[20] Levy-Gigi E, Richter-Levi G: The hidden price of repeated traumatic exposure. Stress; 2014; 17: 343–351. DOI: 10.3109/10253890.2014.923397.

[21] Langan-Fox J, Cooper C: Handbook of stress in the occupations. Massachussets, MA: Edward Elgar Publishing; 2011.

[22] Armstrong D, Shakespeare-Finch J, Shochet I: Predicting post-traumatic growth and post-traumatic stress in firefighters. Aust J Psychol. 2014; 66: 38–46. DOI: 10.1111/ajpy.12032.

[23] Gross JJ: Emotion regulation in adulthood: timing is everything. Curr Dir Psychol Sci. 2001; 10: 214–219. DOI: 10.1111/1467-8721.00152.

[24] Abrahamsen S, Strype J: Are they all the same? Norwegian police officers' personality characteristics and tactics of conflict resolution. Policing Society 2010; 20: 99–123. DOI: 10.1080/10439460903377303.

[25] Twersky-Glasner A: Police personality: what is it and why are they like that? J Police Crim Psychol. 2005; 20: 56–67. DOI: 10.1007/bf02806707.

[26] Black J: Personality testing and police selection: utility of the 'big five'. NZ J Psychol. 2000; 29: 2–9. http://www.biomedsearch.com/article/Personality-Testing-Police-Selection-Utility/65643408.html.

[27] Detrick P, Chibnall J: Prediction of police officer performance with the Inwald Personality Inventory. J Police Crim Psychol. 2002; 17: 9–17. DOI: 10.1007/bf02807111.

[28] Lau B, Hem E, Berg A, Ekeberg O, Torgensen S: Personality types, coping and stress in the Norwegian police service. Personal Individ Differ. 2006; 41: 971–982. DOI: 10.1016/j.paid.2006.04.006.

[29] Detrick P, Chibnall J: NEO PI-R personality characteristics of high-performing entry level police officers. Psychol Serv. 2006; 3: 274–285. DOI: 10.1037/1541-1559.3.4.274.

[30] Vollrath M, Torgersen S, Alnæs R: Neuroticism, coping and change in MCMI-II clinical syndromes: test of a mediator model. Scand J Psychol. 1998; 39: 15–24. DOI: 10.1111/1467-9450.00051.

[31] Hancock P, Desmond P: Stress, workload, and fatigue. London: LEA; 2001.

[32] Folkman S: Personal control and stress and coping processes: a theoretical analysis. J Personal Soc Psychol. 1984; 46: 839–852. DOI: 10.1037/0022-3514.46.4.839.

[33] Folkman S, Lazarus R, Dunkel-Schetter C, DeLongis A, Gruen R: Dynamics of a stressful encounter: cognitive appraisal, coping and encounter outcomes. J Personality Social Psychol. 1986; 50: 992–1003. DOI: 10.1037/0022-3514.50.5.992.

[34] Hart P, Wearing A, Headey B. Police stress and well-being: integrating personality, coping and daily work experiences. J Occupat Organiz Psychol. 1995; 68: 133–156. DOI: 10.1111/j.2044-8325.1995.tb00578.x.

[35] Masel C, Terry D, Gribble M: The effects of coping on adjustment: Re-examining the goodness of fit model of coping effectiveness. Anxiety Stress Coping. 1996; 9: 279–300. DOI: 10.1080/10615809608249407.

[36] Anshel MH: A conceptual model and implications for coping with stressful events in police work. Crim Justice Behav. 2000; 27: 375–400. DOI: 10.1177/0093854800027003006.

[37] Grubb A, Brown S, Hall P: Personality traits and coping styles in UK police officers. Do negotiators differ from their non-negotiator colleagues? Psychol Crime Law. 2015; 21: 347–374. DOI: 10.1080/1068316X.2014.989165.

[38] Briere J, editor: Trauma Symptom Inventory professional manual. Lutz, FL: Psychological Assessment Resources; 1995.

[39] Gambetti E, Bensi L, Nori R, Giusberti F: The trauma symptom inventory: Italian validation of an instrument for the assessment of post-traumatic symptoms. Epidemiol Psychiatr Sci. 2011; 20: 345–355. DOI: http://dx.doi.org/10.1017/S204579601100031X.

[40] Maslach C, Jackson SE: The measurement of experienced burnout. J Occ Behav. 1981; 2: 99–113.

[41] Maslach C, Jackson SE, Leiter MP: Maslach burnout inventory manual (3rd edn.). Palo Alto, CA: Consulting Psychologists Press; 1996.

[42] Sirigatti S, Stefanile C, Menoni E. Per un adattamento italiano del Maslach Burnout Inventory (MBI). Bollettino di Psicologia Applicata. 1988; 187–188: 33–39.

[43] Caprara GV, Barbaranelli C, Borgogni L: Big Five Questionnaire. Firenze: O.S. Organizzazioni Speciali; 1993 (2nd ed. 2000).

[44] Caprara GV, Barbaranelli C, Livi S: Mapping personality dimensions into the Five Factor Model. Eur Rev Appl Psychol. 1994; 44: 9–15.

[45] Goldberg LR: The structure of phenotypic personality traits. Am Psychol. 1993; 48: 26–34.

[46] Endler NS, Parker DA: Coping Inventory for Stressful Situations (CISS): manual (2nd ed.). Toronto: Multi Health Systems; 1999.

[47] Sirigatti S, Stefanile C, Lera S: CISS: Coping Inventory for stressful situations. Firenze: Organizzazioni Speciali, OS; 2009.

[48] Pisanti R, Melchiori FM, Lombardo C, Sagliano T, Violani C, Lazzari L, Lazzari D: Validation of the Italian version of the coping inventory for stressful situations-short version among hospital-based nurses. Psychol Rep. 2015; 117: 457–472.

[49] Tedeschi RG, Calhoun LG: The Posttraumatic Growth Inventory: measuring the positive legacy of trauma. J Trauma Stress. 1996; 9: 455–471.

[50] Prati G, Pietrantoni L: Italian adaptation and confirmatory factor analysis of the full and the short form of the Posttraumatic Growth Inventory. J Loss Trauma. 2014; 19: 12–22. DOI: 10.1080/15325024.2012.734203.

[51] Pisanti R, Lombardo C, Lucidi F, Lazzari D: Psychometrics properties of the Maslach Burnout Inventory for human services among Italian nurses: a test of alternative models. JAN 2012; 69: 697–707. DOI: 10.1111/j.1365–2648.2012.06114.x

[52] Fisher RP, Geiselman RE: Memory enhancing techniques for investigative interviewing: the cognitive interview. Springfield, IL: Charles C. Thomas; 1992.

[53] Milne R, Bull R: Back to basics: a componential analysis of the original cognitive interview mnemonics with three age groups. Appl Cogn Psychol. 2002; 16: 1–11. DOI: 10.1002/acp.825.

[54] Robinson RC, Mitchell JT: Getting some balance back into the debriefing debate. Bull Austral Psychol Soc. 1995; 17: 5–10.

[55] Robinson RC, Mitchell JT: Evaluation of psychological debriefings. J Trauma Stress. 1993; 6: 367–382.

[56] Collwell LH, Lyons PM, Bruce AJ, Garner RL, Miller RS: Police officers' cognitive appraisals for traumatic events: implication for treatment and training. Appl Psychol Crim Justice. 2011; 7: 106–132.

[57] Compas BE, Malcarne VL, Fondacaro KM: Coping with stressful events in older children and young adolescents. J Consult Clin Psychol. 1988; 56: 405–411.

[58] Strutton D, Lumpkin JR: The relationship between optimism and coping styles of salespeople. J Pers Sell Sales Manag. 1993; 13: 71–81.

[59] Folkman S, Lazarus RS: An analysis of coping in a middle-aged community sample. J Health Soc Behav. 1980; 120: 219–239.

[60] Karasek R, Theorell T: Health work: stress, productivity and the reconstruction of life. New-York: Basic Books; 1990.

[61] Anshel MH, Kaissidis AN: Coping style and situational appraisals as predictors of coping strategies following events in sport as a function of gender and skill level. Brit J Psychol. 1997; 88: 263–276.

[62] Violanti JM, Marshall JR, Howe B: Stress, coping and alcohol use: the police connection. J Police Sci Adm. 1985; 2: 106–110.

[63] Ingledew D, Hardy L, Cooper C: Do resources bolster coping and does coping buffer stress? An organizational study with longitudinal aspect and control for negativity. J Occup Health Psychol. 1997; 2: 118–133. DOI: 10.1037/1076-8998.2.2.118.

[64] Ortega A, Brenner S-E, Leather P: Occupational stress, coping and personality in the police: an SEM study. Int J Police Sci Manag. 2007; 9: 36–50. DOI: 10.1350/ijps.2007.9.1.36.

[65] Marchand A, Nadeau C, Beaulieu-Prévost D, Boyer R, Martin M: Predictors of posttraumatic stress disorder among police officers: a prospective study. Psychol Trauma. 2015; 7: 212–221. DOI: 10.1037/a0038780.

[66] Le Scanff C, Taugis J: Stress management for police special forces. J Appl Soc Psychol. 2002; 14: 330–343. DOI: 10.1080/10413200290103590.

Chapter 8

Countertransference in Trauma Clinic: A Transitional Breach in the Therapists' Identity

Mayssa' El Husseini , Sara Skandrani ,
Layla Tarazi Sahab , Elizabetta Dozio and
Marie Rose Moro

Additional information is available at the end of the chapter

http://dx.doi.org/10.5772/64842

Abstract

In line with the theoretical elaboration of countertransference in the trauma clinic, this article addresses the therapist's relationship to the strangeness of the trauma, as well as his/her interaction with the cultural difference of the other, who is in this case, the traumatized patient. Thirty-one therapists were interviewed about their subjective experiences, using the methodology of interpretative phenomenological analysis. This article shows interesting subtleties in countertransference reactions to trauma narratives and sheds light on processes indicative of trauma transmission. Therapists interviewed could express experiencing moments of strangeness and inner disquiet; resonance in the defense mechanisms deployed by therapists and by patients at certain moments of the therapy; resorting to disregarding cultural interpretations/generalizations to make sense of an utterly painful situation and put a protective distance with the patients' culture of origin.

Keywords: countertransference, trauma, humanitarian context, transmission, transcultural psychology

1. Introduction

In line with the theoretical elaboration of countertransference in the trauma clinic, this article addresses the therapist's relationship to the strangeness of the trauma, as well as his/her interaction with the cultural difference of the other, who is in this case, the traumatized patient. Our objectives are to explore the mechanisms implicated in trauma transmission through countertransference reactions in therapists working with traumatized patients and to depict and analyze the processes that could potentially lead to vicarious traumatization.

1.1. Countertransference and trauma clinic

Countertransference is a concept originally coined by Freud [1], referring to the unconscious reactions of therapists to their patients' transference. The classical definition postulates that the implications of a therapist's unresolved childhood conflicts on their reactions require examination in order to be controlled [2].

A broader perspective on countertransference suggests a more totalistic definition [3] and includes the total emotional reactions of the therapist to the patient [4]. Such emotional reactions relate to a variety of factors, such as the therapist's life experiences, inherited internal unknown objects [5], personal psychoanalysis experiences, and theoretical affiliations [2] in interaction with the patient's transference. Therefore, countertransference reactions are bidirectional and refer to the inter-subjectivity of the psychotherapeutic dyad of patient and therapist [6].

In the totalistic perspective of the psychoanalytical theory regarding countertransference, the latter is an essential tool in helping the analyst better understand the patient. The analyst is expected to position himself/herself as a subject of observation and analysis, in order to acquire the required objectivity [4].

Additionally, Balint examines countertransference reactions in non-psychoanalytical situations, focusing on the presence of subjectivity in all therapists and its countertransference mobilization in all types of therapeutic relations [7]. From the same perspective, Devereux [8] broadens the concept of countertransference to include the social sciences and their impact on the findings of research conducted in this domain. Devereux [8] introduces the concept of cultural countertransference, which is related to the position the therapist adopts towards the otherness of the patient and to the latter's cultural codes and perceptions of illness. According to this perspective, cultural transference and countertransference are also influenced by history, politics and geography. Thus, any non-examination of cultural countertransference will compromise the therapeutic alliance and will enhance the risks of aggressive, affective, and racist acting-outs [8].

This aspect of countertransference seems to be of particular interest in the therapy of traumatized patients, although it has sparsely been investigated. Over the past two decades, many studies have investigated the impact of trauma work on therapists who work with trauma patients through the identification of emotional, cognitive, and physical countertransference reactions [9–14] and trauma transmission elements [15]. This accumulation of research has led to innovative concepts such as secondary traumatic stress and compassion fatigue [10], vicarious traumatization [11], and empathic strain [16].

http://dx.doi.org/10.5772/64842

2. Methods

The clinical material in our research was collected through interviews with ten therapists working with traumatized patients, in a humanitarian intervention context, within which the therapeutic encounter is mostly short and intense. The encounter can occur between an expatriate therapist and a patient, or between a foreign therapist and the patient's community of affiliation. The therapists were recruited through humanitarian institutions that provide psychological care programs in critical contexts (natural disasters, war zones) or within their development missions (malnutrition programs in precarious contexts). We have contacted the heads of psychological programs departments in the humanitarian institutions to explain the research. We have then sent an email explaining the research objectives, the interview procedure, and the possibility to withdraw their participation at any stage of the research. Therapists who were interested in participating to the research contacted us by email. All those contacted met the selection criteria as we had targeted NGO's providing programs in trauma clinic. We set an appointment for the interview that would take place at the researcher's office or the participant's office, at his/her convenience. In a later stage, the interview analyses were sent back to the participants to have their validation of the results.

Sex	Age	Nationality	Years of experience	Field of interventions	Countries of missions	Approach	Access to supervision
Five Men and five Women	Mean= 41.9 Standard deviation = 12,4 Range: 30–63 years old	Belgium; French; Iranian; Lebanese	Mean = 10.9 Standard deviation = 8 Range: 5–30 years	Six on Natural disaster (three earthquakes, three tsunami); seven on War zones (five civil war; one invasion; one war in a context of colonization)	Haiti; Indonesia; Lebanon; Occupied Territories of Palestine	Psychodynamic Psychoanalysis Integrative Relaxation Cognitive Behavioral	Eight referred to supervision experience but none had access to supervision on the time of the mission

Table 1. Participants' characteristics.

Our interviews lasted one and a half hours each, were recorded and transcribed, and then analyzed using the interpretative phenomenological analysis (IPA) methodology [17]. IPA provides a dynamic approach of the material and privileges a close access to the participants' experience of the studied phenomenon. The researchers' conceptions of the phenomenon are used to make sense of the participants' personal world through an interpretative activity. Participants' characteristics are described in **Table 1**.

The narratives of humanitarian workers are informative on two levels: (a) the countertransference reaction is one that occurs on-the-spot, in an unusual environment and within an unfamiliar framework for the therapist, and usually in a context wherein certain traumatic events have happened); (b) it allows the observation of a "disquieting strangeness" in the making, throughout the course of the therapeutic relationship, leading to creativity at some times, or to a deadlock in the therapeutic elaboration at other times, and consequently, resulting in a disrupt, or even in the loss of empathy [16, 18]. Finally, it is specifically interesting to see the evolvement of the therapist's narrative and changes in their positions throughout the whole interview.

The objective of our research was to approach the subjective experiences of therapists as closely as possible, through their own narratives. Each interview encompassed the therapist's theoretical background and training, the story of his/her personal traumatic experiences, the context of his/her work, and finally, the description of a specific situation he/she had with a patient. In the last part, the therapist reported the situation, his/her emotional, physical and cognitive reactions, in addition to his/her dreams, and the emergent scenarios towards the trauma narrative.

3. Results

Using the IPA, three themes emerged from the therapists' narratives about their countertransference: (a) personal therapy as a condition and theoretical views on neutrality; (b) attack of the therapists' thinking capacity triggering shame, guilt, and change in worldview; and (c) therapist's issues concerning patients' cultural difference. We will document in the following these three themes reporting when necessary excerpts from certain therapists verbatim. Each therapist is identified by the letter T. followed by a number.

3.1. Personal therapy as a condition and theoretical views on neutrality

The interviewed therapists highlighted the importance of personal analysis as a condition that promotes countenance capacity and elaboration of the countertransference reactions. For instance, T.10 considers that "*the essential part in therapeutic work in general, but especially with persons who have underwent traumatic experiences, is the personal analysis of the therapist. It is about being constantly vigilant and conscious about everything that is happening, of what we are experiencing with the patient, because the narratives are usually very heavy. A narrative loaded with death drive, aggressive drive, a lot of violence, a lot of themes about death and loss. I consider it to be a very dense narrative that the patient can throw in our face, and if we are not protected enough, it is not an obvious task to really treat the verbal expression, the patient's narrative and help him/her elaborate on his/her experience by himself/herself*".

Therapists head into the journey of trauma clinic with theoretical a priori deployed to anticipate more or less such encounters, mobilizing defense mechanisms that are eventually constructive and useful for their thinking and elaboration capacities. "Theoretically," or as some interviewees would say "ideally," the therapist should be in a neutral and welcoming listening position as T.10 explains: *"I believe that in my practice the following was essential: how to be able to dissociate my inner experience of the patient's narrative from his/her experience, in order to be neutral in my work, to have a benevolent listening as they say, to be interiorly available for the patient's account."* In response to the question about being affected by a certain situation reported by the patient, some painted a caricature of the affects that could overwhelm the therapist, such as T.9 who says: *"to be affected and say: oh my god, and start crying with the patient? No, no. I don't believe this is what the patient came to look for, or that it could be of any help. So if it is a demonstration, then no. To let yourself get affected by all cases isn't of any help"*; others imagine a pragmatic schema to protect themselves, such as T.1 *"well, I believe that if you are already well protected, it won't affect you. You come, you already have your barriers and so you have your stuff with you that are solid enough. You are able to separate things, have empathy with the patient, help her, and then clean yourself up afterwards, and you are fine."*

In the same interview for instance, we can notice the gap between the theoretical stance and the lived experience. On that note, T.10 says: *"well yes, during that moment, the limit wasn't clear anymore. For a while, maybe for a minute, I was myself absorbed by what she was saying. It was as if I was in the scene, I was looking at the scene from an outside perspective. And really, there was a feeling of revolt, a feeling of rage. She was sad and I was revolted."* We can also observe this feeling of being within the scene of the traumatic event in T.1's narrative, who, while recounting his experience of the patient's traumatic event narrative, says: *"I saw all the scene happening, I saw all of that, I was there."*

3.2. Attack of the therapists' thinking capacity triggering shame, guilt, and change in worldview

T.1 describes his experience while listening to the trauma narrative of his patient *"in this situation, feelings were all confused. There were my feelings, actually the feelings the patient would give me, and then the feelings that a therapist is not supposed to have: injustice, the need to stop the therapy, disgust, the need to vomit, things like that, well, a therapist is not supposed to feel this, but at that moment, I had them."* He repeats twice that a therapist is not supposed to experience such feelings, thus, leading us to the issues of shame within the community of peers and guilt regarding what the professional superego imposes. He continues *"my stomach was knotted with the need to vomit, I felt disgusted, I was horrified and all. I believe that this is all the countertransference of the other, and the need for injustice."* Herein, we witness an obvious disorganization of the narrative that exposes two Freudian slips: the "countertransference of the other" and the "need for injustice."

The theme of shame recurs in another sequence—in the frame of a post-trauma therapy group interview: a young therapist had of her patient, the image of a Minotaur, a devouring monster. She contemplates the emergence of this image as follows: *"I had a feeling of shame, of disgust by myself, to have had such a feeling that I am not supposed to have. I was a trainee in a learning position, confronted by something that was very disturbing; I know somehow, from what I have learned during my studies, that what I feel towards the patient is good, in the sense of a countertransference reaction that is generally useful working with the patient. But the intensity to that extent was disrupting. In a supervision group, I would express this experience in a more intellectualized way, in terms of dehumanization. I wouldn't have been able to express it as is. I am dealing with an image of an aggressor, to whom I am supposed to be welcoming. I see the patient as an aggressor, like the Minotaur who is aggressive, it devours."* The therapist here is deeply disturbed by her discovery of certain cruel sensations in herself towards this patient and by being prompted into an archaic fantasy of devouring. T.1 had also referred to "something archaic" that was awaken in him in the situation he reported.

In this sense, T.9 says: *"On the long term, it is inscribed in us (…). Thus, it is repetitive, and indeed, we are much more sensitive to what happens in the world around us."* This heightened sensitivity is also reported by T.8 who describes a sense of a widening gap with others once she is back from her mission, she says: *"for example, I go to a movie that takes place in a shantytown. The movie contains lots of scenes happening in the shanty town where I had worked, of which I was an indirect witness with the children. And in the movie, it is so distant from the reality of the spectators, and I had this feeling that people around me were not in the reality. They could almost laugh or… well I had cried as if … I was crying out of shock. (…) It was terrible because the shanty town, at some point, is put on fire, and the shanty town where I was, had been put on fire by the authorities in order to empty the terrain (…) and there were children and families who died there (…). For me, it was serious; it is something that happens in real life. So, not only was there a whole gap between me and the people in the audience, but really I felt almost traumatized."* As shown in these illustrations, therapists report a change in their worldview once they return to their home country in the aftermath of a humanitarian mission.

3.3. Therapist issues concerning patients' cultural difference

In contexts of expatriation and inter-community differences, therapists tend to highlight the cultural differences as a difficulty or sometimes as an impediment to the therapy with the patient. In this sense, T.8 explains " *I am always afraid that they (the target population) see me as a traditional therapist or a priest or something. In my dream, I had that role in the ceremony."* This account clearly reveals a fear of self-loss, of depersonalization.

T.9 recounts a situation wherein she was confronted by a mother who—as T.9 puts it—*"preferred to let her child die"* of malnutrition. T.9 found herself incapable of helping the mother, or of providing her with therapy: *"when it is about a mother who is really 'closed,' I don't understand the culture she lives in, I don't know enough to understand this mother, what motivates this mother to do so. I don't know how to help her get out of this circle. Therefore, I passed it over."* T.9 refers to culture without grounding her account in any etiological theory or cultural genealogy. Moreover, she says: *"well, I mean, I can understand that for some mothers who have five or six children, and who live in economic situations, in some countries where they cannot find ways to nurture their children, the only way would be indeed to have one child who suffers malnutrition, as a way to benefit from food program's help for this child, and then share the food with the others, while letting this one die, because in all cases he is already malnourished, and thus 'uninteresting.' So, in a way, in such situations, mothers can be violent with these children. Well, I understand her functioning modality. I understand why she is like this. Nevertheless, what I can't always do is to find a way to make her understand that this is a child, this is a life. Wouldn't there be other means? Can't we together find other means to help feed the others without letting this child die?"* So for T.9, this mother had been forced to pick and choose between her children, as she was unable to feed them all. This functioning would be grounded in "cultural thing." To another question in the interview, the same therapist responds: *"well... actually, in general, whether it is within a humanitarian action or not, we arrive with a mandate and a specific project. Therefore we cannot accept all of the patients who had been traumatized, not when they do not fit our program. Therefore yes, there are persons that we do not accept in the program. And there are persons whom we accept, because, well, we know it entails other implications."* This statement highlights another cultural specificity that regards the non-governmental organization's culture of implementing programs.

4. Discussion

Our research's results draw attention to some of the established theoretical concepts that therapists acquire through their trainings and hold in their background while working in trauma clinic. Representation of neutrality in psychotherapeutic work refers to the first Freudian conceptualization of countertransference (1910) whereby he urges the analyst to have an attitude analogous to that of a surgeon [1]. Neutrality is to be understood here in the sense of the imperturbable, as Donnet highlighted in his article "Neutrality and the gap subject-function" [19]. Nevertheless, while exploring the therapists' elaborations on specific clinical situations, theoretical stances seem to fade in favor of the clinical experiences as experienced hands on. Therefore, we can note particularly intense countertransference reactions that seem to disrupt the therapist in his/her theoretical assets, consequently unsettling his/her professional identity.

The dread produced by the trauma entails a threat of self-annihilation, hence, mobilizing defense mechanisms that are immediately operated by the person. These defenses—actualized in narratives of traumatic experiences—induce a major part of countertransference reactions. In this sense, actualized defense mechanisms deployed by the patient during the session underpin the countertransference reactions of the therapist, a sort of countertransference that is specific to the encounter with trauma.

The fascinating encounter with the unthinkable of the trauma conveys traumatic substance through infra-verbal channels. This substance is deposited into the therapist's psychological system. Yet, as Bion [20] elaborated, this psyche is the means to transform the beta elements (raw, unthinkable, unlinked sensations) into alpha elements (representable, metabolizable elements). What happens then, within the therapist's psyche, when these unidentified sensations are deposited into him/her through projective identification mechanism, making him/her share the unedited transgressive experience? We witness then an attack of the thinking capacity of the therapist. For instance, the slips highlighted in the results seem to underline a strong resonance with two mechanisms deployed by the patient: one, dissociation, through the therapist's concordant identification with the patient's self; and two, an identification with the aggressor, in an attempt to escape the helpless state of the patient, through mobilizing complementary identification, in the sense that the therapist identified with the object-aggressor incorporated by the patient.

On one hand, trauma seems to revive the "unshaped substance" of an era associated with cruelty, which itself could be the origin of the feelings of shame, and the threat of unsubscribing from the peers community. On the other hand, archaic resurrections of cruelty are hardly bearable by the therapists, at least in the first phase. Such archaic resurrections seem to obstruct the thinking and elaboration capacities of the therapists, even within the framework of supervision, which is supposed to act as a holding and transforming space for these feelings.

As Heimann stated in [21], such elaboration spaces are supposed to render the analyst capable of containing feelings within him/her, instead of simply expelling them as the patient would do, in order to subordinate these feelings to analysis, whereby the therapist functions as a mirror reflection for the patient.

Nevertheless, it would be misleading to believe that the countertransference analysis grants the analyst the possibility to control his/her inner reactions, as Freud urges [1]. Margaret Little [22, 23] formulates the concept of countertransference analysis as an insufficient remedy with inevitable remains unconscious infantile countertransference.

Some of the interviewed therapists, described timidly and with a surprised tone, the resurrection of what they qualified as "archaic," despite the long personal analysis and regular supervision that they have engaged in. It is significant to note here that the supervision space is not always experienced as a room for free and spontaneous expression, but rather, as a space wherein the therapist is required to intellectualize his/her countertransference experiences. This brings to mind what Heimann [21] highlighted regarding the difficulties that analysts face to admit their errors and discuss the issue "we all have our private cemetery, but not all graves have tombstones."

Another aspect of countertransference which emerges in the interviews, is that related to cultural issues. In line with Devereux [8] and Nathan's theories [24], Moro [25] specifies that the cultural countertransference emanates from the inner stance of the therapist and influences this very stance regarding the patient's otherness. The stance is underpinned with the therapist's personal history, as well as the collective, political, geographic, and socioeconomic history. In contexts of expatriation, therapists sometimes describe a phase of loss of cultural references and know-how, and find themselves confronted by a double-layered otherness: the first being the trauma, and the other being cultural otherness. The difficulty facing trauma sometimes resorts in disregarding cultural interpretations and making generalizations to make sense of an utterly painful situation and put a protective distance with the patients' culture of origin. At first level interpretation, the cultural dimension seems to have obstructed the possibility of engaging in therapy: The therapist was confronted by a dead-end that of cultural difference. However, what we observe here is a displacement of the products of traumatic reality lived by the therapist, for instance the unbearable guilt and violence, and relocating them to the "stagnant" and "unchangeable" host culture itself, in a defensive move that consequently maintains security for the therapist, by masking social injustices and deferring the dread for reality until a further notice. The violent socioeconomic reality—which is probably a source of guilt for non-governmental organization staff (who live in relatively comfortable conditions in comparison to the context's reality)—is conflated with the violence of cultural otherness, and probably with the violence of the trauma problematic. Clearly, in humanitarian contexts, expats often find themselves obliged to "pick and choose" the patients they accept in their programs. They too, engage in prioritizing needs/demands, and thus, operate on basis of selectivity. What we observe here is a displacement mechanism: the therapist, deployed in a foreign culture, is confronted by a traumatic encounter with traumatized patients, from a target population that is enduring severe socioeconomic precariousness. Defensively, the therapist assigns to the host culture, the unbearable guilt of having to select and to prioritize. Thus, the culture becomes the platform within which this violence is contained and made sense of. The transgressive aspects of the trauma narratives are the most implicated in the disqualification of the patients' culture of origin. The transitory disruptions in the therapists' beliefs highlight the particularly intense mobilization of countertransference reactions to trauma. Exploring the disorganization in each therapist's narrative structure reflects the style of that therapist's defense mechanisms implicated in countertransference.

This double-layered otherness, trauma and cultural difference, questions the therapist's identity, both, the professional and the human, hence, disrupting their working capacity at certain times.

5. Conclusion

To conclude, we would like to refer to Françoise Davoine [26]: "the trauma asks the analyst: who are you?" Trauma calls into question the very identity of the therapist, disturbing his/her narcissistic assets by evoking questions that concern his/her affiliation to the human community.

This study reflects subtleties in countertransference reactions to trauma narratives and sheds light on processes indicative of trauma transmission. It also provides corroborative evidence to previous study findings in the field of countertransference to trauma work. The findings underline the presence of trauma transmission and depict some of the channels through which it is conveyed within countertransference reactions. However, this transmission is not static and does not necessarily obstruct the therapeutic alliance, insofar as the examination of countertransference reactions helps transform trauma transmission elements into means to better understand the therapeutic process.

Moreover, as seen in some therapists' narratives, the angst triggered by the cultural difference complicates the transforming function of the countertransference. What would be the impending future of the trauma residues deposited in the therapist's psyche? Our results have shown different paths for investigation. Themes of shame and guilt have emerged in therapists' narratives seemingly arising from the transgressive encounter with the not-to-be-seen aspects of the trauma, and hence, entailing counterattitudes and reactions that can be hardly shared with peers. Furthermore, the inscription of un-representable elements of trauma on the therapist's body that can be observed through somatic symptoms experienced by our participants–therapists while working with their patients on the trauma narrative

Author details

Mayssa' El Husseini[1*], Sara Skandrani[2], Layla Tarazi Sahab[3], Elizabetta Dozio[4] and Marie Rose Moro[5]

*Address all correspondence to: mayssa.husseini@gmail.com

1 Maison de Solenn Cochin Hospital, CESP, Descartes-Sorbonne University Paris cité, Paris, France

2 Maison de Solenn Cochin Hospital, Nanterre University, Paris, France

3 Saint Joseph University, Beirut, Lebanon

4 PCPP, Descartes-Sorbonne University Paris cité, Paris, France

5 Maison de Solenn Cochin Hospital, Descartes-Sorbonne University Paris cité, Paris, France

References

[1] FREUD S. (1910). Perspectives d'avenir de la thérapie psychanalytique. In: La technique psychanalytique. trad. fr. A. Berman ed. Paris: PUF; 1953. p. OCF.P, X, 1993; GW, VIII.

[2] MARTIN CABREL J. (2000). La contribution de Ferenczi à la notion du contre transfert. Filigrane; printemps: pp. 7–18.

[3] KERNBERG O. (1965). Notes on countertransference. Journal of the American Psychoanalytic Association. 13. 38–56.

[4] RACKER H. (1957). A contribution to the problem of countertransference. Psychoanalytic Quarterly. 34. 313–324.

[5] DE URTUBEY L. (2006). *Des origines du contre-transfert*. Revue Française de Psychanalyse. LXX. 2. pp. 371–384.

[6] SHUBS C.H. (2008). Countertransference issues in the assessment and treatment of trauma recovery with victims of violent crime. Psychoanalytic Psychology. 25. 156–180.

[7] BALINT A., BALINT M. (1939). On transference and countertransference. International Journal of Psychoanalysis. 20. 223–230.

http://dx.doi.org/10.5772/64842

[8] DEVEREUX G. (1967). From Anxiety to Method in the Behavioral Sciences.Paris: Flammarion. 1980.

[9] DANIELI Y. (1980). Countertransference in the treatment and study of Nazi Holocaust survivors and their children. Victimology: An International Journal. 5. 355–367.

[10] FIGLEY C.R. (1995). Compassion fatigue as secondary traumatic stress disorder: an overview. In C.R. FIGLEY (Ed.).*Compassion Fatigue: Coping with Secondary Stress Disorder in Those who Treat the Traumatized.* New York, NY: Brunner/Mazel. pp. 1–20.

[11] MCCANN I.L. & PEARLMAN L.A. (1990).Vicarious traumatization: a framework for understanding the psychological effects of working with victims. Journal of Traumatic Stress. 3. 131–149.

[12] PEARLMAN L.A. & MACIAN P.S. (1995). Vicarious traumatization: an empirical study of the effects of trauma work on trauma therapists. *Professional Psychology: Research and Practice*. 26. 558–563.

[13] DALENBERG C.J. (2000). Countertransference and the Treatment of Trauma. Washington: American Psychological Association.

[14] SABIN-FARELL R.& TURPIN G. (2003). Vicarious traumatization: implications for the mental health of health workers. *Clinical Psychology Review*. 23. 449–480.

[15] OUSS-RYNGAERT L. (2006). *Transmissions des traumatismes psychiques de la mère au bébé*. In BAUBET T., LACHAL C., OUSS-RYNGAERT L. & MORO M.R. *Bébés et Traumas*. pp. 99–134. Collection Trauma/La Pensée Sauvage éd.

[16] WILSON J.P. LINDY J.D. RAPHAEL B. Empathic strain and therapist defense: type I and II CTRs. In: Countertransference in the Treatment of PTSD. New York, NY: The Guilford Press; 1994. pp. 31–61.

[17] SMITH J.A. FLOWERS P. LARKIN M. Interpretative Phenomenological Analysis, Theory, Method and Research. SAGE ed. London: SAGE; 2009.

[18] WILSON J.P. LINDY J.D. Empathic strain and countertransference. In: Countertransference in the Treatment of PTSD. New York, NY: The Guilford Press ed. 1994. pp. 5–30.

[19] DONNET J.L.(2007) "la neutralité et l'écart sujet-fonction" in Revue Française de psychanalyse, Paris, PUF 2007/3

[20] BION WR. (1962). *Aux sources de l'expérience* — 2nde édition. Paris: PUF. 1991.

[21] HEIMANN P. (1950). A propos du contre-transfert. Le contre-transfert. Paris. Navarin. 1987.

[22] LITTLE M (1951) Countertransference and the patient's response to it. IJP 32, 1951, 32–40.

[23] LITTLE M (1981) Transference Neurosis and Transference Psychosis. Toward Basic Unity. New York u.a. traduit en 1991 Des états-limites: l'alliance thérapeutique.

[24] NATHAN T (1977). Sexualité idéologique et névroses. Essai de clinique ethnopsychanalytique. Grenoble. La Pensée sauvage.

[25] MORO M.R. (1991). Essai d'analyse des propositions thérapeutiques spécifiques en entretien ethnopsychiatrique mère-enfant, Psychologie Française, 36–4, 307–322.

[26] DAVOINE F (2014) Intervention à la journée de l'URFT de Saint-Denis; Quels traitements pour l'effraction traumatique? Le traumatisme dans tous ses éclats.

Chapter 9

"*Growing from an Invisible Wound*" A Humanistic-Existential Approach to PTSD

Mélanie Vachon , Prudence C. Bessette and
Christine Goyette

Additional information is available at the end of the chapter

http://dx.doi.org/10.5772/64290

Abstract

From a humanistic and existential perspective, posttraumatic stress disorder (PTSD) can be understood as a normal response to a threatening existential event. The humanistic-existential approach to understanding and treating PTSD also places particular emphasis on the meaning of the traumatic experience and on the awareness of the existential part of the self. Such an understanding conveys to a different approach to trauma assessment and potential for healing in the clinical encounter. In this chapter, we wish to provide a humanistic-existential understanding of trauma. To do so, we review the key humanistic-existential concepts for trauma conceptualization, assessment, and intervention. Afterwards, we present two different short case studies to illustrate and understand the humanistic-existential psychotherapeutic process and its diversity. In conclusion, we discuss the contribution and limits of a humanistic-existential approach to trauma conceptualization, assessment, and healing.

Keywords: humanistic-existential approach, meaning, posttraumatic growth, post-traumatic stress disorder

1. Introduction

From a humanistic-existential perspective, posttraumatic stress disorder (PTSD) can be understood as a *"normal response"* to a threatening existential experience. Such an experience may disturb our sense of inhabiting the world in a safe, coherent, and meaningful manner. As Greening [1] puts it: *"when we experience trauma, our relationship with existence itself is shattered."*

The term "*Trauma*," from the Ancient Greek "*trauma*," refers to the notion of "*wound*" or "*damage*." In that sense, PTSD may refer to the wound left by an experience that disrupted the person's previous relationship to self, to others, and to the world. Trauma survivors are often said to live with an "*invisible wound*" in a state of relative chaos that may be left unnoticed. The only concrete manifestations of such internal suffering may narrowly be reduced to a visible configuration of symptoms.

As a matter of fact, mainstream approaches to "*assessing*" and "*treating*" PTSD are repeatedly criticized for their propensity to solely focus on the visible aspects of trauma: symptoms [1, 11, 12]. Therefore, the humanistic-existential perspective may be understood as a complement to the pathology-focused model, which may mainly aim at improving symptom management. The humanistic-existential approach to PTSD may not focus primarily on symptom, or even on the traumatic event itself. It may rather emphasize the exploration of the lived experience of the individual and, most importantly, of its existential meaning.

In this chapter, we aim to discuss how PTSD may be conceptualized, recognized, and healed from a humanistic-existential perspective. To do so, we will review the basic foundations of the humanistic-existential approach. We will explore its unique understanding of human being and his potential for growth and healing. We will also suggest how the humanistic-existential approach can offer a different outlook on trauma comprehension and healing through the introduction of two different case studies. Finally, we will discuss the limits and contributions of the humanistic-existential approach and its implications for the therapist's stance.

2. Humanistic-existential approach: introduction and foundations

2.1. History and premises

Known as the "*third force*" in psychology, the humanistic-existential approach was founded in the 1940s in the United States. This movement was created as a distinct complement to the dominating behavioral and psychoanalytic traditions. Inspired by the existential and phenomenological philosophies, the founders of humanistic-existential psychology believed that the subjective experience is the starting point from which all comprehension may emerge [2–4]. A few authors are commonly associated to the humanistic-existential movement, notably Maslow, Rogers, Bugental, Frankl, May, and Yalom.

With such a focus on subjectivity, humanistic-existential psychologists rely on phenomenology to explore and understand the meaning of different human experiences. Phenomenology may be described as the investigation of the "*lived experience*," as opposed to the study of an objective reality. Phenomenology, both as a clinical stance and as a research method, involves bracketing all assumptions about the world (and about the other) to illuminate the essence and the meaning of an experience. Phenomenologists aspire to get as close as possible to "*what it is like*" to be the other person, and to "*what it is like*" to experience the world as he or she does. Thus, humanistic-existential psychology is essentially concerned with the way a patient

http://dx.doi.org/10.5772/64290

experiences his symptoms or illness, as opposed to the actual presence (or absence) of symptoms or diagnosis.

In the 1960s, the founders of the humanistic-existential movement defined their approach by five premises, articulated by Bugental [5]. First, *human beings, as humans, supersede the sum of their parts. They cannot be reduced to components, symptoms, or behaviors*. This premise calls for a holistic comprehension of the human experience. It also calls for the necessity to explore an individual's experience beyond symptoms and behaviors. It aspires to honor and comprehend the uniqueness of each individual, and the unique meaning of one's lived experience.

The second premise states that *human beings have their existence in a uniquely human context*. As a result, the individual experience must be approached and comprehended in the light of its unique contextual reality. Humanistic-existential psychology is concerned with *being*, seen as an expression and influence of societal, cultural, and individual reflections that capture the most personal of experiences [6]. This assumption may remind us that the psychotherapist also develops his subjective comprehension of the reality from his own context.

Third, from a humanistic-existential perspective, it is presumed that *human beings are aware and aware of being aware*. Awareness and consciousness of awareness are major distinctive traits of human beings. Most importantly, it is believed that human potential for growth and healing is possible through the process of increasing awareness of one's experience of self, of others, and of the world. Greater awareness may allow the possibility to make choices and to exert one's existential freedom. As Frankl [7] puts it, humans carry the freedom and the ability to find meaning as long as they are conscious.

Fourth, *human beings also have the ability to make choices and therefore have responsibility*. Awareness and freedom inevitably come with the responsibility to act according to our will and values. It also accounts for recognizing one's responsibility—as opposed to biological or environmental determinism. Existential responsibility is believed to be one of the fundamental challenges of human existence, along with finiteness, isolation, and absurdity [8]. Human being cannot avoid confrontation to the absurdity of the modern world and—to some extent—to the absurdity of the human condition itself. Existential responsibility calls for the recognition of the inherent limitations and possibilities of our human condition. Most importantly, humans have the responsibility to search and create meaning out of life's journey. For Frankl, man's ultimate freedom and responsibility refers to his capacity to choose the attitude toward different life situations. Since death, loss, and suffering are intrinsically a part of what it means to fully experience life, the ultimate freedom and responsibility is to create meaning out of suffering [9].

Consequently, from a humanistic-existential perspective, *human beings are believed to be intentional, to aim at goals, to be aware that they cause future events, and to seek meaning, value, and creativity*. For instance, Frankl believed that (1) human beings carry the ability to find meaning as long as they are conscious; (2) they have a basic will to find such meaning; and (3) they carry within themselves the knowledge that life has meaning.

In summary, humanistic-existential psychology reintroduces the subjective experience as the first instance of the human existence. It relies on phenomenology and emphasizes the importance of the *"here and now"* knowing that the only moment we directly experience is *"right now"*—as we become aware of ourselves in the world. The humanistic-existential psychologist is concerned with the human experience as a whole, and recognizes the meaning and value of nonhedonist emotions and experiences, such as suffering, conflict, grief, guilt, and death. Inevitable loss, mortality, and absurdity are part of the human condition and are recognized as existential universal realities that all beings have to face and adjust to with their unique, creative, yet complex manner [8]. Those existential challenges and the suffering that comes with it are normal, but are also worthy and may be transforming. As such, suffering may open an opportunity for change and for potential healing and growing. Humanistic-existential psychotherapists have genuine interest and curiosity for every individual potential for growing and healing.

2.2. Human potential for growing and healing

The etymology of the term *"healing"* refers to *"wholeness"* or being *"whole."* From the humanistic-existential point of view, psychotherapy may signify *"to make more whole."* Wholeness may therefore be understood as a sense of completeness, integrity, and coherence. It may as well mean to exist more fully as a human being, including with the condition of being mortal. For May [10], health and healing means *"to experience more fully, deeply, consciously, and authentically one's existence."* The psychotherapy process consequently involves the exploration of barriers people may have, preventing them from experiencing and expressing their freedom in choices and will [11, 12]. Healing may as well be understood as a process that leads to a deeper and fuller engagement with the self, with others, and with the world. As Jager [13] puts it, *"being human means standing in a relationship to others, to things, and to the world."* Healing may therefore occur in a relationship that allows the narration and reflection of one's subjective experience. The other's presence can be understood as a key allowing us to become more aware of ourselves, of the other, and of the world [14].

2.3. Healing together: the humanistic-existential encounter

It is within the clinical encounter that the process of healing can occur. The psychotherapeutic relationship involves the validation and value of the individual's unique way of being. It also implies the recognition of the singular contribution of the therapist's subjectivity. Hence, the psychotherapeutic encounter can be understood as a process of shared discovery in which the meaning of the patient's lived experience is explored, understood, and eventually transformed. Repeated events of *"meaning"* and of mutual comprehension of the patient's lived experience may allow a deeper awareness and more freedom of choice and will. New freedom, allowed and supported by the therapeutic relationship, opens up the possibility to seek and cocreate new meanings. The psychotherapist is therefore involved in articulating, comprehending, validating, and contributing to the patient's search of meaning [15].

The humanistic-existential therapeutic encounter, as a unique and intersubjective space of cocreation, aims at supporting, promoting, or restoring the individual's fundamental sense of self-cohesion [16]. As Quintin [15] puts it, psychological suffering is not something that can be fixed with expertise, opinions, or advices. The humanistic-existential stance rather refers to a process of discovery of new meanings to replace one's old assumptions about the world that are no longer true. Previous meanings, as relic of the past, may obstruct the patient's sense of inhabiting the world in a free and meaningful way in his current life's situation. Old meanings cease to be coherent with the patient's actual experience of the world. Disruption of meaning or "*shattered assumptions*" [17] is at the core of the humanistic-existential comprehension of trauma.

3. Trauma: a humanistic-existential perspective

3.1. Trauma: taking a different path

In this section, we will explore how the humanistic-existential approach may shed a different light on the trauma experience and healing process. To do so, we will see how the humanistic-existential perspective can complement the bio-medical model, as both stem from distinct epistemological roots. Hence, we will review the common definitions of PTSD and will introduce the notions of subjectivity and meaning in trauma comprehension, recognition, and healing.

The humanistic-existential approach is concerned with how the individual experiment himself in the world. Therefore, it relies on the subjective experience and on its idiographic meaning as the starting point of comprehension and healing. From its Greek origin "*idios,*" idiographic notably means "*applying to the individual.*" Thus, idiographic exploration focuses on understanding the individual as a unique, holistic, and complex entity. It depends on detailed and descriptive explorations such as biography and case study to develop in-depth and intimate comprehension of the unique individual experience. Idiographic understandings are often contrasted with "*nomothetic*" research or assessment that primarily focuses on uncovering general patterns of behavior having a normative basis. For instance, nomothetic research on PTSD may want to develop an objective description of its symptomatology and to identify its risk factors and predictors of recovery. Such knowledge would apply to people generally as patterns, statements, or laws [18].

Another epistemological distinction may be necessary to understand how the humanistic-existential approach can complement the dominant psychopathology-centered model. Within the biomedical approach, PTSD is considered as a disorder, with universal characteristic features known as "*symptoms.*" It is understood as an entity that exists "*objectively*" as long as its diagnosis criteria are met, despite contexts, nations, or culture. For instance, we may state that *Hannah*—who is a Holocaust survivor—and *Gloria*—who recently witnessed a major car accident—both suffer from PTSD, as they present with similar symptoms such as nightmares, avoidance, flashbacks, difficulty to concentrate, and mood alteration. Such a statement would refer to an "*etic*" approach to PTSD that is not specific to particular contexts, cultures, or nations. On the other hand, an *emic* perspective may try to develop a singular yet complex comprehension of Hannah's and Gloria's lived experiences of trauma. It would deeply explore their subjective world and the different meaning of their experience. It would inquire: "*How is it like to experience trauma for Hannah*"? "*How is it like for Gloria*"?

Based on its basic premises, the humanistic-existential perspective would necessarily approach trauma with an emic-idiographic perspective, as opposed to the etic-nomothetic stance. It may try to look beyond symptom and diagnosis to approach the unique meaning that trauma takes for a specific individual at this particular moment in his life.

3.2. Beyond symptoms: the invisible wound

Commonly accepted descriptions of PTSD involve exposure to a traumatic event that meets specific stipulations and symptoms [19]. The Diagnostic and Statistical Manual of Mental Disorder (DSM-5) currently identifies the trigger to PTSD as exposure to actual or threatened death, serious injury, or sexual violation. Different categories of symptoms characterize PTSD symptoms from each of four symptom clusters: intrusion, avoidance, negative alterations in cognitions and mood, and alterations in arousal and reactivity (p. 271).

By the nature of its definition, DSM-5 identifies a traumatic event as a trigger to the disorder. The resulting disorder may be understood as the indicator of an invisible wound left by the traumatic event. Therefore, the traumatic event is not the pathology, but rather the event that disrupted someone's existence, by revealing major existential threats: finiteness, disintegration, and assaults to integrity and dignity of the self and/or of a fellow human being. As Greening [1] evokes:

> *"What happens when we are traumatized? In addition to the physical, neurological and emotional trauma, we experience a fundamental assault on our right to live, on our personal sense of worth, and further, on our sense that the world (including people) basically supports human life. Our relationship with existence itself is shattered. Existence in this sense includes all the meaning structures that tell us we are a valued and viable part of the fabric of life."*

Greening captures the essence of the lived experience of trauma, and points out the deep disruption of existential meaning that it reveals. Surviving trauma is like waking up in a world that does not make sense anymore. In his book *"Shattered Assumptions,"* Janoff-Bulman [17] argues how trauma devastates our experience and understanding of the world we live in. Healthy human development throughout childhood is indeed facilitated by a perception of the world as being safe, benevolent, and meaningful, and the self as worthy. However, such beliefs could also contribute to the development of an *"illusion of invulnerability"* or, in existential terms, of avoidance of the part of absurdity of the human condition. Trauma reveals something about existence that cannot be integrated in a coherent and meaningful understanding of the self and the world. Symptoms are often seen as the biological, the psychological, and the existential self who is trying to adjust and integrate the meaning of what happened and, most importantly, the meaning of one's existence given a new existential reality.

As such, trauma survivors cannot heal from trauma unless they are supported as whole beings [6], including their existential self. Striving for health, wholeness, and meaning may be facilitated by the humanistic-existential encounter. This psychotherapeutic process first involves the exploration of the lived experience of trauma, of its meaning, and of past existential assumptions that have been shattered. It also involves building and cultivating new awareness of what is still meaningful for an individual. Increasing existential awareness allows the exploration of new, different, and meaningful ways to connect to self, to others, and to the world. As such, it evokes not only healing, but also existential growing.

Humanistic and existential psychology has the premise that the human being has an inner tendency and potential for healing, but also for growing [5]. Hence, we can ask how people grow from trauma. Tedeschi and Calhoun [20] coined the term *posttraumatic growth* to capture the positive psychological changes they had witnessed as clinical psychologists among their patients who were coming to terms with highly stressful and challenging life events. "*Posttraumatic growth*" refers to the transformative process that can lead to positive changes after trauma. It has been a fertile notion to capture the transformation that may occur from gaining more existential awareness, and how it can transform one's relationship to self, to others, and to the world.

Of course, as trauma itself, posttraumatic growth is complex [21]. Its relationship with the trauma itself may be multifaceted. Here, we do not aim at reviewing the concept exhaustively, but explore the type of transformations that may be experienced by individuals who experience trauma. Our synthesis of diverse writings reveals indeed that there are new ways of relating and connecting to self, to others, and the world. Well-known transformation resulting from trauma reported by patients include: "*changes in the self*" or in the "*relationship to the self.*" Such changes may take the form of an increased perception of personal strength, maturity, and spirituality [22]. An increased sense of personal worth and acceptance of one's vulnerability, sensibility, and humanity have also been reported by trauma survivors.

Such personal transformation with the relationship to self may also be mirrored in the experience of relating to others. Patients who survived trauma and healed from it are often moved by the compassion, sensibility, and care of others; feeling better connected to the people surrounding them, and experiencing more deeply or more consciously the preciousness of existing bonds.

Greater awareness and gratitude spread out and contribute to "*a greater appreciation for life*" in general [20, 23]. In fact, in a study examining the role of gratitude in PTSD in a sample of Vietnam War veterans, it is suggested that the experience of gratitude may be integral to this process of healing from trauma. For survivors, more gratitude may mean more pleasure in the small things in life, identification of new possibilities for one's life [22]. Enhanced appreciation of life itself has also been reported. For many, trauma was a trigger to reflect on life's meaning and absurdity. Despite distress, getting more awareness to the suffering aspects of life may also mean more awareness of its humanity and beauty. Existential awareness may allow clarity of life priorities, and more freedom to see "*new opportunities.*" In short, for some people, healing and growing from trauma transformed their experience of the world itself.

3.3. Growing from adversity

A recent review of posttraumatic growth among individuals who had suffered severe physical injuries particularly caught our attention to understand the essential meaning of posttraumatic growth. Based on the meta-synthesis of qualitative research conducted with physically injured trauma survivors, Kampman et al. [24] tried to capture the meaning of such an experience. The analysis highlights essential themes to describe the significance posttraumatic growth may take for physically impaired individuals following trauma.

First, the analysis suggests that the trauma experience forced individuals to question the very basis of their existence. It deeply moved them from their essential core. The findings of Kampman et al. highlight how traumatic injury may trigger existential awareness and force individuals to deeply reflect on the meaning and purpose of their lives. Posttraumatic growth also involves the contemplation and acknowledgment of the unchanged aspects of life, as well as the recognition of the changed aspects of life that are positive. Such an increase in existential awareness may lead to greater sense of meaning and purpose in life. Kampman et al. also noted in individuals a new awareness for physiological and psychological potential despite limitations, and gratitude for the fulfilling meaningful aspects of life that remain unchanged and that can still be part of life (e.g., physical activity, arts, travel). In other terms, it allowed people to experiment their world more fully and more consciously.

Finally, Kampman et al. insist on the deep personal qualities that can be developed from the experience of suffering. In fact, this is reflected in the statement of a participant in Salick and Auerbach (2006) study [cited by 24, p. 289]: "*I guess suffering makes you feel more human. You relate to other people.*" Kampman et al.'s essential theme "*humanity*" tries to capture the increased sense of humanity developed among trauma participants. The authors define this new sense of humanity by altruism, kindness, and act of love toward fellow human beings.

3.4. Posttraumatic growth and existential awareness: making the invisible more visible

Posttraumatic growth can be comprehended as the increased existential awareness that is triggered by the traumatic event. Of course, the experience of trauma is not sufficient in itself to facilitate existential growth [20]. However, one of the recurrent themes in understanding the meaning of posttraumatic growth is the enlargement of existential awareness. Such awareness accounts for fuller appreciation of life and gratitude for the different sources of meaning in life remaining unchanged. Existential awareness may trigger an existential wound, but also reveal existential meaning.

Existential meaning in life was notably introduced in clinical psychology by Viktor E. Frankl (1905–1997). One cannot fully appreciate Frankl's work without considering his exceptional life's story. Austrian and born in Vienna from a Jewish family, psychiatrist and neurologist, Frankl lived for 3 years in different concentration camps during World War II. This period of suffering helped him to pursue the development of the existential approach.

Alongside with the premises of humanistic-existential psychology, the psychotherapeutic approach of Victor E. Frankl is based on meaning and responsibility. It is also based on the premise that human beings need to find a meaning to their life. Like the humanistic-existential movement, Frankl's approach is characterized by a unified understanding of all dimensions of a human being: physical, psychological, and existential. For Frankl, the existential self is the core of the human being, the essence of our humanity. This existential self carries in itself the drive of its expression and recognizes the occasions that allow this expression. It contains resources that the individual can mobilize, allowing him to face disturbing and traumatizing situations.

Frankl had three more deep convictions about human being: (1) *The liberty of choice*, which supports that human beings carry the liberty and capacity of finding a meaning as long as they are conscious. Liberty of choice does not deny biological, psychological, or psychosocial determiners, but rather refers to the human capacity of consciously choosing an attitude when facing conditions of life. Frankl also believed in (2) *the choice of meaning*, which maintains that human beings possess an intrinsic will of finding meaning in life. Last, Frankl put forward the third concept (3) *meaning of life* which states that human beings know deep down inside that life has a meaning. The principle of the choice of meaning reminds us that human beings are motivated to find a meaning to their lives, that they are attracted by this search for meaning, rather than being pushed to act by some force or drive. Finally, the meaning of life refers to the meaning that each person gives to particular moments of his life, and not to a universal ultimate meaning that could be revealed at the end of life.

3.5. Man's search for meaning

For Frankl, three avenues contribute to give meaning to life: (1) *creative*, (2) *attitudinal*, and (3) *experiential values*. All these represent reasons why life has meaning. Deep recognition, concrete embodiment, and full awareness of these values allow human beings to face suffering and absurdity of the modern world.

Creative values represent what we bring to the world and those around us, anything we contribute to and create. Those values include, among other things, the meal that we prepare or the comfort we bring to a patient. What makes those simple actions significant is the level of consciousness in which they are set in. No matter how those actions can seem common, recognizing our contribution to a situation or to someone else's life adds to the meaning of our own life and brings satisfaction.

Experiential values signify that meaning can emerge from experiences as simple as appreciating beauty, whether it is artistic, natural, or in the experience of love; in fact, everything that is given to us, that we did not need to work for. The natural beauty of mountains, masterpieces of artists, as well as encouraging and loving relationships are given gratuitously and help us find a meaning and reasons to live. To Frankl, the salvation of man resides in his capacity to love (and to appreciate). Even if life can be generous and has the possibility to add meaning to our existence, a lack of consciousness and sensibility can keep us from seeing and enjoying it. Therefore, increasing our presence and consciousness is necessary to benefit from experiential values.

For Frankl, the third source of meaning resides in *attitudinal values*. He explains that meaning can come from the acceptance of situations that we cannot change and through a change of attitude toward inalterable situations. For example, death situations that involve physical, mental, and emotional suffering have the potential to bring meaning to the life of an individual and his family. Frankl suggests that human beings develop a greater spiritual and existential maturity and grow out of suffering, which can be enriching and strengthening. As such, Frankl deeply believed that the suffering experienced from trauma may be transformed in an opportunity for growth. When the physical self, or even the psychological self, are threatened by trauma, the individual faces new forms of suffering. To be tolerated, this suffering has to be transformed in opportunities to find meaning. The possibility to give a meaning diminishes psychological suffering. Inevitable suffering can offer the opportunity to discover a meaning. Conscience is the tool that enables the identification or discovery of meaning. For Frankl, despite life experiences, human beings always have an opportunity to discover a meaning through creative, experiential, and attitudinal values.

For Frankl, if living necessarily involves suffering, surviving means giving meaning to suffering. As such, surviving from trauma would mean giving meaning to suffering and searching for new life meanings. Frankl's approach, alongside with humanistic-existential basic premises on human being, healing and growing offers support to explore, identify, and transform the experience of suffering from trauma. In the following section, we will explore how the humanist-existential approach, inspired by Frankl's theory among others, can concretely inspire psychotherapy with PTSD patients.

4. Different path on trauma and healing: two case studies illustrating a humanistic-existential therapeutic process

4.1. From object to subject: Mark's path through healing connexions

I first met Mark while I was working on an oncology ward as a psychologist. Mark had been diagnosed with lymphoma a few months earlier. His tumor had grown fast and spread to major lymph nodes. Mark started his treatment with great energy, hope, and trust to "*fight*" his cancer and go back to his "*normal, busy life.*"

However, one of Mark's lymph nodes, located on the right side of his neck, had grown fast and altered his ability to breathe, talk, and eat normally. Therefore, Mark had to go through surgery to remove the mass. During his surgery, he experienced the so-called "*awareness*"—a rare phenomenon reported by some patients under general anesthesia. Awareness usually occurs when one of the medications given fails. In fact, usually, different types of medications are given: one intends to "*cause unconsciousness*" and the other one to "*relieve pain.*" If the medication to render the patient unconscious fails, awareness may occur, although no pain is experienced. In other words, the patient wakes up, becomes aware of what is going on in the operating room, and of what is being done to his body. However, the patient has no mean to signify his awareness because of the muscle paralysis induced by the anesthesia. Therefore, the medical team does not know about the patient's experience, unless it is reported after anesthesia. In some cases, PTSD may arise after intraoperative awareness, causing the patient to require counseling for an extended period [25].

Mark was referred to me by his oncology nurse to whom he reported that "*he saw everything.*" He was distressed, but also very aggressive and upset about what happened during the surgery. He mentioned that the surgeon was treating him as a dead animal, and that he felt

http://dx.doi.org/10.5772/64290

like *"a piece of fabric under a sewing machine."* In fact, it seemed that Mark's awareness occurred precisely when the surgeon was stitching his neck following tumor removal. Mark wanted to leave the hospital as he no longer felt safe there. He refused meeting his surgeon and oncologist for postoperative follow-ups not trusting them anymore. He mentioned he would rather die home alone than to be assaulted by disrespectful physicians. Mark's medical condition (postoperative, immunosuppressed) and psychosocial situation (living by himself) made it impossible for him to go back home. His nurse convinced him to meet with me and to tell me his story of what happened in the operating room.

I first met Mark 2 days after his surgery, at his bedside. He was quite agitated and hyperaroused. His nurses confirmed that he was awake and agitated most of the time and that he refused all medications. He would take some pain killers, but only if they were administered by a particular nurse he trusted. Our first meetings allowed Mark to tell his story in details and to slowly build alliance with him, as he felt quite threatened by the whole medical team. I spent a few sessions seeing Mark every day, sometimes twice a day, to see how he was doing. Slowly, but surely, he started trusting me. He was still quite hyper and slept very little; despite the pain medication he was taking. At several times, we had multidisciplinary team meetings about his case to facilitate the team's understanding of his situation and to pay more attention to the way they approached him, knowing he felt threatened. As a matter of fact, Mark's young surgeon felt terrible about what had happened. At some point, he mentioned: *"I don't recall being rough or different with this patient… I had no choice to manipulate his body to remove the tumour… I don't know… maybe I wasn't careful enough."* The medical team validated that, indeed, it was a hard procedure and, although every medical gesture was well-intended, it must be traumatizing to experience such body manipulation while being awake. While I was building trust with Mark, I realized that his hyperaroused state made exploration difficult. I started thinking that introducing a light medication may facilitate our therapeutic process. Mark was still sleeping very little and experienced recurrent nightmares of his body being cut into small pieces and thrown away in the garbage as a waste. He would wake up in the dream, realizing that his body was cut into pieces and then, would actually wake up.

Regular sessions with Mark allowed further exploration of his lived experience of the surgery and nightmares. Mark kept asking to go home so he could rest and sleep. I validated his subjective experience of assault to his body during surgery and, as a result, that his body did not feel safe to rest. I mentioned that this state of hyperarousal might in fact be overwhelming for him and for his whole body. Hence, he asked: *"can we do something about it"*? I told him that we had different choices: we could wait a little longer, try relaxation techniques, or introduce a light medication that would help him feel calmer. Mark raised his fear of being asleep at the hospital and that his body would be mistreated. I validated this fear of being mistreated as a result of feeling mistreated by his surgeon. I also shared that I trusted his current medical team. He finally agreed to take a little dose of medication at night, so he could rest.

The following sessions allowed deeper exploration of Mark's experience of being assaulted. Indeed, although no assault to Mark's body was intended, he experienced a fundamental assault by the surgery experience, and it shattered his assumptions that his medical team was there to support him and care for his life. At some point, he reported how he felt like a rotting carcass and, likewise, that is what will happen to him when he dies from his cancer. His body will be thrown away like a waste, with nothing left. At this point, I actually had the thought that Mark may be afraid of dying from his cancer, although he kept emphasizing his hope and trust. I was also stroke by how he experienced himself as a body uniquely, like nothing would be left of him after his death. However, at this stage, such intervention or interpretation appeared to be premature so I gave more reflection to Mark's experience of himself and his body. From a phenomenological stance, the sensitive body is not an object in the world, but the place of anchoring from which it is lived by experience. Mark's PTSD happened notably from the awareness of being treated as an object by individuals he trusted.

I was then able to explore and validate Mark's experience of being treated as a "*thing*." One week after surgery, since nobody had clearly explained to him the "*awareness*" phenomenon, I decided to. Providing a rational explanation of Mark's experience was not used to confront him with the objective reality, but to start exploring other meanings in what had happened. Mark developed the understanding that the medical team did not know about his experience, including the surgeon. Although this information seemed to have partially comforted him, he added:

> *"They should be more careful." – They should care more about people… we are not cars, nor animals and we are not dead yet."*

The day after, I was at Mark's bedside when his surgeon went by to assess the wound. Mark did not say much. He was not very collaborative, but did not display any aggressive behavior. As the surgeon quickly left, still feeling embarrassed about the situation, I asked Mark: "*How was it to see him?*" He responded that "*it was ok, but that the surgeon still doesn't care.*" I asked him: "*How do you think that your surgeon feels about what happened with you experiencing awareness and feeling mistreated in the operating room?*" He responded that "*surgeons don't feel anything; otherwise they wouldn't be able to do their job.*" As of that moment, there was a transformation that allowed Mark to relate differently to his surgeon and to his experience. We could therefore agree that he experienced an assault, but that such assault was not against him as a person, but against his cancer to cure the disease present in his body.

From then on, PTSD symptoms of hyperarousal lowered, but Mark still had nightmares. When he left the hospital after surgery, I continued seeing him as an outpatient, since he still needed to receive chemotherapy treatments. Because he was feeling much better physically, we started a deeper exploration of the story of his life and his experience of illness.

4.1.1. Mark's personal history and psychotherapy process

Mark had been divorced for nearly 10 years and had little contact with his three children, aged between 15 and 20 years. His mother was still alive and he also had a brother. Both lived in a distant city and so family contacts were quite limited. Since his divorce, Mark reported "*having a series of relationships,*" none of which lasted more than 2 years.

Mark describes himself as a "*doer.*" He dedicated the bulk of his time and personal resources to work. He filled many jobs, often in the field of management for various engineering and

http://dx.doi.org/10.5772/64290

telecommunication companies. On several occasions, he attempted to start up his own business, with no success. Mark was curious, a hard worker and very ingenious. He constantly had new ideas for solving all kinds of practical problems, but had a hard time completing his projects. Enthusiasm often led him to become scattered and overloaded. Thus, he accumulated aborted projects despite his innovative ideas. Left with a feeling of failure, he occasionally blamed others and claimed bigger financial rewards for his work. In fact, Mark lived under precarious financial conditions. When he received his cancer diagnosis, he was living with his then-girlfriend who supported him financially. Mark's girlfriend ended the relationship few weeks following the diagnosis, as she felt she could not cope with it. He expressed being concerned and having regrets not having built any material and financial heritage for his children.

During our sessions, it occurred to me that Mark was very labile. He would fluctuate between expansion movements, during which he was extensively discussing about his past accomplishments, and moments of profound distress where he would connect with his terror of death, a feeling of deep solitude, and his suffering of being ill. His chemotherapy treatments made him very symptomatic. It was stealing away his energy and affecting his ability to center himself and concentrate. He came to explicitly question the meaning and goal of his life. Along uncertainty, a constant monitoring of the progression of his tumor led him to first experience total despair and later idealized an improbable future in which he would be fully healed and where he would finally succeed in accomplishing the grandiose projects he was dreaming of.

At one point, I reflected to Mark how success at work had always been an important aspect for him. He agreed and added that it was, until now, the only important thing for him. In some way, it had been the unique source of meaning in his life. After a while, he was able to open up to the idea of having other sources of meaning in life, which were more consistent with the limitations imposed by the disease. In parallel to this exploration, Mark's life experiences led him to open up to various experiential values; he occasionally mentioned being touched by the care he was receiving, although he did not feel safe at first. Moreover, Mark felt good about the fact that the oncology personnel recognized him, remembered his name, and his situation from week to week. He also recalled passing by his surgeon while walking to his chemo treatment. His surgeon asked him how he was doing and, as a mean of connecting with him in a positive way, mentioned he did his best. Mark reported the event with mixed feelings of gratitude and sadness. Afterwards, he did not report having the same recurrent nightmare.

Mark also felt a lot of sadness and compassion toward the other patients he was in contact with and whose situation was sometimes more precarious than his. Often, Mark treated this information as insignificant details. However, during session, we started taking more time to stop and deeply explore these states of compassion and gratitude. By giving it time and attention, these states became more meaningful to a point where they eventually were consciously named as one of the meanings in his life. Because life contained such bursts of compassion and fraternity, it felt worth living.

Thus, the experience of being ill and the psychotherapy allowed Mark to raise his awareness to a new meaning through experiential values. Moreover, we came to identify an important role of suffering in the discovery of new values and sources of meaning. Compassion became possible with the experience of being sick. Suffering could then become a transcending experience and allow for new possibilities of being.

Several months later, Mark had to be hospitalized again for pneumonia. He felt extremely isolated and suffered even more. I continued visiting him at bedside. He could phrase that he was terrified by the idea of dying. His suffering was so important that he even wished to die. However, being accompanied through his solitude allowed him to realize the importance of emotional bond and human connexion. This growing awareness led him to rebuild contact with his children and ask for his mother and brother to visit him. To this day, Mark still has contact with two of his children. The relationship is sometimes hectic, but he satisfies himself from having found the courage to reunite with his family.

Further to his hospitalization, Mark was admitted to a long-term care facility where he currently lives at a relatively independent level. He is assisted in managing his medical situation, which calls for constant monitoring. His gratitude toward life increased. He changed his need to fulfill himself into a modest but concrete implication in the center where he lives. He puts his ingenuity to the service of other residents by improving life conditions, by performing valuable services, and organizing new activities. Sometimes, he mentions that he wished he had *"done more,"* but he realizes that his actions have never been that concrete to contribute to the world around him. Most importantly, this became a source of meaning for him. Mark lives modestly but in a much consistent way.

On several occasions, Mark shared his feeling of failure for not having accumulated a material heritage. In the face of this unchangeable situation, the last stage of the psychotherapy permitted a change of attitude. He certainly did not have money, a house, or any objects to leave behind. Nevertheless, the richness of his experience was invaluable. He had faced illness with courage and committed to a profound transformation through a physical challenge. Hence, he was not leaving anything material behind, but his legacy was one precious teaching. This thought was very comforting for Mark who has now engaged in writing his story for his children.

After just over a year of psychotherapy, Mark still lives with a cancer although currently medically controlled. The progression of his illness is constantly monitored and he is well aware that relapse may occur at any time. However, for the first time, he reports that even if his cancer reoccurred, he could leave with no regret. He also keeps inside the profound truth that he is capable of a humble happiness, that he was able to transcend suffering, and that his illness will never steal away his gratitude, his good actions, and his capacity to love. It is therefore with confidence in his ability to transform psychologically that Mark views the future. He remains sad and sometimes anxious about the suffering that awaits him, but these fears do not dominate him as before.

Mark's psychotherapeutic process allowed the exploration and some transformation of his relationship with himself, others, and his world. It allowed some reintegration and reconstruction of different part of himself. As he said, he metamorphosed from doing to a being. The therapeutic encounter and the support received by the medical team and the exchange with his surgeon enabled him to rebuild and reconnect with a sense of humanity and with a

http://dx.doi.org/10.5772/64290

view of a world as meaningful, caring, and benevolent. Mark no longer defines himself as a doer. He has come to experience himself as a relational and existential being, with a past, a present, and a future. He also sees his current illness as a transformative experience. He considers this transformation as an opportunity for legacy and transmission that is not material, but that may support his children in their own search of meaning and purpose in life.

4.2. Eleanor: meaning of survival

I met Eleanor, 22, a few years ago while I was starting my private practice as a psychologist. Eleanor has lived in Canada for 12 years. She left Rwanda—her country of origin—in 1998, following the 1994 genocide against Tutsis. Eleanor was referred to me by Dr. Lemond, one of my previous clinical supervisors, who had been Eleanor's psychologist a few years ago. Dr. Lemond was now retired and she called me to meet with Eleanor, as she knew I had worked in Rwanda with survivors in the past. With Eleanor's approval, Dr. Lemond sent me a short report of her story and healing process. Dr. Lemond had been involved with Eleanor shortly after she immigrated to Canada as a refugee. She saw Eleanor as an outpatient at the children mental health facility where she was working at the time.

When Eleanor called me, she quickly mentioned being tired and having some nightmares "*again*" but that those "*were not the same as they used to.*" Eleanor mentioned that she would prefer not having to tell her story again, especially since that "*her current situation was not related to her past.*" To Eleanor, it did not make sense to talk so much about the past and she explicitly mentioned seeking consultation to feel better in the present and to go on with her future.

I had considerable hesitation about reading Eleanor's story before actually meeting her, especially given her insistence that her current difficulties were not related to her past. Having worked in Rwanda before, I had heard many stories of trauma: most survivors had witnessed horrors perpetrated by neighbors, had escaped death during weeks, had to deal with grief for an entire family; family they had seen perish in violent deaths… and more… I certainly did not want to have strong preconceptions that may reduce Eleanor's whole experience to her traumatic story. I also wanted to connect with Eleanor's strength and current life experience. Nevertheless, given Eleanor's consent and probable expectations about me knowing her story, I decided to read Dr. Lemond's report. After reading, as consciously and as reflexively as possible, I tried "*suspending all judgments about what would be real*" about the person she had become years after. I wanted to take a phenomenological stance that would allow the exploration of Eleanor's subjective current life experience of the here-and-now.

4.2.1. Eleanor's story

Eleanor was 6 years at the time of the genocide. As a member of a Tutsi family, she had grown in a world of tensions in which her identity as a Tutsi defined her as a minority. The mass killings in Rwanda happened from April to June 1994, following the crash of the presidential plane by extreme Hutu radicals. Then, massacre against Tutsi started.

Six-year-old Eleanor and her family were attacked in mid-April 1994, at home, overnight. Eleanor had witnessed the cruel killing of her mother, father, and big sister as she was hiding under her sister's bed. Being the youngest of a family of four kids, Eleanor did not have her own bed and used to sleep either on cushion, on the floor, or sometimes in her big sister's bed after begging her for a little room. The night of her family killing, Eleanor was on the floor right beside her sister's bed, who was already asleep.

Eleanor could not sleep as she was noticing a conversation between both her parents in the living room who were worried about the recent death of close Tutsi community members. Eleanor recalled being so afraid while listening to her parents' conversation that she could not sleep. At some point, she noticed more and more noises coming from outside. She recalled hearing men yelling and women screaming. Afraid of those distressing noises, she hid under her sister's bed. Noises became louder and louder until she realized that there were people in her house. She recalled hearing her mother's and father's voices, but could not remember what had been said. At that point, her sister woke up and screamed for her mother. Eleanor remembered that people entered the room. She heard screams and hits that seemed to her as not having lasted long. After a while, there were no more noises. Eleanor, terrified and distressed stayed under the bed for hours, as she recalled it. She finally got out of her hiding place and discovered the bodies of her mother, father, and sister. Afraid, she left the house and went hiding into the woods for … *"a while,"* as she remembered.

Somehow, Eleanor made her way—alone—to a refugee camp close to the border of Uganda. She lived there by herself for almost a year, taken care of by nongovernmental organization (NGO)[1] workers. At some point, a Canadian NGO worker named Marissa, accompanied by someone from the Canadian embassy, happened to be looking for her. As mentioned in Dr. Lemond's report, Eleanor reported feeling confused while speaking with Marissa and *"the other Mzungu.*[2] *This Mzungu, she was very nice to me. She just explained to me that I had an aunt in Canada who was looking for her family members here, in Rwanda.*

As a matter of fact, Eleanor happened to have an aunt, Eglantina, in Canada. Eglantina, aged in her early fifties, was actually the sister of Eleanor's grandmother. She had left Rwanda in the 1980s. She had fallen in love with a Canadian humanitarian worker and the couple married in Rwanda in the 1980s. Very aware of the ethnic conflict that was getting increasingly violent, they decided to fly to Canada and live there. Eglantina still had some contact with her family in Rwanda, but could not reach them during the genocide. In the fall of 1994, Eglantina started actively searching for her family by making contact with different Canadian and foreign NGOs. As her research was progressing, she discovered that most of her family had perished. The whole process has been accompanied with great grief and losses.

Fortunately, she was able to find Eleanor and, as a mean to reconnect with her Rwanda origins and traumatic losses, adopted her. Eglantina facilitated her immigration to Canada as a refugee. Eleanor flew to live with Eglantina and her husband, Louis. Both Louis and Eglantina offered a supporting environment to Eleanor. By the time Eleanor started school in Canada, she was almost 10. Needless to say she was struggling with adjusting to this completely new and different world. She experienced more and more anxieties, and struggled with adjusting

[1] Non-governmental organization

[2] This term is a familiar designation given to white people in Rwanda.

to different life areas. She had frequent nightmares and night terrors, panic attacks almost every day, social anxiety, introversion, tear bursts, etc. At school, she could not concentrate and she did not seem to be able to make contact with other kids, nor teachers. Following Eleanor's teacher's advice, Eglantina and Louis sought professional help at the outpatient children clinic close by. From the age of 11–15, Eleanor has been followed by Dr. Lemond.

4.2.2. Meeting with Eleanor

The first meetings with Eleanor allowed the exploration of her current life's situation. I also explored Eleanor's experience of therapy as a kid, and the meaning that therapy have for her. She mentioned feeling very grateful for the help provided by Dr. Lemond. The therapist, who she recalled as a nice, kind, and very patient woman, reminded her of her own mother. From her first psychotherapy process, Eleanor reported that it felt good to have someone knowing her complete story. She also mentioned that although she had a hard time with telling the things she saw, it helped her to stop thinking about it. With time, her images had become blurrier every day, to a point that she could not quite remember her parents' traits. Eleanor had tearful eyes when talking about it, but also stated that she learned to live with it. She mentioned still struggling at times with not knowing what happened to her brothers who were not home the night of the killings as they were studying in a boarding school in another city.

Eleanor said that therapy enabled her to feel calmer about her souvenirs and more "*ok with everything that happened. It took three years for me to be cured from my trauma,*" she said. She added that "*the techniques with the eyes* (EMDR)[3] helped her to feel calmer. Eleanor was aged 16 when she completely stopped seeing Dr. Lemond. She recalled feeling quite well; she was doing well at school and managed to graduate from high school. Excelling in school, Eleanor decided to go to college, and to become a nurse. She was still living with Eglantina and Louis, who kept supporting her in her new life project. Although Eleanor had some difficulty adjusting to "*so much studying,*" she felt happy with her choice.

Eleanor became increasingly anxious as she started her first practical training. Although she felt proud about her career choice, she mentioned feeling sick when being at the hospital. She also reported feeling dizzy, not being able to think clearly, and experiencing confusion in the presence of sick people. She precisely described an event in which she was in the emergency room and had to witness her supervisor do the assessment of a 10-year-old girl who had been in a major bike accident. The young girl had multiple fractures, and blood all over her. The smell of blood made Eleanor instantly sick and she had to leave the room to vomit.

This event made Eleanor even more anxious. She was afraid of falling in front of everybody. As a result of her anxiety symptoms, she started missing days of training. She would stay in her room all day either sleeping or watching TV shows to change her mind. Eglantina and Louis started being concerned about Eleanor's change in mood and behavior. They first interpreted it as a lack of motivation to work hard. Eleanor kept saying that she was tired and

---

[3] EMDR stands for Eye Movement Desensitization and Reprocessing. This type of therapy is commonly used for the treatment of traumatic memories. For more details, see [26].

started to lie about her schedule or obligations. Quite upset about her attitude, Louis and Eglantina tried to confront her. Eleanor recalled a conversation with Louis, in which he mentioned: "*You should feel responsible to do something meaningful with your life.*"

After this conversation, although Eleanor's anxieties were still present, depressive symptoms took over: she was sleeping more and more, staying in her room all day, and not eating. She reported being tearful at times, without understanding why. Following Eglantina's suggestion, Eleanor started to consider psychotherapy again.

4.2.3. Eleanor's current experience and psychotherapy process

I started exploring Eleanor's current situation, as she experienced it. I tried to suspend all my preconceived interpretations, and to inquire about how she felt here and now. I notably asked Eleanor about the reasons that brought her to seek psychotherapeutic help. She responded by asking me if I knew her story. I answered that I had spoken with Dr. Lemond and that I had read about her psychotherapy process with her. Then, Eleanor responded that her current situation was not about her past. So, I asked her what was going on for her. She responded "*I am tired all the time.*" Therefore, I explored Eleanor's fatigue, asking her to further describe her experience of being tired:

M: How is it like for you when you're fatigued?

M: How is it like for you when you're fatigued?

E: I don't know… I just feel like sleeping…

M: And… how is it like when you actually sleep?

E: It depends… sometimes it's good…I don't feel anything, so it's good…but sometimes I have nightmares…again…

M: Again?

E: Yeah… I used to have them when I was younger… But they are not the same. They are not about the past.

M: Do you feel comfortable sharing one of your nightmares with me?

E: …Yeah…it's always the same that keeps coming back…

M: Okay… Tell me about it…

Then, Eleanor explained that she always dream of being at the hospital, as a nurse. In her dream, there are people crying and screaming for help. There are people everywhere and not enough staff to take care of them. At some point, Eleanor's supervisor asks her to be more efficient and to work faster. She tries to get someone's medication and then she freezes. She cannot move. People scream louder and louder and Eleanor's supervisor yells at her to hurry up, but she cannot. She usually wakes up after her supervisors tells her she is fired for being lazy, useless, and worthless.

http://dx.doi.org/10.5772/64290

Eleanor kept her eyes on the floor while narrating her dream. When she finished and looked up at me, her eyes were in tears. I delicately asked her what made her tearful. She responded feeling guilty about not being strong enough to become a real nurse, who actually cares for others. I was surprised with such a statement and further explored what it meant for her not to be "*strong enough*." Then, she reported the incident in the emergency room, where she felt sick seeing the young girl who was injured and covered with blood following her bike accident. She reported feeling bad for the young girl and feeling guilty for not being able to provide a proper response to the situation, as was expected from her.

Although Eleanor mentioned her feeling about the situation, we agreed to discuss it further since the event seemed to have precipitated some of her current suffering. In a following session, we discussed the scene again, with phenomenological exploration. We explored bodily sensations she had experienced back then, as well as the bodily sensations she may experience while remembering the scene. To her, the smell of blood was particularly unbearable and she would be nauseous in the session just remembering it. Gently, I dared to inquire what images came to her mind while smelling blood. She then recalled the view of her family, covered with blood and explained how she ran away from it as a little girl. Crying loudly, she expressed that maybe she should have stayed there and died with them; or maybe they were still alive. She should have tried to save them. She felt like betraying her sister by hiding under her bed. She should have died with them. She described herself as weak and selfish to have escaped instead of facing her destiny. She should have at least tried to save them and to be courageous enough to face death doing so. Why did she think that her life had more value than her parent's or sister's? Why them and not her? She was now stuck to survive. Even worst, she had to do something worth with her life so she could pay back her debt, but was too weak and worthless to actually do it.

Phenomenological and detailed exploration of Eleanor's experience of fatigue, sleep, nightmares, and bodily sensations allowed revealing her feelings of guilt and worthlessness. In fact, Eleanor experienced herself as being guilty to survive and in debt toward life and her family. As she was trying to pay back her debt as a survivor, she felt stuck—again—with a sense of worthlessness and weakness.

With Eleanor, therapy involved slowly trying to reinterpret her past differently and to find new meanings in her experience as a child and as the only survivor of her family. Psychotherapy aimed at exploring and sharing about her story, so that she could slowly build a new understanding of herself, as being resilient, courageous, and compassioned. As a therapist, I started supporting her whole being, including her unique qualities. At some point, I even mentioned that I wished she could see herself as I saw her. We worked on developing her self-compassion. We worked on understanding her sensibility and great empathy toward others as a strength she developed through her own suffering.

We also revisited the strength, discipline, and resilience she had to exert to survive physically and emotionally. We discussed how she had already healed from most of her traumatic experience and that now, there was an opportunity for growing from it by existing more fully as a whole person, not only as a survivor in debt. We discussed how such a process of growth was complex and profound, and that it required time. We worked on reintegrating her story in a different way, so she could try to relate to herself, to others, and to the world more freely.

While Eleanor seemed to slowly get better (having more energy and no more nightmares), she wanted to know more about "*growing*" from trauma. At this point, I decided to lend her my book "*Man's search for meaning*" [27], in which Frankl tells about his own history of concentration camps and in which he extrapolates his theory on life's meaning. Eleanor was particularly moved by the understanding that suffering may have meaning. Following this reading, she initiated rich and deep discussions about the different sources of meaning in her own life. Notably, she mentioned increasing her awareness and gratitude of the value of the relationship she had with her adoptive parents. She would still feel guilty at times for what the world has given her, but would also be able to relate to her experience differently, which motivated her for a fuller engagement toward life. In fact, Frankl's strong thoughts about self-engagement toward life empowered Eleanor to continue to search for and to create her own unique and valuable way of living a purposeful existence.

In the meantime, Eleanor continued to take nursing classes on a part-time basis. She temporarily postponed her practical training and started volunteering at the hospital to see if she could develop a new way to relate to others' illness and suffering. By volunteering, Eleanor experienced rich human contact and compassionate care with patients and got progressively used to witnessing suffering. She created significant bonds with patients and other caregivers, and received good feedback on her listening abilities, kindness, and compassionate way of being. Such bounds may have facilitated her sense of worth and value. Eleanor started giving meaning to her suffering, thinking that her past history contributed to cultivate her sense of humanity and compassion. We worked on cultivating this self-compassion, especially when her feelings of guilt and worthlessness would surface.

After a moment, Eleanor felt that she was ready "*to fly a bit on her own.*" The overall psychotherapy process lasted 18 months, on a regular weekly basis. Before saying goodbye, Eleanor and I identified what her next challenge may be: for the first time, she was thinking in building an intimate relationship with someone. Although the idea pleased her, she was still terrorized by physical and psychological intimacy and quite aware of the challenges it would be to develop attachment toward someone. She fluctuated between states of hope (being with someone), desire for self-protection, and preservation (it is easier to be alone) or self-depreciation (no man would be interested in me). To date, Eleanor still struggles with self-worth at times, but has come a long way from the first time I met her.

5. Discussion

By presenting Mark's and Eleanor's cases in detail, we wanted to show how PTSD can take various forms of expression. Its experience and healing process are complex and unique to every individual, despite common symptoms. PTSD may be understood as a complex experience that has biological and psychological components, but also cultural and existential. A humanistic-existential approach to PTSD emphasizes the exploration of the patient's lived experience, as well as the idiographic meaning that trauma takes for the individual. By relying on phenomenology and on the safety of the therapeutic encounter, a humanistic-existential psychotherapy for PTSD aims at exploring new meanings for the traumatic event and new meanings to surviving, healing, and growing.

In both cases, we wanted to show how the therapeutic process aimed at exploring the history and the lived experience of Mark and Eleanor. In both cases, the exploration process allowed to shed light on the meaning of the traumatic experience itself, as well as the disrupted meanings of life as it was experienced here and now. The co-comprehension enabled by the therapeutic encounter made possible the exploration of other meanings of the event, and of a search for new meanings in life. In both cases, the psychotherapeutic process involved exploration, comprehension, and reconstruction. This sequence should not be seen as linear, but as a repeated and iterative process.

We have chosen cases that honor the diversity and the complexity of PTSD manifestations, origins, recovery, and, most importantly, meaning. In both cases, we offered a humble, yet incomplete view of the meaning of humanistic-existential psychotherapy with trauma patients. With both cases, we also wanted to show how humanistic-existential psychotherapy can be complemented by other approaches.

For instance, in Mark's case, symptom management was first ensured by medication for allowing conditions of deeper exploration. As a matter of fact, exploration may not be possible if the person is constantly in a state of arousal. In Eleanor's case, she had already completed 3 years of psychotherapy before addressing the existential aspects of her traumatic history. Moreover, in the future, Eleanor may again be confronted with life's situation that will reopen her wound. Major grief or loss could trigger PTSD symptoms and another psychotherapeutic process may be helpful at that time. Such experience may not be understood as static conditions that can be treated, but as major existential challenges that may as well be an opportunity for existential growth.

The humanistic-existential psychotherapy has often been criticized for being too intellectual or too abstract. By presenting concrete, yet incomplete case studies, we aimed at illustrating different ways to approach PTSD from a humanistic-existential perspective. That being said, such an approach may not be relevant or helpful with all PTSD patients. In the cases presented above, both Eleanor and Mark were able to verbalize their lived experience and reflect upon their existence. In that sense, they already had significant existential awareness.

However, the therapeutic process being coconstructed between the therapist and the patient, we can imagine how different therapists may have approached Mark's and Eleanor's stories differently. Different path would have been as valuable. The humanistic-existential movement represents a great diversity of approaches that may differ in their philosophical roots, premises, definitions, and views of psychotherapy. Although of crucial importance, more detailed descriptions of those nuances appeared to be beyond the scope of this chapter.

Humanistic-existential psychotherapy may also share theoretical thoughts or even therapeutic techniques with other approaches. In fact, some third wave cognitive psychotherapy may include relaxation techniques such as mindfulness meditation that are congruent with the approach we presented. It is also close to Frankl's description of experiential values. Moreover, Frankl's belief in man's ability to take a different attitude toward situations that cannot be changed may be part of the acceptance and commitment therapy. However, the humanistic-existential approach distinguishes itself from others by its focus on increasing existential awareness and, therefore, freedom of being. Such a freedom accounts for new existential responsibilities: to live a life that is coherent and meaningful.

6. Conclusion

Accompanying patients like Mark and Eleanor, as a humble facilitator of their deep and meaningful transformation was a privilege. For PTSD patients, being in presence of a well-intended witness through the exploration of their suffering may be the first step to allow the reconstruction of human connectedness that is often disrupted by trauma.

For the therapist, the recognition of the other as a sensitive subject, a fellow human being who experienced traumatic suffering, may as well be a transformative experience that should not be left unnoticed. Patients' existential suffering also represents our own suffering as human beings. Others' suffering may as well be the suffering we all share—or will share—as a result of our human condition of being mortal, aware, free, and responsible.

In recent years, there has been increasing interest for the experience of professionals working with individuals who suffered from trauma. In fact, the concept of posttraumatic growth may as well apply to professionals. Arnold et al. [28] claimed that therapists also experience positive changes in many areas of their lives such as relationship to self, others, and to the world. Being in touch with human's profound suffering and transformative growth may be a source of existential meaning for therapist. In a recent study, Ben-Porat [29] actually suggests that secondary exposure to trauma can lead both to distress and traumatic growth. Potential for human connection and supporting work environment may allow therapists to develop and maintain a balance between potential distress and growth.

As a therapist, and as an existential being, both life and work offers intense moments of human connections and may be deeply and existentially meaningful. Cultivating awareness and sensitivity may also help therapists to fully appreciate the beauty and uniqueness of human connections. By allowing ourselves to be existentially touched by our client's lives, we have to be open to also be transformed by the therapeutic encounter. In the tribute to his mentor Rollo May, Pitchford [6] captures the essence of the ultimate, free, and responsible existential engagement we have as humanistic-existential therapists working with suffering and growing individuals:

> *"I had to freely choose whether or not to take risks in my own life, to take responsibility for those risks, or to remain in a state of comfort, avoidance, and security. I knew that if I were to avoid risks, I could potentially miss out on discovering further potentialities about myself."*

http://dx.doi.org/10.5772/64290

Author details

Mélanie Vachon[1*], Prudence C. Bessette[2] and Christine Goyette[1]

*Address all correspondence to: vachon.melanie@uqam.ca

1 Psychology Department, UQÀM, Montreal, Canada

2 SHERPA Research Team/McGill University Health Center, Montreal, Canada

References

[1] Greening T. PTSD from the perspective of existential-humanistic psychology. Journal of Traumatic Stress. 1990;3(2):323–326.

[2] Bühler C. & Allen M. Introduction to Humanistic Psychology. Belmont, CA: Wadsworth Publishing; 1972.

[3] Royce J.R. & Mos L.P. Humanistic Psychology: Concepts and Criticisms. New York: Plenum Press; 1981.

[4] Schneider K.J., Fraser Pierson J.F. & Bugental J.F.T, editors. The Handbook of Humanistic Psychology. Theory, Research and Practice. Thousand Oaks, CA: Sage Publications; 2015. 800 p.

[5] Bugental J.F.T. The third force in psychology. Journal of Humanistic Psychology. 1964;4(1):19–25. DOI: 101177/002216786400400102

[6] Pitchford D.B. The existentialism of Rollo May: an influence on trauma treatment. Journal of Humanistic Psychology. 2009;49(4):441–461.

[7] Frankl V.E. Logotherapy. Israel Annals of Psychiatry and Related Disciplines. 1967;5(2): 142–155.

[8] Yalom I.D. Existential Psychotherapy. New York: Basic Books; 1980.

[9] Frankl V.E. The Doctor and the Soul. An Introduction to Logotherapy. Oxford, England: A.A. Knopf; 1955. 280 p.

[10] May R.E. Existence—A New Dimension in Psychiatry and Psychology. New York: Basic Books; 1958.

[11] May R.E. Freedom and Destiny. New York: Peter Smith; 1999.

[12] Paulson D.S. & Krippner S. Haunted by Combat: Understanding PTSD in War Veterans Including Women, Reservists, and Those Coming Back from Iraq. Westport, CT: Praeger; 2009.

[13] Jager B. Human subjectivity and the law of the threshold: phenomenological and humanistic perspectives. In: Valle R., editor. Phenomenological Inquiry in Psychology. New York: Plenum Press; 1998.

[14] Jager B. Metabletics and the art of psychotherapy. In: Jager B., Mook B., Sipiora & van den Berg J.H., editors. Metabletics: J.H. van den Berg's Historical Phenomenology. Pittsburgh: The Simon Silverman Phenomenology Center, Duquesne University; 1999. Pp. 1–1.

[15] Quintin J. Herméneutique et psychiatrie. Pouvoirs et limites du dialogue. Montréal: Liber; 2005.

[16] Buirski P. & Haglund P. Making Sense Together: The Intersubjective Approach to Psychotherapy. Northvale, NJ: Jason Aronson; 2001.

[17] Janoff-Bulman R. Shattered Assumptions: Towards a New Psychology of Trauma. New York, NY: Macmillan; 1992.

[18] Ponterotto J.G. Qualitative research in counseling psychology: a primer on research paradigms and philosophy of science. Journal of Counseling Psychology. 2005;52(2): 126–136.

[19] Diagnostic and Statistical Manual of Mental Disorders: DSM-5. 5th ed. American Psychiatric Association DSMTF, editors. Washington, DC: American Psychiatric Publishing; 2013.

[20] Tedeschi R.G. & Calhoun L.G. Posttraumatic growth: conceptual foundations and empirical evidence. Psychological Inquiry. 2004;15(1):1–18. DOI: http://dx.doi.org// 10.1207/s15327965pli1501_01

[21] Pat-Horenczyk R. & Brom D. The multiple faces of post-traumatic growth. Applied Psychology: An International Review. 2007;56(3):379–385.

[22] Jayawickreme E. & Blackie L.E.R. Post-traumatic growth as positive personality change: evidence, controversies and future directions. European Journal of Personality. 2014;28(4):312–331.

[23] Calhoun L.G. & Tedeschi R.G., editor. Handbook of Posttraumatic Growth: Research and Practice. Mahwah, NJ: Erlbaum; 2006. 387 p.

[24] Kampman H., Hefferon K., Wilson M. & Beale J. "I can do things now that people thought were impossible, actually, things that I thought were impossible": A meta-synthesis of the qualitative findings on posttraumatic growth and severe physical injury. Canadian Psychology. 2015;56(3):283–294.

[25] Osterman J.E., Hopper J., Heran W.J., Keane T.M. & van der Kolk B.A. Awareness under anesthesia and the development of posttraumatic stress disorder. General Hospital Psychiatry. 1998;23(4):198–204.

[26] EMDR Canada [Internet]. Available from: https://emdrcanada.org/fr/ [Accessed: 2016].

[27] Frankl V.E. Man's Search for Meaning: An Introduction to Logotherapy. New York: NY: Washington Square Press; 1963.

[28] Arnold D., Calhoun G.L., Tedeschi R. & Cann A. Vicarious posttraumatic growth in psychotherapy. Journal of Humanistic Psychology. 2005;45(2):239–263.

[29] Ben-Porat A. Competence of trauma social workers: the relationship between field of practice and secondary traumatization, personal and environmental variables. Journal of Interpersonal Violence. 2015.

Chapter 10

The Impact of Cognitive-Behavioral Therapies for Nightmares and Prazosin on the Reduction of Post-Traumatic Nightmares, Sleep, and PTSD Symptoms: A Systematic Review and Meta-Analysis of Randomized and Non-Randomized Studies

Katia Levrier, Carolyn Leathead,
Delphine-Émilie Bourdon, Sophie Lacerte,
André Marchand and Geneviève Belleville

Additional information is available at the end of the chapter

http://dx.doi.org/10.5772/64224

Abstract

Post-traumatic nightmares (PTNMs) can be treatment resistant to conventional treatments for post-traumatic stress disorder (PTSD). New cognitive and behavioral treatments (CBTs) for nightmares (NM) and pharmacological treatments, such as Prazosin, have been developed to directly reduce PTNMs. *Objectives*: The first objective was to evaluate the impact of CBTs for NM and Prazosin on the reduction of PTNMs in an adult population. A second aim was to explore the impact of these treatments in general PTSD symptoms and sleep. *Method*: A systematic search of English and French clinical studies on any CBTs and Prazosin treatments for PTNMs published from 1980 to 2012 was conducted in PsycINFO, MedLine, PILOTS,and ProQuest Dissertations and Theses. *Results*: The final sample was composed of 26 studies. The combined effect size (ES) for Prazosin was $g = 1.30$, 95% CI [0.61, 2.00], and for CBTs, it was $g = 0.55$, 95% CI [0.38, 0.72]. *Conclusions*: Prazosin had a large impact on PTNM reduction, while CBTs had a moderate impact. Specific NM treatments (Prazosin or CBTs) contribute to PTNM reduction and reduce PTSD and sleep symptoms. These findings are significant to the literature on PTSD and future studies should consider them. Several recommendations are proposed.

Keywords: CBT, meta-analysis, nightmare, Prazosin, trauma

1. Introduction

1.1. PTSD and nightmares

Nightmares (NM) are one of the intrusion symptom clusters of post-traumatic stress disorder (PTSD) in the fifth edition *Diagnostic and Statistical Manual of Mental Disorders* (DSM-5) [1]. The prevalence of frequent NM is 70% in individuals with PTSD compared to only 2–5% in the general population [2]. Post-traumatic nightmares (PTNMs) are different from "normal" dreams as they are recurrent frightening dreams of past traumatic events [3]. Their content may vary from an exact replay to only some components of the trauma, such as changes in time and place [3]. Another distinction is their role in PTSD. In the general population, sleep loss impacts daily functioning due to fatigue and cognitive difficulties [4], leading to poor quality of life [5]. However, in the particular PTSD context, the presence of NM seems to be related to PTSD prevalence and severity [6], and therefore, to contribute to the development of PTSD. They could even contribute to PTSD symptom maintenance [7].

PTSD used to be considered as an anxiety disorder in the fourth edition revised *Diagnostic and Statistical Manual of Mental Disorders* (DSM-IV-TR) [8]. Now, it is part of the trauma- and stressor-related disorders in the DSM-5 [1]. Several meta-analyses, systematic reviews, and guidelines underline that general trauma-focused cognitive and behavioral treatments (CBTs) (through exposure and cognitive restructuring) are superior, or equivalent, to other types of psychological treatments, such as eye movement desensitization and reprocessing (EMDR), psychodynamic psychotherapies, or supportive techniques (e.g., [9]). They also emphasize the efficacy of selective serotonin reuptake inhibitors (SSRIs) as a pharmacological treatment [10]. However, studies also reveal that CBTs and SSRIs do not effectively resolve all PTSD symptoms in individuals who no longer meet PTSD diagnosis criteria. In fact, NMs were found to be treatment resistant, and residual insomnia was also reported [11, 12].

1.2. Emergence of treatments directly targeting nightmares

One approach is to conceptualize NMs in two steps after a traumatic event. First, right after the trauma, NMs would be considered as trauma-induced and would be a PTSD symptom. Later, at a second stage, they would become a learned behavior distinct from PTSD symptoms. The idea is that the person, by fearing and avoiding NM content, cannot process the information related to the event and cannot incorporate it [13]. As these NMs disrupt sleep, it can be difficult for the victims to return to sleep and they may adopt unsuitable sleep hygiene, which could lead to insomnia [14]. Therefore, new psychological and pharmacological treatments are emerging and tested to directly reduce NMs.

Recently, the Standards of Practice Committee (SPC) of the American Academy of Sleep Medicine (AASM) commissioned a task force to assess the literature on the treatment of NM disorder in general. They presented their recommendations in a Best practice guide about pharmacotherapies and CBTs for NM for adults [15, 16]. Their classification was based on study designs from "level 1" (high-quality randomized clinical trials with narrow confidence intervals) to "level 4" (case series or poor case-control studies or poor cohort studies or case reports). Their suggestions were made according to a level of recommendation from "level A" (treatment recommended—level 1 or 2) to "level C" (treatments that may be considered—lever 3 or 4). Their recommendations concerned both psychological and pharmacological treatments.

Regarding the medications conclusions, Prazosin was given an "A level recommendation" compared to antidepressants, anxiolytics, anticonvulsants, and antipsychotics. Prazosin is an α1-adrenergic receptor antagonist, which was first introduced as a treatment for high blood pressure in 1970. It reduces the adrenergic response and has the advantage of crossing the blood-brain barrier. We know that stimulation of α_1 receptors induces the primitive fear response, disrupts rapid eye movement (REM) sleep, and increases non-REM sleep. We believe that Prazosin exerts its effect through a mechanism that blocks the primitive fear responses by antagonizingthe α_1 receptors in the CNS and decreasing PTNMs [17].

In addition, the Best practice guide lists six specific CBTs for NMs: imagery rehearsal therapy (IRT) (Level A), systematic desensitization (Level B), lucid dreaming therapy (LDT) (Level C), exposure, relaxation, and rescripting therapy (ERRT) (Level B), sleep dynamic therapy (Level C), and self-exposure therapy (Level C). These CBTs conceptualize NMs as a learned behavior, but each treatment approaches them differently. The IRT rationale is to select a repetitive NM, to transform and write it into a new dream, and finally to rehearse it in imagination. The idea is to gain control over the NM. The ERRT model is to expose the person to his original nightmare content a little further than IRT. The participant has to write down his original NM and to identify traumatic themes that will be used when rescripting and rehearsing it. Going further than IRT, it also incorporates sleep hygiene education and modification, and relaxation for insomnia. Contrary to IRT and ERRT, LDT will train individuals to become aware that they are dreaming while they are actually dreaming and to change the scenario [18].

1.3. Objectives

The first objective of this chapter is to review and evaluate the impact of CBTs compared to Prazosin for NM reduction, after a traumatic event in an adult population. The secondary objective is to evaluate the impact of both types of interventions on other PTSD symptoms and sleep.

2. Method

2.1. Search strategy

Studies published from 1980 (with the introduction of PTSD in the DSM-III) to the end of December 2012 were identified by searching the electronic databases MedLine, PsycINFO, PILOTS, and ProQuest Dissertations and theses databases [19] to identify relevant studies evaluating the impact of CBT and Prazosin on PTNMs in an adult population. Each search was separately run using the following command in all fields: (treatment OR therapy OR Prazosin OR cognitive OR behav* OR CBT) AND (nightmare* OR dream*) with the asterisk specifying the plural and grammatical variations. We also scanned reference lists of relevant meta-analyses, systematic reviews, and reference lists of each study included in this meta-analysis.

2.2. Eligibility criteria

To be included in the meta-analysis, studies must have met the following criteria: (a) they reported quantitative treatment outcomes for NMs (such as frequencies or questionnaires' scores) occurring after a traumatic event; (b) at least one group received CBT or Prazosin treatment for NM; (c) the study either had a group protocol or was a case study of at least three participants; (d) the participants were 18 years old and above; (e) all the participants presented PTSD symptoms (evaluated by validated questionnaires or by a clinical and structured interview) and PTNM complaints; (f) the study was published between 1980 and 2012; and (g) the study was published in English or in French. Studies were excluded if they were (a) abstracts of posters and (b) did not report original results.

2.3. Data extraction

Information was extracted from each eligible record using a data extraction sheet adapted from previous meta-analyses [11, 20]. Data extracted were : (i) study identification (e.g., authors and publication date); (ii) study description (e.g., protocol sampling, assignment of participants, and research reports following CONSORT statement for randomized studies [21]); (iii) sample characteristics (i.e., sample size, gender, mean age and standard deviation, PTSD and acute stress disorder (ASD) diagnoses, records of PTSD treatments, trauma type, trauma date of occurrence, nightmare definition, nightmare frequency, nightmare intensity, nightmare content, explicit report of sleep difficulties other than nightmares, reports of comorbidity, and attrition rate); and (iv) the type of intervention for NMs at large was also reported (i.e., IRT, IRET, ERRT, LDT, relaxation, exposition, desensitization, EMDR, Prazosin, and any other CBTs for NMs). CBTs for NMs were defined as incorporating cognitive (new dream rehearsal, restructuration, etc.) and/or behavioral strategies (progressive muscle relaxation, gradual exposure, etc.), contrasting with other approaches, such as dream interpretation. We recorded the number of therapy sessions, duration, the therapy modality (i.e., individual psychotherapy, in groups, at distance with or without any contact), the presence of a therapy protocol, the therapist's training (psychologist, graduates in psychology, other medical professionals, other), and whether the CBT treatment also targeted PTSD and insomnia problems in addition to NMs. For Prazosin studies, trade names of Prazosin (Minipress, Vasoflex, Pressin, and Hypovase) were considered in the study screening and we extracted the average prescription (in mg/day), the timing of the prescription, the presence of a protocol for the prescription, and the presence of a washout period at follow-up. (v) In addition, the type of NMs, PTSD and insomnia outcome and measures were coded as either (a) clinic interview, (b) daily self-monitory, (c) EEG for NMs and insomnia, (d) validated questionnaires, (e) subscales from questionnaires, (f) isolated items from questionnaires or interviews, or (g) survey. And, finally, (vi) information was gathered to calculate the following three types of effect sizes: group comparison on post-treatment data (between-group analysis), pre- vs. post-treatment data for groups receiving CBT or Prazosin (within group-group analysis), and pre- vs. post-treatment data for control groups.

2.4. Inter-rater agreement

In order to evaluate inter-rater reliability and to control for data extraction bias, each study was systematically checked by pairs of independent reviewers. Their results were compared and any disagreements were resolved by discussion. Before beginning the coding process, the rating instrument was tested with the four raters going through the coding form and checking one article testing CBT and one trial studying Prazosin together. Judges were students enrolled in a PhD program in psychology. The inter-rater reliability was good and varied from 58.3% to 100%. The strongest agreements were related to sampling method and treatment type while the lowest referred to attrition and female percentages, which may reveal inconsistencies in reporting. The final sample was composed of 26 studies published in English: 8 studies on Prazosin [22–29] and 18 studies on CBT for NM [6, 30–46] (**Figure 1**).

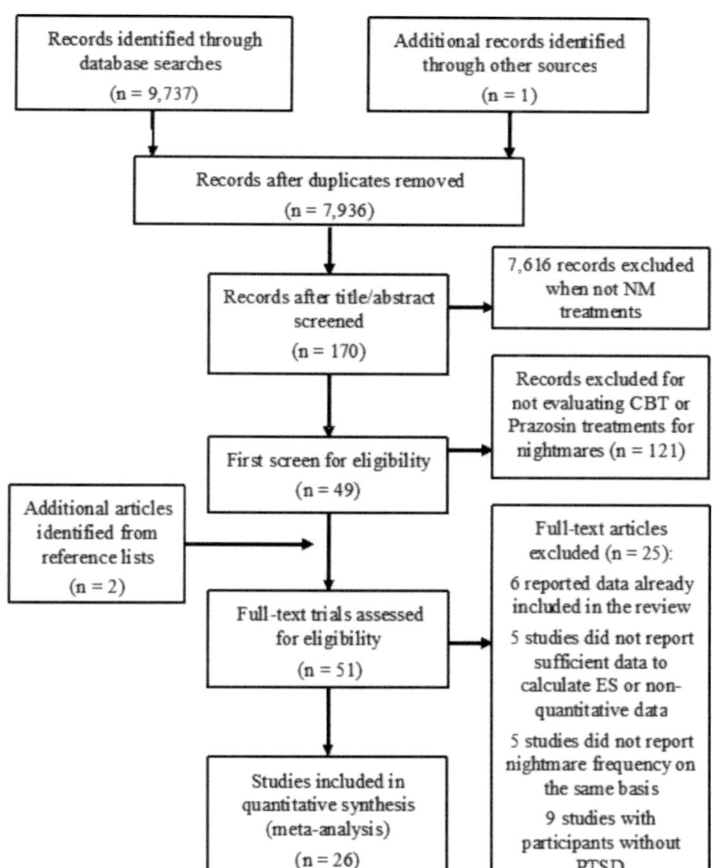

Figure 1. Search strategy flowchart.

2.5. Data analyses

The meta-analyses were performed using the random-effects model [47]. The analyses were conducted with *Comprehensive Meta-Analysis* (*Version* 2) [48]. Effect sizes (ES) were computed with Hedges' g between groups using mean and standard deviation (*SD*) [47] except for one study where they were obtained from t values [37]. When available, quantitative analyses were performed on the difference between the experimental and control groups at post-treatment (between-group); otherwise analyses were computed on pre- and post-data for the same group (within-group). As in the last case, the correlation coefficient r between pre- and post-test for each data is needed, and as this information was missing, r was set to 0 in order to be conservative and to give to these studies the smallest and the same weight, so there will be no bias in weighting [47]. However, we executed sensitivity analysis using a range of plausible correlations (0; 0.5 and 0.95) and the results did not significantly differ between each correlation. The direction of the ES was set as positive when NMs, PTSD symptoms, and sleep variables were improved at post-treatment or for the experimental compared to the control group at post-treatment. ES were not computed at follow-up due to disparities in reporting these data for CBT studies, and only one Prazosin study provided them.

For the NMs variable, effect sizes were calculated based on means and *SD* of weekly NM frequency for CBT studies; and on the CAPS-B2 final scores (item B2 on the *Clinician Administered PTSD Scale*) for Prazosin studies. The CAPS-B2 item sums up the frequency and the intensity (from 0 to 4) of recurrent distressing dreams related to the traumatic event (refer to Blake et al. [49] for a scale description). When these NMs were reported by month or by night, we computed their mean by the week. Effect sizes were also computed for PTSD symptoms. For CBTs, we considered any questionnaire evaluating the construct of PTSD symptoms intensity: *impact of event scale* (IES-R [50]), PTSD *Checklist—Civilian and Military Versions* (PCL [51]), *post-traumatic symptom scale* (PSS [52]), and *post-traumatic diagnostic scale* (PDS [53]). For Prazosin, we used the scores of the PCL and the CAPS. Finally, ES were calculated for sleep difficulties using (1) the CAPS-D1 (CAPS, item D1) final score (sum of the frequency and intensity) for Prazosin and (2) scores on the *Pittsburgh Sleep Quality Index* (PSQI) [54] for CBTs. Computations were also possible for the insomnia construct, as data Pertained only to CBT studies, using scores on the *Sleep Impairment Index* (SII [55]).

We used the data, if available, on an intent-to-treat basis (patients who were enrolled and randomly allocated to treatment), otherwise variables were selected on a completer basis. Also, as a few study designs did not implement immediate post-evaluation and rather evaluated the interventions at follow-up, we decided to include them in the analysis if follow-ups were less than three months after the end of the treatment. Each effect size (and the combined effect size) was calculated with 95% confidence intervals.

We tested for heterogeneity with the Q test and the proportion of true variance was assessed with the I^2 index for each computed ES. Q tests were also used for contrast analyses. Also, due to problems of power in this meta-analysis (less than 20 studies) ($n = 8$ for Prazosin; $n = 18$ for CBT studies), we computed the 95% confidence intervals (95% CI) for the I^2 index [56, 57]. Heterogeneity was detected when Q test was significant ($p < 0.05$) or I^2 index was higher than

50% [56]. In this case, sensitivity analyses and ES comparison across subgroups (subgroup analyses) were performed using the random effect model. Finally, to test for possible publication biases, funnel plots evaluating the association between the Hedges' g and the standard error were visually assessed [58]. In addition, Orwin fail-safe N tests [59] were computed to estimate the number of studies with no effect necessary to reduce the combined ES to a clinically nonsignificant value (0.2).

3. Results

3.1. Characteristics of the studies

Three Prazosin and 10 CBT studies used between-group comparison and randomization to assign participants except for one Prazosin study. However, no randomized Studies specified when they fulfilled CONSORT criteria [21]. Their comparison groups were placebo treatment, waiting list, or no active treatment. All studies used a convenience population sample. Eight Prazosin and 13 CBT studies had immediate post-evaluation. Only one Prazosin and 11 CBT studies reported data at follow-up.

Author, year	Mean dosage achieved (mg/day)(SD)	Time of prescription (in weeks)	Procedure for dosage	Tapering mentioned
Boynton et al., 2009	2.30 (1.40)	8	Yes	–
Calohan et al., 2010	4.10 (2.20)	–	Yes	No
Peskind et al., 2003	2.30 (0.70)	8	Yes	No
Raskind et al., 2002	9.60 (0.90)	8	Yes	No
Raskind et al., 2003	9.50 (0.50)	9	Yes	Yes
Raskind et al., 2007	13.30 (3.00)	8	Yes	No
Taylor et al., 2008	3.10 (1.30)	3	Yes	Yes
Thompson et al., 2008	9.60 (6.00)	–	Yes	–

Table 1. Treatment characteristics for Prazosin studies.

There was a large variation in the total sample sizes from $n = 9$ to $n = 51$, or a total of 181 participants for Prazosin studies; and a variation from $n = 4$ to $n = 278$ for CBTs, or a total of 1169 participants. We also observed a variation in female proportions: from 0% to 84.62% in Prazosin treatments, and from 0% to 100 % in CBTs. Mean ages varied from $M = 26.69$ to $M = 76.00$ for Prazosin, and $M = 36.17$ to $M = 59.42$ for CBTs. The attrition rates varied from 0% to 40% for Prazosin and from 0% to 53.85% for CBTs. The percentage of participants who did not finish the treatment did not differ by type of treatment (Prazosin or CBT) ($p = 0.08$). The first most common trauma for both types of studies was combat experience, followed by sexual assault and mixed trauma. No studies recorded medical comorbidities. To evaluate the impact of Prazosin on PTSD symptoms, only two studies reported global score for PTSD questionnaires. CBTs studies mainly used questionnaires related to PTSD symptom intensity (such as the PTSD Checklist Civilian Version). Finally, four Prazosin studies used the CAPS and more precisely its item D1 for sleep disturbance related to PTSD, and one study used the PSQI to evaluate sleep quality at large.

Author, year	Type of CBT	No. of sessions	Mean duration (min)	Delivery	Therapists	PTSD addressed	Insomnia addressed
Cook et al., 2010	IRT	6	90	GROUP	PSY and OTHER	No	No
Davis & Wright, 2005b	ERRT	3	120	GROUP	–	No	Yes
Davis & Wright, 2007	ERRT	3	120	IND/GROUP	–	No	Yes
Davis et al., 2011	ERRT	3	120	IND/GROUP	–	No	Yes
Forbes et al., 2001	IRT	6	90	GROUP	PSY	No	No
Germain &Nielsen, 2003	IRT	1	180	GROUP	–	No	No
Germain et al., 2012	IRT	8	45	IND	STU	No	Yes
Gerlinde C. Harb et al., 2009	IRT	7.5	–	IND	PSY and OTHER	No	Yes
Krakow, Johnston, et al., 2001	IRT	3	200	GROUP	OTHER	No	Yes
Krakow et al., 2000	IRT	3	140	GROUP	–	No	No
Krakow, Hollifield, et al., 2001	IRT	3	140	GROUP	OTHER	No	Yes
Lancee et al., 2010	IRT/IRT+ SH/IRT +SH+LDT	–	–	REMOTE	–	No	NA
Lu et al., 2009	IRT	6	90	GROUP	PSY and OTHER	No	–
Nappi et al., 2010	IRT	5	90	IND/GROUP	SPY and STU	No	No
Pruiksma, 2011	ERRT	3	105	IND/GROUP	SPY and STU	No	Yes

Author, year	Type of CBT	No. of sessions	Mean duration (min)	Delivery	Therapists	PTSD addressed	Insomnia addressed
Swanson et al., 2009	ERRT	10	90	GROUP	PSY	No	Yes
Thunker & Pietrowsky, 2012	IRT	8	50	–	–	No	No
Ulmer et al., 2011	IRT	6	60	IND	PSY	No	Yes

Note. ERRT: exposure, relaxation and rescripting therapy; IRT: imagery rehearsal therapy; LDT: lucid dreaming therapy; OTHER: other professions (e.g., nurse, physician); NA: not applicable; PSY: psychologist; SH: sleep hygiene; STU: graduate student in psychology; REMOTE: treatment administered remotely (e.g., mail, Internet, video).

Table 2. Characteristics of CBT studies.

Tables 1 and **2**, respectively, present treatment characteristics for Prazosin and CBT studies. In **Table 1**, the mean dosage of Prazosin varies from M = 2.30 to M = 13.30 mg/day with a time of prescription ranging from three to nine weeks. All studies provided a procedure to initiate a stable Prazosin dosage but only two studies described a tapering process.

In **Table 2**, 13 studies looked at IRT efficacy, 5 at ERRT, 1 at IRT incorporating sleep hygiene (SH), and another at IRT incorporating SH and LDT. The mean number of sessions was 5 (from 1 session to 10 sessions), and they lasted from 45 to 140 minutes. They were mainly delivered in a group format by a psychologist. None of the therapies directly addressed PTSD, but half of them specifically addressed insomnia (since the ERRT protocol automatically incorporates the reduction of bad sleep habits).

Regarding NM definitions employed in each study, we noticed that all Prazosin studies used the DSM-IV-TR definition based on the CAPS-B2. It contrasts with CBT studies where they varied between articles, some applying the DSM-IV-TR definition, their own definition, or not providing one. Concerning NM frequency as an inclusion criterion, Prazosin studies employed the CAPS-B2 with a cutoff varying from three to six out of eight. For CBT studies, the criterion used most often was at least one NM per week in the last month or in the last six months. Finally, concerning NM content, as Prazosin studies referred to the CAPS-B2, NMs were related to trauma but it was not specified if they were a replica of the event or only trauma-related. In CBT studies, a few authors gave this information, as in Cook et al. [30] where NM were replica or in Forbes et al. [34] with only trauma-related NM.

3.2. Effect size summary on PTNMs

ES for Prazosin evaluated by the CAPS-B2 (weekly PTNMs in the last month) varied from a small effect (0.28) to a large effect (3.91) (see **Figure 2**). The combined ES was to g = 1.30, 95% CI [0.61, 2.00], which indicates a significant large effect (Z = 3.66, p < 0.001). There was significant heterogeneity in ES across samples (Q (6) = 21.38, $p < 0.001$) and a significant 72% of the total variability among ES indicates that the inconsistency between studies is high ($I^2 = 71.93$, 95% CI [39.21, 87.04]).

Initially, ES was computed with one additional study [25]. After an outcome sensitivity analysis, homogeneity appeared to be affected by the result of this specific study, which also conflicted with the rest of the studies. We, therefore, decided to compute Prazosin combined ES without it.

Regarding subgroup analyses (group comparison and mean dosage subgroups), no significant differences were found. However, the small number of studies and, therefore, the loss of power could explain nonsignificant heterogeneity within each subgroup [56] while differences could be observed (e.g.,"under 5 mg," vs. "between 5 and 10 mg").

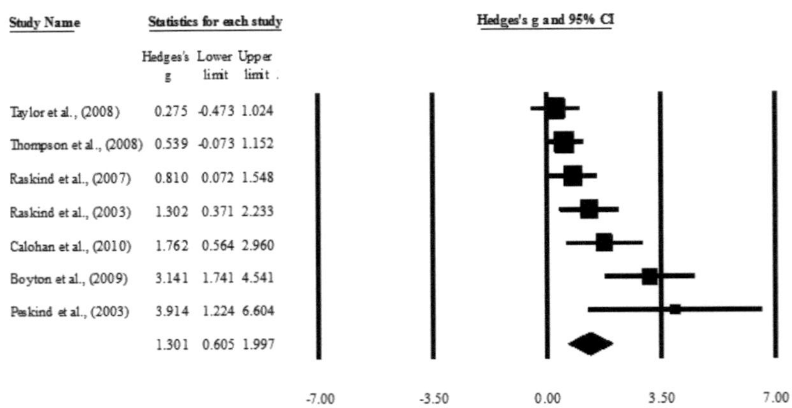

Figure 2. Results of meta-analysis for Prazosin studies using the CAPS-B2 and under the Random-effect model.

Figure 3 reports the ES summary for CBT studies on weekly PTNM frequency. We noticed ES varied from a small effect (0.07) to a large effect (1.75). The combined ES was $g = 0.55$, 95% CI [0.38, 0.72], which indicates a significant moderate effect size for CBTs on weekly PTNM frequency ($Z = 6.21$ $p < 0.001$). There was significant heterogeneity in ES across samples (Q (19) = 35.26, $p < 0.05$) with a moderate amount of observed heterogeneity (46%). The inconsistency between studies was moderately high ($I^2 = 46.12$). Subgroup analyses did not reveal any statistical differences between studies. As mentioned before, this result may be due to loss of power rather than to homogeneity alone.

3.3. Secondary effect size summary

Concerning the PTSD symptoms, the ES for three studies varied from a small effect (0.27) to a large effect (0.88). Their combined ES was $g = 0.58$, 95% CI [0.12, 1.04] and was significant for CBT on PTSD symptoms ($Z = 2.45$, $p < 0.05$). The analysis found homogeneity in ES across samples (Q (2) = 1.18, $p = 0.55$). The amount of observed heterogeneity was null (0%), and therefore, there was no inconsistency between the studies ($I^2 = 0.00$).

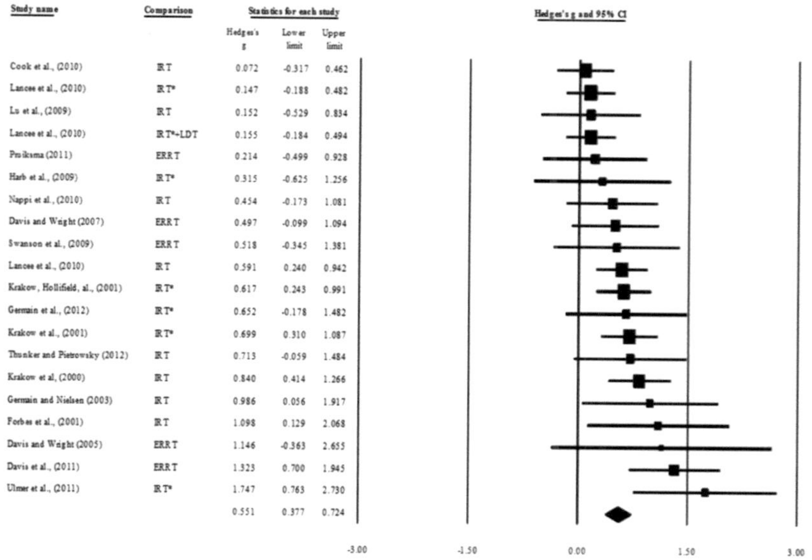

Figure 3. Results of meta-analysis for CBT studies on weekly NM frequency and under the Random-effect model.

For the PSQI variable, ES varied from a medium effect (0.71) to a large effect (0.98). The combined ES was $g = 0.83$, 95% CI [0.32, 1.35], which indicates a significant and large effect of Prazosin treatment on sleep quality ($Z = 3.16$, $p < 0.05$). There was nonsignificant heterogeneity in ES across samples (Q (1) = 0.30, $p = 0.58$). The amount of observed heterogeneity was null (0%), and therefore, there was no inconsistency between the studies ($I^2 = 0.00$).

Regarding the CAPS-D1 variable, ES varied from a medium effect (0.48) to a large effect (1.74). The combined ES was $g = 1.26$, 95% CI [0.62, 1.89], indicating a significant large effect of Prazosin on PTSD sleep difficulties ($Z = 3.88$, $p < 0.001$). There was nonsignificant heterogeneity in ES across samples (Q (3) = 5.59, $p = 0.133$). The amount of observed heterogeneity was moderate (46%) and confirmed that inconsistency between studies was moderately large ($I^2 = 46.36$).

The impact of CBTs on the intensity of PTSD symptoms varied from small ES (0.02) to large ES (1.46). The combined ES in 16 studies was $g = 0.59$, 95% CI [0.38, 0.80], which indicates a significant large effect ($Z = 5.47$, $p < 0.001$). There was significant heterogeneity between studies (Q (15) = 35.24, $p < 0.05$) and a significant 57% of the total of the variance among ES indicates that inconsistency between studies was moderately large ($I^2 = 57.43$). Subgroup analyses did not reveal any statistical differences between them. Previously, the amount of the observed heterogeneity was higher (75%) and could be related to high heterogeneity across studies ($I^2 = 74.68$). There was also a significant heterogeneity in ES across samples (Q (16) = 63.19, $p < 0.001$). ES varied from small ES (0.02) to large (5.70) and the combined ES across 17 studies was $g = 0.69$, 95% CI [0.42, 0.97], which indicated a significant moderate effect for CBTs ($Z = 4.96$, $p < 0.001$). Therefore, an outcome sensitivity analysis between studies was performed. Homogeneity was affected by the result of the Ulmer et al.'s study (2011) [46], which conflicts (5.70) with the rest of the studies and we therefore decided to compute the combined ES without this study.

Concerning the impact on PSQI outcome, ES varied from 0.07 to 4.63. The combined ES computed for 14 studies was $g = 0.95$, 95% CI [0.56, 1.34], which indicated a significant large CBT effect ($Z = 4.78$ $p < 0.001$). There was significant heterogeneity in ES across samples (Q (13) = 66.27, $p < 0.001$). The amount of observed heterogeneity was high (80%) and can be associated with true variance across studies ($I^2 = 80.39$). Therefore, an outcome sensitivity analysis between studies was performed and no studies appeared to influence heterogeneity. No statistical differences between subgroup analyses were found, except for the subgroup insomnia, which was marginally significant with Q (1) = 3.39, $p = 0.07$. It appeared that the addition of one sleep management component has a better effect on PSQI.

Another impact on sleep is insomnia where ES varied from 0.72 to 1.77. The combined ES, computed for six studies, was $g = 1.06$, 95% CI [0.78, 1.34], which represents a significant large effect of CBTs ($Z = 7.41$, $p < 0.001$). There was no significant heterogeneity in ES across samples (Q (5) = 2.69, $p = 0.75$). The amount of observed heterogeneity was null (0%), and therefore, there was no inconsistency between the studies ($I^2 = 0.00$).

3.4. Publication bias

The shapes of the funnel plots of Prazosin outcomes (CAPS-B2, PTSD symptoms, and CAPS-D1) gave some indications of publication bias. The Orwin fail-safe test revealed that 27 studies for CAPS-B2, 6 studies for PTSD symptoms, and 20 studies for CAPS-D1 with a null effect should theoretically be added to the analysis to obtain a combined ES of 0.2. The funnel plots did not reveal any publication biases, and the Orwin fail-safe test results were large for CAPS-B2 and CAPS-D1. Therefore,the results from these two outcomes in this meta-analysis are valid and publication biases are negligible. However, caution is advised when interpreting the results for PTSD symptoms, given that six studies are sufficient to invalidate the analyses. Also, it was not possible to run publication bias analyses for PSQI, as we only had two studies.

The funnel plot shapes for CBTs indicated a limited effect of publication bias on the results. Also, Orwin fail-safe test results were 30 for weekly NM frequency, 30 for PTSD intensity, 43 for PSQI, and 26 for insomnia measure. As the funnel plots did not reveal any publication biases, and the Orwin fail-safe test results were large, we therefore concluded that CBT results from this meta-analysis are valid and publication biases are negligible.

4. Discussion

4.1. Search results

Fifty-one studies considered treatments specifically targeting PTNMs in an adult population, and 26 studies reported data and were, therefore, included in this meta-analysis. Out of eight Prazosin studies, only three reported data on PTSD symptoms, two on sleep difficulties (using the PSQI), and four on insomnia (using the CAPS-D1). Of the 18 CBTs, 17 reported data on PTSD symptoms, 14 on sleep difficulties with the PSQI, and 6 on insomnia (using the ISI and SII). We also noticed a tendency for ERRT, IRT, or Prazosin studies to be conducted by the same research teams [27, 40, 60]. In fact, five out of eight teams working on Prazosin effect were from the University of Washington in Seattle. Of the 18 CBT studies for nightmares, 4 were issued from the University of Tulsa and 2 from the University of Philadelphia. Also, these studies were mostly published after 2000. This small number of studies is not surprising, as PTSD study in psychology and in PTNM research is quite new. It was only in 1980, PTSD was introduced in the DSM-III, and only in 1989 that Ross et al. [61] presented the hypothesis that "sleep disturbances are the hallmark of PTSD," which opened the study of PTNMs. Also, PTNMs are conceptualized as one of the intrusive symptoms of PTSD [3], and therefore, as a secondary symptom of PTSD. In the dreaming field, they are seen as an adaptive function to emotionally adjust to trauma. This main discrepancy hinders their introduction in PTSD treatment and slows down and complicates their inclusion in research. Besides, recommendations concerning NM treatments were only published in 2010 [15], and the first reported open-label study of Prazosin for PTNM treatment was conducted in 2000 [62].

4.2. Treatment efficacy

Looking at the positive results of the impact of Prazosin ($g = 1.30$) and CBTs ($g = 0.55$) on PTNM reduction, we found that treatments specifically targeting NMs are efficient. It was not possible to directly compare CBTs for NMs to Prazosin, but considering the large ES for Prazosin, we may conclude its efficacy is superior to CBTs for NMs in the reduction of PTNMs at post-treatment. However, several considerations on the overall efficacy of each treatment need to be examined and caution in confirming the superiority of Prazosin over CBT is advised.

First of all, only one study [36] has compared both treatments with a placebo group at short and long terms. Prazosin demonstrated slightly better results than CBTs. However, authors reported that their results did not differ at the four-month follow-up assessment.

Another consideration is that most medications have side effects that may force participants to withdraw from one treatment [63]. From a few Prazosin studies, we know researchers sometimes had to stop its administration due to adverse effects, such as dizziness [22], nausea and headache [23], and fainting and nasal congestion [64]. Nevertheless, attrition rates did not statistically differ from Prazosin treatment (0–40.00%) to CBT (0–54.31%). Also, CBT can also present side effects as costs, stigma, etc., but no information was provided. This aspect should therefore be considered in the future for both types of treatments.

Also, the majority of Prazosin studies did not report data at follow-up. It seems the authors' first objectives were to determine the optimal dose to be NM free. It is therefore impossible to evaluate the rate of relapse after stopping this treatment, whereas CBTs reported data at follow-up. In Raskind et al. [26], the authors mentioned that Prazosin effect did not persist after its cessation in a few patients, who returned to their initial NM frequency. This observation reminds us of the broader issue of medications benefits compared to psychological treatments in PTSD [63].

Another concern is related to the characteristics of the studies, which could have influenced the computed combined ES for both types of treatments. First, we noticed large variations in the sample sizes, with a total of 181 participants for Prazosin (from $n = 9$ to $n = 51$) and 1169 participants for CBTs (from $n = 4$ to $n = 278$). In addition, the evaluation of NMs varied between the two types of treatments (CAPS-B2 versus self-reported questionnaires). Moreover, Prazosin effect seems to vary according to its mean dosage, as the effect of a "small" dosage ("under 5 mg," $g = 1.57$) was equivalent or even more efficient than a higher dosage ("between 5 and 10 mg," $g = 1.30$; "over 10 mg," $g = 0.81$) (without reaching a statistically significant difference). On the other hand, some CBT studies did not favor immediate postevaluation and only reported data at follow-up (e.g., [30]).

When analyzing the efficacy of CBTs for NMs, we noticed that variations in their formats (individual compared to group format) or in the type of treatment (ERRT compared to IRT) could influence their impact. For example, even if subgroup analyses did not show any statistical differences, subgroup ES for individual CBT was higher ($g = 0.87$) than the other types of formats. Also, treatment efficacy varied according to the type of CBT, with a slightly higher ES subgroup for ERRT ($g = 0.70$) over IRT ($g = 0.56$). To date, only a few studies have looked at the therapeutic ingredients for these two CBTs, and it would be interesting to directly compare them in the future.

Finally, to attain our second objective, we underlined that the efficacy of these two treatments was not limited to PTNMs and extended to other symptoms. Their impacts were positive and equivalent for PTSD symptoms ($g = 0.58$ for Prazosin; $g = 0.59$ for CBTs), for the PSQI ($g = 0.83$ for Prazosin; $g = 0.95$ for CBTs), and for sleep in general ($g = 1.25$ for Prazosin; $g = 1.06$ for CBTs). No subgroup analysis achieved statistical significance except for the subgroup looking at the efficacy of incorporating a sleep management component, which was marginally statistically significant for the PSQI. This result means therapists or researchers should therefore consider adding this component to IRT or to enhance it in ERRT.

As mentioned before, caution is advised in interpreting these results as discrepancies remained with the type of questionnaires selected. Nevertheless, these secondary effects of treatments specifically targeting NMs are interesting. Even if previous ESs are moderate or high, they are similar to those published in Belleville et al. [20]. The author pointed out that CBT for insomnia had a moderate impact on anxiety in individuals who presented insomnia, with or without a comorbid anxiety disorder. In the case of PTSD, it is therefore important to evaluate the impact of Prazosin and CBTs for NMs on PTSD.

4.3. Implication of results

The large ESs obtained for Prazosin and CBTs demonstrate to clinicians the relevance of using specific NM treatments. From a research point of view, these positive results emphasize the idea that PTNM could become an independent disorder rather than a PTSD symptom that should disappear with conventional CBT or medications. Therefore, it requires a specific treatment, and studies in the PTSD field should focus more on sleep. Moreover, a limited update of the literature search was performed since December 2012, four articles [65–68] were published, as well as new meta-analysis and systematic reviews [69, 70], and still support the present results.

http://dx.doi.org/10.5772/64224

Prazosin, as a medication and because it is linked to PTSD biology and to the neurobiological, correlates between PTSD symptoms and sleep and presents several advantages compared to psychological treatments. First, it seems to offer the possibility of treating nightmares without considering their content compared to CBTs for NM. It represents an interesting option for some patients, for example, when therapy is not available (e.g., soldiers who are still on duty) [63]. It can also have a positive impact on the other PTSD symptoms; and finally, its low cost makes it a promising pharmacological option. However, it seems to take most of the time eight weeks prescription to obtain positive result while observing only one CBT session can be sufficient to train a patient to get rid of his nightmares. Moreover, no standard for Prazosin administration and duration exists.

On the other hand, psychological treatments help to deal with frightening content of NM. It is theoretically believed that CBTs for NM repair the normal sleep process which has been disrupted by NM. In fact, one sleep function is to select, classify, and consolidate information and the emotions lived during the day in the long-term memory [71]. When this process is interrupted by NM because of a strong emotion, the integration of new memories is impeded. In PTSD, individuals live negative emotions during PTNM, and the incorporation of the information related to the traumatic event fails [72, 73]. Compared to Prazosin, the main advantages of ERRT and IRT are easy and rapid learning (sometimes in one session), of how to eliminate NM. But their main disadvantage is that no standards have been proposed to deliver them, and research needs to be conducted for different types of trauma, different types of NM content, and different participant characteristics (such as gender).

4.4. Strength and limitations

Studies may not be exactly the same or perfect. Disparities remained as the two treatments diverge clinically and methodologically, and therefore, heterogeneity had to be expected. However, analyses reflected that no bias could be detected. Nevertheless, caution should be exercised in the interpretation of the efficacy of Prazosin for PTSD symptoms. First, it was not possible to directly compare Prazosin against CBTs for PTNMs. Also, no information was provided on therapeutic maintenance. We observed variations in CBTs format and Prazosin administration. Methodological limits were detected due to a lack of questionnaire standardization to evaluate PTNMs; and NM definitions or NM content were not reported.Finally, variations in the population (sex and age) and in sample sizes were also observed.

There are some limitations including experimental and quasi experimental studies in this meta-analysis as in the latter case, the treatment and control groups may not be comparable at baseline. However, several strategies were used to increase the validity of our results: (1) reviewing each study to carefully interpret our results; (2) grouping outcome by type of questionnaire evaluating the same construct; (3) ES analyses within subgroups was a way of investigating variations; and (4) deciding upon inclusion criteria ahead of the review process and reporting them in a protocol. In spite of all these precautions, a larger *N*, more particularly for Prazosin, would have increased the statistical power of our analysis and would have helped us to highlight interesting results within subgroup analyses. Therefore, the combined ES reported are valid. Also, the "file drawer problem" criticism can be ignored for CBT studies and should be interpreted with caution for Prazosin studies, more particularly for the PTSD symptom variable [47].

Finally, systematic reviews and meta-analysis have previously been published on these new psychological treatments and on Prazosin (e.g., [17, 74–78]). The main advantages of the present study are, compared to the previous ones, to have screened studies written in English and French and to have considered randomized and nonrandomized studies. Also, if looked at all types of nightmares, treatments not only considered imagery rehearsal treatments, in an adult population with PTSD evaluated by validated questionnaires or structured interviews. At last, this study combined both a meta-analysis and a systematic review on CBT for nightmares and Prazosin, which allowed discussing their respective impacts and advantages.

4.5. Further studies

Despite the contribution of this study, future trials should consider some of the weaknesses observed in this meta-analysis when NM is in a PTSD context. First, efforts should be made to standardize the methodology used by including a control group, reporting outcomes at follow-ups, and giving NM definition or content.

Also, the different methods used to evaluate NM frequency in this meta-analysis emphasized that standardization was needed for questionnaire administration, NM definition, and treatment format. In fact, we observed that all Prazosin studies used the CAPS, a retrospective measure to evaluate NM, while CBTs used both self-reported retrospective and prospective measures like home daily logs. More precisely, all Prazosin studies evaluated NM using the CAPS-B2 item, compared to CBTs, which retrieved items evaluating NM from various retrospective questionnaires or home sleep logs. Only two studies, by the same author [36, 79], included objective sleep measurements (polysomnography, PSG). To date, prospective daily logs are considered the gold standard for the measurement of NM frequency [80], as self-reports underestimate current NM frequency [81]. Therefore, results could differ according to the method of measurement used and caution is advised in evaluating to Prazosin impact.

Only a few studies specified NM definition. Even if most studies adhered to a frequency cutoff of one weekly nightmare minimum or an average of two or more NM per week, it is not clear what participants understood by NM. In Prazosin studies, the CAPS-B2 item refers to the frequency and the intensity of recurrent distressing dreams related to the traumatic event. Therefore, we could wonder if the impact of Prazosin was on NM frequency or on NM distress. This could influence the interpretation of results. In addition, we could not retrieve information regarding NM content. As we know, PTNMs may be trauma-related or replicative trauma [3]. Therefore, it would have been interesting to have access to this information in order to evaluate which kind of PTNM contents was targeted and by which CBT. In fact, each treatment has its own rationale and degree of exposure to the selected NM. Therefore, this information would be an indicator of which PTNM contents favor each treatment and could help to refine guidelines.

Disparities were also observed in sample characteristics, with women being less represented than men, more particularly in Prazosin studies; and with combat experience and sexual

http://dx.doi.org/10.5772/64224

assaults being the main considered trauma. Research in the PTSD field is closely linked to war history but it is also important to consider other types of trauma. We could wonder, for instance, if one of the CBTs for NM would be more adapted according to the type of trauma (i.e., PTNM content being different in each case). This will help to generalize the results and to provide guidelines to clinicians in choosing which treatment to apply in a specific situation.

Recommendations on treatment delivery should be proposed (mean dosage, no. of sessions, and NM content) in order to help clinicians and to allow comparison between studies. This meta-analysis raises the possibility to directly treat PTNMs, as a symptom of PTSD, but clinical aspects should be examined. Can we combine any treatment for PTSD with any treatment for PTNMs? Which treatment should be prioritized in complicated PTSD? Could we add Prazosin at any moment in the treatment? Which treatment for PTNMs will be more appropriate in function of individual characteristics (such as gender or type of trauma)? Could we incorporate specific NM treatments in a conventional CBT for PTSD? Many avenues are opened to those who want to participate in standard PTSD treatment improvement.

Finally, secondary measures, such as PTSD scores and sleep, should be recorded.

5. Conclusions

We know CBTs and SSRIs do not effectively resolve all PTSD symptoms, as nightmares were found to be treatment resistant and residual insomnia was reported. From the positive results of this meta-analysis, we know specific NM treatments (Prazosin or CBTs) contribute to NM reduction. These treatments also demonstrate PTSD and sleep symptom reduction. The overall conclusion of this meta-analysis is that treating NM with Prazosin or CBTs directly is interesting and can be a way to improve conventional CBTs for PTSD. However, no consensus or guidelines are available to treat PTNMs. From these outcomes, clinicians can conclude that NM can affect the efficacy of first-line PTSD treatments, and new treatments are developed to solve this problem, while in sleep research PTSD outcomes should be reported.

Author details

Katia Levrier[1], Carolyn Leathead[1], Delphine-Émilie Bourdon[1], Sophie Lacerte[1], André Marchand[1*] and Geneviève Belleville[2]

*Address all correspondence to: marchand.andre@uqam.ca

1 Department of Psychology, Université of Quebec in Montreal, Montreal, Canada

2 Université Laval, Québec, Canada

References

[1] American Psychiatric Association. (2013). Diagnostic and statistical manual of mental disorders (5th ed.). Arlington, VA: American Psychiatric Publishing.

[2] Lancee, J., et al., A systematic review of cognitive-behavioral treatment for nightmares: toward a well-established treatment. J Clin Sleep Med, 2008. 4(5): p. 475-80.

[3] Phelps, A., D. Forbes, and M. Creamer, Understanding posttraumatic nightmares: an empirical and conceptual review. Clin Psychol Rev, 2008. 28(2): 338–355.

[4] Walker, M.P., Cognitive consequences of sleep and sleep loss. Sleep Med, 2008. 9(Suppl. 1): S29–S34.

[5] Caldwell, B.A. and N. Redeker, Sleep and trauma: an overview. Issues Mental Health Nursing, 2005. 26(7): 721–738.

[6] Pruiksma, K.M.E., A randomized controlled trial of exposure, relaxation, and rescripting therapy and relaxation training for chronic nightmares in trauma-exposed persons: findings at one week posttreatment, University of Tulsa, Tulsa, USA, 2011.

[7] Maher, M.J., S.A. Rego, and G.M. Asnis, Sleep disturbances in patients with post-traumatic stress disorder: epidemiology, impact and approaches to management. CNS Drugs, 2006. 20(7): 567–590.

[8] American Psychiatric Association, Diagnostic and statistical manual of mental disorders, 4th ed., text rev., American Psychiatric Association, Washington, DC, 2000.

[9] Ponniah, K. and S. Hollon, Empirically supported psychological treatments for adult acute stress disorder and posttraumatic stress disorder: a review. Depress Anxiety, 2009. 26(12): 1086–1109.

[10] Stein, D.J., J.C. Ipser, and S. Seedat, Pharmacotherapy for post traumatic stress disorder (PTSD). Cochrane Database Syst Rev, 2006(1): p. CD002795

[11] Belleville, G., et al., The impact of cognitive-behavior therapy for anxiety disorders on concomitant sleep disturbances: a meta-analysis. J Anxiety Disord, 2010. 24(4): 379–386.

[12] Galovski, T.E., et al., Does cognitive-behavioral therapy for PTSD improve perceived health and sleep impairment? J Trauma Stress, 2009. 22(3): 197–204.

[13] Krakow, B. and A. Zadra, Clinical management of chronic nightmares: imagery rehearsal therapy. Behav Sleep Med, 2006. 4(1): 45–70.

[14] Lydiard, R.B. and M.H. Hamner, Clinical importance of sleep disturbance as a treatment target in PTSD. Focus, 2009. VII(2): 176–183.

[15] Aurora, R.N., et al., Best practice guide for the treatment of nightmare disorder in adults. J Clin Sleep Med, 2010. 6(4): 389–401.

[16] Aurora, R.N., et al., Revisiting evidence-based guidelines: not such a nightmare standards of practice committee. J Clin Sleep Med, 2011. 7(5): 554–556.

[17] Hudson, S.M., et al., Prazosin for the treatment of nightmares related to posttraumatic stress disorder: a review of the literature. Prim Care Companion CNS Disord, 2012. 14(2). doi: 10.4088/PCC.11r01222

[18] Zadra, A. and R.O. Pihl, Lucid dreaming as a treatment for recurrent nightmares. Psychother Psychosom, 1997. 66(1): 50–55.

[19] Lerner, F. and J.L. Hamblen, Surveying the traumatic stress literature: the effective use of bibliographic databases in preparing reviews and meta-analyses. J Trauma Stress, 2010. 23(6): 819–822.

[20] Belleville, G., et al., Meta-analytic review of the impact of cognitive-behavior therapy for insomnia on concomitant anxiety. Clin Psychol Rev, 2011. 31(4): 638–652.

[21] Altman, D.G., et al., The revised CONSORT statement for reporting randomized trials: explanation and elaboration. Ann Intern Med, 2001. 134(8): 663–694.

[22] Boynton, L., et al., Preliminary findings concerning the use of prazosin for the treatment of posttraumatic nightmares in a refugee population. J Psychiatr Pract, 2009. 15(6): 454–459.

[23] Calohan, J., et al., Prazosin treatment of trauma nightmares and sleep disturbance in soldiers deployed in Iraq. J Trauma Stress, 2010. 23(5): 645–648.

[24] Peskind, E.R., et al., Prazosin reduces trauma-related nightmares in older men with chronic posttraumatic stress disorder. J Geriatric Psychiatry Neurol, 2003. 16(3): 165–171.

[25] Raskind, M.A., et al., Prazosin reduces nightmares in combat veterans with posttraumatic stress disorder. J Clini Psychiatry, 2002. 63(7): 565–568.

[26] Raskind, M.A., et al., Reduction of nightmares and other PTSD symptoms in combat veterans by prazosin: a placebo-controlled study. Am J Psychiatry, 2003. 160(2): p. 371-3.

[27] Raskind, M.A., et al., A parallel group placebo controlled study of prazosin for trauma nightmares and sleep disturbance in combat veterans with post-traumatic stress disorder. Biol Psychiatry, 2007. 61(8): 928–934.

[28] Taylor, F.B., et al., Prazosin effects on objective sleep measures and clinical symptoms in civilian trauma posttraumatic stress disorder: a placebo-controlled study. Biol Psychiatry, 2008. 63(6): 629–632.

[29] Thompson, C.E., et al., Nonnightmare distressed awakenings in veterans with posttraumatic stress disorder: response to prazosin. J Trauma Stress, 2008. 21(4): 417–420.

[30] Cook, J., et al., Imagery rehearsal for posttraumatic nightmares: a randomized controlled trial. J Trauma Stress, 2010. 23(5): 553–563.

[31] Davis, J.L. and D.C. Wright, Case series utilizing exposure, relaxation, and rescripting therapy: impact on nightmares, sleep quality, and psychological distress. Behav Sleep Med, 2005. 3(3): 151–157.

[32] Davis, J.L. and D.C. Wright, Randomized clinical trial for treatment of chronic nightmares in trauma-exposed adults. J Trauma Stress, 2007. 20(2): 123–133.

[33] Davis, J.L., et al., Physiological predictors of response to exposure, relaxation, and rescripting therapy for chronic nightmares in a randomized clinical trial. J Clin Sleep Med, 2011. 7(6): 622–631.

[34] Forbes, D., A. Phelps, and T. McHugh, Treatment of combat-related nightmares using imagery rehearsal: a pilot study. J Trauma Stress, 2001. 14(2): 433–442.

[35] Germain, A. and T. Nielsen, Impact of imagery rehearsal treatment on distressing dreams, psychological distress, and sleep parameters in nightmare patients. Behav Sleep Med, 2003. 1(3): 140–154.

[36] Germain, A., et al., Placebo-controlled comparison of prazosin and cognitive-behavioral treatments for sleep disturbances in US Military Veterans. J Psychosom Res, 2012. 72(2): 89–96.

[37] Harb, G.C., et al., Post-traumatic stress disorder nightmares and sleep disturbance in Iraq war veterans: A feasible and promising treatment combination. J Aggression Maltreatment Trauma, 2009. 18(5): 516–531.

[38] Krakow, B., et al., An open-label trial of evidence-based cognitive behavior therapy for nightmares and insomnia in crime victims with PTSD. Am J Psychiatr, 2001. 158(12): 2043–2047.

[39] Krakow, B., et al., A controlled study of imagery rehearsal for chronic nightmares in sexual assault survivors with PTSD: a preliminary report. J Trauma Stress, 2000. 13(4): 589–609.

[40] Krakow, B., et al., Imagery rehearsal therapy for chronic nightmares in sexual assault survivors with posttraumatic stress disorder: a randomized controlled trial. JAMA, 2001. 286(5): 537–545.

[41] Lancee, J., J. van den Bout, and V.I. Spoormaker, Expanding self-help Imagery Rehearsal Therapy for nightmares with sleep hygiene and lucid dreaming: a waiting-list controlled trial. Int J Dream Res, 2010. 3(2): 111–120.

[42] Lu, M., et al., Imagery rehearsal therapy for posttraumatic nightmares in U.S. veterans. J Trauma Stress, 2009. 22(3): 236–239.

[43] Nappi, C.M., et al., Effectiveness of imagery rehearsal therapy for the treatment of combat-related nightmares in veterans. Behav Ther, 2010. 41(2): 237–244.

[44] Swanson, L.M., et al., A combined group treatment for nightmares and insomnia in combat veterans: a pilot study. J Trauma Stress, 2009. 22(6): 639–642.

[45] Thunker, J. and R. Pietrowsky, Effectiveness of a manualized imagery rehearsal therapy for patients suffering from nightmare disorders with and without a comorbidity of depression or PTSD. Behav Res Ther, 2012. 50(9): 558–564.

[46] Ulmer, C.S., J.D. Edinger, and P.S. Calhoun, A multi-component cognitive-behavioral intervention for sleep disturbance in veterans with PTSD: a pilot study. J Clin Sleep Med, 2011. 7(1): 57–68.

[47] Borenstein, M., et al., eds. Introduction to meta-analysis, John Wiley and Sons, Chichester, UK, 2009.

[48] Comprehensive Meta-Analysis [Computer software]. (2012). Englewood, NJ: Biostat. Available from http://www.comprehensive.com

[49] Blake, D., et al., The development of a Clinician-Administered PTSD Scale. J Trauma Stress, 1995. 8(1): 75–90.

[50] Sundin, E.C. and M.J. Horowitz, Impact of event scale: psychometric properties. Br J Psychiatry, 2012. 180: 205–209.

[51] Weathers, F., T. Keane, and J. Davidson, Clinician-administered PTSD scale: a review of the first ten years of research. Depress Anxiety, 2001. 13(3): 132–156.

[52] Foa, E.B., et al., Reliability and validity of a brief instrument for assessing post-traumatic stress disorder. J Trauma Stress, 1993. 6(4): 459–473.

[53] Foa, E.B., ed. Posttraumatic stress diagnostic scale manual, National Computer Systems Inc., Minneapolis, MN, 1995.

[54] Buysse, D.J., et al., The Pittsburgh sleep quality index: a new instrument for psychiatric practice and research. Psychiatry Res, 1989. 28(2): 193–213.

[55] Morin, C.M., Insomnia. Psychological assessment and management, Guilford Press, New York, 1993.

[56] Higgins, J.P., et al., Measuring inconsistency in meta-analyses. BMJ, 2003. 327(7414): 557–560.

[57] Huedo-Medina, T.B., et al., Assessing heterogeneity in meta-analysis: Q statistic or I2 index? Psychol Methods, 2006. 11(2): 193–206.

[58] Sterne, J. and R. Harbord, Funnel plots in meta-analysis. The Stata Journal, 2004. 4(Number 2): 127–141.

[59] Orwin, R.G., A fail-safe N for effect size in meta-analysis. J Educ Stat, 1983. 8(2): 157–159.

[60] Davis, J.L. and D.C. Wright, Case series utilizing exposure, relaxation, and rescripting therapy: impact on nightmares, sleep quality, and psychological distress. Behav Sleep Med, 2005. 3(3): 151–157.

[61] Ross, R.J., et al., Sleep disturbance as the hallmark of posttraumatic stress disorder. Am J Psychiatry, 1989. 146(6): 697–707.

[62] Dierks, M.R., J.K. Jordan, and A.H. Sheehan, Prazosin treatment of nightmares related to posttraumatic stress disorder. Ann Pharmacother, 2007. 41(6): 1013–1017.

[63] Foa, E.B., T.M. Keane, and M.J. Friedman, Effective treatments for PTSD. Practice guidelines from the international society for traumatic stress studies, 2nd ed., Guilford Publications, Inc., New York, 2008.

[64] Raskind, M.A., et al., A parallel group placebo controlled study of prazosin for trauma nightmares and sleep disturbance in combat veterans with post-traumatic stress disorder. Biol Psychiatry, 2007. 61(8): 928–934.

[65] Ahmadpanah, M., et al., Comparing the effect of prazosin and hydroxyzine on sleep quality in patients suffering from posttraumatic stress disorder. Neuropsychobiology, 2014. 69(4): 235–242.

[66] Balliett, N.E., J.L. Davis, and K.E. Miller, Efficacy of a brief treatment for nightmares and sleep disturbances for veterans. Psychol Trauma, 2015. 7(6): 507–515.

[67] Margolies, S.O., et al., Efficacy of a cognitive-behavioral treatment for insomnia and nightmares in Afghanistan and Iraq veterans with PTSD. J Clin Psychol, 2013. 69(10): 1026–1042.

[68] Raskind, M.A., et al., A trial of prazosin for combat trauma PTSD with nightmares in active-duty soldiers returned from Iraq and Afghanistan. Am J Psychiatry, 2013. 170(9): 1003–1010.

[69] Ho, F.Y., C.S. Chan, and K.N. Tang, Cognitive-behavioral therapy for sleep disturbances in treating posttraumatic stress disorder symptoms: a meta-analysis of randomized controlled trials. Clin Psychol Rev, 2016. 43: 90–102.

[70] Khachatryan, D., et al., Prazosin for treating sleep disturbances in adults with post-traumatic stress disorder: a systematic review and meta-analysis of randomized controlled trials. Gen Hosp Psychiatry, 2016. 39: 46–52.

[71] Stickgold, R. and M.P. Walker, Memory consolidation and reconsolidation: what is the role of sleep? Trends Neurosci, 2005. 28(8): 408–415.

[72] Walker, M.P., The role of sleep in cognition and emotion. Ann N Y Acad Sci, 2009. 1156: 168–197.

[73] Stickgold, R., Of sleep, memories and trauma. Nat Neurosci, 2007. 10(5): 540–542.

[74] Casement, M.D. and L.M. Swanson, A meta-analysis of imagery rehearsal for post-trauma nightmares: effects on nightmare frequency, sleep quality, and posttraumatic stress. Clin Psychol Rev, 2012. 32(6): 566–574.

[75] Escamilla, M., et al., Management of post-traumatic nightmares: a review of pharmacologic and nonpharmacologic treatments since 2010. Curr Psychiatry Rep, 2012. 14(5): 529–535.

[76] Nappi, C.M., S.P. Drummond, and J.M. Hall, Treating nightmares and insomnia in posttraumatic stress disorder: a review of current evidence. Neuropharmacology, 2012. 62(2): p. 576-85.

[77] Harb, G.C., et al., A critical review of the evidence base of imagery rehearsal for posttraumatic nightmares: pointing the way for future research. J Trauma Stress, 2013. 26(5): 570–579.

[78] Augedal, A.W., et al., Randomized controlled trials of psychological and pharmacological treatments for nightmares: a meta-analysis. Sleep Med Rev, 2012. 6(12): 00071–00078.

[79] Germain, A., et al., Effects of a brief behavioral treatment for PTSD-related sleep disturbances: a pilot study. Behav Res Ther, 2007. 45(3): 627–632.

[80] Nielsen, T. and R. Levin, Nightmares: a new neurocognitive model. Sleep Med Rev, 2007. 11(4): 295–310.

[81] Robert, G. and A. Zadra, Measuring nightmare and bad dream frequency: impact of retrospective and prospective instruments. J Sleep Res, 2008. 17(2): 132–139. doi: 10.1111/j.1365-2869.2008.00649.x.

Chapter 11

Post-Traumatic Stress Disorder Outcome Research: Why Moderators Should not be Neglected

Heike Gerger and Jens Gaab

Additional information is available at the end of the chapter

http://dx.doi.org/10.5772/103876

Abstract

Several psychotherapeutic treatments have been developed over the years for treating the symptoms of post-traumatic stress disorder (PTSD). But it remains still unclear which components of the complex treatment packages are necessary and most beneficial for PTSD symptom improvement. In PTSD outcome research, the randomized controlled trial (RCT) design has been applied in order to address this issue. However, meta-analyses repeatedly reported considerable variation between results from individual RCTs (i.e. between-study heterogeneity). Attempts to explain such heterogeneity led to the identification of relevant moderators of treatment effects in PTSD RCTs. This study presents meta-analytic findings, which show that factors, which are not part of the treatment (such as the investigators' preferences for a particular treatment or the complexity of the patients' clinical problems), impact on outcome in PTSD RCTs. We show that considering extra-therapeutic moderators in meta-analyses on PTSD RCTs may impact the conclusions and recommendations that may be deduced. The summarized findings confirm the notion that no PTSD treatment consistently outperforms the others and strengthen the position that even non-trauma-focused treatments may be beneficial PTSD treatments.

Keywords: PTSD, moderators, meta-analysis, randomized controlled outcome research, RCT, personalized psychotherapy

1. Introduction

Over the last decades, different etiological models of post-traumatic stress disorder (PTSD) have led to the design of a number of psychotherapeutic treatments that all target at reducing PTSD symptoms (e.g. exposure therapy [1], cognitive processing therapy [2], for an overview see [3]). Until recently, clinical guidelines and systematic reviews concluded that patients with PTSD require psychotherapeutic treatments that specifically target the trauma experience [4]. However, recent meta-analyses showed that focusing on the trauma experience may not be generally necessary for successful PTSD treatment [5–7].

Randomized controlled trials (RCTs) have typically been conducted in order to identify those components of complex treatment packages that critically impact symptom improvement (i.e. in placebo-controlled studies and comparative or dismantling studies, see [8]). Recently, however, the general validity of RCTs has been criticized in medical as well as in psychotherapy research, by showing that extra-therapeutic factors (such as blinding of outcome assessors or the sample size) may considerably affect the outcome in RCTs [9–12]. Accordingly, meta-analyses, which attempted to explain variation between effect estimates from individual studies—the so-called between-study heterogeneity—identified a number of moderators of treatment effects in PTSD RCTs [7, 13–16].

This paper summarizes meta-analytic findings, which show that in PTSD outcome research extra-therapeutic factors affect the outcome. These findings relate to two questions in the current debate in PTSD outcome research: first, 'Is there evidence that some PTSD treatments consistently outperform others?' and second, 'Is a trauma focus generally necessary for successful PTSD treatment?'. We will briefly describe the research designs that have been used in order to address the abovementioned questions. Then, we will describe common flaws in meta-analyses and we will use examples from PTSD research in order to show how flaws in meta-analyses may lead to invalid conclusions. And finally, we will summarize how the consideration of relevant moderators may alter the conclusions that may be drawn from meta-analyses of RCTs with respect to the two highlighted research questions.

2. What is characteristic in PTSD treatments?

Psychotherapy outcome research aims at identifying treatment components that are critical for symptom improvement. The RCT design has been adopted from medical research and became standard in psychotherapy outcome research. This design relies on the assumption that the overall treatment effect is composed of first, the true effect of the treatment under investigation and second, effects that are due to the context of being in treatment.

Whereas the first type of components has typically been described as 'specific' or 'active' components in psychotherapy outcome research, for the second type of components a number of synonymously used terms occur in the literature, although they may have slightly different connotations [17, 18]. Such terms include 'common,' 'general' or 'non-specific' factors or 'psychological placebos.' For the present review, we will follow the terminology proposed by Grünbaum ([19], p. 159). Grünbaum's definition captures the outlined dichotomy with reference to the presence or absence of a psychological (e.g. etiological) theory, which defines the content of a complex treatment, such as psychotherapy. Accordingly, treatment components will be considered *characteristic* if there is a theoretical model that describes how the respective component will contribute to symptom improvement. In contrast, treatment components will be considered *incidental* if there is no such theory-based link to symptom improvement. Thus, the components that are considered active or specific would be considered *characteristic*, because typically they are deduced from psychological theories, which describe how they will improve the symptoms of a particular disorder. In contrast to the concept of specificity, which has been related to uniqueness of treatment components [18], components may be considered *characteristic* even though they may not be a unique component of a particular treatment package. All other factors that may contribute to a treatment effect but which have not (yet) been specified within a psychological theory would be considered *incidental*, no matter whether they are common to all treatments, shared by some or not at all related to the treatment itself, but, for instance, rather to the patient, therapist or to the conduct of the study.

When looking at PTSD research, a number of etiological models of PTSD led to the definition of a number of *characteristic* components and accordingly to the development of several rival treatment packages (see [3, 5, 20, 21]). However, the classification of PTSD treatments according to the underlying etiological model has been a challenge in previous meta-analyses [14]. An inconsistent terminology and the use of treatment labels that are not clearly defined and thus not exclusive (see [22]) lead to considerable variation in the classification of PTSD treatments across individual meta-analyses. In order to reduce some complexity and despite the differences in the foci of the underlying etiological models (e.g. focusing on cognitions vs. focusing on behavioral aspects), several treatment packages have been summarized under the umbrella term of trauma-focused treatments [23]. But again, the definition of the term remained largely unclear and led to inconsistencies with respect to which treatments were to be considered trauma-focused [22]. In contrast, treatments that clearly do not address the trauma experience or even proscribe talking about the trauma have consistently been used as psychological placebo control conditions.

According to the Grünbaum definition, for the present review, we will consider treatments that provided some theory-driven link between treatment components and symptom improvement as *characteristic* (this includes treatments that have previously been summarized as trauma-focused), whereas the clearly non-trauma-focused interventions would be regarded as relying on *incidental* treatment components. However, we will not be able to resolve the inconsistencies, which appear between different meta-analyses and which are due to the imprecise terminology.

3. Estimating the relevance of characteristic treatment components in meta-analyses of RCTs

The RCT and meta-analyses of RCTs are considered the highest level of evidence for the efficacy of treatments [24], and different types of RCTs are employed in psychotherapy outcome research [8].

First, psychotherapeutic treatments are compared with an untreated control group, such as no-treatment or waiting list (WL) designs. The inclusion of an untreated control group in an

RCT minimizes most threats to the internal validity (e.g. controls for spontaneous remission and regression to the mean). Therefore, such a design may be used for showing that a psychotherapeutic treatment is efficacious. With this study design, a number of meta-analyses demonstrated large effect sizes (ESs) for eye-movement desensitization and reprocessing (EMDR), cognitive treatments, exposure-based treatments and the combination of the latter to cognitive-behavioral treatments (CBT) (e.g. [13, 14, 23]), even though treatment effects may be overestimated in studies with small sample size [14]. However, with respect to the research questions highlighted in the present review, such design does not provide an answer: first, a larger effect size of an assumed study comparing treatment A vs. WL, as compared to a second study comparing treatment B vs. WL, may not be interpreted as superiority of A over B, if A has not been shown to be superior to B in a comparative RCT. A number of study characteristics, which may differentiate between the two assumed studies—A vs. WL and B vs. WL, such as different patient samples, different therapists, different study methodology and design—might explain a larger effect in one comparison than in the other. Second, such design does also not tell which *characteristic* treatment components are critical for symptom improvement, because the amount of the total treatment effect that is due to the *characteristic* vs. *incidental* components cannot be disentangled. Thus, such design may not answer the question whether a trauma focus is necessary for the successful PTSD treatment.

In order to control for the *incidental* effects and to evaluate the impact of *characteristic* treatment components, in a second type of RCTs, psychotherapeutic treatments are compared with psychological placebos. Superiority of the psychotherapeutic treatment over the psychological placebo could be specifically attributed to the *characteristic* treatment components, which were lacking in the placebo control. Thus, by manipulating the presence of a particular component, the incremental value of this component can be estimated. For example, the impact of prolonged exposure on PTSD symptoms was compared to present-centered therapy, which was designed as placebo control. It explicitly excluded exposure to the trauma and thus did not focus on the trauma experience [25]. In this particular study, superiority of prolonged exposure over present-centered therapy was small to moderate, and meta-analyses revealed mixed findings with a small, moderate or large superiority of specific, trauma-focused PTSD treatments over placebo control treatments [7, 13, 14]. While the placebo-controlled RCT in the best case allows for estimating the amount of the treatment effect that may be attributed to the *characteristic* vs. *incidental* components, there is still no information on which out of several rival treatment packages contains the most relevant components, that is which treatment should be considered the treatment of choice for a particular problem or disorder.

Therefore, a third type of control treatments in RCTs may encompass treatments with established efficacy (i.e. comparing treatment A vs. treatment B). Such comparative designs are typically used for demonstrating superiority of a novel treatment compared with an established one. If a novel treatment consists of an amendment to an established treatment, the dismantling or add-on study design may be applied in order to demonstrate the incremental benefit of adding or removing a particular treatment component to or from a complex treatment package. Superiority of the novel treatment over an established one would of course be attributed to the superior efficacy of the unique component(s) of the novel treatment. If, however, such a study demonstrated equivalence in treatment effects of the two compared treatments, symptom improvements in both treatments are most likely mediated by common or shared mechanisms [26, 27]. In PTSD outcome research, for example, prolonged exposure plus cognitive restructuring was compared with exposure alone in one RCT, in order to estimate the incremental effect of adding cognitive restructuring to the established exposure treatment [28]. This particular RCT failed to demonstrate superiority of adding cognitive restructuring to an exposure treatment and also meta-analyses that summarized comparative RCTs of individual PTSD treatments found no statistically significant differences between the effects of two types of PTSD treatments (e.g. [13, 14, 23, 29–34]). The equivalent effects of the diverse PTSD treatments have been explained by the presence of a shared mechanism in all of the successful treatments, namely that all treatments focus on the trauma experience [23].

Thus, regarding the first research question, whether a particular treatment package outperforms the others, meta-analyses on comparative RCTs mostly indicated rather similar effects of different treatment packages and thus no superiority of particular *characteristic* components over other *characteristic* components. Regarding the second research question, the results of placebo-controlled PTSD RCTs at first sight may be considered as confirming the assumption that successful PTSD treatment requires the *characteristic* component of focusing on the trauma experience. However, upon closer examination, a substantial amount of unexplained between-study heterogeneity indicates the presence of moderators in several of the abovementioned meta-analyses [7, 13, 14, 23, 30, 32, 34], which complicates or even precludes drawing valid conclusions [35].

4. Bias and diversity in meta-analytically pooled estimates of treatment effects

Meta-analyses have the potential to provide a precise and valid estimate of an treatment effect on the outcome of interest, as they statistically combine the available evidence relevant for a particular research question. Accordingly, meta-analyses have been established as the top level of the hierarchy of evidence [36]. In a meta-analysis, a pooled estimate of the treatment effect is calculated using the treatment effects obtained from each of the included studies. A meta-analysis thus heavily relies on the necessity of including all relevant studies, or at least a random sample of the relevant studies. This becomes more important, of course, if the total number of relevant studies is small, because each individual study may have a larger impact on the pooled effect size estimate in this case. Therefore, a meta-analysis should be preceded by a systematic review, which intends to identify all studies that addressed a particular research question. A systematic review should be conducted using a documented and systematic approach [37].

Conducting a meta-analysis typically increases the precision of the estimated treatment effect, because the number of patients that contribute to the pooled estimate of the treatment effect is larger in the meta-analysis than in each individual study. But estimates from individual studies may vary considerably. The presence of between-study heterogeneity in effect sizes from individual psychotherapy outcome studies suggests that the total pool of studies may be divided into subgroups of studies that show either larger or smaller treatment effects. The presence of between-study heterogeneity may hint at potential sources of bias or at genuine diversity [38]. Heterogeneity, which is commonly present in meta-analyses of psychotherapy outcome studies, does not necessarily prohibit the conduct of meta-analysis, but rather demands exploration of potential sources of variation [35].

Thus, reducing unsystematic error in the data will result in more precise estimates of treatment effects, while avoiding systematic error—that is bias and genuine diversity—will reduce heterogeneity and increase validity. Thus, bias is different from unsystematic random error and can be regarded as the opposite of validity [39]. Bias has been defined as 'any process at any stage of inference, which tends to produce results or conclusions that differ systematically from the truth ([40], p. 60).' This means that bias may lead to an overestimation or to an underestimation of the true effect. It is important to note that a particular type of bias may lead to opposite deviations from the true effect in different studies [41]. Theoretically, genuine diversity may be differentiated from bias. Nevertheless, the presence of genuine diversity in the studies, which contribute to a pooled effect-estimate in a meta-analysis, may as well reduce the validity of the pooled estimate, because genuine diversity may distort an overall pooled estimate just the same way as bias does.

The issue of bias and diversity in meta-analyses has previously been related to three typically occurring problems in meta-analyses: first, a meta-analysis may not reduce or eliminate bias that has been present in the included studies. For example, if effect estimates from a large number of methodologically flawed studies are combined with only few methodologically sound studies in a meta-analysis, the pooled effect estimate will be biased as well (the so-called *garbage-in, garbage-out problem* [42, 43]). Second, with respect to the potentially present genuine diversity, meta-analysis may even introduce bias in estimating a treatment effect: for example, if the included studies differed regarding study characteristics that may affect the treatment effect (i.e. studies are genuinely diverse), the pooled effect estimate may be invalid (the so-called *apples-and-oranges problem* [42, 43]). If, for example, studies with patients that fulfill diagnostic criteria of two or more mental disorders had systematically larger treatment effects than studies that included patients who fulfill diagnostic criteria of one mental disorder only, combining treatment effects from both subsets of studies would result in an invalid pooled effect estimate. Thus, genuine diversity in the studied samples, treatments, treatment providers or study methodology may reduce the validity of the pooled estimate of the treatment effect. Finally, the validity of meta-analyses may be reduced if the sample of studies that is considered for meta-analytic pooling of treatment effects is not representative of all relevant studies (the so-called *file-drawer problem* [43, 44]). This problem is related to difficulties to publish studies with negative or non-significant results, especially if the study samples are small. In published articles of small-sized studies, treatment effects thus tend to be large and significant. If only published articles are considered for meta-analysis, the obtained effect estimates may only poorly reflect the true treatment effect. The *file-drawer problem* has consequently also been described as publication bias. The problems that may occur from including mainly small and underpowered studies in a meta-analysis have been summarized nicely by

Cuijpers ([9], p. 2): 'If a therapy is found to be superior to an existing therapy in an underpowered trial that would rather raise doubts about the validity of the trial than trust that this new therapy is indeed more effective.'

Thus, all three briefly introduced problems in meta-analyses threaten the validity of the pooled effect estimate. They differ, however, with respect to the interpretation of the estimated treatment effects (**Figure 1**): first, the *garbage-in, garbage-out problem* reflects the bias that has

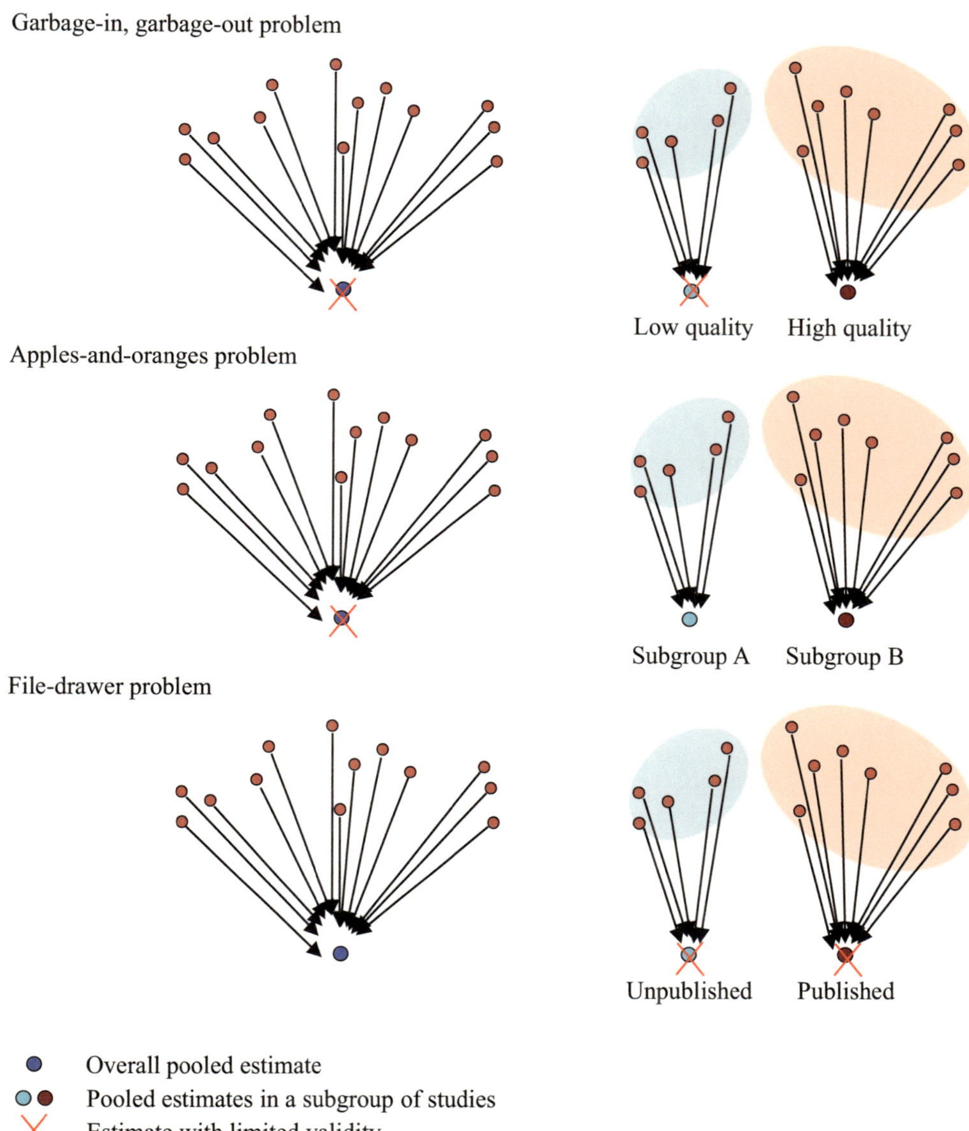

Figure 1. Interpreting pooled effect estimates in the presence of between-study heterogeneity. The validity of the pooled effect estimates depends on the type of problem, which is responsible for the observed between-study heterogeneity.

already been present in a subgroup of poor-quality studies. The pooled effect estimate across all studies as well as the pooled effect estimate of the poor-quality subgroup of studies will be biased. In this case, only the effect estimate of the high-quality subgroup of studies may be regarded as valid. Second, the *apples-and-oranges problem* reflects meaningful variation between effect estimates due to dissimilarity between studies on relevant study characteristics (i.e. genuine diversity). That is, the pooled effect estimate across all included studies may be invalid whereas the pooled effect estimates in each subgroup of studies may be valid. Third, if the *file-drawer problem* was present, the pooled effect estimate of published studies is expected to differ from the pooled effect estimate of unpublished studies, as study results may more likely be published if they have statistically significant results. Many of the unpublished studies may, therefore, have non-significant results. Thus, a meta-analysis restricted to the published studies would probably provide a higher result compared to a meta-analysis restricted to the unpublished studies [45]. Only including both, published and unpublished studies, would warrant the validity of the effect-estimate. The difference between published and unpublished studies should particularly be the case if the study samples are small [46], which further complicates the issue. If a meta-analysis considers only published studies and non-significant results are most likely to be lacking if a study was small in scale, publication bias should be most potent in the small-scale studies and less pronounced or even not present in the large-scale studies. In this case (i.e. when including only published studies), the pooled effect estimate including all studies as well as the pooled effect estimate restricted to small-scale studies might be biased, whereas the effect estimate in the large-scale studies will be most valid with respect to publication bias. It is important to note, however, that the presence of any of the three problems indicates only an increased probability of bias in a meta-analysis rather than being necessarily associated with bias in the meta-analytically pooled effect estimates.

5. Addressing between-study heterogeneity in meta-analyses of PTSD RCTs

Meta-analyses on the effectiveness of psychotherapeutic treatments for PTSD revealed between-study heterogeneity in any kind of RCTs—those that compared psychotherapy with wait list, with a psychological placebo control and those that compared two types of rival PTSD psychotherapies. But not all meta-analyses reporting heterogeneous results made attempts to explore potential sources of the observed heterogeneity (e.g. several of the comparisons in Bisson and Andrew [23]).

A typical approach in meta-analyses to deal with the presence of between-study heterogeneity is to identify characteristics of the included studies that systematically differentiate studies with larger or smaller effect sizes (i.e. so-called moderators or effect modifiers [43, 47]. Every characteristic of a study that is associated with the treatment effect may also act as a moderator in a meta-analysis. Two statistical approaches are used in order to identify relevant moderators: stratification of analyses by potential moderators and meta-regression analyses [35]. In stratified meta-analysis, the effect estimates of the subgroups of studies with and without a particular characteristic are contrasted. If effect estimates differ significantly in the contrasted subgroups or heterogeneity is reduced in at least one of the contrasted subgroups, the respective study characteristic may be interpreted as relevant moderator. Meta-regression analysis provides a statistical test for the exploration of sources of heterogeneity in meta-analyses [48].

The following paragraphs will give examples of different kinds of study characteristics that have been shown to moderate the pooled effect estimates in meta-analyses on PTSD treatments. We will focus on meta-analytic findings that summarized data from placebo-controlled and comparative RCTs as those two designs are informative with respect to the identification of *characteristic* treatment components in PTSD treatments and thus to the two highlighted research questions.

5.1. Moderators in placebo-controlled PTSD RCTs

One meta-analysis [7] summarized RCTs which compared treatments that somehow focused on the trauma with treatments lacking a trauma focus. The initial overall analysis showed a moderate superiority of the trauma-focused over the non-trauma-focused treatments with moderate between-study heterogeneity. On closer examination, the extent of structural equivalence (i.e. that therapists in both treatment conditions were equally trained and supervised and that the number of sessions was equivalent in both treatment conditions) substantially moderated the initially observed differences when all studies were included in the analysis. In the stratified meta-analyses, the superiority of trauma-focused treatments over the placebo controls was larger in studies without equivalence between the two treatment conditions, which was most likely due to an underestimation of the efficacy of the placebo control. Heterogeneity was considerably reduced in the stratified analyses. Furthermore, the initially observed superiority of trauma-focused treatments over placebo controls was moderated by patient characteristics: by combining several indicators of more complex clinical problems (e.g. the presence of comorbid disorders in addition to the PTSD symptoms or trauma history, as suggested by Cloitre and colleagues [49]), the moderator analysis conducted by Gerger and colleagues [7] revealed that patients with more complex clinical problems benefited equally from trauma-focused PTSD treatments as well as from the psychological placebo control. In contrast, in studies with less complex problems (e.g. PTSD symptoms without comorbid symptoms following a single trauma), patients benefited more from the trauma-focused treatments than from the placebo control. Again, the inclusion of the moderator reduced heterogeneity, and only a small amount of between-study heterogeneity remained unexplained. Importantly, in studies with less complex clinical problems and structural in-equivalence, a clear superiority of trauma-focused over placebo control treatments was observed (ES = 0.93; $p = 0.001$), whereas this was not the case in studies with complex clinical problems and structural equivalence of the trauma-focused treatment and placebo control (ES = 0.11; $p = 0.28$).

5.2. Moderators in comparative PTSD RCTs

A concrete example of the presence of between-study heterogeneity, i.e. contradicting findings from individual studies that compared two rival PTSD treatments, can be found in the review by Bisson and Andrew [23]. In one of the conducted meta-analyses out of six studies that compared CBT and EMDR, three studies reported moderate to large superiority of CBT on clinician-rated PTSD scores, while the remaining three studies reported the exact opposite effect, namely moderate to large superiority of EMDR over CBT. Overall, the meta-analysis indicated no difference between the effects of the two treatments, but a large amount of between-study heterogeneity (ES = 0.03, $p = 0.92$, $\tau^2 = 0.28$). Without further exploration of the observed heterogeneity, no valid conclusions may be drawn from such data [35].

Several meta-analyses aimed at explaining such heterogeneity between individual study estimates in PTSD RCTs. Two meta-analyses [14, 34] included different types of PTSD treatments, but found no evidence for the type of psychotherapeutic PTSD treatment to explain between-study heterogeneity. Rather, Gerger et al. [14] found evidence for the presence of publication bias with respect to the trauma-focused PTSD treatments: a meta-analysis that was restricted to large-scale studies demonstrated considerably reduced treatment effects compared to the effects found in the overall analysis or in an analysis that was restricted to small-scale studies. The between-study heterogeneity, which was very large in the initial analysis ($\tau^2 = 0.29$), was considerably reduced in the analysis restricted to large-scale trials ($\tau^2 = 0.08$).

One possible explanation for the striking differences in the direction of effects between two treatments as in the EMDR-CBT comparison by Bisson and Andrew [23] is the presence of researchers' preferences for one over the other treatment, the so-called researcher allegiance [50]. Accordingly, the intriguing pattern of results in the EMDR-CBT meta-analysis by Bisson and Andrew [23] could simply be explained by the fact that in one half of the studies researchers preferred CBT and in the other half researchers preferred EMDR. While, by chance, in this particular case, the distribution of researcher allegiance appears balanced across the six included studies, an unbalanced preference for one particular treatment may be more problematic. In fact, a meta-analysis on trauma-focused PTSD treatments found researcher allegiance to significantly correlate with effect-size differences between the trauma-focused PTSD treatments ($r = 0.35$) and to explain between-study heterogeneity [15]. Further, Munder and colleagues presented evidence for the assumption that the association between researcher allegiance and outcome was due to bias [16] and against the assumption that true differences in the effectiveness of different types of PTSD treatments explained the association between researcher allegiance and outcome [15].

Thus, meta-analyses on comparative PTSD RCTs failed to demonstrate the superiority of particular *characteristic* components, but demonstrated the relevance of researcher allegiance —a factor that is *incidental* to the treatment—in explaining differences between individual study results. Thus, in the case of PTSD outcome studies, comparative RCTs run a considerable risk of providing biased estimates of the contribution of *characteristic* treatment components to the entire treatment effect. Furthermore, while on first sight meta-analyses of placebo-controlled PTSD RCTs appeared to support the claim that focusing on the trauma is necessary for successful PTSD treatment, a closer examination of potential moderators of treatment effects indicated that a trauma focus might be necessary for some but not all patient samples. A thorough implementation of the assumed psychological placebo might further enhance its effectiveness and, hence, reduce the superiority of trauma-focused treatments over placebo controls. The finding of only a small and non-significant superiority of established PTSD treatments over present-centered therapy in a meta-analysis [6], as well as a recent meta-analysis on counseling treatments for PTSD [5], confirm the objection regarding a general necessity of a trauma focus in psychotherapeutic PTSD treatment.

6. Conclusion

Our analysis of PTSD outcome research demonstrates the presence of considerable conceptual problems in PTSD RCTs, which limit the validity of the conclusions that may be drawn from these studies when trying to identify the most beneficial treatment components. In placebo-controlled RCTs, an inappropriate implementation of the placebo control led to an overestimation of the superiority of the PTSD treatments over the placebo control, and in comparative RCTs, the presence of unbalanced researcher allegiance led to biased estimates of treatment effect differences. Besides such conceptual issues, which hamper valid conclusions from PTSD RCTs, the moderating role of patient characteristics confirms the recent conclusion that 'one size does not fit all' in PTSD treatment [49]. Thus, moderators of treatment effects in PTSD RCTs may include genuine diversity, which contributes to the *apples-and-oranges problem* and that indicates a need for differential treatments, but may also include factors that contribute to bias—that is the *garbage-in, garbage-out problem* as well as the *file-drawer problem*.

Future attempts to identify the most beneficial treatment components of PTSD treatments should therefore consider not only the theory-driven *characteristic* components but must also further investigate how the assumed *incidental* factors may impact on outcome in order to warrant the validity of conclusions from PTSD outcome research. The underlying etiological theories may need revisions if moderators indicated genuine diversity and study methodology may need to be adapted in order to ensure the validity of psychotherapy outcome studies. Neglecting extra-therapeutic moderators may threaten the validity of RCTs and meta-analyses and may result in misleading recommendations for researchers, practitioners and policymakers, who base their treatment decisions on empirical findings. On the other hand, the possibility of exploring sources of genuine diversity between RCTs when conducting a meta-analysis (i.e. conducting moderator analyses in order to explain between-study heterogeneity) may be seen as an important step towards personalized psychotherapy [51].

It is important to note, however, that moderator analyses in meta-analyses, even if they include only high-quality RCTs, should always be considered as retrospective and observational in nature, because the studies were not randomly assigned according to their characteristics (e.g. studies have neither been randomly assigned to being of high vs. low quality nor to having included patients with complex vs. non-complex problems). Thus, the results from moderator analyses in meta-analyses should be considered as hypothesis generating, which would, if possible, at best to be confirmed by high-quality experimental research.

Acknowledgements

We thank Sebastian Hasler for providing editorial help with the manuscript.

Author details

Heike Gerger* and Jens Gaab

*Address all correspondence to: heike.gerger@gmail.com

Department of Psychology, Clinical Psychology and Psychotherapy, University of Basel, Basel, Switzerland

References

[1] Foa EB, Rothbaum BO, Riggs DS, Murdock TB. Treatment of posttraumatic stress disorder in rape victims: A comparison between cognitive-behavioral procedures and counseling. Journal of Consulting and Clinical Psychology. 1991;59:715–723. DOI: 10.1037/0022-006X.59.5.715

[2] Resick PA, Schnicke MK. Cognitive processing therapy for sexual assault victims. Journal of Consulting and Clinical Psychology. 1992;60:748–756. DOI: 10.1037/0022-006X.60.5.748

[3] Schnyder U, Ehlers A, Elbert T, Foa EB, Gersons BPR, Resick PA, et al. Psychotherapies for PTSD: What do they have in common? European Journal of Psychotraumatology. 2015;6:28186. DOI: 10.3402/ejpt.v6.28186

[4] Cusack K, Jonas DE, Forneris CA, Wines C, Sonis J, Middleton JC, et al. Psychological treatments for adults with posttraumatic stress disorder: A systematic review and meta-analysis. Clinical Psychology Review. 2016;43:128–141. DOI: 10.1016/j.cpr.2015.10.003

[5] Erford BT, Gunther C, Duncan K, Bardhoshi G, Dummett B, Kraft J, et al. Meta-analysis of counseling outcomes for the treatment of posttraumatic stress disorder. Journal of Counseling & Development. 2016;94:13–30. DOI: 10.1002/jcad.12058

[6] Frost ND, Laska KM, Wampold BE. The evidence for present-centered therapy as a treatment for posttraumatic stress disorder. Journal of Traumatic Stress. 2014;27:1–8. DOI: 10.1002/jts.21881

[7] Gerger H, Munder T, Barth J. Specific and nonspecific psychological interventions for PTSD symptoms: A meta-analysis with problem complexity as a moderator. Journal of Clinical Psychology. 2014;70:601–615. DOI: 10.1002/jclp.22059

[8] Schnurr PP. The rocks and hard places in psychotherapy outcome research. Journal of Traumatic Stress. 2007;20:779–792. DOI: 10.1002/jts.20292

[9] Cuijpers P. The future of psychotherapy research: Stop the waste and focus on issues that matter. Epidemiology and Psychiatric Sciences. 2015:1–4. DOI: 10.1017/S2045796015000785

[10] Cuijpers P, Cristea IA. How to prove that your therapy is effective, even when it is not: A guideline. Epidemiology and Psychiatric Sciences. 2015:1–8. DOI: 10.1017/S2045796015000864

[11] Ioannidis JPA. Why most published research findings are false. PLoS Medicine. 2005;2:e124. DOI: 10.1371/journal.pmed.0020124

[12] Ioannidis JPA, Greenland S, Hlatky MA, Khoury MJ, Macleod MR, Moher D, et al. Increasing value and reducing waste in research design, conduct, and analysis. Lancet. 2014;383:166–175. DOI: 10.1016/S0140-6736(13)62227-8

[13] Bradley R, Greene J, Russ E, Dutra L, Westen D. A multidimensional meta-analysis of psychotherapy for PTSD. American Journal of Psychiatry. 2005;162:214–227. DOI: 10.1176/appi.ajp.162.2.214

[14] Gerger H, Munder T, Gemperli A, Nüesch E, Trelle S, Jüni P, et al. Integrating fragmented evidence by network meta-analysis: Relative effectiveness of psychological interventions for adults with post-traumatic stress disorder. Psychological Medicine. 2014;44:3151–3164. DOI: 10.1017/S0033291714000853

[15] Munder T, Flü ckiger C, Gerger H, Wampold BE, Barth J. Is the allegiance effect an epiphenomenon of true efficacy differences between treatments? A meta-analysis. Journal of Counseling Psychology. 2012;59:631–637. DOI: 10.1037/a0029571

[16] Munder T, Gerger H, Trelle S, Barth J. Testing the allegiance bias hypothesis: A meta-analysis. Psychotherapy Research. 2011;21:670–684. DOI: 10.1080/10503307.2011.602752

[17] Critelli JW, Neumann KF. The placebo: Conceptual analysis of a construct in transition. American Psychologist. 1984;39:32–39. DOI: 10.1037/0003-066X.39.1.32

[18] Kirsch I. Placebo psychotherapy: Synonym or oxymoron? Journal of Clinical Psychology. 2005;61:791–803. DOI: 10.1002/jclp.20126

[19] Grü nbaum A. The placebo concept. Behaviour Research and Therapy. 1981;19:157–167. DOI: 10.1016/0005-7967(81)90040-1

[20] Cukor J, Olden M, Lee F, Difede J. Evidence-based treatments for PTSD, new directions, and special challenges. Annals of the New York Academy of Sciences. 2010;1208:82–89. DOI: 10.1111/j.1749-6632.2010.05793.x

[21] Foa EB, Keane TM, Friedman MJ, Cohen JA, editors. Effective Treatments for PTSD. 2nd ed. New York: Guilford Press; 2009. 658 p.

[22] Wampold BE, Imel ZE, Laska KM, Benish S, Miller SD, Flü ckiger C, et al. Determining what works in the treatment of PTSD. Clinical Psychology Review. 2010;30:923–933. DOI: 10.1016/j.cpr.2010.06.005

[23] Bisson JI, Andrew M. Psychological treatment of post-traumatic stress disorder (PTSD). Cochrane Database of Systematic Reviews. 2007;3:CD003388. DOI: 10.1002/14651858.CD003388.pub3

[24] Jones DS, Podolsky SH. The history and fate of the gold standard. Lancet. 2015;385:1502–1503. DOI: 10.1016/S0140-6736(15)60742-5

[25] Schnurr PP, Friedman MJ, Engel CC, Foa EB, Shea MT, Chow BK, et al. Cognitive behavioral therapy for posttraumatic stress disorder in women: A randomized controlled trial. JAMA. 2007;297:820–830. DOI: 10.1001/jama.297.8.820.

[26] Asnaani A, Foa EB. Expanding the lens of evidence-based practice in psychotherapy to include a common factors perspective: Comment on Laska, Gurman, and Wampold. Psychotherapy. 2014;51:487–490. DOI: 10.1037/a0036891

[27] Rosenzweig S. Some implicit common factors in diverse methods of psychotherapy. American Journal of Orthopsychiatry. 1936;6:412–415. DOI: 10.1111/j. 1939-0025.1936.tb05248.x

[28] Foa EB, Hembree EA, Cahill SP, Rauch SAM, Riggs DS, Feeny NC, et al. Randomized trial of prolonged exposure for posttraumatic stress disorder with and without cognitive restructuring: Outcome at academic and community clinics. Journal of Consulting and Clinical Psychology. 2005;73:953–964. DOI: 10.1037/0022-006X.73.5.953

[29] Benish SG, Imel ZE, Wampold BE. The relative efficacy of bona fide psychotherapies for treating post-traumatic stress disorder: A meta-analysis of direct comparisons. Clinical Psychology Review. 2008;28:746–758. DOI: 10.1016/j.cpr.2007.10.005

[30] Davidson PR, Parker KC. Eye movement desensitization and reprocessing (EMDR): A meta-analysis. Journal of Consulting and Clinical Psychology. 2001;69:305–316. DOI: 10.1037/0022-006X.69.2.305

[31] Mendes DD, Mello MF, Ventura P, de Medeiros Passarela C, de Jesus Mari J. A systematic review on the effectiveness of cognitive behavioral therapy for posttraumatic stress disorder. International Journal of Psychiatry in Medicine. 2008;38:241–259. DOI: 10.2190/PM.38.3.b

[32] Powers MB, Halpern JM, Ferenschak MP, Gillihan SJ, Foa EB. A meta-analytic review of prolonged exposure for posttraumatic stress disorder. Clinical Psychology Review. 2010;30:635–641. DOI: 10.1016/j.cpr.2010.04.007

[33] Seidler GH, Wagner FE. Comparing the efficacy of EMDR and trauma-focused cognitive-behavioral therapy in the treatment of PTSD: A meta-analytic study. Psychological Medicine. 2006;36:1515–1522. DOI: 10.1017/S0033291706007963

[34] Watts BV, Schnurr PP, Mayo L, Young-Xu Y, Weeks WB, Friedman MJ. Meta-analysis of the efficacy of treatments for posttraumatic stress disorder. Journal of Clinical Psychiatry. 2013;74:e541–550. DOI: 10.4088/JCP.12r08225

[35] Deeks JJ, Higgins JPT, Altman DG (editors). Chapter 9: Analysing data and undertaking meta-analyses. In: Higgins JPT, Green S (editors). Cochrane Handbook for Systematic Reviews of Interventions Version 5.1.0 (updated March 2011). The Cochrane Collaboration, 2011. Available from www.cochrane-handbook.org

[36] Guyatt GH, Sackett DL, Sinclair JC, Hayward R, Cook DJ, Cook RJ. Users' guides to the medical literature: IX. A method for grading health care recommendations. Journal of the American Medical Association. 1995;274:1800–1804. DOI: 10.1001/jama.1995.03530220066035

[37] Liberati A, Altman DG, Tetzlaff J, Mulrow C, Gøtzsche PC, Ioannidis JPA, et al. The PRISMA statement for reporting systematic reviews and meta-analyses of studies that evaluate health care interventions: Explanation and elaboration. BMJ. 2009;339:b2700. DOI: 10.1136/bmj.b2700

[38] Salanti G, Higgins JPT, Ades AE, Ioannidis JPA. Evaluation of networks of randomized trials. Statistical Methods in Medical Research. 2008;17:279–301. DOI: 10.1177/0962280207080643

[39] Rothman KJ, Greenland S, Lash TL. Validity in epidemiologic studies. In: Rothman KJ, Greenland S, Lash TL, editors. Modern Epidemiology. 3rd ed. Philadelphia: Lippincott Williams & Wilkins; 2008. p. 128–147.

[40] Sackett DL. Bias in analytic research. Journal of Chronic Diseases. 1979;32:51–63. DOI: 10.1016/0021-9681(79)90012-2

[41] Higgins JPT, Altman DG, Sterne JAC (editors). Chapter 8: Assessing risk of bias in included studies. In: Higgins JPT, Green S (editors). Cochrane Handbook for Systematic Reviews of Interventions Version 5.1.0 (updated March 2011). The Cochrane Collaboration, 2011. Available from www.cochrane-handbook.org.

[42] Eysenck HJ. An exercise in mega-silliness. American Psychologist. 1978;33:517. DOI: 10.1037/0003-066X.33.5.517.a

[43] Sharpe D. Of apples and oranges, file drawers and garbage: Why validity issues in meta-analysis will not go away. Clinical Psychology Review. 1997;17:881–901. DOI: 10.1016/S0272-7358(97)00056-1

[44] Rosenthal R. The "file drawer problem" and tolerance for null results. Psychological Bulletin. 1979;86:638–641. DOI: 10.1037/0033-2909.86.3.638

[45] Turner EH, Matthews AM, Linardatos E, Tell RA, Rosenthal R. Selective publication of antidepressant trials and its influence on apparent efficacy. New England Journal of Medicine. 2008;358:252–260. DOI: 10.1056/NEJMsa065779

[46] Egger M, Smith GD, Schneider M, Minder C. Bias in meta-analysis detected by a simple, graphical test. BMJ. 1997;315:629–634. DOI: 10.1136/bmj.315.7109.629

[47] Lipsey MW, Wilson DB. Practical meta-analysis. 1st ed. Thousand Oaks: Sage Publications; 2001. 264 p.

[48] Thompson SG, Higgins JPT. How should meta-regression analyses be undertaken and interpreted? Statistics in Medicine. 2002;21:1559–1573. DOI: 10.1002/sim.1187

[49] Cloitre M, Bryant RA, Schnyder U. What works for whom? In: Schnyder U, Cloitre M, editors. Evidence Based Treatments for Trauma-Related Psychological Disorders. Cham: Springer International Publishing; 2015. p. 499–512. DOI: 10.1007/978-3-319-07109-1_27

[50] Luborsky L, Singer B, Luborsky L. Comparative studies of psychotherapies. Is it true that "everyone has won and must have prizes"? Archives of General Psychiatry. 1975;32:995–1008. DOI: 10.1001/archpsyc.1975.01760260059004

[51] Cuijpers P, Ebert DD, Acarturk C, Andersson G, Cristea IA. Personalized psychotherapy for adult depression: A meta-analytic review. Behavior Therapy. 2016. DOI:10.1016/j.beth.2016.04.007